Sally McKee

A NEW LATIN SYNTAX

A NEW LATIN SYNTAX

E. C. WOODCOCK, M.A.

Published by Bristol Classical Press (U.K.)
General Editor: John H. Betts
and by
Bolchazy-Carducci Publishers (U.S.A.)
(by arrangement with Methuen & Co. Ltd.)

Printed in Great Britain

First published by Methuen & Co. Ltd., 1959
Reprinted, with permission, 1985, by

U.K.
Bristol Classical Press
Department of Classics
University of Bristol
Wills Memorial Building
Queens Road
BRISTOL BS8 1RJ

ISBN 0-86292-042-6

U.S.A.
Bolchazy-Carducci Publishers
8 S. Michigan Ave.
CHICAGO
Illinois 60302

ISBN 0-86516-126-7

© *E.C. Woodcock, 1959*

Preface

This book began as a series of notes on Latin syntax drafted at the request of Professor W. H. Semple of Manchester for the purpose of standardizing the teaching to the numerous sections of the then large Intermediate Class. These notes have been supplemented by sections of more advanced discussion drawn from lectures on historical Latin syntax to Honours classes.

In a work drawn up with a view to specific teaching requirements it is to be expected that there will be examples of unevenness and omissions. If some sections appear to be laboured, it is because they deal with constructions in which mistakes continue to be made even by Honours students right up to the end of their course.

It is natural that much is owed to the criticism and advice of colleagues at weekly meetings. I owe much to colleagues at both Manchester and Durham, and it would be difficult to make acknowledgement to individuals. Nevertheless my thanks are due to the following in particular. Without the encouragement of Professor Semple this work might never have been attempted. To Professor W. B. Anderson of Cambridge I owe a special debt. As a lecturer under him in Manchester I learned the meaning of accurate scholarship. When I first began this book, he consented to read through the earlier draft of the first eight chapters, and in the light of his careful, searching, but kindly criticism these chapters have been re-written several times. For any errors that remain in them he is certainly not to blame. For these, as for the rest, I must take full responsibility.

Finally, I must acknowledge my debt to my colleague at Durham, Mr. N. E. Collinge, who has read through the proofs and given me the benefit of his philological knowledge.

E. C. WOODCOCK

Durham, September 1958.

Contents

Introduction

It has long been the tradition in Great Britain to teach Latin syntax through the medium of Latin prose composition, and not by reading only. The general educational advantages of this method are far too great to be discarded, but it has accompanying disadvantages. The author of a text-book on composition is naturally anxious to equip the learner as soon as possible with the means to express common ideas in sentences which a reasonable human being might be expected to utter. There is a consequent temptation to ignore the historical order of syntactical development and to produce over-simplified rules which bear no relation to any scientific explanation. For example, rules are devised for the expression of purpose and result in subjunctive clauses many lessons ahead of the independent uses of the subjunctive from which such subordinate clauses are derived. To make matters worse, the adverbial clauses are usually widely separated from relative clauses in which the subjunctive is of the same type. In order to make indirect reports, the accusative and infinitive noun-phrase (usually wrongly called a noun *clause*) is introduced before the other uses of either the accusative or of the infinitive have been explained. Under such circumstances, Latin syntax must seem to the average student a collection of irrational peculiarities which can be mastered only by memorizing disconnected rules based on statistics. But in most Grammar Schools nowadays Latin is not begun till the age of twelve, by which time the faculty of memorizing is beginning to wane. The faculty of reason is beginning to take its place, and therefore a thread of reason ought to be supplied in the presentation of Latin syntax.

It might be thought that the deficiencies of the average text-book on composition could be supplied by reference to the relevant sections in a fully documented scientific grammar. But this is difficult, so long as the traditional order of dealing with constructions is kept; and no existing authoritative work on Latin syntax is suitable for pedagogic purposes by itself. One could not take the learner through a dozen chapters dealing exhaustively with the functions of cases, adjectives and adverbs, pronouns, prepositions, voices, tenses, moods, gerunds and participles, before arriving at the composition of a simple sentence with a finite verb. Furthermore, although few verbs are confined to a single construction, but require different constructions, according to the idea to be expressed, scientific grammars tend to divide constructions vertically into watertight compartments. For example, in a full account of the accusative and infinitive noun-phrase, verbs of resolving such as *constituo* and *decerno* will appear on the list of verbs to which it may stand as object, but one may have to travel through another hundred pages before one learns that these same verbs may be followed by a final *ut*-clause. In a still earlier chapter, these verbs will have been mentioned in connexion with the prolative infinitive. But the prolative infinitive, the accusative and infinitive, and the final *ut*-clause have different semantic values, and this wide separation makes it very difficult for the learner to sort things out. The only way to save the learner from error, whether in composition or in the interpretation of texts, is to mention at once the different constructions which may follow such verbs, and to point out the different forces of each.

In the following account of Latin syntax a compromise has been attempted, both between the vertical and the horizontal method of presentation, and between the scientific and the artificial order of constructions. It seemed necessary to give an account of the functions of the cases at the beginning of the work. But if an account of the infinitive is given immediately after the accusative, the accusative and infinitive construction can be brought in at an early stage, and sentences containing indirect reports can give reasonable interest to the exercises. A chapter on the independent uses of the subjunctive is put before its subordinate developments in final and consecutive clauses. Relative clauses containing a final or consecutive subjunctive are not separated from the corresponding adverbial clauses. Elementary remarks on agreement of adjective with noun and verb with subject have been omitted, since these things are usually pointed out at an earlier stage, when the accidence is being learned. Pronouns and prepositions also are dealt with only incidentally, only when it has been necessary to discuss particular usages in the text. An attempt has been made to substitute, as far as possible, historical explanation for cut-and-dried rules, and awkward examples have not been suppressed, in the hope that the student may thus be equipped to interpret his texts, as well as to write correct sentences himself.

But the difficulties in the way of a historical account of Latin syntax are formidable. The origin of many constructions is disputed. Not all developments are due to rational extension, but illogical analogy and formal extension play a large part. There are psychological gaps to be bridged, and it is not always possible to trace the successive shifts in meaning whereby a construction acquires a new force. To give examples: it is easy enough to show how the jussive subjunctive in parataxis issues in the final subordinate clause, whereby the intentions or motives of the subject of the main clause may be reported indirectly; and it is possible to connect this further with the extension of the subjunctive into other subordinate clauses in indirect speech, in which not motives but statements of fact are being quoted. But what is the grammarian to do with the use of the subjunctive in consecutive clauses of fact? The German authorities on Latin grammar and their followers attribute this to purely formal extension of the subjunctive in final clauses, on the ground that the difference between willed result and accidental result is negligible. What would the praetor in a Roman court of law have said to that? In any case, how can we tell that final subjunctives developed first, when both final and consecutive subjunctives occur as early as Plautus? For analogical extension of a linguistic formula to take place, there must be a close and repeated association of ideas, as when the etymologically unjustifiable form *noctu* was invented to accompany *diu*. Similarly, it would be useless to appeal to any original sense of the dative case to account for the construction *pecuniam tibi eripio*, since the usage is due simply to the inability of the human mind to dissociate the ideas of give and take. In such a case formal extension is a valid explanation and is intellectually satisfying. But could association of ideas make a method of attributing motive to someone else appear a natural method of expressing one's own ideas about the causal connexion of two events? Besides, such an explanation fails to account for the negative *non* in consecutive clauses, or for the difference in the use of the tenses. The explanation of purely formal extension cannot be justified by *a posteriori* argument, because the evidence does not begin early enough to determine which of the two constructions developed first. *A priori* argument, on the other hand, suggests that, since the need to distinguish between the two ideas so often assumed a legal importance, care would have been taken to express them differently, had not the two constructions developed concurrently, and acquired a resemblance by accident.

This misconception as to the origin of the consecutive subjunctive causes utter confusion when the same type of subjunctive in relative clauses comes to be explained. Most grammars are reduced to the expedient of drawing up lists of antecedents such as *is*, *nemo*, *nihil*, *nullus*, *solus*, *unus*, etc., after which they say the consecutive subjunctive may or must be used. This is the statistical method again, and it explains nothing. Yet some authorities have already recognized the independent potential subjunctive as the origin of the generic subjunctive in *qui*-clauses, and they have commented on its descriptive effect (e.g. Bennett, *Syntax of Early Latin*, vol. I, pp. 288 ff.; Ernout-Thomas, p. 286). What seems to have escaped observation is that, if the *qui*-clause is attributive or parenthetic, the subjunctive, if not merely descriptive, can suggest only cause or contrast. If, on the other hand, the clause is predicated or predicative, the same subjunctive can express only result (cf. §§ 155–6 below). There is no need to draw up lists of antecedents or to memorize a meaningless rule.

These are some of the difficulties encountered by anyone who tries to adopt the historical method of presentation, and examples might be multiplied. What is the origin of the subjunctive in temporal *cum*-clauses, or in frequentative clauses in Silver Latin? And how can one give the learner an account of the sequence of tenses in *Oratio Obliqua* to which Cicero and Caesar themselves will not seem to give the lie on every other page? (cf. Excursus, § 279). It is not surprising that compilers of school text-books have found it safer to stick to the statistical method of classification and to keep awkward examples dark. They are concerned to transmit knowledge of the main facts, and this they do very well. Nevertheless, the method of tabulating the facts in the order of numerical preponderance is apt to obscure the true explanation and the order of development. A most natural expression which is in complete conformity with the genius of the language and may be the only method by which an author can express a particular nuance, will be treated as a deviation, if it is not allowed for in the main statement of principle. For example, both Caesar and Livy drive a coach and horses through Roby's rule about the expression of rhetorical questions in *Oratio Obliqua* (cf. §§ 267 ff.). The real force of exceptions to such grammar-book rules will not be understood by the pupil, and far from being equipped to interpret human thought, he is actually being trained to misinterpret.

On balance, therefore, in spite of the gaps in our knowledge and disputes arising through the lack of evidence, a case can be made out for changing the method and order of the presentation of the syntax, particularly in books that teach through the medium of composition. Roby said long ago, in the introduction to his syntax: 'Few things can be more important in the treatment of language than an historical method: what appears hopelessly intricate and irritational, when judged from a scientific point of view which is not that of historical development, becomes intelligible and almost simple, when we look along the line of growth. No doubt there is much about Latin constructions which will always be dark, because we come upon the language not in its youth, but in its maturity, when it was no longer a mere rustic dialect, but a literary language.' There Roby has put his finger on the spot. Nevertheless, what both he and Draeger meant by 'Historical Latin Syntax' was the observation and explanation of the changes in usage and style which took place in a historical series of authors from Plautus to Tacitus. What we really need is a historical explanation of syntax as we already find it in Plautus; for the changes that take place in the three hundred years of Latin with which we are mainly concerned are relatively slight. We can see the use of the subjunctive extending as time goes on, but the main subordinate uses, such as the final and consecutive, and in subordinate clauses in *O. O.*, are already fully fledged in Plautus. We can see the Genitive of Quality extending from a mere couple of examples in Plautus and Terence, but it is already there. The changes that take place are almost matters of style rather than of syntax. Cicero's achievement consisted, not in developing Latin syntax, but in developing a style which made the syntax of Plautus capable of expounding the philosophy of Greece.

To satisfy modern conditions, it is clearly necessary for historical explanation of syntax to be carried back a good deal further than has been customary, further even than the findings of scientific philology would warrant. There does not seem to be any other way of explaining to modern pupils, many of whom have been handicapped at the primary stage by the banning of formal grammar by educational cranks, what syntax is for. It seems to be thought nowadays that understanding of syntax is something that grows with the flesh. Pupils are pushed on to specialize in various branches of learning and science, before they have received sufficient formal training in the use of language to enable them either to learn from books or to achieve clarity of thought and expression themselves. No programmes of wireless talks or visual aids will ever compensate for this neglect. Somehow pupils have to be persuaded that only by command of language can they give evidence of the possession of mind or make an individual contribution to the study of whatever other subject they may have chosen.

Some inkling of the importance of the study of grammar might be imparted by appealing to the history of early Greek philosophy. That accuracy of thought and validity of conclusions entirely depend on the understanding of syntax was early revealed in the history of scientific thought. The attempt of the early Greek philosophers to think out an explanation of what the world was made of, and how it had reached its present stage, broke down because the vehicle of their thought had not yet itself been subjected to scientific investigation. Heracleitus and Parmenides between them made all knowledge appear incapable of attainment. Concluding that movement and change are the only permanent reality, Heracleitus denied the validity of any statement about phenomena, because the subject of a statement has changed, before a sentence about it can be completed. Parmenides and the Eleatic Monists went to the opposite extreme. In their search for permanence and unity they assumed that only the objects of thought are real, and that the words of language have a permanent and consistent relation to this objective existence. If the words 'Queen of England' are not meaningless, they must refer to something that exists here and now. To say 'There *was* a Queen of England' is to say that a Queen of England does not exist. But one cannot think or name what does not exist. Therefore there is no 'nothing', no empty space for something to move into, and movement and change must be popular illusions. All that exists is unchanging in a continuous present, and all that can be said or known about it is that *it is*. To say 'grass is green' is to say that grass is something other than grass, which again is unthinkable.

The Eleatics froze the universe into a solid motionless plenum, because the nature of language was not yet understood. Further advance was possible only when Protagoras and his successors laid the foundations of scientific grammar. Educationists who think we can get along without it have all the less excuse, because modern philosophers are well enough aware that fallacious arguments can be avoided only by the careful study of language. Bertrand Russell, in the chapter on the philosophy of logical analysis in his *History of Western Philosophy*, says:

> 'It gradually became clear that a great part of philosophy can be reduced to something that may be called "syntax", though the word has to be used in a somewhat wider sense than has hitherto been customary. Some men, notably Carnap, have advanced the theory that all philosophical problems are really syntactical, and that, when errors in syntax are avoided, a philosophical problem is thereby solved or shown to be insoluble.'

If a student has been persuaded that syntax is something which he ought to learn about, how is he to be persuaded that it is worth his effort to begin with Latin or Greek, rather than with English, or French, or German? There are those who will tell him that the study of Latin will injure and not help his command of English, that the grammatical categories handed down to us from the rhetoricians of Greece and Rome do not fit, and that the study of formal grammar is an attempt to force English into an alien mould. There is enough truth in this argument to make it specious. But it is itself based on a misconception, that the Greek philosophers and rhetoricians invented a formal grammar that was applicable only to Greek. They did nothing of the sort; they merely invented names for the functions which they found their own language performing, and their classifications have survived, because they were correct. The functions which they identified are those which have to be performed by every human language on earth, to whatever group it belongs, whether inflexional like Indo-European or Semitic, polysynthetic like American Indian, agglutinative like Bantu or Turkish, or isolating like Chinese. In consequence of this misconception the Parts of Speech are still defined in current modern text-books as 'the various classes, or headings, under which all words used in speaking or writing may be arranged'. A single word in Latin or Greek may be performing the functions of all the Parts of Speech required to express a complete thought, i.e. a sentence may consist of a single word, without any other words being left to be understood. Also the same word may perform the functions of different Parts of Speech in different contexts. Under what single class or heading can such a word be put? It cannot be insisted too strongly that the Parts of Speech are not classes of words, but syntactical functions, and that the human mind does not care what means it seizes upon to perform these functions. It is prepared to use an adjective as an adverb, or as a noun (*Invitus hoc scribo. Bona fugientium diripiebantur*); it is prepared to use a noun as a verb (*That will fox you!*), or a verb as a noun (*'Habet!' exclamant*); it is prepared to defy all attempts to classify words, provided only that the intended meaning is conveyed. The fact that Latin employs a somewhat different machinery from English in its syntax makes it more, not less, useful as a medium in which to practise how to convey clear meaning. Both English and Latin belong to the same (Indo-European) group of languages, which begin by being inflexional and tend to develop analytically. Inflexions are discarded and separate words or word-order take their place. That is to say that syntax extends at the expense of accidence. The more component parts you have to play with, the easier it is to be untidy and inaccurate. It is easier to acquire skill in putting together a jigsaw picture, if you begin with one that is divided into fewer component parts.

The scientific methods of modern comparative philology have succeeded in establishing the main lines along which language develops, so that it has been possible to argue back beyond the period of recorded language and to reconstruct with reasonable probability the grammatical structure of the parent Indo-European. We find that, far from being rudimentary and simple, Indo-European was already possessed of a grammatical apparatus even more complicated than that of Latin and Greek. There were at least eight cases of the noun, which Latin and Greek have reduced to six and five respectively; and at least four moods of the verb, which Latin has reduced to three. All the same, it is difficult not to believe that the beginnings of language were of the simplest, and that the syntactical developments of particular languages or groups of languages have some connection with the intellectual achievements of the peoples speaking them. The science of philology cannot penetrate to these first beginnings, any more than the physical sciences can tell us how energy first came to be harnessed, or account for the existence of the universe. Science can investigate and explain only what we have, and how it works; it cannot explain how or why it came to be.

Lucretius in the *De Rerum Natura* and Darwin in *The Descent of Man* assume that human language is the natural development of animal cries in the ordinary course of evolution. Nothing could be further from the truth. There is a whole world of difference between noises that are conditioned reactions to physical stimulus and noises that are deliberately organized into an artificial system of signals. The language-barrier between man and the animals does exist. It consists in the power to sort out and classify sense-impressions. Animals live in a world of particulars. If they could classify and generalize, they would need labels for their classifications, and they would have had to invent some form of articulate language. The idea of equating an identifiable sound with an identified class of sense-impressions is the sort of flash of inspiration that can have happened only to an individual. In this sense there must have been a first man. According to the biblical account, in *Genesis* ii, 19, Adam laid the foundations of language by inventing nouns.

The physical universe which language was first invented to represent is a universe of space–time relations. To represent it completely, not only names for the ideas of *things* were needed, but names for distinguishable types of movement or state, and some means of indicating the space–time relations between the ideas which the nouns represented. The latter function is performed in existing languages by grammatical apparatus, but something could be done merely by the order in which the names or nouns were produced. If *x* was the sound representing the idea of a wolf, *y* a lamb, and *z* the act of killing, then *x y z* or *x z y* could be a comprehensible sentence, representing the idea of a wolf killing a lamb. It is possible that the earliest form of language was a 'newspaper-headline' language of this sort. But it too greatly lacked precision to remain long in this state. Only the particular context could determine what view the pronouncer of the sound *z* was taking of the act of killing, whether he wished to indicate that he had seen or was seeing it take place, or whether he conceived it as a future possibility, or whether he desired it to take place. So it must have been that, among some tribes of mankind, space-relations and others began to be represented by case-inflexions of *x* and *y*, while mood, tense, and person modifications took place in *z*, until it developed into the finite verb.

It is true that *a priori* speculation of this sort is very hazardous, where language is concerned. The philological evidence suggests that the most primitive languages are the most complicated and irregular, so that one must suppose that, if language did have simple beginnings, it soon sprouted into a jungle growth. The refinements of historical times have all been in the direction of simplification. There is, however, some scanty *a posteriori* evidence that the finite verb is a later acquisition than the noun or the verbal noun. There existed both in northern Semitic dialects and in Old Egyptian a simple uninflected form of the infinitive called the Infinitive Absolute,[1] which functioned sometimes as a verb, sometimes as a verbal noun. The Canaanite form became a fossilized relic, but the Egyptian parallel formed the basis of further developments. These two infinitive forms, because of their wide application and refusal to be tied down to a single syntactical function, seem likely to be relics of the most primitive stages of proto-Semitic and Old Egyptian speech. Such evidence, coming from the twin cradles of civilization, is not without significance. It suggests that the oldest use of the infinitive in Latin is not the Prolative Infinitive, wherein the case-inflexion indicates a locatival relation, but the Historic Infinitive. That, too, though the infinitive used in it is of the current inflected form, functions as if it were a finite verb. Its development as a trick of style by the historians

[1] See T. W. Thacker, *The Relationship of the Semitic and Egyptian Verbal Systems* (O.U.P. 1954), pp. 128 ff., 318, 323, 324–31.

is no evidence of its age, for it already exists in Plautus, and it seems likely to be the sole surviving relic in Latin from the time when neither had Indo-European yet developed a system of finite verbs.

The examples of usage quoted in the following chapters are taken from the series of authors from Plautus to Tacitus who are usually studied in classical courses in schools and universities. That is to say, account is taken only of three of the periods into which the development of Latin is usually divided. References to subsequent developments in the period of decadence are only incidental. The periods into which the development of Latin, as illustrated by extant literature, may be conveniently divided, are the following:

(1) 240 B.C.–88 B.C. Although the Latin of this period, from the end of the First Punic War to the end of the Social War, is usually called early or archaic, the main constructions are already standardized. 240 B.C. is a convenient date from which to begin, because it was the year in which Livius Andronicus produced his first play on the Greek model. From this point on, recorded Latin begins to differ from the spoken language. For example, Livius himself, in translating Homer's *Odyssey*, copies the archaism of the Greek by using Latin words and forms which were already obsolete in his own time. Ennius made this archaic style traditional for Epic, and he was followed by Lucretius and to some extent by Virgil. However, the only authors extant from this period, except in fragments, are Plautus and Terence. Prose is represented only by Cato's handbook *de Agri Cultura*, which is written in short and pungent sentences, with no attempt at literary style. Nevertheless, during this century and a half literary styles were emerging from the spoken language. Conscious choice was being exercised among the available methods of expression. The use of some, such as the gerund of transitive verbs and certain uses of the infinitive, begins to be restricted, while other constructions are extended and exploited. There is a groping after greater precision in the use of the tenses, particularly of the subjunctive. The nuances of the subjunctive begin to be extended and exploited in subordinate clauses. As political and forensic oratory flourished in this age, there is no doubt that Greek rhetoric was studied and applied to Latin, and that artistic oratorical style had been developed by the time of Sulla. But of this there are only fragmentary quotations. There is as yet no literary narrative prose.

(2) 87 B.C.–A.D. 14. This is the 'Golden' or 'Classical' Age in both prose and verse. In this age oratorical and philosophical prose is perfected by Cicero, and narrative prose by Caesar. Accidence and vocabulary are now carefully standardized. In the search for purity and clarity of expression, many syntactical doublets are weeded out. For example, the functions of *ad* with the accusative as opposed to the dative are regulated; the use of the preposition with the Ablative of Time is dropped; for reporting speech and thought indirectly preference is finally given to

the accusative and infinitive over a clause introduced by a conjunction such as *quod* or *ut*; the method of expressing purpose by means of the infinitive is discarded, and so on. Finally, the naïve juxtaposition of simple sentences is discarded except for particular effect. Complex thought finds expression in complex sentences in which the less important constituent parts are carefully subordinated, so that the completed period is clear, coherent, and rhythmically balanced. As the purity of Cicero and Caesar set the standard for many generations, it is usual to regard their Latin alone as strictly 'classical', and to sub-divide the period into (*a*) 'Classical' (87 B.C.–30 B.C.) and (*b*) 'Augustan' (30 B.C.–A.D. 14). But the periodic style of Cicero and the strict purity of Caesar did not win universal acceptance. Sallust regarded historical writing as the composition of a prose-epic, and accordingly sought to dignify his narrative by adopting some of the archaism of Ennian epic, both in vocabulary, phraseology, and to some extent in syntax. For example, he freely uses neuter plural adjectives with partitive genitives (cf. *strata viarum*), and the infinitive instead of an *ut*-clause after verbs of exhorting, demanding, persuading. Although such constructions had continued to be used in colloquial Latin, Sallust's use of them is to be attributed to poetic archaism. His style is as artificial as that of Cicero and Caesar, and he set the fashion for subsequent historical writing. Livy also rejects the exclusive purity of Caesarean syntax, but prefers the fuller periodic style of Cicero to the shorter pointed sentences of Sallust. In the wider sense, Sallust, Livy, and Cornelius Nepos must be counted as classical.

(3) A.D. 14–A.D. 180. The 'Silver' Age of the early Empire. The chief prose-authors of this age are Seneca, Petronius, Quintilian, Tacitus, Pliny the Younger, Suetonius, Fronto, Aulus Gellius, and Apuleius. The distinction between the language and style of prose and poetry is blurred in this age. The chief characteristics of both prose and verse are rhetoric and a striving after effect. Seneca writes short epigrammatic sentences, Quintilian prefers the Ciceronian period, and Tacitus elaborates and brings to perfection the style of Sallust. The admission into 'Silver' prose of constructions which were permissible only in verse in the classical period, but undoubtedly continued to be used in the spoken language of the people, may suggest that literary prose was being influenced by vulgar Latin. On the contrary, it is more likely that the gulf between literary and spoken Latin was widening. Authors continue to model themselves on their great predecessors, on the language of Virgil's *Aeneid* no less than on Ciceronian or Livian prose. By the age of the Antonines literary Latin had become completely artificial. It was handed on by Christian writers to the mediaeval priesthood, while vulgar Latin, when the unifying influence of the official language of the central bureaucracy was removed, broke up into the Romance vernaculars of modern Europe.

I

The Accusative Case

1. The functions of the accusative case can be divided broadly into two groups:

I. The word in the accusative, with or without the aid of a preposition, performs the function of an *adverb*, indicating the goal, direction, or extent of a movement or action, in space or time.

In this local sense, the accusative answers the questions whither? how far? how long? It is to be contrasted with the local senses of the ablative, which answers the questions whence? where? when?

II. The accusative is used as a mere grammatical sign, to indicate the direct object of a verb. This accusative is of two kinds:

(*a*) The word in the accusative indicates an *external* object (person or thing) upon which the action denoted by the verb is directly brought to bear, as in 'Brutus *Caesarem* occidit'.

(*b*) The word in the accusative denotes something inherent in the action of the verb itself, and merely helps to amplify or define the verbal notion, as in *cursum currere*, 'to run a course', *vitam vivere*, 'to live a life', *ludum ludere*, 'to play a game'. This is called the accusative of the Cognate, or Internal Object.

Note. Of these two types of accusative object, the cognate or internal is mostly used with intransitive verbs, and might therefore seem more fittingly to come under the same heading as the adverbial accusatives. Indeed, an example such as *vivere longam vitam* would seem to have some connexion with the accusative denoting extent or duration. But a word that was truly adverbial in function could not be used as the nominative subject of the passive verb (*vita vivitur, ludus luditur*, etc.). Furthermore, the use of the accusative of the internal object is extended until it appears to merge into type (a), e.g. *verba loqui*. It seems best, therefore, to classify it with the purely grammatical object-accusative.

2. At first sight there seems to be no connexion between the two groups of accusative functions indicated in the preceding section. Hence some grammarians hold that the Latin accusative is an amalgamation of two

original Indo-European cases, a 'grammatical' case, and a 'local' case. Although amalgamation accounts for the variety of the functions performed by the ablative, this explanation of the variety of accusative functions is most unlikely. Words and word-forms do not become mere grammatical signs, with no independent meaning of their own, except as the result of very long usage. The accusative denoting the object of a verb is therefore not original. On the other hand, simple space-relations must have needed to be expressed by most primitive man. We can be sure, therefore, that the earliest function of the accusative was an adverbial one, perhaps to indicate the goal of motion, and that the other uses developed gradually out of it. For example, the accusative denoting the external object of a transitive verb may have developed out of an original 'accusative of the goal' in some such way as follows. It is likely that in the early stages of language all verbs had a complete and independent significance of their own, i.e. that there were, to begin with, no transitive verbs at all. But a word in the accusative would so often be required to indicate the direction or goal of an action, particularly of a verb of motion, that in course of time it would come to be expected, and the verb would be felt to be incomplete without it. How the transitive verb was born in this way can be shown by a simple example. The verb *peto*, 'I seek', in extant Latin, is transitive, but the root *pet-*, seen in the Greek verb πέτομαι, 'I fly', originally signified merely rapid motion. But one rarely moves rapidly without an object in view, and soon the sense of the verb was felt to be incomplete without the accusative direction-giving word. Then *peto urbem* no longer meant 'I fly *to* the city', but 'I seek the city'. The verb had changed its meaning by absorbing the meaning of the case-ending, which thus became superfluous, but remained as the traditional shape of a word, when it denoted the object. Once this construction had arisen, linguistic usage would extend it indefinitely, and the number of transitive verbs would go on growing.

3. It is more difficult to account for the accusative denoting extent or duration. It may have developed directly out of the 'goal' notion, for 'He walked *to* the city' may mean 'He walked *as far as* the city', the adverbial phrase indicating the limits of the motion. But the limits of a motion can be indicated by a word expressing space or time, as well as by a word indicating a goal. So we can say 'He walked *as far as* ten miles', or 'He walked ten miles'. Compare also the expressions 'He lived to a great age', 'He lived as long as eighty years', and 'He lived eighty years'.

On the other hand, it is impossible not to suspect a connexion between the accusative of extent or duration and an internal accusative of the type 'He went *a long journey*', 'He lived *a long life*'. The substitution of a more particular expression such as 'He went *ten miles*', 'He lived *eighty years*', would be parallel to the substitution of *aleam ludere*, 'to play dice', for *ludum ludere*, 'to play a game'. (See 13 (ii).)

Accordingly, some grammarians derive the accusative of extent or duration from the accusative of the internal object. If this is right, the wheel has come full circle, for out of a grammatical function has developed a new adverbial one. It is particularly difficult with neuter singular adjectives and pronouns (*id*, *hoc*, *illud*, *aliquid*, etc., *multum*, *aliquantum*, etc.) to know whether they represent an extended use of the accusative of the internal object, or whether they are adverbial accusatives of extent. Does *aliquid gaudeo* mean 'I feel some joy', or 'I rejoice *to some extent*'? One cannot even decide the matter by turning the expression passively, for *aliquid gaudetur* may mean either '*Some joy* is felt' (nominative subject), or 'There is rejoicing *to some extent*' (adverb). When the neuter adjective or pronoun is plural, as in *multa peccat*, 'He makes many mistakes', it is obviously an internal object. It seems right, therefore, to classify the singulars under this heading. For examples, see Section 13 (iv).

4. *Prepositions*

When a case such as the accusative or ablative had acquired a variety of different functions, the danger of ambiguity arose. For instance, the intransitive verb *cedere*, 'to retire', came to be used also transitively in the sense 'to yield', 'give up'. Then *cedit urbem* would have been ambiguous, for it might have meant either 'He retires to the city', or 'He surrenders the city'. In such circumstances it became necessary to add another word, an adverb of place, to the accusative, in order to distinguish the former sense from the latter. Words like *ad*, *in*, *ab*, *ex*, *de* were originally such adverbs of place. When it had become necessary for them regularly to accompany an accusative or ablative, to express a certain sense, it began to be felt that a word in the accusative or ablative must *always* accompany them, and they ceased to be used as independent adverbs. They had become prepositions. The sense of the old case-ending was now expressed by a prepositional phrase, in which the preposition was capable of doing all the work. As after a transitive verb, so after a preposition, the case-ending had lost a good deal of its importance. But so long as the same preposition could accompany different cases, the case-ending did remain important. In English and Romance languages this development has been carried to its logical conclusion. Prepositions do all the work, and the shape of the noun is not changed.

5. *The Accusative answering the question 'Whither?' (Accusative of the Goal)*

The accusative indicating the goal or direction of movement is normally helped by prepositions such as *ad*, 'to', 'towards'; *in*, 'into', 'on to', 'against'; *sub*, 'up to'.

But throughout extant Latin literature particular expressions remain as relics from the time when the accusative could function alone. These are:

(i) Names of towns and small islands.
(ii) The words *domum*, 'to one's home', 'home'; *rus*, 'into the country'; *foras*, 'out of doors', 'out'.
(iii) Verbal nouns of the fourth declension, including the Supine, e.g. *venum ire* (*venire*), 'to go for sale', 'be sold'; *pabulatum ire*, 'to go a-foraging'. On the Supine, see 152–4.
(iv) The expression *infitias, exsequias, suppetias ire*, 'to deny', 'to go to a funeral', 'to go to the aid'.
(v) The poets omit the preposition freely with nouns other than those indicated above.

6. *Examples and Notes*

Cic. *Fam.* 12, 23, 2 *Antonius cogitabat legiones ad urbem adducere.* 'Antonius was thinking of bringing the legions to the city.' Caes. *B. C.* 1, 74, 4 *Varro Cordubam ad Caesarem venit.* 'Varro came to Corduba to Caesar' or '. . . to Caesar at Corduba.' (In the normal English, the prepositional phrase *at Corduba* is not an adverbial phrase indicating the goal of motion of the verb *came*, but is loosely attached as an adjectival phrase to the noun *Caesar*. Latin has not the equivalent of this idiom, but puts both the person and the place in the accusative of the goal.) Caes. *B. C.* 1, 37, 1 *Caesar legiones in Hispaniam praemiserat.* 'Caesar had sent forward the legions into Spain.' *Ibid.* 3, 35, 2 *Pompeius in Thessaliam pervenit.* 'Pompey arrived in Thessaly.' (Here the English prepositional phrase *in Thessaly* is misleading, for 'in' normally expresses place 'where', not 'whither'. The equivalent Latin expression of 'place where', *in Thessalia*, could never be used with a verb of motion to indicate the goal.) *Ibid.* 2, 14, 4 *Illi sub murum se recipiunt.* 'They retire beneath the wall.' (i.e. *up to the foot of* the wall.) Cic. *Font.* 12 *Sub populi Romani imperium ceciderunt.* 'They fell under the dominion of the Roman people.'

In the last example the 'goal' is abstract, and it is to be noticed that the goal-notion of the accusative is capable of a wide metaphorical extension, to express ideas such as purpose, tendency, and result: Cic. *Q. fr.* 1, 1, 26 *ad templum pecunias decreverunt.* 'They decreed funds for a temple.' *Id. Verr.* 2, 137 *pecuniam contulerunt in statuam.* 'They contributed money for a statue.' Liv. 9, 37, 12 *indutias in triginta annos impetraverunt.* 'They obtained a truce for thirty years.' Ter. *Ph.* 327 *deverberare ad necem.* 'To beat to death.' Cic. *Cl.* 188 *in familiae luctum nupsit.* 'She married to her family's grief.'

7. *Names of Countries*

The use of a preposition with the name of a country is regular, as in the examples in Section 6. *In* with the accusative means 'into' the country, *ad* means 'to the borders' of it. Nevertheless the preposition is occasionally omitted, even by the best prose-authors, particularly with Greek names, including *Aegyptus*: Caes. *B. C.* 3, 106, 1 *coniectans eum Aegyptum iter habere.* 'Guessing that he was on his way to Egypt.' But authors are not consistent with these exceptions, and no rule can be laid down.

Livy and later authors sometimes omit the preposition with names of countries other than those indicated above. This is probably due to the influence of the poets: cf. Virg. *Aen.* 1, 2–3 *Italiam, fato profugus, Lavinaque venit/litora.* 'Doomed to exile, he came to Italy and the Lavinian shores.'

8. *Names of Towns*

(i) The bare accusative of the name of a town which is the destination of a journey is regular, as in the second example in Section 6. Similarly the bare ablative is used of the name of a town which is the starting-point (Section 41 (1), 42): Cic. *T. D.* 5, 109 *Damaratus fugit Tarquinios Corintho.* 'Damaratus fled to Tarquinii from Corinth.' Nevertheless, when both the starting-point and the destination are thus given, it is common to find a preposition with the ablative name: Cic. *Verr.* 2, 99 *non ego a Vibone Veliam venissem.* 'I should not have come from Vibo to Velia.'

(ii) The preposition *ad* is regularly used by all prose-authors, if the motion is conceived as stopping short at the boundary of the town, *i.e.* to express the vaguer notion of 'towards', 'to the neighbourhood of', 'near': Caes. *B. G.* 7, 79, 1 *Commius reliquique duces ad Alesiam perveniunt.* 'Commius and the rest of the chiefs arrive *before* Alesia.' (They cannot *enter* the town, for Caesar's lines are between.)

However, authors are not consistent, for the verb *proficisci*, 'to set out', seems to involve the vaguer notion of 'direction', and yet it is more often accompanied by the bare accusative (and bare ablative) of the place-name: Caes. *B. C.* 1, 24, 1 *Pompeius Luceria proficiscitur Canusium atque inde Brundisium.* 'Pompey sets out from Luceria to Canusium and thence to Brundisium.' Yet cp. *B. G.* 7, 76, 5 *ad Alesiam proficiscuntur; B. C.* 1, 41, 2 *ad Ilerdam proficiscitur.*

It is not always possible to observe any distinction in sense, when the preposition instead of the bare case is used. All authors seem to waver to some extent, but Livy in particular: Liv. 8, 19, 13 *ad Privernum flexit iter.* 'He bent his march towards Privernum.' *Id.* 23, 2, 1 *Capuam flectit iter.*

All that can be said is that the idea of going to and entering a town is normally expressed by the bare accusative of the place-name, while the idea of going 'towards', 'in the direction of', 'to the boundary of', is normally expressed by the preposition *ad* with the accusative of the name.

(iii) A common noun like *oppidum* or *urbem* in apposition to the name normally has the preposition, though the preposition is sometimes omitted, if the name comes first. When the common noun is further qualified by an adjective, it regularly follows the name, and has the preposition: Caes. *B. G.* 2, 12, 1 *ad oppidum Noviodunum contendit.* 'He hastened to the town of Noviodunum.' Cic. *Rep.* 2, 34 *Demaratus fugisse dicitur Tarquinios, in urbem Etruriae florentissimam.* 'Demaratus is said to have fled into the most flourishing Etruscan city of Tarquinii.'

9. Domum, Rus, Infitias, etc.

(i) The bare accusative of *domus* is used both in the singular and in the plural, and even when qualified by a possessive adjective or genitive: Caes. *B. G.* 2, 10, 4 *constituerunt optimum esse domum suam quemque reverti.* 'They decided that it was best for each to return to his own home.' Nep. 16, 2, 5 *domum Charonis devenerunt.* 'They came to Charon's house.' Sall. *Jug.* 66, 3 *alius alium domos suas invitant.* 'They invite them severally to their homes.'

But prepositions are used in the following circumstances:

(*a*) When both the starting-point and the goal are given: Nep. 25, 22, 1 *ut non ex vita, sed ex domo in domum videretur migrare.* 'so that he did not seem to be departing from life, but from one home to another'. (Cf. the usage with place-names in 8 (i) above.)

(*b*) When *domus* means 'house', not in the sense of 'home', but of 'family': Cic. *Off.* 1, 138 *in suam domum consulatum primus attulit.* 'He was the first to bring the consulship into his family.'

(*c*) When the actual building or place is meant: Cic. *Mil.* 75 (*dixit*) *mortuum se in domum eius inlaturum.* 'He said he would bring a dead man into his house.'

(*d*) When *domum* is qualified by an adjective other than the possessive: Cic. *Ac.* 1, 13 *remigrare in domum veterem e nova.* 'to come back to an old home from a new one'.

But the poets, Livy, and later prose writers often use the preposition in any circumstances: Liv. 25, 10, 9 *recipere se in domos suas quemque iussit.* 'He ordered them to retire to their several homes.'

(ii) *Rus, Foras*: Ter. *Eun.* 216 *Ego rus ibo atque ibi manebo.* 'I shall go into the country and stay there.' Plaut. *Cas.* 211 *I foras, mulier.* 'Woman, leave the house!'

(iii) The phrase *infitias ire* is not used by Caesar or Cicero. It is usually negatived: Livy 9, 9, 4 *neque ego infitias eo foedera sancta esse.* 'Nor do I deny that treaties are sacred.'

The phrases *suppetias ire, exequias ire* occur mostly in early and in colloquial Latin.

10. *The Accusative answering the questions 'How far?' 'How long?'* (*Accusative of Extent or Duration*)

The accusative is used adverbially with both verbs and adjectives; with verbs, to indicate the extent of space or time covered by an action, or to indicate at what distance of space or time an action takes place; with adjectives, to give the dimensions of things:

Cic. *Quinct.* 78 *Nemo potest triduo septingenta milia passuum ambulare.* 'No one can walk seven hundred miles in three days.' *Id. Att.* 13, 20, 6 *A recta conscientia traversum unguem non oportet discedere.* 'One should not depart a nail's breadth from a good conscience.' *Id. T. D.* 1, 94 *Aristoteles ait bestiolas nasci quae unum diem vivant.* 'Aristotle says that little creatures are born which live for one day.' Caes. *B. G.* 4, 1, 8 *Maximam partem lacte vivunt.* 'For the most part they live on milk.' (In the last example there is no particular reference to space or time, but merely to extent or degree.) Caes. *B. G.* 1, 22, 5 *Milia passuum tria ab eorum castris castra ponit.* 'He pitches his camp three miles from theirs.' Caes. *B. G.* 7, 72, 4 *Turres pedes octoginta inter se distabant.* 'The turrets were eighty feet apart.' Cic. *T. D.* 5, 57 *Duodequadraginta annos tyrannus Syracusanorum fuit Dionysius, cum quinque et viginti natus annos dominatum occupavisset.* 'Dionysius was tyrant of Syracuse for thirty-eight years, having seized power at the age of five and twenty years.'

With adjectives: Livy 21, 28, 7 *Ratem ducentos longam pedes, quinquaginta latam in amnem porrexerunt.* 'They thrust out into the river a raft two hundred feet long and fifty broad.' Caes. *B. G.* 7, 24, 1 *Milites aggerem altum pedes octoginta exstruxerunt.* 'The soldiers raised a mound eighty feet high.'

Notes (i) The use of *natus* with the accusative, to give the age of a person, as *puer decem annos natus*, 'a boy ten years old' (lit. 'born ten years'), is an illogical extension of the usage, for it does not mean that the boy's birth extended over ten years.

(ii) *altus* is used in the sense of both 'high' and 'deep'. *Profundus* is not used with the accusative, and *crassus*, 'thick', only in early Latin.

(iii) Instead of an adjective with the accusative of extent, the Genitive of Quality or Description may be used, as Caes. *B. G.* 7, 46, 3 *sex pedum murus*, 'a wall of six feet' or 'a six-foot wall'. (See Sections 84–5.)

11. To indicate *how long ago* something happened, the accusative is used preceded by *abhinc*: Cic. *Verr.* II, 1, 34 *Quaestor fuisti abhinc annos quattuordecim.* 'You were quaestor fourteen years ago.' The normal word-order is (1) *abhinc*, (2) noun, (3) cardinal numeral. The same idea is often expressed by *ante*, either as a preposition with the accusative: Livy 39, 28, 4 *ea mihi paucos ante dies ademistis.* 'You took those away from me a few days ago.' – or as an adverb, with the ablative of the measure of difference, e.g. *biennio ante*, 'two years ago' (= '*earlier* by two years').

Like the English adverb 'ago', *abhinc* can be used only to measure backwards from the present moment. To express how long before some point of time already past, *ante* must be used.

The few instances that occur of *abhinc* with the ablative are probably due to a conflation of the construction of *abhinc* with the accusative and that of *ante* with the ablative.

12. To indicate how long something has or had been going on, the accusative is usually accompanied by *iam*. The verb must be in a tense of incomplete action, i.e. present or imperfect: Cic. *Flacc.* 70 *Annos iam triginta in foro versaris.* 'You have been practising at the bar for thirty years.' *Id. Man.* 7 *Annum iam tertium et vicesimum regnat.* 'He has now been reigning for twenty-two years.' (Lit. 'He reigns for the twenty-third year').

13. *The Accusative of the Internal Object*

(i) The simplest type of internal object is an accusative abstract noun of kindred origin with the verb. It does little more than add the name of the action which is being performed, e.g., *pugnam pugnat*, 'He fights a fight', *vitam vivit*, 'He lives a life', etc. In such examples the object is truly 'cognate', but when the noun is not of kindred origin with the verb, it is better to call it an 'internal' object.

An internal object without any epithet to give it added point is almost as rare in Latin as it is in English. Most of the examples that occur are archaic legalistic formulae, e.g. Livy 9, 10, 9 *noxam nocuerunt*, 'they have done a wrong' (a phrase occurring in the XII tables). English normally substitutes a general verb of 'doing' for the kindred verb, as '*make* a mistake', '*do* a wrong', etc.

Examples: Cic. *pro Mur.* 61 (*huius sententia est*) *solos sapientes esse, si servitutem serviant, reges.* 'His view is that only the wise, even in a state of bondage, are kings' (*servitutem servire* is a legal phrase). Plaut. *Pers.* 494 *faciam ut mei memineris dum vitam vivas.* 'I will make you remember me so long as you live your life.' (Such use of words that add nothing to the sense is characteristic of colloquial language.)

(ii) Much commoner is the type of internal object by which the action of the verb is further defined either by the presence of an epithet attached to the noun, or by a noun of narrower sense being substituted for the cognate noun. The livelier colloquial language of Plautus and Terence and the more emotional language of poetry provide the most examples. There are, however, a fair number in the prose of Cicero, but none in Caesar, and only a few in Livy and later prose: (*a*) Cognate noun with epithet: Plaut. *Pseud.* 525 *istam pugnam pugnabo.* 'I shall fight that battle of yours.' Ter. *Eun.* 586 *consimilem luserat ludum*, 'He had played a similar game.' Cic. *Agr.* 2, 44 *cur non eosdem cursus cucurrerunt?* 'Why did they not run the same courses?' Cael. in Cic. *Fam.* 8, 2, 1 *ut suum gaudium gauderemus.* '. . . that we might share his joy'. Cic. *Clu.* 17 (*vitam*) *quam tum ille vivebat.* 'The life which he was then leading.' (*b*) Noun of different root or narrower application: Plaut. *Aul.* 830 *garrire nugas.* 'To chatter nonsence.' Cic. *Phil.* 2, 63 *vinum redolere.* 'to smell of wine' (for *vini olorem*). Suet. *Claud.* 33, 2 *aleam studiosissime lusit.* 'He played dice most assiduously.' Cic. *Phil.* 5, 20 *sanguinem nostrum sitiebat.* 'He was thirsting for our blood.'

In the last example *sanguinem* is substituted for *sanguinis sitim* – a particular kind of thirst – but as it denotes something concrete, it tends to give the verb a transitive meaning 'to thirst *for*' instead of 'to be thirsty'. The poets can be very bold in their use of internal accusatives, e.g. Virg. *Aen.* i, 328 *nec vox hominem sonat.* 'Nor has your voice a human sound' (for *hominis* or *humanum sonum*).

Note 1. Instead of an internal accusative, it is often possible to use the instrumental ablative of means, cause, or respect, and this is the commoner prose-construction. So instead of *aleam ludere* it would be more usual to say *alea ludere*, 'to play *with* dice', and with Gell. 2, 11, 4 *triumphavit triumphos novem*, 'he celebrated nine triumphs', compare Livy 10, 46, 2 *triumphavit insigni triumpho.*

Note 2. For the passive equivalent of *pugnare pugnam*, etc., see Plaut. *Amph.* 253 *haec pugnata pugna est*, 'this battle has been fought'. The following suggest that the Roman mind, at any rate, connected the accusative of the internal object with the accusative of extent or duration: Cat. 5, 6 *nox est perpetua una dormienda*, 'one eternal night is to be slept through'; Ov. *Met.* 12, 188 *annos/vixi bis centum, nunc tertia vivitur aetas.* 'I have lived two hundred years, now my third century is being lived.' In the active form of the latter, *nunc tertiam vivo aetatem*, the accusative would certainly have to be classed as an accusative of extent or duration.

(iii) When the object is not an abstract cognate noun, but a noun that denotes some external manifestation of the action, or a result that remains after the action has ceased, as *dicta dicere*, *verba loqui*, *scribere epistulam*, *aedes aedificare*, etc., it is difficult to know whether to class the object as external or internal. Hence such an accusative is sometimes put in a separate category and called 'The Accusative of the Result produced'.

(iv) For a noun may be substituted a neuter pronoun or neuter adjective used substantivally: Cic. *Phil.* 1, 4, 11 *Pauca querar.* 'I shall make a few complaints.' *Id. N. D.* 1, 31 *Xenophon eadem fere peccat.* 'Xenophon makes almost the same mistakes.' *Id. de Sen.* 32 *vellem idem posse gloriari quod Cyrus.* 'I should have liked to be able to make the same boast as Cyrus.' Nep. 15, 6, 1 *in oratione sua multa invectus est in Thebanos.* 'In his speech he uttered much invective against the Thebans.'

The singular of pronouns and adjectives is far commoner than the plural. In classical prose only pronouns such as *id*, *hoc*, *illud*, *quod*, *quid*, *aliquid*, *nihil*, etc., are used, and adjectives denoting quantity or degree, such as *multum*, *plus*, *plurimum*, *tantum*, *quantum*, *aliquantum*, etc. In the singular, these are often indistinguishable from adverbs, as remarked in Section 3.

The poets and later prose-writers extend the usage to adjectives other than those mentioned above, which then usually have to be translated by adverbs: Hor. *Sat.* 1, 4, 76 *suave locus voci resonat.* 'The place echoes pleasantly to the voice.' Virg. *Aen.* 6, 288 *horrendum stridens.* 'Shrieking horribly.' Tac. *Ann.* 4, 60 *falsum renidens.* 'Smiling falsely.'

14. *The Internal Accusative with transitive verbs*

A transitive verb may have two accusative objects, one external, the other internal. The external object is usually a person, e.g. *docet me musicam.* 'He teaches me music.' The internal object is more often a neuter pronoun or adjective than a noun, e.g. *multum te amo,* and is often indistinguishable from an adverb. The construction, at least when the second accusative is clearly an internal object and not adverbial, is much less common in Latin than in Greek. The only transitive verbs which commonly govern a second *noun* in the accusative are certain verbs of *asking, teaching,* and *concealing* (see Section 16). In the passive, it is always the external object which becomes the subject, while the internal accusative is retained, as *rogatus sententiam,* 'being asked his opinion'.

Examples of neuter pronoun or adjective: Ter. *Hec.* 766 *Hoc te moneo unum.* 'I give you this one piece of advice.' *Id. Heaut.* 982 *neque me quicquam consilio adiuvas.* 'You give me no help with your counsel.' Cic. *Att.* 13, 22, 4 *Illud accuso non te, sed illum.* 'I make that accusation not against you, but him.' *Ib.* 1, 1, 5 *multum te amamus.* 'We have much love for you.' (But in the last example *multum* is best regarded as a fully-fledged adverb, so also *plus, plurimum, tantum, quantum,* etc.)

15. *Accusative in apposition to the sentence.* An extended use of the accusative of the internal object is to be found in the 'accusative in apposition to the sentence' whereby a word or words in the accusative are added as an amplification of the whole predicate: Sall. *H.* 4, 69, 8 *Eumenem prodidere Antiocho, pacis mercedem.* 'They betrayed Eumenes to Antiochus (as) the price of peace.' Virg. *A.* 6, 222 *pars ingenti subiere feretro,/ triste ministerium.* 'Some took up the mighty bier, a sad service.' Tac. *Ann,* 1, 27 *deserunt tribunal . . . manus intentantes, causam discordiae et initium armorum.* 'They deserted the tribunal . . . using threatening gestures, the cause of strife and the beginning of conflict.'

16. *The Construction of* rogo (posco *etc.*), doceo, *and* celo

(i) With *rogo,* 'inquire', 'ask a question', the only type of internal accusative normally used is that of a neuter pronoun or adjective, e.g. *id te rogo,*

'I ask you that question'. If the thing asked about is denoted by a noun, *de* with the ablative is used (*rogare aliquem de aliqua re*).

Note 1. The noun-clause of an indirect question after *rogo* is an *internal object*.

Note 2. The construction of *quaero* is *aliquid ab* (or *ex*) *aliquo*.

(ii) With *rogo*, 'request', 'ask *for*', and other verbs of requesting and demanding, e.g. *oro, posco, postulo, flagito*, a second (internal) accusative, whether of a pronoun or of a noun, is rare. A second object after these verbs is usually a noun-clause introduced by *ut* or *ne* (see 134, 146). In classical Latin a second *noun* in the accusative is regular only in the following technical phrases: *rogare aliquem sententiam*, 'to ask someone for his opinion' (of procedure in the senate), and *rogare populum magistratus*, 'to propose magistrates to the people for election': Cic. *Q. F.* 2, 1, 3 *Racilius me primum sententiam rogavit.* 'Racilius asked me first for my opinion.' Livy 6, 42, 14 *Factum est senatus consultum ut duumviros aediles dictator populum rogaret.* 'A senatorial decree was passed that the dictator should propose the election of two aediles to the people.' In the passive, the second accusative is retained: Cic. *Dom.* 16 *rogatus sum sententiam.* 'I was asked my opinion.'

Only in early Latin, in poetry, and in later prose is a noun sometimes found as a second object after *rogo*: Plaut. *Pseud.* 1070 *Roga me viginti minas.* 'Ask me for twenty minae.' Hor. *C.* 2, 16, 1 *otium divos rogat.* 'He asks the gods for rest.' Sen. *Contr.* 1, 7. 9 *Te similem sortem rogo.* 'I ask you for a similar chance.'

With the exceptions mentioned above, such examples as the latter are not to be found in Caesar or Cicero, but Cicero does occasionally use the construction after *posco*: *Verr.* II, 1, 44 *magistratum Sicyonium nummos poposcit.* 'He demanded money of a magistrate of Sicyon.'

With *oro* the construction is not classical, but there are isolated examples in Livy and later authors: Livy 28, 5, 6 *auxilia regem orabant.* 'They were begging the king for help.'

With *flagito* the double accusative is found only once in Cicero and once in Caesar: Cic. *de Dom.* 14 *me frumentum flagitabant*; Caes. *B. G.* 1, 16, 1.

N.B. The normal construction of *posco, postulo, flagito*, and also of *peto*, is *aliquid ab aliquo.*

(iii) After *doceo* a second accusative of a noun is not really common in classical Latin. The commonest construction is an external object (person) with an infinitive: *Docet me scribere.* 'He teaches me to write.' Examples of double accusative: Plaut. *Tr.* 1016 *Is hunc hominem cursuram docet.* 'That (his gullet) is instructing this fellow in the art of running.' Sall. *Cat.* 16, 1 *Catilina iuventutem mala facinora edocebat.* 'Catiline was teaching the youth evil ways.' Passive equivalent: Hor. *C.* 3, 6, 21 *motus doceri gaudet Ionicos.* 'She rejoices to be taught Ionic dances.' Livy 6, 32, 7

Latinae legiones longa societate militiam Romanam edoctae . . . 'The Latin legions, taught Roman military methods by their long association . . .'

Instead of *doceri* Cicero and Caesar use *discere*, and with the past participle *doctus* classical prose prefers the ablative of respect, e.g. *homo litteris Graecis doctus*, 'a man learned in Greek literature'.

When *doceo* means 'inform', 'tell', the thing told is either expressed in an accusative and infinitive noun-phrase, as after other verbs of speaking, or by a neuter pronoun, or *de* with the ablative is used (*docere aliquem de aliqua re*): Caes. *B. G.* 7, 10, 3 *Praemittit qui Boios de suo adventu doceant.* 'He sends forward men to inform the Boii of his arrival.'

(iv) *Celo*, besides meaning 'conceal', can mean 'to keep someone in the dark'. The normal construction in the latter sense is the accusative of the person and *de* with the ablative of the thing (*celare aliquem de aliqua re*): Cic. *Fam.* 7, 20, 3 *Bassus noster me de hoc libro celavit.* 'Our friend Bassus kept me in the dark about this book.'

But in early and in colloquial Latin *celo* is sometimes made to express both senses at once, and is accordingly followed by two accusatives, one of the person, the other of the thing: Plaut. *Bacch.* 375 *Ut celem patrem tua flagitia?* 'I conceal your misdeeds from your father?' Of this construction with *celo* there is only one example in Cicero (Letters), and one in Livy, but none in Caesar.

17. *Other constructions which involve two accusatives with the same verb are the following:*

(i) A factitive verb is accompanied by a second accusative of the predicate, as *Ciceronem consulem creaverunt.* 'They made Cicero consul'; *me matrem tuam appellant.* 'They call me your mother.'

(ii) Transitive verbs implying motion (sending, carrying, etc.), when compounded with a preposition, may have a second accusative of the 'place over which', 'through which', etc. The second accusative depends on the preposition contained in the verb, as *milites flumen transportare*, 'to ferry soldiers across a river'. The second accusative will naturally be retained in the passive: *milites flumen transportati*, 'soldiers ferried across a river'.

(iii) A verb-phrase like *animum advertere*, 'to turn one's attention to', may be felt to be equivalent in sense to a single transitive verb, and may then take an accusative object in addition to the accusative which is already present in the phrase: Cic. *T. D.* 3, 48 *animum advertit Gracchus in contione Pisonem stantem.* 'Gracchus noticed Piso standing in the assembly.' So with the phrases *manum inicere aliquem*, 'to lay hands on someone', 'arrest someone'; *ius iurandum adigere aliquem*, 'to bind someone on oath'.

18. (i) A number of intransitive verbs, when compounded with a preposition, acquire a transitive meaning and take an accusative object:

adire aliquem, 'to approach someone', *adloqui aliquem*, 'to address someone', *praeterire aliquem* or *aliquid*, 'to pass over, neglect, someone or something'. This is natural enough, when the preposition is one that itself takes the accusative, but it also happens occasionally when the preposition is one that takes the ablative: *egredi pueritiam*, 'to leave one's boyhood behind', *congredi aliquem*, 'to meet someone'. In some cases this construction is an alternative to the use of a prepositional phrase: *congredi cum aliquo*.

(ii) A number of verbs expressing emotion, such as *dolere*, *flere*, *gaudere*, *laetari*, etc., which are primarily intransitive, developed a transitive sense and were followed by an accusative of the thing causing the emotion. *gaudere* then means 'to rejoice *at*', *flere* 'to weep *over*' or 'bewail', and so on. This is a development of the internal object-accusative of the type dealt with in Section 13 (ii) (cf. *sitire sanguinem*, 'to be thirsty *for* blood'). The usage is mainly poetic, but some of these verbs are so used in good prose: Cic. *pro Sest.* 60 *flens meum casum*, 'weeping over my misfortune'; *ibid.* 145 *meum casum luctumque doluerunt*, 'They grieved over my misfortune and grief'. Caes. *B. G.* 1, 32, 4 *quod Ariovisti crudelitatem horrerent*, 'because they shuddered at Ariovistus' cruelty'.

(iii) Of the deponents *fruor*, *fungor*, *potior*, *utor*, *vescor*, in early Latin *fungor* regularly takes an accusative object, the rest occasionally. It is possible that this early transitive use accounts for the existence of a *passive* gerundive of these verbs. In classical Latin they are all regularly constructed with the ablative.

19. *Poetic uses of the Accusative under the influence of Greek*

By the poets, and occasionally by later prose-writers imitating them, an accusative is used:

(i) with adjectives, to denote that in respect of which the adjective is applied: Ov. *Met.* 9, 307 *flava comas*, 'fair as to her hair'; Virg. *Aen.* 5, 97 *nigrantes terga iuvencos*, 'bullocks dusky as to their backs'; Tac. *Germ.* 17 *feminae nudae bracchia et lacertos*, 'women bare as to their forearms and upper arms'. So also *Cressa genus*, 'Cretan as to her race'.

(ii) with passive participles, and occasionally with a finite verb, to denote a part of the body affected: Virg. *Aen.* 12, 64 *lacrimis perfusa genas*, 'bedewed as to her cheeks with tears'; *ibid.* 468 *hoc concussa metu mentem*, 'smitten in mind by this fear'; Lucr. 3, 487 *tremit artus*, 'trembles in his limbs'; Livy 21, 7, 10 *femur tragula ictus*, 'struck in the thigh by a javelin'.

(iii) with passive participles, and occasionally with finite passive forms, especially of verbs connected with the donning of clothing (*induor*, *succingor*), to denote that with which the action of the passive verb was effected: *Indutus pallam*, 'clothed with a robe'; *flores inscripti nomina*, 'flowers inscribed with names'.

The normal Latin method of expressing these ideas is by the ablative case, whether instrumental or of respect (e.g. Virg. *Aen.* 10, 775 *indutus spoliis*, 'clothed with spoils', cf. also *oculo captus*, 'blinded in the eye'), and the accusative was introduced and developed by the poets in imitation of Greek. The examples of the first group are obviously an imitation of the Greek Accusative of Respect, and so probably are those of the second group. But those of the third group, and possibly examples such as *femur ictus* of the second group, look like an attempt to revive, under Greek influence, the sense of the 'middle' voice, which had become obsolete in Latin.

The Middle Voice, out of which the Passive originally developed, had a quasi-reflexive sense. Its inflexions in Greek are, in most tenses, the same as those of the passive. It denotes an action that the subject does to himself, or for his own profit, or that he gets done for himself; and so we come finally to the passive sense, of an action done to the subject without any design on his part. The middle sense is sufficiently active for the verb to take an external accusative object: διδάσκομαι τὸν υἱόν, 'I have my son taught'; βοστρύχους κεκαρμένη, 'having had her locks shorn'.

This middle voice survives in early Latin, but only in examples such as *indutus pallam.* The following examples undoubtedly represent a revival and extension of it: Virg. *Aen.* 7, 640 *loricam induitur.* 'He dons his breastplate.' *Id. Aen.* 2, 510 *ferrum cingitur.* 'He girds on his sword.' Hor. *Sat.* 1, 6, 74 *laevo suspensi loculos tabulamque lacerto.* 'Dangling from their left arms their satchels and slates.' Virg. *Geor.* 4, 13 *picti squalentia terga lacerti.* 'Lizards coloured on their scaly backs' ('having had their backs painted'). Sall. *Hist.* 3, 24 *inulti terga ab hostibus caedebantur.* 'They had their backs slashed by the enemy without avenging themselves.' Tac. *Ann.* 1, 50 *frontem ac tergum vallo munitus.* 'Having guarded his front and rear with a rampart.' Virg. *Ecl.* 3, 106 *flores inscripti nomina regum.* 'Flowers that have had inscribed on them the names of kings.' Id. *Aen.* 2, 273 *perque pedes traiectus lora tumentes.* 'And having had thongs thrust through his swelling feet.'

II

The Infinitive Mood. Accusative and Infinitive

20. The Infinitive is not, strictly speaking, a mood of the verb, but an abstract verbal noun. *Currere*, 'to run', or 'running', is the *name* of a type of activity. One can imagine a very primitive stage of linguistic development in which actions and states could only be named, when the finite forms of verbs had not yet grown out of these verbal nouns. In such circumstances a speaker, wishing to draw someone's attention to a wolf

running across a field, could only utter the word for 'wolf' and associate it with the word for 'running'. *Lupus currere* would be the Latin equivalent of this primitive man's statement 'A wolf is (*or* was) running'. Although the Latin forms of the Infinitive are morphologically recent, the present infinitive has inherited this primitive method of expression, which is known as the *Historic Infinitive.*

21. The *Historic Infinitive* is used in excited narrative to describe an unfolding scene, a state of feeling, or the beginning or repetition of striking actions: Plaut. *Amph.* 229 *clamorem utrimque ecferunt. imperator utrimque Iovi vota suscipere, utrimque hortari exercitum.* 'They raise a shout on either side. On either side the general proceeds to offer vows to Jove and exhort his army.' *Id. Bacch.* 289 *ubi portu eximus, homines remigio sequi, neque aves neque venti citius.* 'When we get outside the harbour, the men row after us, fast as a bird, fast as the wind.' But historic infinitives are seldom used singly. There are usually two or more, as in the first example, and in the following: Ter. *Hec.* 181 *si quando ad eam accesserat confabulatum, fugere e conspectu ilico, videre nolle.* 'Whenever she approached to speak to her, she would straightway fly from her sight and refuse to see her.' Cic. *Verr.* II, 2, 188 *postulo ut mihi respondeat qui sit is Verrucius. clamare omnes neminem unquam in Sicilia fuisse Verrucium. ego instare ut mihi respondeat* . . . 'I demand that he tell me who this Verrucius is; all begin to shout that there was never any Verrucius in Sicily; I continue to insist on a reply . . .'

Possibly evidence of the antiquity of this method of expression is to be found in the fact that in Plautus and Terence the historic infinitive is still not used in the passive form. Passive forms begin to appear only in the literary language. The historians in particular developed the construction as a stylistic device for painting a scene with a few rapid strokes: Sall. *Jug.* 101, 11 *tum spectaculum horribile in campis patentibus: sequi, fugere, occidi, capi.* 'Then a dreadful scene in the open plains: pursuit – flight – (men) being slaughtered and taken prisoner.' Although the infinitive in this construction acts as if it were a finite verb, its original substantival nature is clear in the last example, for the infinitives are in apposition to the noun *spectaculum.*

22. *The Prolative Infinitive.* In Indo-European languages the infinitive verbal nouns acquired case-inflexions like other nouns. The Sanskrit infinitive has an accusative termination identical with the Latin Supine, while Greek and Latin infinitives have terminations which were originally locative or dative. Nouns with the locative or dative inflexion have an *adverbial* function, denoting the sphere in which, or the end for which, a person or thing acts or moves or exists. *Possum currere* must have meant originally something like 'I have power in the sphere of running', *volo currere,* 'I exercise my will in running', and so on.

The infinitive used in this way with a finite verb is called the *Prolative Infinitive* because it 'carries on' or extends the sense of the finite verb.

23. Verbs taking a prolative infinitive had been extending and interacting upon one another for so long before Plautus that it is no longer possible to classify them according to their historical order of development. The following are some of the most important: verbs expressing will, wish, purpose, endeavour: *volo, nolo, malo, cupio, iubeo, veto, constituo, cogito, paro, cogo, sino, prohibeo, conor, nitor, studeo*; verbs expressing daring and the reverse: *audeo, timeo, metuo, vereor*; power and the reverse: *possum, nequeo, scio* ('Know how to'), *nescio, disco*; duty and habit: *debeo, soleo, assuesco, consuesco, assuefacio*; hastening, continuing, hesitating: *propero, festino, maturo, insto, persevero, pergo, cesso, dubito* ('hesitate'); beginning and ending: *coepi, incipio, desino, desisto.*

The infinitive can also stand as the subject of a number of so-called 'impersonals': *decet, dedecet, iuvat, delectat, licet, libet, piget, pudet, paenitet, praestat, prodest, obest,* and many phrases of equivalent sense, such as *aequum est, difficile est, necesse est,* etc. Examples: Cic. *Br.* 206 *Aelius Stoicus esse voluit, orator autem nec studuit* (*sc. esse*) *unquam nec fuit.* 'Aelius wished to be a Stoic, but was neither keen to be an orator nor ever was one.' Caes. *B. C.* 1, 64, 3 *Caesar timebat tantae magnitudinis flumini exercitum obicere.* 'Caesar feared to expose his army to a river of such magnitude.' Livy 22, 51, 4 *vincere scis, Hannibal, victoria uti nescis.* 'You know how to conquer, Hannibal, but you do not know how to use your victory.' Cic. *Att.* 16, 16C, 10 *suos quisque debet tueri.* 'Each ought to protect his own.' Caes. *B. G.* 1, 7, 1 *Caesar maturat ab urbe proficisci.* 'Caesar hastens to set out from the city.' Plaut. *Bacch.* 481 *alia memorare dispudet.* 'It shames (me) to mention other things.' Tac. *Ann.* 1, 73 *haud pigebit referre . . .* 'It will not be irksome to relate . . .' (Other constructions of impersonal verbs will be dealt with later.)

24. The habitual association of an infinitive with a particular group of finite verbs had a twofold effect, comparable with that of the association of an accusative of the goal with verbs of movement, referred to in Section 2. Firstly, some of the finite verbs lost their independence and could no longer express a complete idea without the help of an infinitive (the so-called 'modal' or 'indeterminate' verbs). Secondly, the significance of the infinitive's case-inflexion was lost to sight, and its function became purely grammatical. Used with verbs which had become transitive, it appeared to be an accusative object (cp. *timeo pugnare* and *timeo pugnam*). Even when the prolative infinitive was added as an extension of the predicate to verbs such as *iubeo, veto, sino,* which already took an accusative object (*iubeo te ire*), the adverbial function and the purposive sense of the infinitive's inflexion was no longer felt, but it came to be regarded as a second accusative object.

25. *The Accusative and Infinitive Noun-phrase.*

The next step in syntactical development was an associational shift, whereby the infinitive with a verb which already had an object was dissociated from the finite verb and associated with the accusative object, so that the word in the accusative together with the infinitive formed a noun-phrase in which the accusative appeared to be the subject of the infinitive. Thus, in a sentence like *cogo te abire*, the meaning was no longer felt to be something like 'I force you *into going away*', wherein *you* is alone the object, while *into going away* is an adverbial extension, but something like 'I compel *your departure*', the accusative and infinitive phrase *te ire* standing as a composite object-noun. Such phrases could be used not only as objects, but also as subjects, and one could say: *Te abire mihi displicet*, 'Your departure displeases me', or 'It displeases me *for you to go away*'.

Both the infinitive alone and the infinitive in combination with an accusative 'subject' could now be used substantivally as the subject or object of a finite verb: *errare est humanum*. 'To err is human.' Cic. *T. D.* 5, 111 *docto homini et erudito vivere est cogitare*. 'To a learned and cultivated man to live is to think.' Ter. *Phor.* 913 *viduam extrudi turpe est*. 'It is disgraceful for a widow to be thrust out.' Plaut. *Mer.* 1010 *nunquam te patiar perire*. 'I shall never suffer you to perish.'

These developments had taken place before extant Latin literature begins, and from the beginning of our records the infinitive is treated as an indeclinable neuter verbal noun, which, with few exceptions, could be used substantivally only as subject or object in the nominative or accusative.

26. *The Infinitive with Adjectives.*

The original adverbial function of the infinitive is still clear when it is used to explain or limit the application of an adjective, e.g. *paratus mori*, 'prepared for dying'. This construction is not common in Latin, but was extended in poetry and later prose in imitation of Greek. In classical Latin prose the only adjectives followed by this 'explanatory' infinitive are participles, used adjectivally, from some of the verbs indicated in section 23, e.g. *paratus, assuetus, solitus*. When the construction is extended to other adjectives, they are usually such as suggest a verbal notion, and can be treated as almost synonymous with some of the participles mentioned above, e.g. *cupidus, avidus* (cf. *cupiens*), *peritus, nescius*. The use of the infinitive in poetry and later prose with adjectives such as *audax, blandus, callidus, fortis, lentus, piger, dignus*, etc., is probably to be attributed to the influence of Greek (cf. δέξιος λέγειν, 'clever at speaking'; ἄξιος ἰδεῖν, 'worth seeing'). Examples: Hor. *Od.* 1, 3, 25 *audax omnia perpeti*. 'Bold to endure all things.' *Ibid.* 12, 11 *blandus . . . ducere quercus*. 'With charm to draw the oak-trees after him.' *Id. Sat.* 1, 4, 12 *piger . . . ferre laborem.* 'Slothful in enduring toil.' Ov. *Met.* 5, 146 *sagax futura videre.* 'Sagacious in seeing the future.' *Ibid.* 1, 240 *digna perire.* 'Worthy to perish.' Pliny, *Pan.* 7 *dignus erat eligi.* 'He was worthy to be chosen.'

The prose equivalent of the infinitive after most of the above adjectives would be *in* with the locatival ablative of the gerund or gerundive (*audax in perpetiendo*, etc.).

27. *Less usual uses of the Infinitive.*

When the infinitive had come to be regarded as an indeclinable neuter, usable only in the nominative and accusative, other forms of verbal nouns had to supply the other oblique cases. Hence most grammars give the following scheme of declension: N. A. *scribere* (but *ad scribendum*), G. *scribendi*, D. A. *scribendo.*

Other restrictions on the use of the infinitive as a noun are probably to be attributed to its close association with the verbal system: (i) Its use as object of verbs other than those of the types indicated in Section 23 is much restricted. (ii) It is not normally qualified by an adjective or by a word in the genitive. (iii) It is not normally made to depend upon a preposition.

Nevertheless exceptions are to be found both in colloquial and in literary Latin: Plaut. *Bacch.* 158 *hic vereri perdidit.* ('has lost his *feeling of respect*'); Cic. *Br.* 140 *ipsum Latine loqui.* 'the very fact of speaking (correct) Latin.' *Id. de Or.* 2, 24 *me hoc ipsum nihil agere delectat.* 'as for me, this very fact of doing nothing delights me.' Val. Max. 7, 3, 7 *cuius* (sc. *Fabii Cunctatoris*) *non dimicare vincere fuit.* 'whose abstention from fighting was tantamount to victory.'

From Cicero onwards the infinitive is sometimes governed by the preposition *inter*, and in the poets by *praeter*: Sen. *de Ben.* 5, 10 *multum interest inter dare et accipere.* 'There is a great difference between giving and receiving.' Hor. *Sat.* 2, 5, 65 *inveniet nil sibi legatum praeter plorare.* 'He will find that nothing has been bequeathed to him except to lament.'

All the above examples may owe something to the Greek use of the infinitive with the article.

28. *The Infinitive expressing Purpose.*

The loss of perception of the original locative-dative sense of the infinitive inflexion may account for the reluctance of literary Latin to avail itself of the infinitive to express purpose (except for the phrase *dare bibere*). The notion of 'the end aimed at' is inherent in the dative, as *auxilio venire alicui*, 'to come to someone's aid'. But the very natural use of the infinitive to express purpose is found in early Latin, and continues in colloquial Latin and in poetry: Plaut. *Bacch.* 631 *venerat aurum petere.* 'He had come to seek the gold.' *Id. Pseud.* 642 *reddere hoc, non perdere erus me misit.* 'My master sent me to pay this back, not to lose it.' Virg. *Aen.* 1, 527 *non . . . Libycos populare penates venimus.* 'We have not come to plunder Libyan homes.' Hor. *Od.* 1, 2, 7 *Proteus pecus egit altos visere montes.* 'Proteus drove his flock to visit the high mountains.'

It is to be noticed that this use of the infinitive occurs only after verbs of motion, after which, in literary Latin, the Supine, a verbal noun in the accusative 'of the goal', may be used (*pabulatum ire,* 'to go a-foraging').

29. *The Accusative and Infinitive after verbs of Saying, Thinking, and Perceiving. Indirect Statement* (Oratio Obliqua)

The composite noun-phrase consisting of an accusative with an infinitive, of which the development was described in Section 25, came to be the characteristic Latin method of turning a statement of fact into a noun-equivalent which could stand as the object of verbs of saying, thinking, or perceiving. In order to report a statement indirectly, the nominative subject of the statement is put into the accusative, and the indicative verb into the infinitive. Thus *Caesar proficiscitur* becomes (*dico, puto, video*) *Caesarem proficisci.* 'I say, think, see, *that Caesar is setting out.*' When the subject of the indicative of the original direct statement was contained in the verb, and not separately expressed by a noun or pronoun, the accusative of the appropriate pronoun is regularly supplied with the infinitive. Thus *Erro,* 'I am making a mistake', becomes *Dico me errare,* 'I say that I am making a mistake', or *dicis te errare,* 'you say that you are making a mistake', or *dicit se errare,* 'he says that he (himself) is making a mistake'. *Erras* becomes *dico, dicit, te errare*; *errat* becomes *dico, dicis, dicit eum errare,* and so on, according to the person of the verb in the statement to be reported, and the point of view of the subject of the verb of saying, thinking, or perceiving.

30. *Tenses of the Infinitive in Indirect Statement*

As there are only three tenses of the infinitive, while there are seven tenses of the indicative finite verb, it will be seen that Indirect Speech (*Oratio Obliqua*) cannot always accurately reproduce the full sense of Direct Speech (*Oratio Recta*), since three tenses have to do the work of seven. The three tenses of the infinitive are: (i) the present (*scribere*), (ii) the perfect (*scripsisse*), (iii) the future (*scripturum esse*). These tenses of the infinitive, in *O. O.*, have no independent or absolute time-significance of their own, but indicate time relative to that of the verb of saying, thinking, or perceiving on which they depend. The Present indicates that an action is going on, or state obtaining, at the time of speaking; the Perfect indicates an action that has already taken place, and the Future an action that is yet to take place at the time of speaking. The tenses of the infinitive, therefore, are present, past, or future only in relation to the tense of the main verb of their sentence or clause.

The verb of the *O. R.* which, when reported indirectly, has to be put into one of these three tenses of the infinitive, may have been in any one of the following tenses of the finite verb:

(i) Present: *scribo*, 'I am writing'.
(ii) Present-Perfect: *scripsi*, 'I have written'.
(iii) Aorist-Perfect: *scripsi*, 'I wrote'.
(iv) Imperfect: *scribebam*, 'I was writing', 'used to write'.
(v) Pluperfect: *scripseram*, 'I had written'.
(vi) Future Simple: *scribam*, 'I shall be writing', 'shall write'.
(vii) Future Perfect: *scripsero*, 'I shall have written'.

The rule for converting these into *O. O.* is as follows:

(1) *Scribo epistulam*, 'I am writing a letter', becomes:

<table>
<tr><td>Dicit</td><td rowspan="3">se epistulam scribere</td><td>'He says that he is writing a letter'.</td></tr>
<tr><td>Dixit</td><td>'He said that he was writing a letter'.</td></tr>
<tr><td>Dicet</td><td>'He will say that he is writing a letter'.</td></tr>
</table>

(2) *Scripsi*, *scribebam*, *scripseram epistulam*, 'I have written, wrote, was writing, had written a letter', ALL become:

<table>
<tr><td>Dicit</td><td rowspan="3">se epistulam scripsisse</td><td>'He says that he has written, wrote, was writing, had written a letter'.</td></tr>
<tr><td>Dixit</td><td>'He said that he had written, had been writing a letter'.</td></tr>
<tr><td>Dicet</td><td>'He will say that he has written, wrote, was writing, a letter'.</td></tr>
</table>

(3) *Scribam epistulam*, 'I shall write a letter', becomes:

<table>
<tr><td>Dicit</td><td rowspan="3">se epistulam scripturum (esse)</td><td>'He says that he will write a letter'.</td></tr>
<tr><td>Dixit</td><td>'He said that he would write a letter'.</td></tr>
<tr><td>Dicet</td><td>'He will say that he will write a letter'.</td></tr>
</table>

Notes. (i) Verbs of speaking or thinking such as those meaning 'promise', 'swear', 'threaten', 'hope', can, in English, be followed by a present infinitive, even when the reference is to the future. Latin is normally more accurate, and requires the accusative with the *future* infinitive: *promittit (pollicetur), iurat, minatur, sperat se iturum esse*, 'He promises, swears, threatens, hopes, that he will go' (or 'promises etc. to go').
(ii) *Iuro* and *spero* may, of course, also be followed by the accusative with a present or perfect infinitive, for one can 'swear' or 'hope' (i.e. 'have good

hopes', 'feel sure') that something is happening or has happened: Cic. *Fam.* 5, 2, 7 *populus me vere iurasse iuravit.* 'The people swore that I had sworn truly.' Caes. *B. C.* 3, 8, 3 *reliquos deterreri sperans . . .* 'feeling sure that the rest were frightened'. It is to be noticed that *spero* with a present or perfect infinitive does not express a *Wish.*

(iii) The Latin construction which is really parallel to the English 'He promises (or threatens) *to go*' is the following colloquial usage, which does, however, occur occasionally in good prose: Plaut. *Men.* 843 *minatur mihi oculos exurere.* 'He threatens to burn my eyes out.' Caes. *B. G.* 2, 32, 3 *legati veniunt qui polliceantur obsides dare.* 'Envoys come to promise to give hostages' (or 'to promise *the giving* (of) hostages').

It is to be observed that with the present infinitives *exurere* and *dare* in the above examples there is no accusative 'subject'. The verbs *minatur* and *polliceantur* could have an accusative *noun* as object, and that noun is, in the above examples, an infinitive.

31. It will be observed from the scheme given in the previous section that the Perfect Infinitive has to represent all the four kinds of past tense of the finite verb. Latin has no special infinitive form to express continuous action in the past, like the English 'to have been writing', and until late times, when *quod*-clauses became serious rivals of the Acc. and Inf. construction in *O. O.* (see Section 35), there was nothing better than *dicit se scripsisse* to represent 'he says that he was writing'. But *scripsisse* tells us only that the writing took place before the time of speaking; it does not, like 'was writing', express clearly the idea of incomplete or progressive action in the past. If it was really important to bring out this shade of meaning, some other way had to be found. For 'he says that he was writing a letter when your message arrived' one might say *dicit se tum in epistula scribenda occupatum fuisse cum nuntius tuus advenerit,* 'he says that he was engaged in writing a letter, when your message arrived'. Other methods would be possible in certain circumstances. Sometimes, especially with a verb or verbal phrase which contained in itself an idea of continuance, such devices would be unnecessary, e.g. *dicit Numam eo tempore regnasse,* where the context might make it clear that the meaning was "he says that Numa was reigning at that time".

32. If the main verb of the *O. R.* refers to the future and is one which has no future participle in use, the sense of the future infinitive is produced by the periphrasis *fore ut* with the Consecutive Subjunctive, e.g. *dico fore ut metuas,* 'I say that you will be afraid'. (lit. 'that it will be the case that, come to pass that, you are afraid'). This periphrasis is also widely used, instead of the Supine with *iri,* to represent the Future Passive, e.g. *dixit fore ut urbs caperetur,* 'he said that the city would be captured'.

If the tense of the main verb in *O. R.* is Future Perfect, e.g. *tribus diebus epistulam scripsero,* 'in three days I shall have written a letter', there is no means of reporting it indirectly, if the verb is active. But the idea is sometimes expressed passively by using the Perfect Participle with *fore: dicit tribus diebus epistulam a se scriptam fore*, 'he says that in three days a letter will have been written by him' (lit. 'will be in a written state', see on Perfect Participle, Section 103).

33. *Nominative with Infinitive after passive verbs of speaking, etc.*

When a verb of saying, thinking, or perceiving is used passively ('It is said, thought, observed that . . .'), it would be logical to expect the Acc. and Inf. noun-phrase to stand as its subject; i.e. along with *dicunt Homerum caecum fuisse*, 'they say that Homer was blind', we should expect *dicitur Homerum caecum fuisse*, 'it is said that Homer was blind'. This, the so-called impersonal construction, is common in early and in colloquial Latin, and it never died out. But already in Plautus the accusative noun is beginning to be detached again from the infinitive and used in the Nominative as the personal subject of the passive verb of speaking, thinking, etc. Thus we get: *dicitur Homerus caecus fuisse*, 'Homer is said to have been blind'; *Terentii fabellae putabantur a C. Laelio scribi*, 'the plays of Terence were thought to be written by C. Laelius', or 'it was thought that the plays of Terence were being written by C. Laelius'.

Except in circumstances to be noted below, with a number of verbs the personal construction had become the rule in classical Latin. In Plautus and Terence it is regular only with *dicor* and *videor*. Caesar extends it to *audior*, *existimor*, *nuntior*, and *ostendor*. Cicero, in addition to the above, uses *negor*, *demonstror*, *scribor*, *perhibeor*, *putor*, *invenior*, *reperior*, *intellegor*, *iudicor*, *perspicior*, *cognoscor*, and occasionally a few other verbs.

34. The impersonal construction never died out, even with the verbs listed above, but remained commoner in certain circumstances than the personal construction: viz. (i) when the verb of saying was a compound form of the passive. Thus, with Cic. *T. D.* 5, 7 *Lycurgi temporibus Homerus fuisse traditur*, 'Homer is related to have existed in the times of Lycurgus', compare *ibid.* 5, 4 *traditum est Homerum caecum fuisse*, 'It has been related that Homer was blind'. (ii) The impersonal construction is commoner with the Gerundive, though the personal is found also: Cic. *de Rep.* 3, 43 *ubi tyrannus est, ibi dicendum est plane nullam esse rem publicam.* 'Where there is a tyrant, there it must be said that there is no commonwealth at all.' But cf. *Id. de Domo* 93 *non sum existimandus de rebus gestis gloriari.* 'I am not to be thought to be boasting about my exploits.' (iii) Finally, if an indirect report which begins with the personal construction is continued to any length, the personal construction passes over to the impersonal: Cic. *de Or.* 2, 229 *ad Themistoclem quidam doctus homo accessisse*

dicitur eique artem memoriae pollicitus esse se traditurum; cum ille quaesisset quidnam illa ars efficere posset, dixisse illum doctorem, ut omnia meminisset; et ei Themistoclem respondisse . . . etc. 'A certain learned man is said to have approached Themistocles and to have promised to pass on to him the art of memory; and when Themistocles asked what that art could effect, the teacher said it could make him remember everything; and Themistocles replied . . . etc.'

35. Of the several methods of turning a sentence into a noun-equivalent, so as to make it a subordinate part of a larger sentence, a clause introduced by the conjunction *quod* used in the sense of 'the fact that', seems eminently suitable for reporting statements of fact. There is, indeed, evidence that this method of reporting speech indirectly was common in colloquial Latin even in classical times, since it occurs in less well-educated authors, e.g. *Bell. Hisp.* 36 *renuntiaverunt quod Pompeium in potestate haberent.* 'They reported that they had Pompey in their power.' This became the general method in 'Vulgar' Latin, whence it passed to the Romance languages (e.g. *Il dit que* . . .). When it occurs in classical authors, the verb of saying, thinking, or perceiving seems always to have already a neuter pronoun (e.g. *id, hoc, illud*) as object, to which the *quod*-clause is in apposition: Cic. *Fam.* 3, 8, 6 *an mihi de te nihil esse dictum unquam putas? ne hoc quidem, quod Taurum transisti?* 'Do you think that I am never told anything about you? Not even this, that you have crossed Mt. Taurus?' In the following example we find the acc. and inf. used side by side with a *quod*-clause: Tac. *Ann.* xiv, 6 *Illic reputans ideo se fallacibus litteris accitam (esse), quodque litus iuxta* . . . *navis* . . . *concidisset* . . . 'There, reflecting that it was for that purpose that she had been summoned by the deceitful letter, and that the ship had fallen to pieces near the shore . . .' *Concidisset* is subjunctive, being in a subordinate clause reporting the thought of the main subject (cf. the use in *qui*-clauses and in causal *quod*-clauses, Sections 240, 285). Contrast Tac. *Ann.* iii, 54 *nemo refert quod Italia externae opis indiget.* 'no one recalls that Italy needs supplies from abroad.' Here the Indicative *indiget* records a fact as a fact, viewed apart from any observer or reporter. Some such distinction as this between the Indicative and the Subjunctive is still found in later authors, but the practice varied a great deal, and it is often hard to find any fixed principle of choice. As might be expected, the Indicative is commoner in clauses which are anticipated by a neuter pronoun. This use of *quod*-clauses instead of the accusative and infinitive in *O. O.* begins to be common from the second century of our era.

Note. Quia, quoniam, quomodo, and *quemadmodum* are found mostly in ecclesiastical writers, instead of *quod* in this sense. Here we see the influence of Greek, where ὅτι means both 'that' and 'because', and ὡς means both 'that' and 'as'.

36. *The reflexive pronoun and adjective* Se *and* Suus

When a speaker is referring to himself or to something belonging to himself, the indirect reflexive *se, sui, sibi, se,* and its adjective *suus, sua, suum* are used. *Se* and *suus* therefore have two uses: (i) As direct reflexives: *Brutus se suo pugione interfecit.* 'Brutus killed himself with his own dagger.' (ii) As indirect reflexives: *Caesar dixit Gallos a se victos esse.* 'Caesar said that the Gauls had been defeated by him(self)' (Here *ab eo* would mean by someone other than Caesar.)

Notes. (i) The direct reflexive is often used in an emphasizing sense, referring not to the grammatical subject, but to the logical subject, i.e. to the person or thing which is the centre of the thought: Cic. *pro Sest.* 142 *Hunc (Hannibalem) sui cives e civitate eiecerunt.* 'Him his own fellow-citizens expelled from the community.' Livy 21, 50, 4 *Romanis multitudo sua auxit animum.* 'Their own numbers raised the spirit of the Romans.' *Suus* is much more freely used in this way than *se,* though the latter is regular in the emphasizing rather than reflexive sense after prepositions such as *per, propter, inter,* e.g. *virtutem amamus propter se,* 'we love virtue for its own sake'; *omnia sunt amicis inter se communia,* 'all things are common to friends among themselves'. When neither the reflexive nor the emphasizing sense is required, the appropriate case of *is* is regularly used: Cic. *T. D.* 1, 70 *Deum agnoscis ex operibus eius.* 'You recognize God from His works.'
(ii) A subordinate clause does not need to be in *formal* Indirect Speech to require the use of *se* and *suus* to refer to the subject of the main verb; i.e. the main verb need not be a verb of speaking. It is enough if the subordinate clause represents the words, thought, or intention of the main subject, e.g. Livy 23, 7, 7 *Misit qui vocarent Magium ad sese in castra.* 'He sent men to summon Magius to him in the camp.' Here *sese* refers to the subject of *misit,* since the subordinate clause *qui vocarent* etc. represents his intention. Cf. also Cic. *ad Att.* 2, 1, 12 *Paetus omnes libros quos frater suus reliquisset mihi donavit.* 'Paetus presented to me all the books which (he said) his brother had left.' Here the subjunctive *reliquisset* marks the words of the subordinate clause as being those of Paetus, not Cicero's; hence *suus* is required. Had the clause been an explanatory remark of Cicero's, *eius* would have been required, and the indicative *reliquerat.*
(iii) The use of the indirect reflexive avoids the ambiguity which has to be helped out in English by awkward parentheses such as the following: 'Mr Smith said that he (Mr Jones) had insulted him (Mr Smith)', which in Latin would be simply: *Cicero dixit eum sibi maledixisse.* But when both the direct and the indirect reflexive are required in the same sentence, ambiguity arises. One cannot say in Latin without ambiguity 'Cicero ordered his slave to wash his (Cicero's) feet', for in the sentence: *Cicero servum suum iussit pedes suos lavare,* the reflexive *suos* might be either direct

or indirect, referring either to Cicero or to the slave. If there was no hope of the context making the sense clear, some other method of expression would be adopted, e.g. it would be easy to say: *Cicero pedes suos a servo lavari iussit.* But Latin authors do not, in fact, seem to have been much worried by the ambiguity, if the sense was clear from the context. Cf. Cic. *de Or.* 2, 273 *cum rogaret eum* (sc. *Maximum*) *Salinator ut meminisset opera sua se Tarentum recepisse* . . . 'When Salinator asked him to remember that it was by his (Salinator's) aid that he (Maximus) had recovered Tarentum . . .' Also Caes. *B. G.* 1, 36, 6 *Ariovistus respondit neminem secum sine sua pernicie contendisse.* 'Ariovistus replied that no one had opposed him (Ariovistus) without bringing about his own downfall.'

(iv) The statement sometimes made, that the ambiguity is avoided by the use of *ipsum* for the indirect reflexive, is erroneous, at least for classical Latin. On this, see below.

37. Ipse

Ipse is an intensifying pronoun which can be used to emphasize any noun or pronoun and is particularly often used with the reflexive: *Consul ipse hoc fecit,* 'The consul himself did this'; *ipse hoc feci,* 'I did this myself', etc.

(i) When used in conjunction with the reflexive pronoun, *ipse* may either agree with the reflexive, or be nominative in agreement with the subject; but the sense differs accordingly. Thus: (*a*) *Sibi ipse nocet* = 'He himself does himself hurt' (i.e. it is no one else who is harming him). (*b*) *Sibi ipsi nocet* = 'He is harming *himself*' (i.e. and not harming anyone else). Nevertheless Latin authors show an increasing tendency to use (*a*), even where the sense would seem to demand (*b*). Cf. Cic. *ad Q. fr.* 1, 1, 7 *facile est continere alios, si te ipse contineas.* 'It is easy to restrain others, if you restrain *yourself.*' Here one would expect *te ipsum.*

(ii) When used to intensify the possessive adjectives *meus, tuus, suus, noster, vester,* which are equivalent in sense to a possessive genitive of the pronoun, *ipse* is put in the possessive genitive: *meus ipsius pater,* 'my own father'; *suos ipsorum patres amant,* 'they love their own fathers'.

(iii) In classical Latin *ipse* is not regularly used as a substitute for *se* to distinguish the direct from the indirect reflexive. If it does sometimes appear to be so used, it is because the reflexive is understood, while *ipse* is there in its own right, because the emphasizing sense is required. Cf. Sall. *Jug.* 46, 2 *Iugurtha legatos mittit qui tantummodo ipsi liberisque vitam peterent.* 'Jugurtha sent envoys to beg for life only for himself *personally* and his children.' Here *ipsi* has point, and *sibi* is understood. It is customary to omit *se* and *suus* in such circumstances. This holds good even in the following example: Caes. *B. G.* 1, 40, 4 *cur de sua virtute aut de ipsius diligentia desperarent?* 'Why did they lose faith in their own courage or in his (Caesar's) watchfulness?' Even here *ipsius* does not stand *instead of* the indirect *sua*, in order to avoid the ambiguity, but is required to emphasize the *sua* which is understood. One or other of the reflexives needs to be emphasized, in order to point the contrast, and that which is emphasized by *ipse* is omitted according to usage.

It is only in later Latin that *ipsum* is sometimes used for *se*, without the intensifying sense being intended: e.g. Q. Curtius 7, 6, 8 *illi nec de fide nec de potentia regis ipsos dubitare respondent*. 'They replied that they did not doubt either the king's good faith or his power.'

III

The Functions of the Ablative Case

38. The ablative case in Latin is used to express three different groups of ideas, which are roughly represented by the English prepositions *from*, *with*, and *in*.[1] The name 'Ablative' means the 'taking-away' case, and therefore covers only the first of these meanings. These different ideas were originally, in the parent language, expressed by three different cases:

I. The true Ablative, or 'from'-case.
II. The Sociative-Instrumental, or 'with'-case. This name was coined to include the ideas of instrumentality and of accompaniment, or 'togetherness', both of which were expressed by this case, as by our preposition 'with'.
III. The Locative, or 'in'-case. This case expressed position, both in space and in time.

The ablative may thus be said to answer the questions: (1) Whence? (2) By what means? Under what circumstances? (3) Where? or When?

39. As the Latin ablative represents a fusion or assimilation of different case-forms, its functions will be more readily comprehensible if they are arranged under the three above-mentioned headings. But the ideas of source, instrumentality, and place-where occupy a certain amount of common ground in the field of thought; which no doubt aided the fusion or syncretism of the cases which originally expressed them. In addition, usage continued to develop after the fusion had taken place. There are therefore some uses which it is hard to classify. For example, the cause of an action or state may be regarded either as the source, or as the means whereby something is brought about, and one finds accordingly both *ex*

[1] The traditional rendering of the ablative by the prepositions 'by', 'with', and 'from' does not give the right picture.

vulnere and *vulnere interire*; the environment in which an action is performed may be at the same time the means whereby it is done, and we find both *curru vehi* and *in curru*. Some uses in which there is no preposition to serve as a guide are particularly hard to classify. Under which heading should one put ablatives of 'respect' such as *moribus praestare* or *oculis captus*, which may contain either the idea of instrumentality or of place-where? Such uses, of uncertain or composite origin, may reasonably be placed in a separate category. On the other hand, when the derivation of an extended usage can be traced with reasonable certainty, it can be placed under the appropriate heading. For example, the Ablative of Comparison can be assigned to the true Ablative, and the Ablative of Price to the Instrumental.

40. I. *The true Ablative or 'From'-Case*

The ablative expressing the general idea of source or separation is usually accompanied by one of the prepositions *ab*, *ex*, or *de*, unless the verb with which it goes contains in itself the idea of separation, as *metu liberare*, 'to set free from fear'. Sometimes the preposition is already attached as a prefix to the verb, as *castris expulsus*, 'expelled from the camp', in which case it need not be repeated, though it often is. Other usages where the preposition is omitted are noted below.

41. The chief uses of the ablative that contain or are derived from the idea of source or separation are the following:
(1) The ablative denotes the *starting-point of motion*: *Ab urbe proficiscitur.* 'He sets out from the city.' For the omission of the preposition with place-names, etc., see Section 42. With this use should be included figurative extensions, as when the ablative denotes the source or origin of a person or thing: *ex improbo patre nasci*, 'to be the son of a wicked father'; *a Deucalione ortus*, 'descended from Deucalion'. With *natus* the preposition is often omitted, as Caes. *B. G.* 4, 12, 4 *amplissimo genere natus*, 'born of a distinguished family'.
(2) The ablative with *ab* denotes the *agent* with the passive verb. The agent is regarded as the *source* of the action. Only the real author of the action, whether a person, other living creature, or a personified thing, is designated by *ab* with the ablative: Caes. *B. G.* 5, 34, 2 *ab duce et a fortuna deserebantur.* 'They were being deserted by their leader and by fortune.'
(3) The *material* out of which a thing is made us usually regarded as the source of the thing, and is then denoted by *ex* or *de* with the ablative: Cic. *Fin.* 4, 19 *ex animo constamus et corpore.* 'We are composed of mind and body.'

Notes. (i) If the speaker decides to regard the material as the *means* of producing the thing, he will use the instrumental ablative, which does not

require a preposition: Cato, *R. R.* 14, 1 *faber faciat parietes calce et caementis, pilas ex lapide.* 'Let the workman make the walls with lime and cement, but the pillars out of stone.' Here we find both uses.
(ii) If the material is something abstract which may be regarded as comprising or containing the thing, *in* with the locatival ablative may be used (cp. English 'consist *in*'): Caes. *B. G.* 6, 21, 3 *vita omnis Germanorum in venationibus atque in studiis rei militaris consistit.* 'The whole life of the Germans consists in hunting-expeditions and military pursuits.'
(iii) For the genitive designating material, see Section 72 (4).

(4) The notion 'on this or that side', 'in this or that quarter', is often expressed in Latin by *ab*, sometimes by *ex*; that is to say, the Latin expression has an eye on the quarter *from* which a thing presents itself. A similar feature appears in the Romance languages, e.g. in French *de près, de loin, de l'autre côté,* etc. So in Latin *a fronte,* 'in front', *a tergo,* 'in the rear', *a dextra,* 'on the right', *ab oriente,* 'on the east side', 'in the east', *ex utraque parte,* 'on each side', etc. Such expressions are indeed often used where the meaning 'from' is obviously suitable, e.g. Caes. *B. C.* 3, 93, 6 *eos a tergo sunt adorti,* 'they attacked them in (or 'from') the rear'; but this is by no means always the case. A notable instance of the idiom in question is *ab aliquo stare,* 'to be on someone's side', 'to stand by someone'; so also *facere ab, esse ab,* etc.
(5) That with which an action or state is in *conformity* is usually regarded as the starting-point or standard from which one starts, and is denoted by *ex* with the ablative: Cic. *Rosc. Am.* 26 *ex sua natura ceteros fingunt.* 'They fashion others (imagine others to be) *according to* their own nature.' Similarly *ex senatus consulto,* 'in accordance with a decree of the senate'; *e legibus,* 'according to the laws'; Cic. *Phil.* 10, 25 *Brutus bene et e re publica fecit.* 'Brutus acted well and in accordance with the public interest'; etc.
(6) The Ablative of Source with *ex* or *de* is naturally used to express the idea of *partition,* as *unus ex iis,* 'one (out) of them'; Hor. *Odes* III, xi, 33–4 *una de multis face nuptiali digna,* 'one alone out of many who was worthy of the marriage-torch'. So also *homo de plebe,* 'a man of the people'.

Under this heading ought probably to be put the use of *de* with the ablative in the sense of 'of', 'about', 'concerning', 'in connexion with': *de aliqua re dicere, cogitare, queri,* 'to speak, think, complain *about* something'; Plaut. *Most.* 271 *in mentem venit de speculo.* 'The thought of the looking-glass occurred (to her).' Cic. *Off.* 1, 39 *Regulus de captivis commutandis Romam missus est.* 'Regulus was sent to Rome in connexion with an exchange of prisoners'.

Note. As *de* with the ablative is an alternative to the genitive in some of the above expressions (cf. *unus eorum, in mentem venit alicuius rei*), it is easy to see how this preposition came to be used in Romance languages in the sense of 'of' or 'about' (*Ile de la cité, parler de quelque chose*), when the case-inflexions had become obsolete. In Vulgar Latin, *de* begins to be used with the accusative as a general oblique case from the fourth century.

(7) With verbs and adjectives denoting *difference* or disagreement, the person or thing from whom or from which the subject differs is often denoted by *ab* with the ablative, e.g. *a te dissentio*, 'I disagree with you'; Cic. *pro Caec.* 39 *quid hoc ab illo differt?* 'In what does this differ from that?' So *alienus ab*, 'a stranger to', 'foreign to'.

Note. With these verbs and adjectives the ablative with *ab* is not usually the only construction. Thus one can say *dissentio tibi* (Dat. of Disadvantage), or *dissentio tecvm.*

(8) With verbs (and some adjectives) whose sense involves the idea of separation, including verbs compounded with the prepositions *ab*, *ex*, *de*, the Ablative of Separation is often used without a preposition. However, no rule can be laid down, for sometimes, as stated in Section 40, the preposition is used, though there would be no ambiguity without it. Examples of such verbs are *cedere*, 'give way', 'retire'; *movere*, remove'; *pellere*, 'drive out', with its compounds; *arcere*, 'ward off', 'keep out'; *liberare*, 'set free'; *solvere*, 'loose'; *levare*, 'relieve'; *privare*, 'deprive'; *orbare*, 'bereave'; *se abdicare magistratu*, 'resign from a magistracy'; and many others. Examples of adjectives: *liber*, 'free'; *vacuus*, 'empty'; *orbus*, 'bereaved'; *nudus*, 'bare'.

(9) As the comparative of adjectives implies difference, the ablative (without *ab*) can be used to denote that with which something is compared, i.e. *from* which it differs. For this Ablative of Comparison, see Sections 78 ff.

42. *Further Remarks on the Ablative of the Starting-point*

The ablative indicating the starting-point of motion is normally helped by one of the prepositions *ab*, *ex*, or *de*, except when the starting-point is indicated by the name of a town or small island, or by the words *domo*, 'from home'; *rure*, 'from the country'; *humo*, 'from the ground' (mostly poetical).

The bare ablative of these words, without *ab*, is to be regarded as the normal usage. Nevertheless the preposition is used in circumstances similar to those in which *ad* is used with the Accusative of the Goal (cf. Sections 8 and 9), viz.:

(i) When both starting-point and goal are given (for examples see 8 (i) and 9 (i) (a)); but this rule is not invariable.

(ii) When the motion starts, not from within the town, but from the neighbourhood of it: Caes. *B. C.* 3, 24, 4 *Libo discessit a Brundisio.* 'Libo departed from Brundisium' (i.e. not from within the town, but from the harbour). *Id. B. G.* 7, 43, 5 *consilia inibat quem ad modum ab Gergovia discederet.* 'He began to form plans as to how he might retire *from before* Gergovia.'

But this distinction is not observed in colloquial Latin, nor by Livy and post-classical authors generally: Sulp. in Cic. *Fam.* 4, 12, 2 *cum ab Athenis proficisci in animo haberem,* 'when I had in mind to start from Athens'. It is to be noted that this is in the more colloquial style of letters, and it is not by Cicero himself. But Cicero does use the preposition (with a verbal noun) in *Fam.* 12, 25, 4 *Antonii reditus a Brundisio.* Livy 22, 24, 12 *speciem praebuerunt novi praesidii ab Roma venientis.* 'They gave the appearance of a new garrison coming from Rome.' With Livy, in fact, the bare ablative is exceptional.

(iii) When a common noun is in apposition to the name, the preposition is regular, if the name comes second. When the common noun is further qualified, it regularly follows the name and has a preposition (cf. 8 (iii)): Caes. *B. G.* 7, 4, 2 *Vercingetorix expellitur ex oppido Gergovia.* 'Vercingetorix is expelled from the town of Gergovia.' Cic. *Font.* 41 *Tusculo ex clarissimo municipio,* 'from the most famous township of Tusculum'.

Notes. (1) To denote the point from which distance is measured, e.g. with the verbs *abesse* and *distare,* when there is no motion implied, the preposition *ab* is regularly used with place-names: Cic. *Clu.* 27 *Teanum abest a Larino XVIII milia passuum.* 'Teanum is 18 miles distant from Larinum.' But when *abesse* means 'to be absent', the bare ablative is used, e.g. *Roma aberat.* 'He was absent from Rome.'

(2) The poets omit the preposition freely with nouns other than those indicated above, even when the verb is not one of those noted in Section 41 (8). The result is that the type of the ablative is often vague. The context may often admit of its being either separative or instrumental or even locative. The poet's point of view is then left to be interpreted in the light of the context. Occasionally the preposition is similarly omitted by Livy and subsequent prose-writers, possibly under the influence of the poets. Examples: Virg. *Geor.* 3, 203 *spumas aget ore cruentas.* 'He will drive forth blood-stained foam from his mouth.' Val. Fl. 5, 253 *lapsus montibus anguis,* 'a snake gliding from the mountains'. For prose examples, cf. Livy 9, 3, 3 *num montes moliri sede sua paramus?* 'Are we preparing to move mountains from their place?' Tac. *Hist.* 3, 29 *cum tela testudine laberentur,* 'as the javelins were glancing from the locked shields'.

II. *Sociative-Instrumental Functions of the Ablative*

43. The ablative performing the functions of the older *with*-case is distinguished from the *from*- and the *in*-case either by the absence of any preposition or by the use of the preposition *cum,* 'with'. The following are the chief sociative-instrumental uses:

(1) The ablative without a preposition denotes the *Means* or *Instrument* whereby some act is performed or a situation or state brought about: *hostem gladio ferire*, 'to strike the enemy *with* the sword'; Caes. *B. G.* 1, 40, 8 *Ariovistum magis ratione et consilio quam virtute vicisse*. 'Ariovistus had conquered more *by* scheming and strategy than by valour.' See further Section 44.

(2) *The Ablative of Price and Value*. That which is given in exchange for something may be regarded as the means by which the thing is acquired. Hence the instrumental ablative (without a preposition) came to be used to denote the price at which something is bought or sold, and, through extension by analogy, to denote value with verbs of valuing. The genitive also is used in certain expressions of Price and Value. For the classical usage and examples, see Sections 72 (7), 86–7.

(3) The *Ablative of the Measure of Difference*. The amount or degree *by which* things differ is expressed by the instrumental ablative. See Section 82.

(4) The *Ablative of Route* is also of instrumental origin, e.g. *recta via ire*, 'to go by the straight way'; Livy 23, 26, 8 *diversis itineribus cum in castra se recepissent*, 'when they had returned to the camp by different routes'.

(5) *The Ablative of Accompaniment*

(i) When the ablative denotes a person or thing *in association with* whom or with which an act is performed, the preposition *cum* is regularly used. When the ablative noun is qualified by an epithet, the preposition is often omitted. For examples and notes, see Section 46.

(ii) The word or words in the ablative may denote, not a concrete accompaniment, but the circumstances under which the action is performed, or even circumstances resulting from it: e.g. 'He did this *with my blessing*'; 'He returned *with great risk*'. If the circumstances may be viewed as a result of the action, English is apt to use the preposition 'to', e.g. 'to his danger', 'to his ruin'. This type of ablative is usually called the Ablative of Attendant Circumstances. For rules with regard to the use or omission of *cum*, and for examples, see Section 47.

(iii) The Ablative Absolute is best regarded as a special type of Ablative of Attendant Circumstances. See Sections 49, 93.

(iv) When the ablative expresses the manner in which an action is performed, e.g. 'He returned *with great speed*', it is called the Ablative of Manner. See Section 48.

(6) *The Ablative of Description* (*or Quality*). The ablative of a noun with an epithet may be attached to another noun, to describe the thing denoted by the qualified noun: e.g. *summa virtute adulescens*, 'a young man of the highest courage'. For the development and use of this construction, see Sections 83–5.

(7) The ablative which completes the meaning of the Deponents *utor*, *fruor*, *fungor*, etc. is usually counted as instrumental. With *vescor*, 'feed

on', *potior*, 'make oneself master by means of', this is perhaps clear, but with *fruor* and *fungor* the ablative may well be one of source or separation, the sense of these verbs being: 'reap profit (from)'; 'rid oneself (of)'.

44. *Further Remarks on the Ablative of Means or Instrument*

The instrumental ablative of means is mostly used of things. A personal agent employed by another is usually denoted by *per*, 'through' (i.e. 'through the agency of'), with the accusative: e.g. Caes. *B. G.* 1, 4, 2 *per eos, ne causam diceret, se eripuit.* 'By their means he saved himself from standing trial.'

Nevertheless the bare instrumental ablative, without *ab*, is used of persons, if they are regarded as the mere instruments in the hands of another: e.g. Cic. *Att.* 4, 3, 2 *armatis hominibus expulsi sunt fabri de area nostra.* 'The workmen were driven from my building-site by means of armed men.' Here the real author of the deed was Clodius, and the armed men were his hired tools. But an unconscious or unwilling agent also may be regarded as an instrument, e.g. Cic. *Mil.* 54 *uxore paene constrictus.*

45. *The Ablative of Cause.*

How nearly allied the idea of instrument or means may sometimes be to that of cause can be seen from such an expression as *morbo perire*, 'to die of disease'. The disease may be regarded as the means by which the death was brought about or as the source or cause of the death. We can see from such instances that the Ablative of Cause may reasonably be traced, at least in part, to an 'instrumental' origin. Examples: Cic. *Att.* 5, 20, 3 *vulnus accepit eoque interiit.* 'He received a wound and died from it.' Livy 21, 26, 2 *abscesserant metu hostes.* 'The enemy had departed in (or 'through') fear.' Sall. *Cat.* 6, 6 *ei vel aetate vel curae similitudine patres appellabantur.* 'They were called "Fathers", either because of their age, or because of the similarity of their responsibilities.'

Note. That the true ablative with a preposition may be an alternative method of expression has been already mentioned in Section 39. The idea of cause can also be expressed by the prepositions *ob*, *propter*, 'on account of', and *per*, 'through', with the accusative.

46. *Further Remarks on the Ablative of Accompaniment*

The ablative with *cum* expresses a variety of ideas besides that of mere accompaniment. Examples: Caes. *B. G.* 4, 27, 2 *una cum his legatis Commius venit.* 'Together with these envoys came Commius.' *Ibid.* 24, 2 *cum hostibus erat pugnandum.* 'It was necessary to fight with the enemy.' *Id. B. C.* 1, 18, 4 *Caesar eas cohortes cum exercitu suo coniunxit.* 'Caesar joined those cohorts with (to) his own army.' Cic. *Off.* 3, 1, 1 *secum loqui*, 'to converse with, talk to, oneself'. *Id. Cat.* 1, 13, 32 *desinant obsidere cum gladiis curiam.* 'Let them cease to beset the senate-house with swords (in their hands).' (It is to be noted that *cum* is not used in classical Latin to denote an instrument.)

Exceptions to the use of *cum*:

(i) When the accompaniment is a thing, and the ablative is qualified by an epithet, *cum* is sometimes used, sometimes omitted (cf. the ablative of attendant circumstances below, Section 47): Cic. *Pis.* 92 *veste servili navem conscendit.* 'He went on board the ship in (with) slave's attire.' Cic. *Div.* 1, 119 *cum purpurea veste processit.* 'He went in procession in purple vestments.'

(ii) In military language, in expressions denoting marching with troops, the Ablative of Accompaniment is often used without *cum*, even though the accompaniments are persons, so long as there is an epithet attached. This is sometimes called the *Ablativus Militaris*: Caes. *B. C.* 1, 41, 2 *omnibus copiis ad Ilerdam proficiscitur.* 'He sets out for Ilerda with all his forces.'

But *cum* is omitted only if the verb is intransitive. After a transitive verb, e.g. *mitto*, *cum* is always used: Caes. *B. C.* 2, 38, 1 *audit Saburram, cum mediocribus copiis missum, Uticae appropinquare.* 'He hears that Saburra, sent with moderate forces, is approaching Utica.'

cum is used also if the epithet is a cardinal numeral: Caes. *B. G.* 7, 57, 1 *cum quattuor legionibus Lutetiam proficiscitur.* 'He set out with four legions to Lutetia.'

47. The rule with regard to the use of *cum* with the *Ablative of Attendant Circumstances* is that it is always used if the ablative noun has no epithet, but often omitted if there is an epithet: Caes. *B. G.* 7, 74, 2 *ne cum periculo ex castris egredi cogatur*, 'lest he be compelled to go out of the camp with the attendant danger (or 'to his danger')'. Cic. *Br.* 164 *nulla est altercatio clamoribus unquam habita maioribus.* 'No dispute ever took place to the accompaniment of louder shouting.' But cf. *ibid.* 242 *verborum copiam praebebat populo cum multa concursatione magnoque clamore.* 'He used to pour out a flood of words before the people, to the accompaniment of a great concourse and a great deal of shouting.'

48. The word or words in the ablative may express not so much attendant circumstances as the *manner* in which the action is performed. For the use or omission of *cum* the same rule holds good as for the ablative of attendant circumstances: Cic. *Fin.* 3, 39 *honeste, id est cum virtute, vivere*, 'to live honourably, that is with virtue'. Here Cicero plainly equates *cum* and an ablative noun with the adverb of manner *honeste.* Caes. *B. G.* 2, 19, 7 *incredibili celeritate ad flumen decucurrerunt.* 'They ran down to the river with incredible speed.' Here the presence of the epithet *incredibili* accounts for the omission of *cum*; but there are plenty

of examples of both *cum* and an epithet, as Cic. *N. D.* 2, 97 *admirabili cum celeritate moveri*, 'to move with marvellous speed'.

Notes. (i) The place of an epithet may be taken by an attributive genitive; then, too, *cum* may be omitted: Caes. *B. C.* 2, 40, 2 *imperat ut simulatione timoris paulatim cedant.* 'He orders them to retreat gradually with a pretence of fear.'
(ii) A number of nouns in very common use are used in the Ablative of Manner without either *cum* or an epithet, e.g. *iure*, 'rightfully'; *iniuria*, 'wrongfully'; *lege*, 'by law', 'lawfully'; *consilio*, 'by design', 'purposely'; *vi*, 'by force'; *casu*, 'by chance'; *voluntate*, 'voluntarily'. Some of these ablatives are clearly instrumental in character, so that *cum* would not be required with them in any case. The explanation of the absence of *cum* with the rest is that the words have practically become adverbs.

49. *The Ablative Absolute*

Although the Ablative Absolute construction is usually regarded as of mixed origin, there is little doubt that it is merely a special type of Ablative of Attendant Circumstances. In the absolute construction the ablative noun (or pronoun) has with it an epithet (either adjective, participle, or appositional noun) which is not attributive but *predicative*. That is to say, the epithet adds something to the predicate and makes an additional statement. For example, the sentence *Ex urbe exibant capitibus opertis* may mean, according to the context, either 'They went out of the city with covered heads', or 'With their heads covered (i.e. having covered their heads), they went out of the city'. With the former meaning *opertis* is attributive, and the phrase *capitibus opertis* is the equivalent of an adverb (cf. *veste servili navem conscendit* in Section 46). In the latter sense *opertis* is predicative, and the phrase *capitibus opertis* is equivalent to a subordinate clause (e.g. 'When they had covered their heads, they went out') or to a separate sentence (e.g. 'They covered their heads and went out'). But the fact that the epithet in the absolute construction is predicative does not prevent the ablative from being of essentially the same type as that which denotes accompaniment or attendant circumstances.

50. The relation of the thought expressed in an ablative absolute phrase to that of the main clause may vary greatly, according to the context. Besides expressing mere situation or attendant circumstances, the absolute phrase can express Time, or Cause, or Concession, or even Condition. Examples: Cic. *Prov. cons.* 32 *Bellum Gallicum C. Caesare imperatore gestum est.* 'The Gallic war was fought under the generalship of Gaius Caesar' ('with Caesar *as general*'). Cic. *Cat.* 3, 10 *Cethegus, recitatis litteris, repente conticuit.* 'When the letter had been read out, Cethegus

suddenly fell silent.' Caes. *B. G.* 1, 2, 1 *Is, M. Messala et M. Pupio Pisone consulibus, coniurationem fecit.* 'He, in the consulship of M. Messala and of M. Pupius Piso, raised a conspiracy.' Cic. *N. D.* 2, 8 *C. Flaminius religione neglecta cecidit apud Trasumenum.* 'Gaius Flaminius fell at Trasimene, because he had neglected religious usage.' Caes. *B. G.* 4, 20, 1 *exigua parte aestatis reliqua Caesar tamen in Britanniam proficisci contendit.* 'Though a small part of the summer remained, Caesar nevertheless hastened to set out for Britain.'

Note. As an adjective, participle, or appositional noun may be used predicatively without being in the absolute construction, the Ablative Absolute may not be needed if the epithet applies to a noun or pronoun which plays an integral part in the syntax of the sentence. E.g. the normal Latin for 'They hate Caesar as leader' is *Caesarem ducem oderunt* and not *Caesare duce, eum oderunt*; similarly the Latin for 'With the city captured, the soldiers proceeded to plunder it' is *Urbem captam milites diripiebant,* and not *Urbe capta, milites eam diripiebant.* For exceptions to this rule, and a fuller discussion of the predicative use of participles, see Ch. VII, Sections 88, 91–3.

III. *Locatival Functions of the Ablative*

51. The case which, in Indo-European, expressed *position* in space or time is called the Locative, but it survives in Greek and Latin only in isolated forms. In the first or *-ā* declension *-ĭ* was added to the stem, which produced in Old Latin *Romai*, etc. By a regular phonetic development this had become *Romae* by the beginning of the second century B.C., and was then indistinguishable in form from the genitive. Similarly the locative of the second, or *-o* declension was *-oi* (cf. Greek οἴκοι, 'at home'), which became *-ī* (e.g. *Arimini*, 'at Ariminum', *domi*, 'at home'), and was again indistinguishable from the genitive. A few third declension words borrow this *-i* from the second declension, as *ruri*, 'in the country', *tempori*, 'in time'.

Except in singular place-names of the first and second declension and a few other words such as *domi*, etc. the function of the locative was taken over by the ablative, which, with common nouns and pronouns, needs to be distinguished in this sense by the prepositions *in*, 'in' or 'on', and *sub*, 'under': e.g. *in urbe*, 'in the city'; *in mensa*, 'on the table'; *sub terra*, 'under the earth'. But the following exceptions should be noted:
(i) The preposition is regularly omitted with the locatival ablative of place-names (including names of small islands).
(ii) The bare ablative (or locative) is used of a few common words or phrases, e.g. *terra marique*, 'by land and sea'; and often of words which themselves denote a place or district, when they are qualified by an epithet: e.g. *loco* and *locis*, *regione*, *parte* and *partibus*, *litore*, etc.

(iii) The preposition is often omitted with a noun qualified by *summus*, *imus*, *medius*, *totus*, *omnis*, *cunctus*, *universus*.
(iv) The locatival ablative is used freely without a preposition by the poets in any circumstances.

52. Examples and notes: Caes. *B. G.* 2, 19, 6 *in silvis abditi latebant.* 'They were lying hidden in the woods.' *Ibid.* 29, 3 *saxa in muro conlocarant.* 'They had placed stones on the wall.' *Ibid.* 3, 29, 3 *exercitum in hibernis conlocavit.* 'He placed his army in winter quarters.' Caes. *B. C.* 3, 13, 5 *sub pellibus hiemare constituit.* 'He decided to pass the winter under canvas.'

Notes. (i) With verbs of placing the ablative of the 'place on or in which' is usually preferred, though if the speaker or author has in mind the picture of something being moved into or on to a place, he will naturally use *in* with the accusative: Cato, *R. R. oleas in solem ponito.* 'Set the olives in the sun' (i.e. 'put them into the sunlight'). Caes. *B. G.* 1, 12, 3 *reliqui sese in proximas silvas abdiderunt.* 'The rest hid themselves in the nearest woods.' Livy 41, 20, 7 *Cyzici in Prytaneum vasa aurea posuit.* 'He placed golden vessels in the Council-chamber at Cyzicus.' Sall. *Jug.* 61, 2 *exercitum in provinciam collocat.* 'He stationed an army in the province.' The accusative presents a different mental picture from the ablative, but it is difficult to make the distinction in English.
(ii) The idea of 'position' is widely extended in a figurative sense: Cic. *leg. agr.* 3, 12 *non parvum sub hoc verbo furtum latet.* 'No petty theft lurks beneath this word.' Caes. *B. G.* 1, 31, 7 *quominus sub illorum imperio essent*, 'that they might not be under their rule'. Cic. *Fam.* 1, 2, 4 *dignitatem nostram, ut potest in tanta hominum perfidia, retinebimus.* 'We shall retain our dignity, as far as that is possible amidst such great treachery of men.' Livy 21, 10, 11 *scio meam levem esse in Hannibale auctoritatem.* 'I know my influence is slight in the case of Hannibal.'

53. Place-names: Nep. 23, 7, 4 *ut Romae consules, sic Carthagine quotannis bini reges creabantur.* 'As at Rome the consuls, so at Carthage two kings used to be created every year.' Cic. *Fam.* 8, 17, 1 *me potius in Hispania fuisse tum quam Formiis!* 'To think of my having been in Spain at that time rather than at Formiae!' It is to be noted that the preposition is used with the names of countries.

An adjective qualifying a name in the locative usually agrees with the locative form: Cic. *Clu.* 27 *alter filius Teani Apuli educabatur.* 'The other son was being educated at Apulian Teanum.' Livy 32, 9, 3 *Suessae Auruncae natum*, 'born at Auruncan Suessa'. Similarly with *domi*: Cic. *Fam.* 4, 7, 4 *nonne mavis sine periculo tuae domi esse quam cum periculo alienae?* 'Do you not prefer to be without danger at your own home rather than in danger at someone else's?' But if a name in the locative has another noun in apposition to it, the appositional noun has to be in the locatival ablative, usually (not always) with the preposition: Cic. *Phil.* 4, 6 *milites Albae constiterunt, in urbe opportuna.* 'The soldiers halted at the conveniently situated town of Alba.' But for the omission of the preposition cf. Cic. *Arch.* 4 *Archias poeta Antiochiae natus est, celebri quondam urbe et copiosa.* 'The poet Archias was born in the once populous and wealthy city of Antioch.'

Note. For examples of the omission of prepositions under exceptions (ii) and (iii) noted in Section 51, cf. Caes. *B. C.* 1, 81, 1 *iniquo loco castra ponunt.* 'They pitch camp in a disadvantageous position.' *Id. B. G.* 4, 23, 6 *aperto ac plano litore naves constituit.* 'He stationed his ships on an open and level shore.' Cic. *Rep.* 6, 18 *terra ima sede semper haeret.* 'The earth always clings to (stays in) the lowest position.' Livy 1, 33, 8 *carcer media urbe aedificatur.* 'A prison was built in the middle of the city.' Caes. *B. C.* 1, 2, 2 *delectus tota Italia habiti.* 'Levies were held in (throughout) the whole of Italy.' Cic. *Off.* 3, 80 *omnibus vicis statuae (erant).* 'There were statues in all the streets.'

Other examples will be found, however, in which the preposition is inserted.

54. *The Ablative of Time*

The locatival ablative denoting position in time is normally used without a preposition. This ablative can indicate: (*a*) a point of time *at which* something happens; (*b*) a period of time *within which* something happens. Examples: (*a*) Caes. *B. G.* 4, 23, 2 *hora diei circiter quarta Britanniam attigit.* 'He reached Britain at about the fourth hour of the day (i.e. at about 10 a.m.).' (*b*) Caes. *B. C.* 2, 21, 4 *Tarraconem paucis diebus pervenit.* 'He reached Tarraco within a few days.' Cic. *Rosc. Am.* 74 *Roscius Romam multis annis non venit.* 'Roscius did not come to Rome for many years.' (Cf. colloqu. 'I have not seen him *in* years'.)

Notes. (1) In the last example the ablative is still answering the question 'within what time?' rather than 'how long?' It denotes the period of time *within the limits of which* Roscius did not come. Had the intention been to tell 'how long' he was away, the Accusative of Duration would have been used, with another verb, e.g. *multos annos Roma abfuit.*

Nevertheless there are isolated examples, even in classical Latin, where the ablative seems to be encroaching on the function of the Accusative of Duration: Cic. *de Or.* 3, 138 *Pericles quadraginta annis praefuit Athenis.* 'Pericles was in control of Athens for forty years.' Caes. *B. G.* 1, 26, 5 *tota nocte continenter ierunt.* 'They went continuously throughout the whole night.' From the time of Livy onwards this use of the ablative becomes more frequent. In the following sentence it alternates with *per* with the accusative: Livy 21, 2, 1 *ita se Africo Bello per quinque annos, ita deinde novem annis in Hispania se gessit . . .* 'He so behaved for five years in the

African war, and then for nine years in Spain . . .' Tac. *Ann.* 1, 53 *quattuordecim annis exsilium toleravit.* 'He endured exile for fourteen years.'

It is to be noticed, however, that the verb in all these examples is in a tense of completed action, so that the ablative may denote the limits within which the action was completed. A tense of incomplete or progressive action more obviously answers the question 'How long?', and seems to entail the Accusative of Duration.

(ii) With the ablative denoting time 'within which', the preposition *in* is sometimes used: Cic. *de Or.* 1, 168 *in his paucis diebus nonne homo postulabat* . . .? 'Within these last few days was not a man demanding . . .?'

(iii) With nouns denoting a period of time, e.g. *tempus, aetas, dies,* when they are qualified by an epithet, *in* usually denotes not time, but situation or circumstance, e.g. *in tali tempore,* 'under such circumstances'. The Latin for 'in (good) time' is either *in tempore, tempore,* or *tempori.* (Note the locative form of the latter.)

(iv) The preposition *in* is regularly used when a distributive or numeral adverb is present: Cic. *Fam.* 15, 16, 1 *ternas epistulas in hora darem.* 'I should be posting three letters an hour.' Plaut. *Stich.* 501 *deciens in die mutat locum.* 'He shifts his ground ten times a day.'

55. *The Ablative of Respect*

As indicated in Section 39, the origin of the ablative used in this sense cannot be determined with certainty. Examples: Cic. *Phil.* 2, 23 *non tota re sed temporibus errasti.* 'You were wrong not *in* (or *with regard to*) the whole business, but with regard to your dates.' Here *de* with the ablative would be equally possible. With adjectives: *uno oculo captus,* 'blind in one eye'; *umero saucius,* 'wounded in the shoulder'; *maior natu,* 'older in age', or 'elder by birth'; *Cicero nomine,* 'Cicero by name'; *lingua melior,* 'better (more skilful) with his tongue'; etc. Some of these examples may be locative, others instrumental in origin.

IV

The Functions of the Dative Case. Impersonal Passive of Verbs

56. *General Remarks*

The chief function of the dative is to denote the person or, more rarely, the thing for whose benefit (or the reverse) the action of the verb is performed, or for whose benefit a thing or a state exists, or whom the quality of a thing affects: e.g. *librum mihi dat.* 'He gives a book *to me.*' *est mihi liber.* 'There is a book *for me* (or 'I have a book').' *donum mihi suavissimum,* 'a gift most acceptable *to me*'. With verbs, the dative denotes a remoter object of the action than is denoted by the accusative. It does not, like the accusative, denote that upon which the action of the verb is directly brought to bear, but that which is less directly affected. In this sense the dative may be called the case of the Indirect Object. The name 'dative' (*casus dativus*) means 'the case of *giving*' and is derived from the fact that one of its commonest uses is to indicate the indirect object after a verb of giving. But the dative is really the case that denotes the recipient.

Almost any verb, whether transitive or intransitive, may be modified by a dative indicating a person interested (see Section 64), but a number of intransitive verbs are regularly accompanied by a dative which completes their sense (Section 59), and a number of transitive verbs regularly have a dative of the indirect object in addition to their direct accusative object (Section 61).

When the noun in the dative denotes a thing, whether concrete or abstract, it may indicate that *for which* something serves, or the end or purpose for which something is intended or an act performed, or the result to which something tends: e.g. *haec res exemplo est.* 'This thing *serves as* an example' ('is *for* an example'). *constituit diem conloquio.* 'He fixed a day *for* a conference.' *haec res exitio est.* 'This thing *results in* (makes for) ruin', etc. (See Sections 67–8.)

It will be seen that, on the whole, the English preposition 'for' gives a better idea of the sense of the dative than the preposition 'to'.

57. The original significance of the dative is much disputed. Some grammarians (the 'Localists') maintain that all Latin uses of the dative can be derived from an original sense of 'direction towards a goal'. It is true that the dative often modifies a sentence of which the verb implies motion, e.g. *misit subsidia militibus,* 'He sent reinforcements to the soldiers', but here the indication of the goal of the motion is not really the chief point. The dative indicates the people *for whose benefit* the sending took place. If the soldiers were regarded as merely marking the spot to which the reinforcements were sent, the normal Latin would be *ad milites,* not *militibus.* But the receiver of something sent to him is at once the beneficiary and the goal of the motion. To that extent the function of the dative overlaps that of the Accusative of the Goal, and it was inevitable that there should be some interchange of function in the end.

There are three strong arguments against regarding the indication of the goal of physical motion as being the original function of the dative: (1) If one excludes the dative of nouns denoting persons, who may be regarded as beneficiaries, examples in which the dative is used to mark the goal of motion are as rare in early as in classical Latin. They occur mostly in poetry, e.g. Virg. *Aen.* 5, 451 *it clamor caelo,* 'The shout goes to heaven'. The explanation of this use is probably that poets are prone to endow inanimate things with life and feelings to be affected. When Virgil says *it clamor caelo,* the dative *caelo* pictures the sky as something sentient which is affected by the shout, but it denotes the goal of the motion at the same time. The purely analogical justification would be common phrases like *dare leto,* 'to consign to death', then *mittere leto,* 'to send to death'; also a phrase like *manus tendere alicui,* 'to stretch out the hands (in supplication) to someone', suggests direction as well as the person to whom the prayer is addressed. (2) One would expect our earliest texts to show a preponderance of nouns denoting concrete things or places in the dative, particularly after verbs of motion. This is not so. Throughout Latin the dative is preponderantly used of nouns or pronouns denoting persons. (3) The history of the truly local cases (accusative and ablative) suggests that, if all the uses of the dative developed out of an original goal-notion, prepositions would have been called in, to distinguish the various senses. But the dative in Latin is never used with a preposition.

58. *Summary of the Uses of the Dative*

(1) The dative with verbs: (*a*) with intransitive verbs with which the dative is the sole complement, e.g. *noceo tibi,* 'I am injurious to you' (Section 59). (*b*) With transitive verbs, marking the indirect object, e.g. *do, monstro tibi librum,* 'I give, show you a book'; *hoc dico tibi,* 'I say this to you' (Section 61). (*c*) With a number of verbs compounded with certain prepositions, e.g. *inicio terrorem tibi,* 'I cast fear into you'; *circumdat murum urbi,* 'He sets a wall around the city'; etc. (Section 62). (*d*) With certain impersonal verbs, e.g. *licet mihi hoc facere,* 'It is allowable for me to do this' (Sections 59 (iv); 211, 212).
(2) The dative denoting possession, e.g. *est mihi liber,* 'I have a book'; *malam mihi percussit,* 'He smote my cheek' (Section 63).
(3) The Dative of Advantage and Disadvantage, loosely used with any verb, e.g. *tibi me exorno,* 'I am decking myself for you' ('for your pleasure') (Section 64).
(4) The dative with adjectives, e.g. *homo amicus mihi,* 'a man friendly to me'.
(5) The Dative of the Person Judging (Section 65).
(6) The Ethic Dative (Section 66).
(7) The Dative of the Agent (Sections 202; 207, Note).
(8) The Dative of Purpose and Result (Sections 67–8).
(9) Poetic use of the dative to mark the goal of motion (cf. Section 57).

59. *Intransitive verbs normally accompanied by a dative*

It was suggested in Section 2 that the transitive verb was a comparatively late acquisition of syntax. The 'transitivisation' of verbs had not gone quite so far in Latin as it has in English, and a number of verbs whose sense is represented by transitive verbs in English were still intransitive in Latin. Although an intransitive verb by its nature expresses a complete sense by itself, there are many which are rarely used without mention of the person or thing in relation to whom or to which the action is performed. With the majority of such verbs in Latin this relation is naturally expressed by the dative, but a few have their meaning completed by an ablative (see Section 43, (7)), and a few by the genitive (see Sections 71, 73).

It is difficult to classify the intransitive verbs which take the dative, but they may be grouped as follows:

(i) Many verbs denoting activities which involve the conferring of advantage or benefit on someone will naturally be accompanied by a dative of the person interested, e.g. *prodesse*, 'to be useful', or 'to benefit'; *auxiliari*, *opitulari*, *subvenire*, 'to bring help', 'come to the aid'; *favere*, 'to be favourable'; *studere*, 'to be zealous'; *mederi*, 'to apply a remedy'; *consulere*, 'to take counsel (for someone)', 'consult the interest'; *placere*, 'to be pleasing'; *indulgere*, 'to be indulgent'; *credere*, 'to be trustful', 'to believe'; *assentiri*, 'to give assent', 'agree with'; *cedere*, 'to yield'; *parcere*, 'exercise restraint', 'spare'; *ignoscere*, 'to be forgiving'; *parere*, 'to obey' (originally 'to appear at someone's behest', but the meaning 'to appear' is confined in classical Latin to the compound *apparere*); *servire*, 'to be a servant', 'to serve'; *nubere*, 'to take the veil' (of a woman marrying a man – she takes the veil *for* him).

(ii) As constructions tend to develop in pairs of opposites (cf. Introd. p. xvii), many verbs of a meaning opposite to that of those above take the dative: e.g. *obesse*, 'to be prejudicial'; 'hinder'; *obstare*, 'to stand in the way'; *nocere*, 'to cause injury', 'be harmful'; *resistere*, *repugnare*, 'to stand against', 'resist', 'fight back', 'oppose'; *displicere*, 'to be displeasing'; *diffidere*, 'to distrust'; *dissentire*, 'to think differently', 'disagree'; *invidere*, 'to cast envious looks', 'envy'; *minari*, 'to threaten'; *irasci*, *suscensere*, 'to be angry'.

(iii) With several verbs which imply the exerting or imposing of one's will on someone, the person whom it is sought to influence is indicated by the dative: e.g. *imperare*, 'to issue orders', 'command'; *praecipere*, 'to give instructions', 'prescribe'; *suadere*, 'to urge'; *persuadere*, 'to persuade', 'convince'.

(iv) The dative is used with a number of impersonal verbs such as *licet*, 'it is allowable'; *libet*, 'it is one's fancy'; *placet*, 'it pleases'; *expedit*, 'it is expedient'; *accidit*, 'it befalls'; *contingit*, 'it falls to one's lot'; etc. See further Sections 211, 212.

Notes. (1) A number of the intransitive verbs which take the dative have transitive synonyms. Others can be used in both an intransitive and in a transitive sense. A few can be seen becoming transitive in the course of

Latin literature, e.g. Horace has *invideor*, and in colloquial and later Latin *persuasus est* is found.

It is useful to compare the following constructions:

subvenio tibi: adiuvo te, 'I help you'.
placeo tibi: delecto te, 'I please you', 'I delight you'.
obsto tibi: impedio te, 'I hinder you'.
noceo tibi: laedo te, 'I injure you'.
impero tibi ut hoc facias: iubeo te hoc facere, 'I order you to do this'. With these cf. *imperat Gallis frumentum*, 'He requisitions corn from the Gauls'.
suadeo tibi: moneo te, 'I urge, advise you'.
permitto tibi ut hoc facias: sino, patior te hoc facere, 'I permit you to do this'.
consulo tibi, 'I take counsel for you', 'consult your interests': *consulo te*, 'I consult you', 'ask your advice'.
timeo tibi, 'I fear for you': *timeo te*, 'I fear you'.
credo tibi, 'I believe you': *credo tibi pecuniam*, 'I entrust money to you'.

(2) *Moderor* and *tempero* have both an intransitive or quasi-reflexive sense 'to exercise self-restraint', with a dative of the person or thing in view of which the restraint is exercised (e.g. *moderari linguae*, 'to restrain one's tongue'), and also a transitive sense 'to temper', 'govern', 'control': Cic. *T. D.* 1, 2 *rem publicam nostri maiores melioribus temperaverunt legibus*, 'Our ancestors tempered (or governed) the state with better laws'.

Tempero in its intransitive sense is also used with *ab* and the ablative: Caes. *B. G.* 1, 7, 5 *neque homines temperaturos ab iniuria existimabat*, 'Nor did he think the men would refrain from wrong-doing'.

(3) *Minor* and *minitor*, in addition to the dative of the indirect object, can have an accusative object of the thing: Cic. *T. D.* 1, 102 *cui cum rex crucem minaretur*, 'when the king was threatening him with crucifixion . . .'

(4) The history of *invideo* is as follows: (*a*) In early Latin it took the accusative like *video* and meant 'look upon (with envy)': Cic. *T. D.* 3, 20 (quoting Accius) *quisnam florem liberum invidit meum?* 'Who has envied my flourishing children?' (*b*) By classical times it has come to be classed with the *verba nocendi*, and takes a dative either of the person envied or of the thing begrudged: Cic. *Fam.* 1, 7, 2 *qui honori inviderunt meo*, 'those who begrudged (me) my honour'. So, too, in Livy 38, 47, 5 *nullius equidem invideo honori.* 'I begrudge no man's honour.' (*c*) The poets Virgil, Horace, and Ovid revive the earlier use of the accusative of the thing, but join with it a dative of the person, so that we get the construction *invidere alicui aliquam rem*, 'to begrudge somebody something'. This construction does not appear in classical prose. Its first appearance in prose seems to be Livy 44, 30, 4 (one example only); thereafter it is found in Valerius Maximus,

Curtius, and Pliny the Elder, e.g. *N. H.* 15, 2, 8 *(Africae) natura oleum ac vinum invidit.* 'Nature has begrudged Africa oil and wine'; also Petr. *Sat.* 129 *homini misero non invideo medicinam.* 'I do not grudge a poor man a cure.' (*d*) The regular post-classical construction (cf. Quint. 9, 3, 1) is the dative of the person and the ablative of the thing. This begins with Livy 2, 40, 11 *non inviderunt laude sua mulieribus viri Romani.* 'Roman men did not begrudge the women their praise.' The ablative is probably one of Separation rather than Respect, possibly on the analogy of *interdicere alicui aqua et igni.*

60. *The Impersonal Passive*

As an active intransitive verb has no direct object to become the subject of the passive form, it follows that intransitive verbs, including those which take the dative, cannot be used 'personally' in the passive, i.e. they cannot have first- and second-person, or plural forms. But the third person singular passive of intransitive verbs is very common in Latin. The explanation of this form (which is, in fact, the earliest passive form) is that an intransitive verb can have a cognate or internal object (cf. Section 1), and this, whether expressed or understood, can become the subject of the 'impersonal' passive. Hence *curritur* means '*running* is taking place', i.e. 'people run'; *cursum est*, 'running took place'; *currendum est*, 'running is to take place'. The subject, in fact, is the abstract noun, the *name* of the action, implied in the root of the verb. This is true also of impersonal verbs of active form such as *tonat*, 'It thunders', *pluit*, 'It rains'. When the abstract noun implied by the verb is not expressed it is assumed to be of neuter gender, which explains the neuter form of *cursum*, *currendum*; and of *pugnatum est*, 'a battle was fought', beside *pugna pugnata est.* As with the personal passive, an agent with the impersonal passive (except for the gerundive, see Section 202) is expressed by *ab* with the ablative.

It follows that the Latin equivalent of 'I am being obeyed, harmed, spared, resisted, etc.' must be *paretur, nocetur, parcitur, resistitur mihi*, which mean literally 'obedience is being shown, harm is being done to me; restraint is being exercised towards me; resistance is being made to me; etc.' Examples: Cic. *de Sen.* 80 *mihi nunquam persuaderi potuit animos emori.* 'I could never be persuaded that our souls died.' *Id. Att.* 2, 14, 2 *a nobis non parcetur labori.* 'Toil will not be spared by us.' Livy 22, 22, 14 *vult sibi quisque credi.* 'Each man wishes to be believed.' Caes. *B. C.* 1, 4, 1 *omnibus his resistitur.* 'All these are resisted.'

61. *Dative of the Indirect Object with transitive verbs*

Transitive verbs taking a dative of the indirect object are mostly verbs of 'giving', 'showing', and 'telling'. But the idea of 'giving' must be interpreted very widely. As the dative denotes the *receiver*, even *mitto* would come under this heading in a sentence such as *mitto tibi epistulam* (cf. remarks in Section 57). Again, as already remarked in 59 (ii), constructions are apt to develop in pairs of opposites. This is the explanation of the dative with certain verbs of 'depriving'. On the analogy of *do tibi librum* one said *adimo, demo, eximo, eripio, aufero, detraho tibi librum*, 'I take the book away from you, withdraw it, snatch it from you, etc.' The dative denotes the person to whose *disadvantage* the act is performed. Logically one would expect the Ablative of Separation of the person from whom the thing is taken. In classical Latin the ablative (with preposition) is the normal construction when it is a thing or a place, and not a person or personified thing, from which the withdrawal takes place. Compare the following: Cic. *Div. in Caec.* 19 *quod auri in meis urbibus fuit, id mihi tu, C. Verres, eripuisti atque abstulisti.* 'All the gold there was in my cities, you, Gaius Verres, have snatched away and taken from me.' *Id. Att.* 7, 21, 2 *attulit mandata ad consules ut pecuniam de aerario auferrent.* 'He brought orders to the consuls that they should take the money away from the treasury.' But the poets, Livy, and later prose-writers often use the dative of things also.

Notes. (i) In English the direct and the indirect objects, as they are not distinguished by their forms, are apt to be confused. Only the direct accusative object can become the subject of the passive verb, yet it is possible to say in English 'I was given a book'. This, if logically analysed, is sheer nonsense. The Latin must be *liber mihi datus est.*

(ii) The verb *donare* has two constructions. It can have either the person or the thing as the direct object. In the former case the thing 'with which' one is presented is expressed by the instrumental ablative: *donare aliquem aliqua re*, 'to present someone with something'. The construction *donare aliquid alicui* is on the analogy of *dare.*

62. *The Dative with compound verbs*

A number of verbs, both intransitive and transitive, which in their simple form would require a prepositional phrase to express indirect relation, have their meaning modified, when they are compounded with certain prepositions, so that they either come within the categories of the verbs mentioned in Sections 59 and 61 or at any rate are naturally modified by a dative of the person or thing in view of whom or of which the action takes place. Thus the Latin for 'A tree fell on him' would be *arbor in eum cecidit*, but 'Terror fell upon the army' is *terror incidit exercitui*; similarly cp. *sequor te*, 'I follow you', but *obsequor tibi*, 'I comply with, obey you' (cf. *pareo*). With some of these compounds, e.g. *subvenire, obstare, praeesse* ('be in charge'), *praestare* ('surpass'), *praeficere aliquem alicui* ('put someone in charge of something'), etc., the dative is the only classical construction. With most of them, however, the dative is an alternative to the repetition of the preposition with its appropriate case; and with a few, e.g. compounds of *cum* (*con-*), *ex*, *de*, the dative is the less usual construction.

It will be noticed that many of these verbs imply motion, but in the compound verb the sense is often figurative (cp. *arbor cecidit* and *terror incidit*). In classical Latin, when the motion is only figurative, the dative is more often used; but when real motion is implied, the preposition is repeated with the appropriate case. Examples: Caes. *B. C.* 3, 23, 2 *magnum nostris terrorem iniecit.* 'He cast great fear into our men.' (The idea of motion is figurative.) Cic. *Dom.* 64 *legeram clarissimos viros se in medios hostes iniecisse.* 'I had read that most famous men had cast themselves into the midst of the enemy.' (Real motion is implied.) Caes. *B. G.* 1, 2, 4 *finitimis bellum inferre*, 'to make war on their neighbours' (figurative motion). Cic. *Fam.* 15, 2, 1 *nuntii de bello a Parthis in provinciam Syriam illato*, 'messages about the carrying of the war by the Parthians into the province of Syria'. (The extending of the war into the province, is in mind. I.e. real motion is implied.) Cic. *Fam.* 15, 11, 2 *cui me studia communia coniunxerant*, 'to whom our common pursuits had joined me'. *Cic. Fam.* 7, 30, 3 *eam epistulam cum hac epistula coniunxi.* 'I have joined that letter to this one.' (The latter is probably the more usual construction, though when the joining is only figurative, as in the previous example, the dative is common enough.)

Notes. (i) The distinction between the dative denoting the person or thing affected and the preposition repeated, with the accusative, denoting the goal of real motion, was never observed by the poets. In Caesar and Cicero the distinction is usually observed, though the verb *appropinquare*, 'to approach', is regularly constructed with the dative at all periods. But Livy and later prose-writers use the dative freely with compounds, even when real motion is implied. Examples: Virg. *Geor.* 1, 316 *cum flavis messorem induceret arvis/agricola*, 'when the farmer was bringing the reaper into the yellow fields'. Livy 2, 53, 1 *porta cui signa intulerat*, 'the gate against which he had advanced the standards'.

Such examples are due to extension by analogy, and are not to be regarded as evidence of an original 'goal' notion in the dative.

(ii) Some transitive compounds of *circum* (e.g. *circumdare*, *circumfundere*, *circumicere*) have a double construction like *dono*: Livy 21, 55, 3 *consul equites circumdedit peditibus.* 'The consul set the cavalry round the infantry.' Cic. *Tim.* 20 *deus animum circumdedit corpore.* 'God surrounded the mind with a body.'

63. *The Dative denoting Possession*

The dative of a noun or pronoun denoting a person can, with the verb 'to be', indicate for whose benefit something exists, i.e. something which the person possesses, e.g. *Est mihi magna domus.* 'I have a large house' (Lit. 'There is for me a large house'); Plaut. *Poen.* 84 *illi duae fuere filiae.* 'He had two daughters.' The verb 'to be' asserts the existence of the thing possessed as not being previously known. This use of the dative is common at all periods and in all types of Latin. The dative thus used differs from a predicated Genitive of possession or from a possessive adjective, for *Illius duae fuere filiae* would mean 'The two daughters were *his*' and *Est mea magna domus* would mean 'The large house is *mine*', implying that the existence of the thing possessed is already known.

The use of the dative instead of a Possessive Genitive or possessive adjective in the latter sense is common in colloquial Latin and in poetry but comparatively rare in literary prose. It is usually classed apart from the Dative of Possession and called the Sympathetic Dative. Examples: Plaut. *Mil.* 271 *illic est Philocomasio custos.* 'There is Philocomasium's guardian.' Caes. *B. G.* 1, 31, 2 *sese Caesari ad pedes proiecerunt.* 'They threw themselves at Caesar's feet.'

The effect of this dative cannot be reproduced in English, because it has to be rendered by the possessive case. It differs from the possessive genitive in denoting a warmer interest of the person concerned; hence the name 'sympathetic' dative. The use of the dative is normally adverbial, and grammatically it qualifies the verbs *est* and *proiecerunt* in the above examples. Nevertheless one feels that it belongs rather to the nouns *custos* and *pedes*, and so it came to be used adjectivally with nouns, when there was no verb for it to qualify: Plaut. *Mil.* 1431 *Quis erat igitur? – Philocomasio amator.* 'Who was it, then?' – 'Philocomasium's lover.' (Cf. 'Pindarus, servant to Cassius'; 'Calpurnia, wife to Caesar', etc., in a list of Dramatis personae.) So Virg. *Geor.* 3, 313 *miseris velamina nautis*, 'sails for wretched sailors'; Livy 9, 19, 7 *scutum, maius corpori tegumentum*, 'the shield, a greater protection to the body'.

Note. When the thing possessed is a *name*, as with the phrase *nomen est mihi*, it was the custom to attract the name also into the dative, e.g. Plaut. *Rud.* 5 *nomen Arcturo est mihi.* 'My name is Arcturus.' This attraction takes place in classical prose also: Cic. *Rosc. Am.* 17 *duo isti sunt T. Roscii, quorum alteri Capitoni cognomen est.* 'There are two T. Roscii, one of whom has the surname of "Capito".' But the nominative is also correct, and Cicero seems to prefer it in his later speeches and works.

The English use of the defining 'of' is not paralleled by the Latin Defining Genitive, except with adjectives used as nicknames, e.g. Cic. *de Sen.* 6 *cognomen habebat Sapientis.* 'He had the nickname of "The Wise".' But this defining genitive begins to be used of other names in Silver Latin: Tac. *Hist.* 4, 18 *castra quibus Veterum nomen est*, 'the camp which has the name of "Castra Vetera"'.

64. *The Dative of Advantage and Disadvantage*

The dative can be used quite loosely with almost any verb to indicate a person for whose benefit (or the reverse) an action is performed: Cic. *Rosc. Am.* 49 *praedia aliis coluit, non sibi.* 'He cultivated the estate for the benefit of others, not for himself.' Cic. *Pis.* 26 *an tibi quisquam in curiam venienti assurrexit?* 'Did anyone rise in your honour (i.e. "for your benefit") as you came into the senate-house?'

65. *The Dative of the Person Judging*

Another aspect of the 'interest' idea is to be seen in the dative denoting the person in whose eyes or in whose judgement the statement of the sentence is true: Cic. *Para.* 36 *an ille mihi liber cui mulier imperat?* 'Can that man be free in my eyes, whom a woman governs?' Caes. *B. C.* 3, 80, 1 *Caesar Gomphos pervenit, quod est oppidum primum Thessaliae venientibus ab Epiro.* 'Caesar came to Gomphi, which is the first town of Thessaly to people coming from Epirus.'

This dative is essentially of the same type as that used with *videri*, e.g. *vir bonus mihi videtur*, 'He seems to me a good man'.

66. *The Ethic Dative*

When the dative of a pronoun is used very loosely in the syntax of the sentence to indicate a person who regards, or who may be expected to regard the action with interest, it is called the Ethic Dative; cf. English 'Come, knock *me* at that door', where 'me' is almost equivalent to 'Please!' or 'I beg you'. The usage is essentially colloquial. The dative of the first person usually means 'please!' or 'pray'; the second person means 'For your pleasure I tell you this', or 'You will be surprised to hear', or 'Lo and behold!' It is hard to find two examples that can be translated alike: Hor. *Ep.* 1, 3, 15 *quid mihi Celsus agit?* 'How, pray, doth Celsus fare?' Cic. *Fam.* 9, 2, 1 *at tibi repente venit ad me Caninius mane.* 'But, lo and behold, Caninius suddenly came to me in the morning.' Livy 22, 60, 25 *haec vobis istorum per biduum militia fuit.* 'This, please your worships, was how yonder men served their country during the two days.'

67. *The Dative of the 'End aimed at' or 'Result achieved'*

As indicated in Section 56, when the use of the dative indicating the person who is the indirect object, i.e. whom it is the aim of the action to *affect*, is extending to things, especially if the thing is denoted by an abstract verbal noun, the dative marks not that which is affected, but that which is *effected*: e.g. *receptui canere*, 'to sound the signal *for retreat*'. Here the dative *receptui* no longer denotes something affected by the action, for it has not yet been brought about, but something that it is the aim of the action to effect. This use of the dative seems to belong particularly to the technical language of the crafts and professions. It is only such phrases as lend themselves to a general application or metaphorical use that are to be found in literary prose: e.g. *auxilio, subsidio, praesidio (aliquem) mittere*, 'to send someone to the relief' or 'as a reinforcement', or 'as a garrison or defence'. Such military phrases are naturally common in the historians. In writers on agriculture we find phrases like *alimento serere*, 'to sow for food'. An obviously medical phrase is *remedio adhibere*, 'to apply as a remedy', which could easily be extended to other spheres. So could the financial phrase *quaestui habere*, 'to have as a source of income'. This came to be used in the general sense of 'levy toll on', 'make a good thing out of': Cic. *Off.* 2, 77 *habere quaestui rem publicam turpe est.* 'To make a profit out of public affairs is disgraceful.' Similarly *usui esse*, 'to be for use', became general in the sense of 'to be useful'.

It is mostly abstract verbal nouns that are so used, but the usage could be extended to nouns denoting concrete things, if they were not yet in existence but intended to be brought about, or if the dative denoted a concrete thing for which something was intended to serve. So Caesar can say *locum deligere castris*, 'to choose a site for a camp', and the phrase *aliquid dono dare*, 'to give something as a gift', is fairly common: Sall. *Jug.* 85, 38 *virtus sola neque datur dono neque accipitur.* 'Virtue alone is neither given nor received as a gift.' Nep. 4, 2, 3 *Pausanias regis propinquos tibi muneri misit.* 'Pausanias has sent the king's relatives to you as a boon.'

Note. For the use of a gerundive phrase in the dative of 'the end aimed at' see Section 207 (4), and cf. Livy 24, 11, 6 *Q. Fabius comitia censoribus creandis habuit.* 'Q. Fabius held an assembly for the electing of censors.' *Id.* 25, 16, 9 *dies composita gerendae rei est.* 'A date was arranged for the conducting of the affair.'

68. *The Predicative Dative*

The dative marking the end, whether intended or simply resulting, is most commonly used in combination with a dative of the person interested, and predicated with the verb 'to be', or with a verb like *dare*, 'assign', 'attribute'; *ducere, habere*, 'consider'; *vertere*, in the sense of 'construe', 'interpret': Cic. *Verr.* II, 1, 16 *nemini meus adventus labori aut sumptui fuit.* 'To no one was my arrival a (source of) burden or expense.' *Id. T. D.* 1, 2, 4 *si Fabio laudi datum esset quod pingeret*, 'had it been attributed as a source of credit to Fabius that he was a painter' ('had it been considered creditable to him . . .'). Plaut. *Amph.* 492 *nemo id probro ducet Alcumenae.* 'No one will consider that as a reproach to Alcmena.' Cic. *Mur.* 56 *Catonis opes et ingenium praesidio multis, exitio vix cuiquam esse debet.* 'Cato's resources and talent ought to serve as a protection to many, as a source of ruin to scarcely anyone.' *Id. Fam.* 7, 6, 1 *persuasit ne sibi vitio verterent quod abesset a patria.* 'She persuaded them not to construe it as a fault against her that she was absent from her country' ('turn it to her discredit that . . .' or 'condemn her for being absent').

Notes. (i) The list of words that are used in the predicative dative as in the above examples is much restricted. A list of just over two hundred words is given by Roby, *Latin Grammar,* Vol. ii, Introd. pp. xli ff., but hardly more than two score of these are really common. Among these are the following: *adiumento esse,* 'be an aid'; *argumento esse,* 'be a proof', 'serve as evidence'; *auxilio esse, venire, mittere aliquem,* 'be a help', etc.; *bono esse,* 'be an advantage' (cf. the legal phrase *cui bono?* 'to whose advantage?' lit. 'to whom is it for a good thing?'); *calamitati esse,* 'be calamitous'; *causae esse,* 'serve as a reason'; *cordi esse,* 'be dear' (usually given amongst predicative datives, though *cordi* is probably locative, so that *hoc mihi cordi est* = 'This lies near to my heart'. 'This is to me for a heart' would be nonsense); *crimini esse,* 'be a ground for a charge'; *curae esse,* 'be a subject for anxiety'; *damno esse,* 'be a cause of loss'; *decori esse,* 'be a source of honour', 'be creditable', also *dedecori,* 'discreditable'; *detrimento,* 'a loss'; *documento,* 'an argument' or 'object-lesson', cf. *argumento*; *dolori,* 'a grief', 'grievous'; *dono dare, accipere, offerre,* etc., 'give as a gift', etc.; *emolumento,* 'a gain'; *exemplo,* 'an example'; *exitio,* 'a ruin', 'ruinous'; *fraudi,* 'a source of risk, or damage'; *fructui,* 'a source of revenue', 'fruitful'; *gloriae,* 'a glory', 'glorious'; *honori,* 'an honour'; *impedimento,* 'a hindrance'; *laudi esse, dare, ducere,* 'be, consider creditable'; *lucro,* 'a source of gain'; *ludibrio,* 'an object of mockery'; *malo,* 'a disadvantage', cf. *bono*; *muneri,* 'a boon', cf. *dono*; *odio,* 'hateful' (used regularly to give the passive of *odi,* e.g. *odi odioque sum Romanis,* 'I hate the Romans and am hated by (hateful to) them'); *oneri,* 'burdensome'; *opprobrio,* 'subject of reproach'; *pignori,* 'a pledge'; *praedae,* 'an object or source of plunder'; *praesidio,* 'a protection'; *probro,* cf. *opprobrio*; *pudori,* 'a thing to be ashamed of'; *quaestui,* 'a source of gain'; *receptui,* 'a retreat'; *religioni,* 'a ground of pious scruples'; *remedio,* 'a remedy'; *saluti,* 'a source of safety'; *solacio,* 'a consolation'; *subsidio,* 'a reserve', 'reinforcement', 'support'; *sumptui,* 'source of expense'; *terrori,* 'an object of terror'; *testimonio,* 'witness', 'evidence', cf. *argumento, documento*; *timori,* 'an object of fear'; *vitio esse, dare, ducere, vertere,* 'a fault'; *voluptati,* 'pleasurable'; *usui,* 'useful'.

(ii) Nouns in the predicative dative are very rarely accompanied by adjectives other than those of quantity, and very rarely by a qualifying genitive. Thus one finds *hoc mihi magnae, parvae, maiori, minori, maximae, minimae curae est,* 'This is a source of great, little, etc. care to me', but an example like Cic. *Fam.* 2, 7, 1 *ut sempiternae laudi tibi sit iste tribunatus*, 'that your tribunate may be an everlasting credit to you', is very rare indeed. Similarly the Latin for 'This redounds to my father's credit' is *hoc patri meo laudi est*, and not *hoc patris mei laudi est*. Examples like Caes. *B. G.* 1, 44, 6 *eius rei testimonio esse quod nisi rogatus non venerit*, 'as evidence of that was the fact that he had only come when asked' can be counted on the fingers of one hand.

(iii) When a word is commonly used in the predicative dative, it is very seldom found predicated in the nominative. As being less usual, the nominative has a more striking effect, and consequently there are more examples in poetry than prose, e.g. Virg. *Ecl.* 3, 101 *idem amor exitium est pecori pecorisque magistro*. 'The same love is a ruin to the flock and to the master of the flock.' After the poets Silver Latin prose-writers, from Livy onwards, begin to use the nominative: Qu. Curt. 3, 2, 18 *tu documentum eris posteris*. 'You will be an object-lesson to posterity.'

V

The Functions of the Genitive Case

69. The chief function of the genitive in Latin is to qualify nouns. The word or words in the genitive define, describe, or classify the thing (or person) denoted by the noun qualified. The genitive inflexion thus turns a noun or a pronoun into a sort of indeclinable adjective, which is sometimes interchangeable with an adjective: compare, for example, *fratris mors* with *fraterna mors*, 'a brother's death'; *domus regis* with *domus regia*, 'the king's house'.

The genitive defines or describes the thing or person denoted by the noun which it qualifies by indicating that with which the thing or person is in some way connected. The kinds of connexion or relation denoted by the Latin genitive include, but extend more widely than, those indicated by the English Possessive case or by the English adjectival phrase with the preposition 'of'. English can use a noun to define another noun either by putting it in the Possessive case ('the king's house') or, sometimes, by using it as an adjective without any inflexion ('the London-road', 'a sea-breeze'), or by using a preposition with it. The commonest preposition so used is 'of', but other prepositions may be used also, e.g. 'the road *to* Misenum', 'Roscius *from* Ameria', 'Damascus *in* Syria', 'anger *at* their flight', etc. The similar adjectival use either of a prepositional phrase or of any case other than the genitive is much restricted in Latin. To express the above ideas Latin uses either an adjective, if there is one, or else the genitive case: e.g. *via Miseni*, *Roscius Amerinus*, *Damascus Syriae*, *ira fugae*.

It will be seen that the genitive appears capable of expressing *adjectivally* all the relations which the other cases express adverbially.

70. As the genitive can express so many different relations, some of which are logically opposite to one another, it seems useless to look for any common sense-value underlying the various uses. The connexion between them is not to be found in meaning but in function. The genitive has become a 'grammatical' case, i.e. a syntactical device for enabling a noun or a pronoun to perform the function of an adjective. The genitive could then be used to express any relation suggested by the context.

It is possible that the Latin genitive, like the ablative, acquired some of its variety of functions by the process of syncretism. Some of the Latin genitive terminations are descended from Indo-European formations which served as ablatives as well as genitives, and it is noteworthy that the genitive case continues to perform ablatival functions in Greek. It would be contrary to the usual course of linguistic development if there were no survivals in Latin from this earlier state of things. Forms that were originally used adverbially would be likely to retain some of their adverbial functions in particular expressions, even after they had come to be regarded as genitive terminations. These adverbial uses would be extended to all forms of the genitive, and new adverbial uses also might arise by analogical extension. Therefore the adverbial uses of the genitive that will be noted below cannot all be explained as derived from the adjectival uses.

71. *The Genitive with Verbs and Adjectives*

Although the genitive is mainly used to qualify nouns, it is also used to modify or complete the meaning of a number of verbs and adjectives. With verbs such as *memini*, 'remember', *potior*, 'gain power over', and *misereor*, 'pity', the genitive appears to denote the object of the activity denoted by the verb. With other verbs, such as *compleo*, 'fill', *accuso*, 'accuse', *condemno*, 'condemn', *taedet*, 'it wearies', etc., the genitive is an adverbial extension or complement additional to the accusative object.

There is no single sense-value underlying these adverbial uses of the genitive, any more than the adjectival. With *compleo*, *taedet*, and *egeo*, 'need', 'lack', the genitive suggests source, cause, or separation; with verbs of accusing and condemning it suggests the locatival or sociative-instrumental ideas of the 'sphere within which' or 'matter in connexion with which'. It is to be noted that an ablative of separation (as with *egeo*), or an instrumental ablative (as with *compleo*), is often an alternative construction; and with *memini* and *obliviscor* an accusative of the object is an alternative. There is no evidence that these adverbial uses of the genitive are later developments, or that they are in any way derived from the adjectival uses. As indicated in Section 70, it is more likely that they are original and older than some of the adjectival uses.

72. *Summary of the uses of the Genitive*

I. *Adjectival uses*

(1) *Possessive Genitive.* The genitive denotes the possessor: *domus Ciceronis*, 'Cicero's house'; *Hasdrubal Gisgonis*, 'Hasdrubal (son) of Gisgo'; *coniuratio Catilinae*, 'Catiline's conspiracy'; *belli pericula*, 'the dangers of war'; *hominis periculum*, 'the man's danger'; etc. It should be noted that the relation between the possessor and the possessed may be very varied. On the one hand, the author or source of a thing may be regarded as its possessor, on the other, the person affected by a thing (e.g. 'the danger *to* the man') may be regarded as having a proprietary interest in it.

Notes. (i) Instead of the possessive genitive of the first, second, and reflexive pronouns, the possessive adjectives *meus*, *tuus*, *suus*, *noster*, *vester* are used. But the genitives *nostrum* and *vestrum* are usually used, if the pronoun is further qualified by *omnium*: Cic. *Cat.* 1, 14 *quae ad omnium nostrum salutem pertinent*, 'things that concern the safety of us all'. Cf. *Id. pro Mil.* 92 *in nostro omnium fletu*, 'amidst the tears of us all'. The latter is less usual.

(ii) The pronoun *ipse*, or any word in apposition to the person implied by the possessive adjective, must be in the possessive genitive: *meus ipsius pater*, 'my own father'; Cic. *Fam.* 15, 13, 1 *tuum studium adulescentis*, 'your zeal as a youth'.

(iii) The possessive genitive, like an adjective, may be predicated, either with *esse* or a factitive verb: *domus est patris mei*, 'the house is my father's'; *horti appellantur Caesaris*, 'the gardens are called Caesar's'. Under this heading belongs the idiomatic *Sapientis est hoc facere*, 'It is (the part of) a wise man to do this'. The possessive adjective may be similarly predicated: *meum est hoc facere*, 'It is my business to do this'.

(2) *The Subjective Genitive.* With a verbal noun, or a noun implying activity, the genitive may denote the author of the activity, who would be expressed as the nominative subject of the active verb or would be denoted by *ab* with the ablative with the passive verb, cf. *coniuratio Catilinae* above. This is a subdivision of the possessive genitive, but deserves a separate heading. See further, Sections 74–5.

(3) *The Objective Genitive.* The genitive may also denote the object of the activity implied by a noun or adjective. Thus *metus hostium* may, according to the context, mean either 'fear of the enemy' (objective, cf. *metuimus hostem*), or 'the enemy's fear' (subjective, cf. *hostes metuunt*).

Neither from the Objective Genitive is the idea of possession wholly absent, as indicated with reference to *hominis periculum* above, or cf. *hominis supplicium*, 'punishment *inflicted on* the man'. See further, Sections 74–6.

(4) *Partitive Genitive.* The genitive may denote the larger whole, of which something forms a part, or the larger stock from which something is drawn: *pars Galliae*, 'part of Gaul', *multi militum*, 'many of the soldiers', *cadus vini*, 'a cask of wine'. Here again the idea of 'belonging' can still be seen. When the genitive denotes the material drawn on, as in the last example, it may be called Genitive of Material. See further, Section 77.

(5) *Genitive of Definition.* The genitive may define a common noun by giving a particular example of the class of things denoted: *virtus iustitiae*, 'the virtue of justice' (i.e. that particular virtue which consists in justice); *praemium laudis*, 'the reward of praise'; *nomen amicitiae*, 'the noun *friendship*'; Cic. *Fin.* 2, 2 *Epicurus non intellegit quid sonet haec vox voluptatis*, 'Epicurus does not understand the meaning of this word "pleasure"'; *Id. Leg. agr.* 2, 36 *duae sunt huius obscuritatis causae: una pudoris, altera sceleris*, 'there are two motives for this vagueness, one consisting of shame, the other of criminal intention'. As this genitive denotes the same thing as the more general term which it qualifies, it is sometimes called the Appositional Genitive.

Notes. (i) This genitive corresponds to the English use of the preposition 'of' in expressions like 'the city of London'. Latin, however, does not normally use the appositional genitive of place-names, but puts the common noun and the place-name in apposition in the same case, as *urbs Roma*. The use of the genitive is poetic and post-Augustan: Virg. *Aen.* 1, 247 *urbem Patavi*, 'the city of Patavium'.

(ii) Conversely, the defining genitive is used sometimes of the *general* term which may be applied to the particular thing, and is then called Genitive of the Rubric: Caes. *B. C.* 1, 3, 6 *sex dies ad eam rem conficiendam spatii postulant*, 'they demand six days of interval for completing the business' (instead of *spatium sex dierum*); Cic. *Verr.* 3, 116 *ad singula medimna multi sestertios binos accessionis cogebantur dare*, 'many were compelled to pay two sesterces a bushel as an extra charge'. So one might say *decem sestertii mercedis*, or *lucri*, or *compendi*, 'ten sesterces by way of wages, *or* of profit,' *or* 'a saving of ten sesterces'. When the genitive is made predicative, we get the common phrases *lucri facere, compendi facere aliquid*, 'to make a profit of, *or* a saving of', or 'count as a gain': Plaut. *Poen.* 771 *me esse hos trecentos Philippos facturum lucri*, '(the thought that) I am going to make a gain of these three hundred Philips'.

(6) *Genitive of Description* (*Quality*). A noun *with an epithet* in the genitive may describe a person or thing by indicating size or measure (*res decem talentum*, 'an estate of ten talents', *res eius modi*, 'a thing of that

measure') or by indicating some distinctive quality, as *vir summi ingenii*, 'a man of the highest talent'. For the history and extension of this use of the genitive, see Sections 84–5.

(7) *Genitive of Value and Price.* The genitive singular of certain neuter adjectives and pronouns, and one or two nouns, is used in expressions of value and price (*magni facere aliquid*, 'to value something highly', *pluris vendere aliquid*, 'to sell at a higher price'). Although this use is adverbial, it may be mentioned here, because it probably arose out of the predicative use of the above defining or descriptive genitives. See further, Sections 86–7.

73. II. *Adverbial Uses*

(1) A genitive, usually reckoned as partitive in origin, is used to denote the object, whether person or thing, of certain verbs of remembering, forgetting, reminding, and equivalent expressions: *memini, obliviscor, venit in mentem, commonefacio, mentionem facio*: Plaut. *Capt.* 800 *faciam ut huius diei semper meminerit*, 'I will cause him always to remember this day'; Cic. *Fin.* 5, 3 *vivorum memini, nec tamen Epicuri licet oblivisci*, 'I remember the living, nor yet may I forget Epicurus'; *Ib.* 5, 2 *venit mihi Platonis in mentem*, 'the thought of Plato came into my mind'; *Id. Verr.* 5, 112 *nemo est quin tui sceleris et crudelitatis commonefiat*, 'there is no one but is reminded of your crime and cruelty'.

Notes. (i) With verbs of remembering and forgetting (except the participle *oblitus*) the accusative of the object is also used, mostly of things, less often of persons, and particularly when the object is a neuter pronoun or adjective. It is said that the genitive suggests groping in the mind after something, without grasping it in its entirety, while the accusative suggests that something is completely remembered or forgotten. With the example from Plautus above cp. *Men.* 45 *illius nomen memini facilius*, where the adverb suggests complete recollection. But it is doubtful whether the analysis of all examples would substantiate this distinction. It should, perhaps, be pointed out that the genitive construction goes far back, and is not a particularly Latin development.
(ii) *recordor*, 'call to mind', 'recollect', regularly takes an accusative object in classical Latin, or else *de* with the ablative. The genitive is found with it in later Latin, on the analogy of *memini*.
(iii) With verbs of reminding other than *commonefacio* the regular classical construction is *de* with the ablative. With *admoneo* and *commoneo* the genitive is rare in Cicero and Caesar, but commoner in poetry and in historical prose from Sallust onwards; with *moneo* the genitive is used only by Tacitus: Livy, 23, 18, 7 *Cannarum Trasumennique et Trebiae singulos admonens universosque*, 'reminding them one and all of Cannae, Trasimene, and the

Trebia'; Tac. *Ann.* 1, 67 *iussos dicta cum silentio accipere temporis ac necessitatis monet*, 'bidding them listen to his words in silence, he warned them of the crisis and urgency'.

(2) From the earliest times the genitive was used as an alternative to the ablative after *potiri*, 'to become master of', 'gain control or possession of': Plaut. *Rud.* 1337 *viduli ubi sis potitus*, 'when you have gained possession of the bag'; Caes. *B. G.* 1, 3, 8 *totius Galliae sese potiri posse sperant*, 'they hope to be able to gain control of the whole of Gaul'. Sallust regularly uses the genitive, but most authors prefer the ablative.

(3) A genitive which has obvious 'partitive' connexions is used after compounds of *pleo*, 'fill', and certain other verbs and adjectives denoting fulness or abundance, and their opposites: *compleo*, *impleo*, *abundo*, *egeo*, *indigeo*; *plenus*, *refertus*, *inanis*, *inops*; and occasionally, by analogy, with other verbs and adjectives of similar meaning: Cato, *R. R.* 88, 1 *amphoram puram impleto aquae purae*, 'fill a clean jar with clean water'; Cic. *de Sen.* 46 *convivium vicinorum cotidie compleo*, 'I fill up my company with neighbours every day'; *Id. pro Cl.* 189 *domum scelerum omnium adfluentem*, 'a house overflowing with every crime'; Sall. *Cat.* 51, 37 *maiores nostri nec consilii neque audaciae eguere*, 'our ancestors lacked neither policy nor boldness'; Cic. *de Or.* 1, 37 *omnia plena consiliorum, inania verborum videmus*, 'we see all full of ideas, but empty of words'.

Notes. (i) Examples such as the following may be regarded as extensions by analogy: Plaut. *Rud.* 247 *ut me omnium iam laborum levas!* 'how you relieve me of all my troubles!'; Hor. *Odes* 2, 9, 17 *desine querellarum*, 'cease from your complaints'; and poetical combinations such as *dives opum*, 'rich in resources'; *pauper aquae*, 'poor in water'.

(ii) With verbs and adjectives denoting fulness, an instrumental ablative is more common than the genitive, and an ablative of separation with verbs and adjectives of the opposite meaning: Cic. *Tim.* 9 *deus bonis omnibus explevit mundum*, 'God has filled the world with all good things'; *Id. Sest.* 23 *vita plena et conferta voluptatibus*, 'a life full and crammed with pleasures'; *Id. T. D.* 5, 102 *nos ipsa natura admonet quam paucis, quam parvis rebus egeat*, 'nature herself reminds us how few and how small things she lacks'. *egeo* regularly takes the genitive in early Latin, but with this, as with most of the other verbs and adjectives, the ablative gradually becomes more common. *careo* prefers the ablative from the first.

(4) With verbs denoting emotion, such as *misereor*, 'pity', and the impersonals *miseret*, *paenitet*, *piget*, *pudet*, *taedet*, the genitive is used to indicate the matter with regard to which the emotion is felt: *taedet me vitae*, 'I am weary of life'; *piget me laboris*, 'reluctance affects me with regard to work'. See further, Sections 208–9. The genitive here denotes the 'sphere within which' the activity takes place, and is essentially of the same type as the genitives indicated in the following sections.

(5) A genitive of the matter involved is used with verbs and expressions denoting judicial procedure, such as *accuso*, 'accuse'; *insimulo*, 'invent a charge against'; *ago*, 'bring an action'; *arcesso*, 'summon'; *postulo*, 'impeach'; *arguo*, 'show up', 'censure', 'charge'; *convinco*, 'convict'; *damno*, *condemno*, 'condemn'; *absolvo*, 'acquit'; and with adjectives such as *reus*, 'charged', 'on trial'; and (from Livy onwards) *obnoxius*, 'liable'; *suspectus*, 'under suspicion'; *manifestus*, 'proved guilty', 'apprehended in'; etc.: Nep. 1, 7, 5 *Miltiades proditionis accusatus est*, 'Miltiades was accused of treachery'; Cic. *Verr.* II, 1, 128 *Fannius C. Verrem insimulat avaritiae*, 'Fannius charges C. Verres with avarice'; *Id. Inv.* 2, 59 *agit is, cui manus praecisa est, iniuriarum*, 'he whose hand has been cut off brings an action for injury (damages)'; Suet. *Caes.* 4, 1 *Caesar Dolabellam repetundarum postulavit*, 'Caesar impeached Dolabella for extortion'; Cic. *Flacc.* 43 *pecuniae publicae est condemnatus*, 'he was condemned for embezzlement' (lit. 'in connexion with public money'); *Id. de Or.* 1, 233 *Socratis responso sic iudices exarserunt ut capitis hominem innocentissimum condemnarent*, 'the jury were so incensed at Socrates' reply that they condemned that most innocent man to death'; *Id. Verr.* II, 1, 72 *video non te absolutum esse improbitatis, sed illos damnatos esse caedis*, 'I see, not that you are acquitted of dishonesty, but that they are convicted of murder'.

It will be seen that the genitive may indicate either the crime (e.g. *proditionis*), or the penalty (e.g. *capitis*), or the matter involved in the case (e.g. *pecuniae publicae*, or *repetundarum* – *sc. pecuniarum* – 'in connexion with moneys to be reclaimed').

Notes. (i) With the above-mentioned judicial verbs and expressions may be used the instrumental ablatives *crimine*, 'on a charge of', *nomine*, 'under the heading', 'on account of'; *lege*, 'under the law of'; *iudicio*, 'by proceedings for . . .', and these ablative words will naturally have genitives depending on them. But it is by no means necessary to postulate the ellipse of these ablative words, when the genitives stand alone.

(ii) The sense of the genitive denoting the crime or the claim involved can be expressed equally well by a prepositional phrase such as *de* or *in* with the ablative, or *propter* with the accusative. Thus one can say either *maiestatis* or *de maiestate aliquem accusare, damnare*, etc. But to express 'to accuse of assault and battery' only the prepositional phrase *de vi* can be used, because *vis* has no gen. sing. in use: Cic. *Phil.* 1, 21 *de vi et maiestatis damnati*, 'condemned for violence and treason'.

(iii) The only genitives of the *penalty* regularly in use are the following: *capitis*, 'death', 'capital punishment', or 'disenfranchisement'; *dupli, quadrupli, octupli*, 'a fine of double, four times, eight times, the amount involved'; *tanti, quanti, pluris, minoris*, 'so great, how great, a greater, smaller, fine'. Any other word denoting a fine or punishment is normally put in the instrumental ablative, and with it *multare*, 'to fine, sentence, punish', is rather more usual than *damnare*: Nep. 4, 2, 6 *Pausanias accusatus capitis absolvitur, multatur tamen pecunia,* 'Pausanias, accused on a capital charge, was acquitted, but was sentenced to a money-fine'; Cic. *Verr.* 3, 69 *quinque milibus damnari,* 'to be condemned to a fine of 5,000 sesterces'; Livy 10, 1, 3 *Frusinates tertia parte agri damnati,* 'the people of Frusino were condemned to the loss of a third part of their land'.

(6) *Genitive of Reference.* In the poets and later prose-writers a genitive is used with many adjectives, other than those under headings (3) and (5), to denote that with respect to which the adjective is applicable: Tac. *Ann.* 12, 22 *atrox odii Agrippina,* 'Agrippina, unrelenting in her hatred'; Stat. *Silv.* 3, 2, 64 *audax ingenii,* 'bold of intellect'; *Id. Ach.* 2, 237 *blandus precum,* 'charming in entreaty'; Tac. *Ann.* 14, 19 *ut par ingenio, ita morum diversus,* 'equal in intellect, but different in respect of character'; *Ib.* 4, 12 *ferox scelerum,* 'ruthless in crime'; Virg. *Aen.* 5, 73 *maturus aevi,* 'mature in respect of age'; Vell. 1, 12, 4 *modicus virium,* 'moderate in strength'; Tac. *Ann.* 4, 7 *occultus odii,* 'secretive in his hatred'; *Ib.* 16, 14 *occasionum haud segnis,* 'not slow in seizing opportunities'; etc.

In classical Latin an Ablative of Respect (cf. *par ingenio*) would normally be used with such adjectives. The use of the genitive is to be regarded as an extension of some of the types already indicated, e.g. partitive, objective, or of matter involved. Such extensions of the genitive are not without early and classical precedent: Plaut. *Asin.* 459 *quoi omnium rerum ipsus semper credit,* 'whom he himself always trusts in all things' (cf. Caes. *B. G.* 1, 19, 3 *cui summam omnium rerum fidem habebat,* 'in whom he had the greatest confidence in all matters', where, however, the genitive may depend on the noun *fidem*); Plaut. *Epid.* 239 *nec sermonis fallebar tamen,* 'nor yet was I cheated of their conversation' (i.e. it did not escape my ears); Ter. *Ad.* 695 *ceterarum rerum socordem,* 'slothful with regard to other matters'; Cic. *pro Quinct.* 11 *ceterarum rerum prudens et attentus,* 'wise and attentive with regard to other matters' (with *prudens* alone an objective genitive would be regular).

74. *Further remarks on the Subjective and Objective Genitive*

The connexion of the subjective and objective sense of the genitive with the possessive has already been noticed. The subjective genitive further resembles the possessive in that the possessive adjectives *meus, tuus, suus, noster, vester,* are used instead of the genitive forms in the *subjective* sense. On the other hand, the genitives *mei, tui, sui, nostri, vestri,* are regularly used in the *objective* sense. Thus the Latin for 'my love for you' is *meus amor tui.*

Notes. (i) The above-mentioned genitive forms are never used in a subjective sense in classical prose, any more than they are normally used to express possession. There are, however, occasional examples in poetry and post-Augustan prose: Tac. *Ann.* 15, 36 *testificatus non longam sui absentiam fore,* 'proclaiming that his absence would not be long'. Also the genitive form *vestrum* is occasionally used by Cicero in a subjective sense: *Phil*, 5, 2 *recordamini quantus consensus vestrum fuerit*, 'recollect how great was your unanimity' (for *vester*).

(ii) On the contrary, the possessive adjectives in agreement are sometimes used in an objective sense, where one would expect the genitive form: Cic. *Att.* 1, 29, 7 *vir bonus amatorque noster*, 'a good man and my lover'; *Id. pro Planc.* 2 *vester conspectus reficit et recreat mentem meam*, 'the sight of you refreshes and renews my spirit' (for *vestri*). This happens when the possessive idea is uppermost ('*my* lover', '*your* appearance') and is fairly common.

75. When both the subject and the object of the verbal activity implied by a noun are expressed by nouns, ambiguity may be avoided by substituting for the objective genitive a prepositional phrase with *erga*, *in*, or *adversus*: Cic. *Q. Fr.* 3, 1, 26 *voluntas Servilii erga Caesarem*, 'the goodwill of Servilius towards Caesar'. But if the context shows which is the subject and which is the object, both a subjective and an objective genitive may depend on the same noun: Caes. *B. G.* 1, 30, 2 *pro veteribus Helvetiorum iniuriis populi Romani*, 'in requital for the injuries inflicted *by* the Helvetii *on* the Roman people'. In such examples the subjective genitive usually comes first.

76. *Extensions of the Objective Genitive*

The objective genitive is not confined to use only with nouns connected with transitive verbs. With nouns which are connected with transitive verbs the genitive expresses the same relation to the noun that the object-accusative expresses to the verb, as, for example, *ruptor foederum*, 'a breaker of treaties', corresponds to *foedera rumpit*. But from the earliest extant literature we find the genitive also used to represent what would have been the cognate or internal object, or the indirect object, of the verb. That is to say, we find objective genitives qualifying nouns connected with intransitive verbs, such as may require a dative, or an ablative, or a prepositional phrase, to complete their sense. Thus we find *fiducia tui*, 'reliance upon you', though *fido* takes the dative or ablative; *usus alicuius rei*, 'the use of something', though *utor* takes the ablative; and *consensio alicuius rei*, 'agreement about something', though one would have to say *consentire de aliqua re*. This is the light in which it is necessary to consider the following examples: Cic. *Leg.* 2, 16 *quam multos divini supplicii metus a scelere revocavit*, 'how many the fear of divine punishment has restrained from crime'. (A straightforward example corresponding to *metuunt supplicium.*) Livy 6, 4, 1 *Camillus in urbem triumphans rediit trium simul bellorum victor*, 'Camillus returned in triumph to the city, the victor in three wars at once'. (Here *bellorum* represents what would have been an *internal* object of the verb *vincere.*) Cic. *Man.* 3 *semper appetentes gloriae atque avidi laudis fuistis*, 'you have always been thirsty for glory and eager for praise'. (With participles used as adjectives the objective genitive is regular.) Caes. *B. G.* 7, 64, 8 *civitati imperium totius provinciae pollicetur*, 'he promises the community command over the whole province'. (But the verb *imperare* takes the dative.) Virg. *Aen.* 1, 132 *tantane vos generis tenuit fiducia vestri?* 'Has such confidence in your birth possessed you?' Cic. *Off.* 1, 87 *miserrima est honorum contentio*, 'most abject is competition for office'. (But *contendere de honoribus.*) *Id. Phil.* 2, 23 *Pompeium a Caesaris coniunctione avocabam*, 'I was trying to recall Pompey from his connexion with Caesar'. (But *coniungere aliquem cum aliquo.*) Caes. *B. C.* 1, 4, 1 *Catonem veteres inimicitiae Caesaris incitant et dolor repulsae*, 'Cato was urged on by his ancient feud *with* Caesar and chagrin *at* his defeat'. Cic. *de Or.* 1, 98 *patefecit earum ipsarum rerum aditum quas quaerimus*, 'he has opened an approach *to* the very things we are seeking' (cf. *via Miseni*, 'the road *to* Misenum').

77. *Notes on the Partitive Genitive*

(i) A partitive genitive may qualify any noun, pronoun, adjective, or even adverb which, in its context, denotes a part, measure, quantity, or number of persons, things, or stuff, as *pars Galliae*, 'part of Gaul'; *modius frumenti*, 'a peck of corn'; *magnus numerus eorum*, 'a great number of them'; *quis vestrum?* 'who of you?'; *uterque horum*, 'each of these (two)'; *multi militum*, 'many of the soldiers'; *tria milia militum*, 'three thousand soldiers' (the plural *milia* is a noun and always requires a genitive after it; the singular *mille* is normally treated as an indeclinable adjective in agreement: *mille milites*, *cum mille militibus*, but there are exceptions); *altior horum montium*, 'the higher of these (two) mountains'; *optimus civium*, 'the best of the citizens' (the comparative and superlative of adjectives naturally imply partition); *satis alicuius rei*, 'enough of something'; *nusquam gentium*, 'nowhere among men'; *ubi terrarum?*, 'where on earth?'.

(ii) A partitive genitive is often used after neuter adjectives and pronouns such as *multum, plus, plurimum, tantum, quantum, aliquid, quid, quod, id, hoc*, etc., instead of an adjective in agreement: *multum auri*, 'much gold'; *quid negotii?* 'what business?'; *aliquid novi*, 'something new' (third declension genitives are rarely so used; cf. *aliquid memorabile*, 'something memorable', *nihil tale*, 'no such thing'); Caes. *B. G.* 3, 16, 2 *navium quod fuerat coegerant*, 'they had gathered together what ships there were'; Ter. *Hec.* 643 *quid mulieris uxorem habes!* 'what a woman you have as wife!'

Some of these genitives are similar to the genitives of the rubric, and do not always produce quite the same effect as an adjective in agreement; e.g. *quid praemii erit?* means 'what will there be *by way of* reward?', and is not quite the same as *quod praemium erit?*

Apart from the expressions *eo, eodem, quo loci*, 'up to that point', 'up to the same point', 'up to which point', the partitive genitive is not used with neuter pronouns in an oblique case, nor do Cicero and Caesar use it with pronouns depending on a preposition, though the latter becomes fairly common later on, as Sall. *Cat.* 45, 3 *postquam ad id loci venerunt*; Livy 27, 28, 10 (*cataractam*) *subducunt in tantum altitudinis ut subire recti possent*, 'they raised the portcullis to such a height that they could pass under without stooping' (= *in tantam altitudinem*).

(iii) The adjectives *omnis, omnes, cuncti, totus* are not followed by a partitive genitive, because they do not imply partition, but are used in agreement with the noun or pronoun, e.g. *nos omnes*, 'all of us'; *tota urbs*, 'the whole of the city'; etc.

On the other hand, adjective and noun may agree in some cases where a partitive meaning is present. This is found with such adjectives as *summus, imus, extremus, medius, primus*, e.g. *summa aqua*, 'the surface of the water'; *summus mons*, 'the top of the mountain' (but cf. *summus montium*, 'the highest of the mountains') *in media urbe*, 'in the middle of the city' (but cf. *media trium rerum*, 'the middle one of three things'); *primo vere*, 'at the beginning of spring'; etc.

With such adjectives the use of the neuter and a partitive genitive is rarely found in prose before Sallust, as *Jug.* 93, 2 *ad summum montis*, 'to the top of the mountain'; Livy 28, 9, 1 *extremo aestatis*, 'at the end of the summer'. In poetry and post-Ciceronian prose neuter plural adjectives also are found with the genitive: Livy 5, 29, 4 *per aversa urbis*; 4, 1, 4 *extrema agri*.

(iv) The partitive genitives *nostrum, vestrum* are used with reference to groups of persons, as *multi nostrum, pars nostrum*, 'many of us, some of us', whereas the genitives *nostri, vestri* are used in a partitive sense only with reference to individuals, e.g. *nostri melior pars animus est*, 'the mind is the better part of ourselves'.

(v) *Uterque* (cf. *uter, neuter*) can be used either as an adjective or as a pronoun. With a noun it is used as an adjective in agreement: *uterque consul*, 'each consul', 'both consuls'; with a pronoun it is itself a pronoun, and requires the partitive genitive: *uterque nostrum*, 'each of us (two)'.

(vi) A singular positive adjective is used occasionally with the partitive genitive in poetry, but is unclassical in prose, e.g. *sancte deorum*, 'O holy among gods' (probably imitated from Greek). With a plural positive adjective such genitives are fairly common in the historians: Sall. *reliqua cadaverum*, 'the rest of the corpses'; Livy 26, 51, 3 *cum delectis peditum*, 'with chosen of the infantry'; *Id.* 42, 65, 5 *revocato equite et reliquis peditum*, 'recalling the cavalry and the rest of the infantry'.

(vii) The whole out of which a part is taken can obviously be expressed equally well by *ex* or *de* with the ablative, and this construction is usually an alternative to the partitive genitive: *multi, pauci, centum ex iis*, 'many, few, a hundred of them'; Cic. *de Or.* 2, 357 *acerrimus ex omnibus nostris sensibus est sensus videndi*, 'the keenest of all our senses is the sense of sight'; Hor. *Od.* III, xi, 33 *una de multis face nuptiali digna*, 'alone out of many worthy of the marriage-torch'.

VI

Further Uses of the Ablative and Genitive

78. *The Ablative of Comparison.* The ablative is used after comparative adjectives, more rarely after comparative adverbs, to denote the person or thing used as the standard of comparison: Cic. *de Am.* 42 *Quis clarior Themistocle?* 'Who was more famous than Themistocles?'; *Ibid.* 28 *nihil est amabilius virtute*, 'Nothing is more lovable than virtue'; Livy 29, 15, 11 *alii aliis magis recusare*, 'Some objected more than others'; Cic. *Inv.* 1, 109 *lacrima nihil citius arescit*, 'Nothing dries more quickly than a tear'.

The use of the ablative in expressions of comparison, however, is more restricted than that of the conjunction *quam*, as will be indicated below.

79. There is now little doubt that the Ablative of Comparison is an offshoot of the 'from'-case or true ablative. Thus the original sense of *haec res pulchrior est illa* must have been something like 'from the standpoint of that thing, this thing is more beautiful'. This is supported by the fact that the ablatival genitive is used to express comparison in Greek, and by the introduction in later Latin of the prepositions *ab* and *de*. The use of *ab* begins in classical times: Ovid, *Her.* 17, 69 *a Veneris facie non est prior ulla*, 'there is no beauty more outstanding than that of Venus'.

80. *The Conjunction* Quam *in expressions of comparison*

Except in a limited range of expressions, the conjunction *quam* is far commoner than the ablative as a method of expressing comparison in all periods of Latin.

Quam is the relative adverb to *tam*, and can have been used in the beginning only to indicate that two persons or things are equal in some respect (*tam . . . quam* = 'so . . . as' or 'as . . . as'): *Hic tam clarus est quam ille*, 'This man is as famous as that'. But we sometimes find comparative adjectives mixed with or substituted for the positive after *tam* or *quam* (e.g. Cic. *Deiot.* 8 *per dexteram istam te oro . . . non tam in bellis quam in promissis et fide firmiorem*; Plaut. *Poen.* 825 *neque peior alter est quam erus meus . . . neque tam luteus*). Such passages suggest that the *tam–quam* construction was contaminated with the ablative of comparison, examples like *hic tam clarus est quam ille* with *hic clarior est illo*, so as to produce *hic clarior est quam ille*, 'This man is more famous that that'.

The *quam*-method of expressing comparison is handier, capable of a wider application, and avoids the ambiguity which would often be caused by the ablative. E.g. in Hor. *Sat.* I, 1, 96 *ita sordidus ut se non unquam servo melius vestiret* might mean either 'He was so mean that he never dressed himself better than he dressed his slave' (= *quam servum*) or '. . . than his slave dressed' (= *quam servus se vestiebat*).

For these reasons the *quam*-construction soon came to be commoner than the ablative. The circumstances under which the ablative is a regular alternative or commoner than *quam* are explained in Section 81.

81. (i) In both positive and negative expressions of comparison the ablative is an alternative to *quam* only when it represents what would be a nominative or an accusative in a *quam*-clause: cf. Hor. *Sat.* I, 1, 96 quoted above, and Cic. *N. D.* 3, 25 *qui id efficit melior est homine*, 'he who accomplishes that is better than a man' (= *quam homo*); *Id. Att.* 10, 11, 1 *habet me se ipso cariorem*, 'he holds me dearer than himself' (= *quam se ipsum habet*); Sall. *Jug.* 14, 15 *morte graviorem vitam exigunt*, 'They pass a life more burdensome than death' (after *quam* Latin would probably attract *mortem* into the accusative, though strictly *graviorem quam mors* (sc. *est*) would be correct). Hence the ablative cannot be used to say, e.g. 'He is dearer to me than to you' (*carior est mihi quam tibi*), for *carior est mihi te* could be an alternative only to *carior est mihi quam tu* (*es*).

But it is to be noted that, in expressions of comparison which are not negative and imply no negative (e.g. 'I am taller than my brother'), Plautus, Caesar, Cicero, Sallust, and Tacitus prefer *quam* (there are only four examples of the ablative in Caesar). Pliny the Younger, on the other hand, has a leaning towards the ablative.

(ii) In *negative* expressions of comparison, and in rhetorical questions that imply a negative answer, the ablative is commoner than *quam*: Plaut. *Most.* 1072 *alter hoc nemo doctior*, 'there is no other man more learned than this'; Cic. *de Or.* 2, 37 *non tulit ullos haec civitas clariores P. Africano, C. Laelio, L. Furio*, 'this country has not produced any men more famous than P. Africanus, etc.'; Plaut. *As.* 557 *qui me vir fortior?* 'What man is braver than I?'; Cic. *Div.* 2, 116 *Herodotum cur veraciorem ducam Ennio?* 'Why should I consider Herodotus more truthful than Ennius?'

(iii) The ablative is regular in a number of stereotyped proverbial expressions such as *stultior stultissimo*, 'fool of fools'; *opinione melius*, 'better than expected'; *plus iusto*, 'more than is right'; *melle dulcior*, 'sweeter than honey'; etc.

(iv) Only the ablative, never *quam*, is used when the word denoting the standard of comparison is a relative pronoun: Cic. *Rep.* 2, 27 *Polybium sequamur, quo nemo fuit diligentior*, 'let us follow Polybius, than whom no one was more accurate'. So always *quo nihil melius*, etc., and never *quam quod . . .*

(v) After *plus, amplius, minus*, with numerical measurements of time and space, sometimes the Ablative of Comparison is used, sometimes the Accusative of Extent or Duration with or (more often) without *quam*: Caes. *B. G.* 2, 7, 3 *castra amplius milibus passuum octo in latitudinem patebant*, 'the camp extended more than eight miles in width' (= *amplius* (*quam*) *octo milia*); *Ibid.* 4, 37, 3 *nostri milites amplius horis quattuor pugnaverunt*, 'our soldiers fought for more than four hours' (= *amplius* (*quam*) *horas quattuor*); *Ibid.* 7, 19, 1 *palus non latior pedibus quinquaginta*, 'a swamp not broader than fifty feet' (= *latior quam pedes L*).

82. *The Ablative of Measure of Difference*

In expressions of comparison or which imply comparison, the amount of difference is expressed by the ablative: e.g. *hic murus decem pedibus altior est quam ille*, 'This wall is higher than that *by ten feet*'. The type of ablative is clearly instrumental.

This ablative is used:

(i) With comparative and superlative adjectives and adverbs: Curt. 5, 1, 26 *turres denis pedibus quam murus altiores sunt*, 'The turrets are each ten feet higher than the wall'; Cic. *N. D.* 2, 92 *sol multis partibus maior est quam terra*, 'The sun is many sizes larger than the earth'; Plaut. *Men.* 680 *redimam tibi bis tanto pluris pallam*, 'I will buy you a dress worth twice as much' (lit. 'worth more (*pluris*) by twice so much'). So *ter*, *quater*, *quinquiens*, etc., *tanto altior*, 'three times, four times, five times higher'. Instead of *bis tanto*, sometimes *altero tanto* (lit. 'by another such amount') is found.

With superlatives only *multo*, 'by much', 'by far', is regular, for which *longe* is commoner: Cic. *Div. in Caec.* 36 *adrogantia ingenii multo molestissima*, 'intellectual arrogance is by far the most annoying'.

(ii) With verbs that imply comparison or difference, such as *praestare*, *antecellere*, *superare*, *vincere*, 'to surpass'; also occasionally (especially from Livy on) with *abesse* and *distare*, 'to be distant from', instead of the Accusative of Extent: Cic. *N. D.* 2, 102 *sol, cuius magnitudine multis partibus terra superatur*, 'the sun, by whose size the earth is surpassed many times'; Livy 22, 40, 7 *parte dimidia auctas hostium copias cernebat*, 'He began to discern that the enemy's forces were increased by a half'; Caes. *B. G.* 1, 41, 5 *certior factus est Ariovisti copias a nostris milibus passuum quattuor et viginti abesse*, 'He was informed that the forces of Ariovistus were twenty-four miles distant from ours'; *Ibid.* 1, 43, 1 *hic locus aequo fere spatio ab castris Ariovisti et Caesaris aberat*, 'This place was about an equal distance from the camp of Ariovistus and that of Caesar'.

Sometimes the ablative instead of the accusative is used to indicate the amount of distance away, even when the verb is not *abesse* or *distare*: Caes. *B. G.* 1, 43, 2 *legionem Caesar passibus ducentis ab eo tumulo constituit*,

'Caesar halted the legion two hundred paces from that mound'; so also *B. G.* 1, 48, 1; 2, 23, 4; and fairly often. In *passibus ducentis* it is difficult to decide whether we have an extension of the Ablative of Measure, or a locatival ablative ('at' or 'within' 200 paces).

(iii) With *ante*, 'before', 'earlier', and *post*, 'after', 'later', Cic. *de Sen.* 10 *Quaestor quadriennio post factus sum*, 'I was made quaestor four years later'; *Id. de Am.* 42 *viginti annis ante*, 'twenty years before'; *Id. de Or.* 2, 154 *Numa annis ante permultis fuit quam Pythagoras*, 'Numa lived many years earlier than Pythagoras'. In these examples *ante* and *post* are adverbs. As adverbs they are normally placed either after or in between the ablative words denoting the measure of difference, as *tribus ante* (*post*) *diebus*, 'three days before (after)'; rarely in front, as Livy 32, 5, 10 *post paucis diebus*.

But *ante* and *post* can also be used as prepositions with the accusative in the same sense, in which case they naturally precede the accusative words: Cic. *Mil.* 44 *post diem tertium* (= *tribus post diebus*) *gesta res est quam dixerat*, 'the affair took place three days after he had spoken'.

The addition of the conjunction *quam* to the adverbs *ante*, *prius*, and *post*, turns them into compound conjunctions of time which may be written as one word: *antequam*, *priusquam*, *postquam*.

(iv) The words most commonly used in the Ablative of Measure of Difference are the neuter singular pronouns or adjectives *multo*, *paulo*, *nihilo*, *eo*, *hoc*, *quo*, *tanto*, *quanto*, *aliquanto:* Cic. *Off.* 1, 90 *quanto superiores sumus*, *tanto nos geramus summissius*, 'by as much as we are superior, by so much the more humbly let us behave', or 'let our humility be in proportion to our superiority'. So *aliquanto maior*, 'somewhat larger', etc. Rarely are the adverbial accusatives of extent *multum*, *aliquantum*, etc., used with comparatives.

83. *The Ablative of Description* (*Quality*)

As indicated in Section 43 (6), an ablative noun with an epithet may be used adjectivally to describe a person or thing. This use arose from the ablative denoting accompaniment or attendant circumstances. In a sentence like *serpens immani corpore labitur*, 'The serpent glides along with its huge body', the *immane corpus* is treated as a distinct accompaniment, and the ablative words are grammatically adverbial with *labitur*. But it was easy for such words to be detached from the verb and loosely attached to the noun *serpens*, so that one could speak of *serpens immani corpore*, 'a serpent with a huge body'. This adjectival use having arisen, the ablative words could be used either attributively or predicatively, like any other adjective: Plaut. *Rud.* 316 *nullum ista facie venisse huc scimus*, 'we know that no one of that appearance has come here'; *Id. Most.* 1148 *sunt capite candido*, 'they are white-headed'.

It will be obvious from the origin of the construction that such ablatives can have been used in the first instance to indicate only external characteristics, as in the above examples. It was soon extended, however, to describe internal qualities also, or any sort of observable characteristics, whether transitory or permanent. The following examples show the range: (*a*) External characteristics: Caes. *B. G.* 5, 14, 3 *Britanni capillo sunt promisso atque omni parte corporis rasa praeter caput et labrum superius.* 'The Britons are long-haired and with all parts of the body shaved except the head and upper lip.' (*b*) Internal but not necessarily permanent qualities: Plaut. *Pseud.* 322 *animo bono es.* 'Be of good cheer'; *Id. Capt.* 105 *ille antiquis est adulescens moribus.* 'He is a young man with old-fashioned manners.' (*c*) Inherent and permanent qualities: Cic. *Fam.* 4, 8, 1 *vir praestanti prudentia et maximi animi*, 'a man of outstanding wisdom and the highest spirit'. In describing permanent and inherent qualities, as can be seen from the last example, the ablative is an alternative to the genitive.

84. *The Genitive of Description (Quality)*

The Genitive of Description or Quality is an outgrowth of the general idea of 'belonging' inherent in the genitive. The genitive of a noun with an epithet may indicate that class or type to which a person or thing belongs, as Caes. *B. G.* 5, 2, 2 *naves eius generis*, 'ships of that sort'; *Id. B. C.* 3, 74, 2 *superioris ordinis nonnulli*, 'some men of higher rank'. But the nouns in the genitive need not themselves designate a class or type. Persons or things may be distinguished by reference to many external things, or ideas, or circumstances which they partake of, or involve, or with which they are in some way connected, e.g. by words denoting size, measurement, worth, capacity, or what is required or involved: Caes. *B. G.* 2, 30, 4 *tanti oneris turrim*, 'a siege-tower of such great weight'; *murus centum pedum*, 'a wall of a hundred feet' or 'a hundred-foot wall'; *cibaria decem dierum*, 'ten days' food-supply'; *puer decem annorum*, 'a boy of ten years' or '. . . ten years old'; *res nullius pretii*, 'a thing of no value'; *magni sunt oneris*, 'they are (beasts) of great burden'; *vir magni laboris*, 'a man of mighty labour' (i.e. 'hard-worked' or 'hard-working'); *res magni laboris*, 'an affair involving great toil'; *servus minimi cibi*, 'a slave requiring little food.'

The descriptions expressed by the above genitive phrases are all quantitative rather than qualitative, and the epithets are all either demonstrative or adjectives of number or quantity. But most of them do, in fact, suggest the secondary idea of *internal* qualities possessed by the persons or things described: *magni laboris*, applied to a person, suggests industry, diligence, endurance; *minimi cibi* suggests abstinence, etc. When this secondary idea comes to the fore, nouns such as *industria*, *prudentia*, *virtus*, *animus*, *ingenium*, *consilium*, etc., begin to be used in the genitive construction, and the epithets need no longer be confined to quantitative ones. This stage had just been reached by the time of Plautus and Terence, but there are only two examples in them (Plaut. *Men.* 269 *homo iracundus, animi perditi*, 'a quick-tempered man of uncontrollable spirit'; Ter. *Andr.* 608 *tam nulli consili sum*, 'so devoid of (good) counsel am I').

The extending circles of genitive and ablative usage have now intersected and the segments enclose a certain amount of common ground. The Ablative of Description could already convey the idea of internal qualities, and we begin to find words in both cases qualifying the same noun (*vir magni ingenii summaque prudentia*), without any apparent distinction in meaning. It is to be noted, however, that the genitive cannot yet be used to express *external* characteristics or appearance. *mulier eximiae formae* is not classical. Furthermore, authors up to the time of Livy tend to avoid using in the Genitive of Description nouns of third, fourth, and fifth, and adjectives of third, declensions, and to prefer the ablative when the phrase is predicative.

Finally, in poetry and from the Augustan period onwards in prose, the genitive usurps the function of expressing external characteristics also, and begins to gain ground at the expense of the ablative.

This line is followed in the classification of the following examples.

85. *Examples of the Genitive of Description*

I. The genitive does not denote inherent qualities, but classifies by reference to some external category:

(*a*) Class, rank, type: *Res eius modi, huius modi*, etc. 'a thing of that sort, this sort, etc.'; Caes. *B. G.* 5, 2, 2 *sescentas eius generis naves invenit instructas*, 'He found that 600 ships of that type had been equipped'; Sall. *Jug.* 47, 1 *ubi incolere consueverant Italici generis multi mortales*, 'where many persons of Italian nationality had been wont to live'; (the ablative, as in *summo genere homines*, 'men of the highest birth', does not classify in the same way as the genitive); Caes. *B. C.* 1, 23, 2 *erant quinque senatorii ordinis*, 'there were five men belonging to the senatorial order' or 'of senatorial rank'.

(*b*) Quantity, numerical measurement, weight, value: Nep. 1, 7, 1 *classem septuaginta navium Athenienses Miltiadi dederunt*, 'The Athenians gave Miltiades a fleet of seventy ships'. *Id.* 2, 2, 5 *Xerxis classis mille et ducentarum navium longarum fuit*, 'Xerxes' fleet was one thousand two hundred warships strong'. (These genitives are not 'defining' or 'appositional' or of 'material', because their object is to indicate the *size* of the fleet, not of what it consisted.) Caes. *B. G.* 2, 29, 3 *magni ponderis saxa in muro collocabant*. 'They were placing boulders of great weight upon the wall'; *Ibid.* 30, 4 *quibus viribus tanti oneris turrim in muros posse se collocare confiderent?* 'with what strength did they think they could station against the walls a siege-tower of such burden?' (It is observable that, while the genitive is regularly used of weight, which is invisible and intrinsic, the ablative is used of height and breadth, which are outward appearances, e.g. Caes. *B. C.* 3, 112, 1 *Pharus est in insula turris magna altitudine*, 'The Pharos is a tower of great height upon an island') Caes. *B. G.* 2, 29, 3 *aditus in latitudinem non amplius ducentorum pedum relinquebatur* (= *non amplius quam latitudinem ducentorum* . . .) 'An approach was left to a breadth of not more than 200 feet.' The genitive of the measurement is an alternative to the Accusative of Extent with *latus* or *longus*, and, of age, with *natus*, e.g. *murus centum pedum*, 'a wall of a hundred feet' or 'a hundred-foot wall' (= *centum pedes longus*); *puer decem annorum*, 'a boy of ten years' (= *decem annos natus*). Sometimes the noun which the genitive qualifies is understood from the context: Nep. 17, 8, 2 *cum octoginta annorum in Aegyptum iisset*, 'having gone to Egypt (as a man) of eighty years'; Livy, 30, 37, 9 *novem annorum a vobis profectus post sextum et tricesimum annum redii.* 'Having set out from you (as a boy) of nine years, I have returned thirty-six years later.' Plaut. *Most.* 81 *paucorum mensum sunt relictae reliquiae.* 'Remnants for a few months are left' (i.e. 'a few months' supply'); Livy 44, 35, 13 *decem dierum cocta cibaria habere iussit.* 'He ordered them to have cooked food for ten days'; Plaut. *Aul.* 790 *nullust tam parvi preti*, 'No one is of so little worth'; *Id. Epid.* 502 *fateor me esse minimi preti*, 'I confess that I am of very little worth'; *Id. Bacch.* 630 *mortuus pluris preti est quam ego sum.* 'A dead man is of greater value than I am'; Ter. *H. T.* 64 *agrum meliorem neque preti maioris nemo habet.* 'No one has better land or of greater value'; Cic. *Verr.* 4, 88 *signum ab sociis pecuniae magnae sustulit.* 'He stole from the allies a statue of great monetary value'; *Id. T. D.* 3, 18 *nequitia (dicitur) ab eo quod nequicquam est in tali homine, ex quo idem 'nihili' dicitur.* 'Naughtiness is termed from the fact that there is naught in such a man, hence he is called "a man of naught".' (In *nihili* the negative component takes the place of the epithet.)

(*c*) What a person or thing is capable of, requires, or involves: Plaut. *Most.* 782 *habeo homines clitellarios; magni sunt oneris.* 'I have men as baggage-carriers; they are (beasts) of great burden.' Cic. *Cael.* 64 *fabella plurimarum fabularum poetriae*, 'the petty drama of a lady-poet with many romances to her credit'; *Id. Br.* 246 *M. Messala diligens, magni laboris, multae operae, multarumque causarum fuit.* 'M. Messala was painstaking, hard-working, of much service, and had many cases to his credit.' (When the natural qualities implied by these words are in mind, the ablative may be used, cf. Cic. *Br.* 113 *multaque opera multaque industria Rutilius fuit.* 'Rutilius was very energetic and industrious.') Cic. *Fam.* 9, 26, 3 *non multi cibi hospitem accipies sed multi ioci.* 'You will be receiving a guest requiring not much food, but of much joviality'; Caes. *B. G.* 5, 49, 6 *erat magni periculi res tantulis copiis iniquo loco dimicare.* 'It was a matter of great danger to fight with such small forces in a disadvantageous position'; Livy, 38, 4, 1 *consuli advenienti magni operis oppugnatio visa est.* 'To the consul on his arrival it seemed that an assault would cost a great effort'; Cic. *de Or.* 1, 257 *stilus ille tuus multi sudoris est.* 'That style of yours involves much effort'; *Ibid. disputatio non mediocris contentionis est.* 'The discussion involves no mean effort.'

In the last three examples, in spite of the fact that the descriptive phrases are predicative, and some of the nouns and adjectives of the third declension, the ablative would not do, because it would denote *accompanying circumstances* and imply that the actions were taking place, which they were not. The genitive expresses only the potentialities of the situation.

II. The genitive denotes inherent potentialities and qualities, and is often interchangeable with the ablative: Cic. *Sest.* 36 *nimium me timidum, nullius animi, nullius consilii fuisse confiteor.* 'I confess that I was too timid, of no spirit, of no wit' (*nullo consilio* here would mean 'with no plan or policy on this particular occasion'); Caes. *B. G.* 2, 15, 5 *Nervios esse homines feros magnaeque virtutis,* 'that the Nervii were fierce men and of great courage'; Cic. *Leg.* 3, 45 *vir magni ingenii summaque prudentia,* 'a man of great intellect and the highest wisdom'.

III. In poetry and post-Augustan prose the genitive is extended to express external characteristics also: Hor. *Ep.* I, 1, 76 *belua multorum es capitum.* 'You are a many-headed beast'; *Id. Sat.* II, 8, 84 *redis mutatae frontis.* 'You come back with changed countenance'; Juv. 11, 154 *ingenui vultus puer ingenuique pudoris,* 'a boy of noble face and noble modesty'; Phaedr. 1, 5, 5 *cervus vasti corporis,* 'a stag of huge body'; Suet. *Dom.* 10 *lanceas novae formae,* 'spears of new shape'; Nep. 14, 3, 1 *hominem maximi corporis terribilique specie,* 'a man of very large body and terrifying appearance'.

86. *The Ablative and Genitive in Expressions of Price and Value*

The ablative denoting the price at which something is bought, sold, exchanged, or valued, is instrumental in origin. The ablative first denoted the means by which something was acquired or purchased, and this use was then extended by analogy to expressions of selling, valuing, costing, etc.

The genitive expressions of price and value are most probably derived from the Genitive of Description in expressions such as those given in Section 85 under I (*b*). Expressions such as *haud magni pretii, pluris pretii, parvi pretii, nihili,* etc., are very common, and it would be very easy for the noun *pretii* to be understood, giving *magni esse, parvi esse,* etc., 'to be of great, small value, etc.'.

87. The regular classical usage in expressions of price and value is as follows:

(i) When the price or valuation is expressed as a precise numerical sum, or by means of a noun, the ablative is always used, whatever the verb: Cic.

Verr. 3, 220 *ternis denariis aestimare*, 'to value at three denarii apiece'; *Ibid.* 214 *cum esset tritici modius denariis quinque, aestimavit denariis tribus*, 'when a peck of corn was worth five denarii, he assessed it at three denarii'; Plaut. *Curc.* 344 *emi virginem triginta minis.* 'I bought the maiden for thirty minae'; Val. Max. 5, 4, 1 *magno ubique pretio virtus aestimatur.* 'Virtue is valued at a high price everywhere'; Caes. *B. G.* 7, 39, 3 *levi momento aestimare*, 'to consider of slight importance'; Cic. *Inv.* 1, 94 *Eriphyle auro viri vitam vendidit.* 'Eriphyle sold her husband's life for gold'; *Id. Mil.* 87 *pecunia se a iudicibus redemerat.* 'He had ransomed himself from the jury with money'; Livy 23, 30, 2 *multo sanguine ac volneribus ea Poenis victoria stetit.* 'That victory cost the Carthaginians much blood and many wounds.'

(ii) With *esse*, 'be worth' (or, sometimes, 'cost'), and verbs of valuing such as *aestimo*, 'value', 'assess', and *habeo, facio, duco*, 'consider', the following adverbial genitives are used: *magni, parvi, plurimi, maximi, permagni, minimi, nihili; tanti, quanti, pluris, minoris:* Cic. *Off.* 3, 82 *est ulla res tanti ut viri boni nomen amittas?* 'Is anything worth the price of losing the name of good man?'; *Id. Par.* 51 *si prata et areas magni aestimant, quanti est aestimanda virtus?* 'If they value meadows and plots of land at a high price, at what price is virtue to be valued?'; Caes. *B. G.* 4, 21, 7 *cuius auctoritas in iis regionibus magni habebatur*, 'whose influence in those districts was considered valuable'; Cic. *Fin.* 2, 24 *nec Laelius eo dictus est sapiens quod non intellegeret quid suavissimum esset, sed quia parvi id duceret*, 'nor was Laelius called wise because he did not understand what was most pleasant, but because he considered it of little value'.

(iii) With verbs of buying, selling, exchanging, hiring, costing, the following ablatives are used: *magno, plurimo, parvo, permagno, minimo, nihilo, tantulo:* Cic. *Verr.* 3, 40 *magno decumas vendidi.* 'I sold the tithes at a high price'; *Id. Cael.* 18 *Caelius conduxit in Palatio non magno domum.* 'Caelius rented a house on the Palatine for a reasonable price'; *Id. Fin.* 2, 92 *consequatur summas voluptates non modo parvo, sed per me nihilo, si potest.* 'Let him procure the greatest pleasures not only for a small sum, but as far as I am concerned, for nothing, if he can.'

(iv) The four words *tanti, quanti, pluris, minoris*, in expressions of price and value are always used in the genitive, whatever the verb: Cic. *Verr.* 3, 43 *multo minoris vendidit quam tu.* 'He sold at a much lower price than you'; Plaut. *Epid.* 295 *quanti potest minimo illa emi?* 'What is the lowest price you will take for her?' (lit. 'At how much can she be bought at the lowest price?'); Hor. *Sat.* 2, 3, 155–6 *sume hoc tisanarium oryzae. 'Quanti emptae?' 'Parvo' 'Quanti ergo?' 'Octussibus'*, 'Take this mess of rice pudding'. 'How much did it cost?' (lit. 'bought at how much') 'A small sum.' 'How much, then?' 'Eightpence.'

Notes. (1) The following phrases are colloquial (they occur mostly in Plautus, Cicero's Letters, and lighter poetry): *non flocci facere, non habere nauci*, 'to consider not worth a straw'; *non assis*, or *unius assis aestimare*, 'to think not worth a penny', 'to rate at one penny': *Cat.* 5, 2–3 *rumoresque senum severiorum/omnes unius aestimemus assis*. Here we have the genitive of nouns used instead of the strictly correct *nihili* or *parvi*.

(2) As the genitives *tanti, quanti, pluris, minoris,* usurped the function of the ablative in expressions of Price, so the ablative of adjectives occasionally usurped the function of the genitive in expressions of Value, e.g. Cic. *T. D.* 3, 8 *ista sapientia non magno aestimanda est*, 'that wisdom of yours is not to be greatly valued'.

(3) With verbs of buying and selling the adverbs *bene, male, melius, optime,* etc., are sometimes used instead of *magno, pluris,* etc. The adverbs *care*, 'dearly', *viliter*, 'cheaply', are occasionally found, though not often in the best authors: Cic. *Off.* 3, 51 *quam optime vendere*, 'to sell to the best advantage'; *Ibid. melius emere*, 'to buy more cheaply'; Varr. *R. R.* 1, 16, 3 *care emere*, 'to buy dearly'; Cic. *de Dom.* 115 *carius emere*, 'to buy more dearly'.

VII

The Use of Participles

88. Participles are verbal adjectives. As adjectives, they qualify nouns. At the same time they are non-finite forms of the verb and have some of the characteristics of a verb. They can be active or passive, transitive or intransitive; they can be modified by, or 'govern' the oblique cases; and they can express the tense-ideas of progressive, completed, or future action. But they are not verbs, because they do not agree in Person with a 'Subject', neither can they express the ideas of 'present', 'past', or 'future', except in relation to the time of the action expressed by the finite verb of their sentence or clause. The uses of the Participle can be divided broadly into two groups: I. Adverbial. II. Adjectival. Of these the former is by far the more important.

To say that a participle is *adverbial* in function is not to deny that it is still an adjective, for an adjective is performing the function of an adverb in the sentence when it is used predicatively as an *extension* to the predicate, i.e. when it is answering, not the question 'what?' or 'what sort of?', but 'how?', 'under what circumstances?', 'when?', 'why?', 'in spite of what?' E.g., in the sentence 'Hannibal retired *beaten*', *beaten* is an adjective, not qualifying the subject *Hannibal*, though it agrees with it, but qualifying a noun such as 'man', which is understood. The sentence stands for 'Hannibal retired (as) a beaten *man*'. But the words 'as a beaten man' describe the manner or the circumstances in which Hannibal retired, and do not qualify the subject *Hannibal*.

Therefore they are syntactically equivalent to an adverb, and so is the adjective *beaten*, when used predicatively in this way.

From this *predicative* use of an adjective or participle is to be distinguished the *predication* of an adjective or participle by a link verb or factitive verb, as *Hannibal victus est*, 'Hannibal *is beaten*'. Here *beaten* is a predicated adjective, and is not adverbial in function, for it is an *essential* complement, not a mere extension. It would be better to call a participle that is an essential complement 'predicated', and reserve the term 'predicative' for that which is a mere extension.

Participles are more often used predicatively than in any other way, and failure to realize this is apt to cause mistakes in the interpretation of Latin sentences containing participles, and, conversely, in the rendering of ideas into Latin by means of participles.

Note. Besides participles, a number of adjectives are often used predicatively, i.e. adverbially, rather than adjectivally. Such are those denoting position in place or time, e.g. *superior, summus, extremus, medius, proximus*, etc.; denoting quantity or numerical order, e.g. *prior, primus, postremus, solus, totus*; and denoting attitude of mind or manner, e.g. *laetus, maestus, libens, invitus, sciens, prudens, inscius, incautus*, etc.: Cic. *Br.* 173 *Crasso et Antonio L. Philippus proximus accedebat.* 'L Philippus came next to Crassus and Antonius.' Virg. *Geor.* 4, 134 *primus vere rosam atque autumno carpere poma.* 'He was the first to pluck the rose in spring and apples in the autumn.' Cic. *Fam.* 13, 63, 1 *eum ego a me invitissimus dimisi.* 'I sent him away most unwillingly.' (*Invitus* is regularly so used.)

It will be seen that adjectives so used must be translated in English by an adverb or adverbial phrase, or they must be made the predicate ('He was the first to . . .'). This usage is not a merely Latin peculiarity, but is a relic from the time before adverbs had evolved.

89. *The Tenses of the Participles.* The Latin participles are only three in number: (i) Present Active: *faciens*, 'doing'; (ii) Perfect Passive: *factus*, 'done'; (iii) Future Active: *facturus*, 'about to do', 'going to do'. Only deponent verbs have a perfect participle active, e.g. *hortatus* means 'having exhorted'.

Latin is therefore much poorer in participles than Greek, which has participles belonging to every tense-stem of the verb, both active and passive. Thus Greek has participles which mean: (1) 'doing', (2) 'being done', (3) 'having done', (4) 'done', (5) 'going to do', (6) 'going to be done'. All the same, Latin has one more participle than English, for only 'doing' and 'done' are real participles. The rest are participle-phrases built up with the aid of auxiliaries. Latin cannot in this way build up substitutes for the missing present participle passive, perfect participle active, and future participle passive, but there are other ways of expressing the ideas which they represent.

90. *Uses of the Participle. I. Adverbial*

Participles are most commonly used predicatively so that they form extensions to the predicate, as indicated in Section 88. In this use they are equivalent in sense to an *adverbial clause*. The type of adverbial clause to which they are equivalent varies according to the context. As participles contain a tense-idea which expresses time-relation to the finite verb, they are very often equivalent to a temporal clause, expressing circumstances attending (present participle), or leading up to (perfect participle), the action of the main verb: Cic. *de Sen.* 5 *Plato scribens est mortuus.* 'Plato died writing' ('while he was writing'); *Id. T. D.* 3, 27 *Dionysius tyrannus Syracusis expulsus Corinthi pueros docebat.* 'The tyrant Dionysius, expelled from Syracuse, taught boys at Corinth' ('after he had been expelled'); Tac. *Germ.* 3 *Germani Herculem ituri in proelia canunt.* 'The Germans, when about to enter battle, sing of Hercules.'

Note. The predicative use of the *future* participle is rare before Livy. (See Section 104.)

The participle so used may agree with a noun or pronoun in any case: Cic. *Manil.* 23 *hunc Tigranes excepit diffidentemque rebus suis confirmavit, et adflictum erexit perditumque recreavit.* 'Tigranes welcomed him and, while he was distrustful of his fortunes, encouraged him, and when he had been cast down, raised him up, and when he was lost, restored him';  Curt. 8, 1, 52 *haec dicentis latus hasta transfixit.* 'While he was saying this, he pierced his side with a spear'; Cic. *de Sen.* 11 *C. Flaminio restitit agrum Gallicum dividenti.* 'He resisted Gaius Flaminius, who was trying to apportion the Gallic territory.' (On the translation of a participial phrase by means of a parenthetic relative clause, see Section 91.) Often the perfect participle is best translated by a separate co-ordinate sentence in English: Nep. 23, 5, 3 *Hannibal Gracchum in insidias inductum sustulit.* 'Hannibal led Gracchus into an ambush and destroyed him' ('destroyed him *after he had been led* . . .').

91. This predicative use of the participle is usually gravely misrepresented. If *Urbem captam incendit* means 'He captured the city and burned it', it does *not* mean 'He burned the captured city', nor 'He burned the city which he had captured'. The latter two renderings take *captam* as adjectival to *urbem*, which it is not. In other contexts *captam* might be so taken, but, in the sort of context we have in view, it is adjectival not to *urbem*, but to another noun or pronoun, which is understood, and which belongs to the predicate. I.e. the meaning is 'He burned the city *as a captured one*'. The sense can certainly be rendered by a relative clause, but it must be of the co-ordinate or parenthetic type, which is in effect a parenthetic sentence, and is preceded by a comma: 'He burned the city, which he had

(previously) captured'. The participle or adjective, so used, does not define the subject or object, but *extends the statement* about the subject.

92. *Participial phrases expressing Cause, Concession, Condition, Purpose*

In the following examples the context is such that the participle or participial phrase expresses some other notion than that of mere time or circumstances under which the action of the main verb takes place: (*a*) Cause: Cic. *Off.* 2, 25 *Dionysius cultros metuens tonsorios candente carbone sibi adurebat capillum.* 'Dionysius, fearing the barber's shears, used to singe his hair with a glowing coal' (= '*because* he feared . . .' or '*through* fear of'). Nep. 7, 7, 2 *Athenienses Alcibiadem corruptum a rege capere Cymen noluisse arguebant.* 'The Athenians claimed that Alcibiades had been unwilling to capture Cyme *because he had been bribed* by the king.' (*b*) Concession: Cic. *T. D.* 1, 67 *ut oculus sic animus se non videns alia cernit.* 'As the eye, so the mind, though not seeing itself, perceives other things'; *Id. Cat.* 3, 12 *vehementissime perturbatus Lentulus tamen et signum et manum suam cognovit.* 'Though gravely shaken, Lentulus nevertheless recognized his own seal and hand.' (*c*) Condition: Cic. *de Or.* 3, 179 *haec tantam habent vim, paulum ut immutata cohaerere non possint.* 'These (arrangements) have such force that, (if) slightly changed, they could not hold together'; *Ibid.* 2, 180 *non mihi nisi admonito venisset in mentem.* 'It would not have occurred to me, unless reminded.'

Note. That the participial phrase is often used as a conscious abbreviation for the equivalent causal, concessive, or conditional clause, is shown by the fact that the participle itself is often introduced by a conjunction such as *ut, tamquam, etsi,* or *nisi.* The English equivalent would be the attachment of 'while' or 'when' to a participle. In Latin, however, purely temporal conjunctions such as *cum* or *dum* are never so used.

(*d*) Purpose: The future participle *from the time of Livy onwards* is often used predicatively to express intention or purpose: Livy 10, 26, 7 *Galli ad Clusium venerunt legionem Romanam oppugnaturi,* 'the Gauls came to Clusium intending to attack the Roman legion'. As a rule, the future participle so used is the last word of the sentence or clause.

93. *Participial phrases in the Ablative Absolute*

The predicative use of a participle (adjective, or appositional noun) with a noun or pronoun in the Ablative Absolute has been explained in Sections 49 and 50.

The 'absolute' construction is necessary only when the noun or pronoun with which the participle agrees is not playing an integral part in the syntax of the sentence, e.g. as subject or object, as Plaut. *Bacch.* 1070 *urbe capta, domum reduco exercitum.* 'With the city captured (or 'having captured the city . . .'), I am leading my army home.' Thus to express the idea 'Having captured the city, he burned it', a Latin author usually wrote *urbem captam incendit*, rather than *urbe capta, hanc incendit.*

Nevertheless, the apparently unnecessary use of the absolute construction is not so uncommon as is sometimes implied. The effect of it is to lay greater stress on the circumstance or action expressed in the participial phrase. The difference is as the difference in English between 'He captured and burned the city' and 'When he had captured the city, he burned it': Caes. *B. G.* 6, 4, 4 *Caesar obsidibus imperatis hos Haeduis custodiendos tradit.* 'Caesar, having ordered hostages, handed these over to the Haedui to guard.' Cf. also *B. G.* 3, 14, 4; 5, 4, 3; 5, 44, 6; *B. C.* 1, 36, 5; and fairly often in Caesar. Tac. *Ann.* 14, 10 *a Caesare perfecto demum scelere magnitudo eius intellecta est.* 'Only when the crime had been completed was its enormity understood by the emperor.' Here *perfecti demum sceleris magnitudo* . . . would not have the same force at all.

Notes. (1) The ablative noun or pronoun with which the participle agrees is sometimes omitted and left to be understood from the context. This happens especially when the noun or pronoun is antecedent to a relative, and denotes a person or persons indefinite: Livy 21, 23, 1 *Hiberum copias traiecit, praemissis qui specularentur.* 'He transported his forces across the Ebro, (men) having been sent ahead to reconnoitre.'

(2) The perfect participle of a few verbs was used impersonally in the Ablative Absolute from the earliest times, e.g. *consulto,* 'consultation having taken place' (i.e. 'deliberately', 'purposely'); Tac. *H.* 4, 16 *nec diu certato,* 'no long struggle having taken place'; etc. The ablative noun is here implied in the participle, and is 'cognate'. This construction is parallel to the impersonal passive *curritur,* 'running is taking place'. Most of such ablative singular participles have practically become adverbs, cf. *consulto* above, and *falso,* 'falsely' ('deception having taken place').

In the course of time this impersonal construction spreads to more verbs, and we find ablative singular participles followed by the Acc. and Infin., or with noun-clauses depending on them: Cic. *Fin.* 2, 85 *concluso neque virtutibus neque amicitiis usquam locum esse* . . . 'it having been conclusively proved that there is no place anywhere for virtues and friendships . . .'; *Id. Inv.* 2, 34 *cur locus praetereatur demonstrato,* 'it having been demonstrated why the point is being passed over . . .'. In these examples the indeclinable Acc. and Infin. noun-phrase, and the Indirect Question noun-clause are taking the place of the ablative nouns with which the participles *concluso* and *demonstrato* agree. This latter development begins in Cicero, but becomes frequent only from Livy on.

94. *The Participle after verbs of Perceiving*

Verbs of seeing and perceiving, chiefly *video* and *audio,* may be followed by a predicative participle instead of by an Accusative and Infinitive noun-phrase, e.g. *video puerum currentem,* 'I see the boy running', instead of *video puerum currere*. This must be counted as an adverbial use of the participle, for *currentem* is not here a predicated adjective; i.e. *video* is not acting as a factitive verb, for *video puerum* is a complete sentence and *currentem* is an extension, not an essential complement.

The inner difference between a participle so used and the Acc. and Infin. construction is that the participle expresses a more vivid and physical experience on the part of the subject. The Acc. and Infin. expresses a less vivid intellectual realization. The difference is as in English between 'I see the boy running' and 'I see that the boy is running'. Nevertheless the two constructions soon became interchangeable, without any intended distinction in sense, probably because the lack of a present participle passive made the Acc. and Infin. construction the only one possible, whenever the passive form was required. It follows, however, that *audivi eum loquentem*, 'I heard him speaking', always implies the presence of the subject, whereas *audivi eum loqui* may mean either 'I heard him speak' or 'I heard that he was speaking'. Examples: Plaut. *Rud.* 163 *mulierculas video sedentis in scapha*. 'I see some young women sitting in a boat'; *Id. Most.* 934 *tibicinam cantantem audio*. 'I hear the flute-girl singing.' (But the Acc. and Infin. is equally common in Plautus.) Livy 1, 25, 8 *respiciens videt magnis intervallis sequentes, unum haud procul ab sese abesse*. 'Looking back, he saw them following at long intervals, and that one was not far from him.' (It is impossible to know whether any distinction is intended here, because *abesse* has no present participle.) *Ibid.* 7, 6 *vestigia omnia foras versa videt nec in partem aliam ferre*. 'He saw all the footprints turned outwards, and that they were not leading in any other direction.'

Even when distinction in sense is not intended, the feeling of greater vividness imparted by the participle remains, and when the participle is the perfect passive without *esse*, it is by no means certain that *esse* should be understood.

95. *Participial phrases doing the work of Noun-clauses*

Out of the predicative use of the participle or its equivalent (predicative adjective or appositional noun), whereby the participle does the work of an adverbial clause, there developed an idiom whereby the participle in agreement with a noun or pronoun does the work of a noun-clause. On the analogy of *Hannibal victus sese recepit*, 'Hannibal retired beaten', where *Hannibal* is logically as well as grammatically the subject of *recepit*, it became possible to say, e.g., *Hannibal victus Romanos metu liberavit*, 'Hannibal *beaten* freed the Romans from fear', i.e. '*The fact that Hannibal* was beaten . . .' or '*The defeat of* Hannibal . . .'. Here, though grammatically *Hannibal* is still the subject, the logical subject is the abstract idea conveyed by *Hannibal* and *victus* together. In other words, the noun together with the predicative participle forms an abstract noun-phrase wherein the leading idea is conveyed by the participle (adjective, or appositional noun). Once this idiom had arisen, its apparent concreteness recommended it to the Latin mind, and it came to be preferred to an abstract noun with a dependent genitive. The idea of "the loss of the city" presented itself to the Roman not as *amissio urbis*, but as *urbs amissa*. Such an abstract noun-phrase also enjoyed an advantage over a noun-clause introduced by *quod* in that it could be declined, and its use in the oblique cases and with prepositions is very common. A typical example is *post urbem conditam*, 'since the foundation of the city'.

The beginning of this idiom can be seen in early Latin: Plaut. *Bacch.* 424 *ante solem orientem*, 'before the rising of the sun'; *Id. Cas.* 84 *post transactam fabulam*, 'after the performance of the play'; but it was not widely developed till classical times. Cicero provides a fair number of examples, but there are few in Caesar or Sallust. The authors who provide most examples are Livy and Tacitus.

Examples: Sall. *Cat.* 48, 4 (*dixit*) *se missum qui Catilinae nuntiaret ne eum Lentulus et Cethegus deprehensi terrerent.* 'He said he had been sent to tell Catiline that the exposure of Lentulus and Cethegus was not to frighten him'; Cic. *Phil.* 9, 7 *auctorem senatus exstinctum laete tulit.* 'He greeted with joy the death of the senate's adviser'; Livy 4, 34, 1 *capti oppidi signum ex muro tollunt*, 'They hoisted from the wall the signal that the town had been taken' (or 'the sign of the capture of the town'); *Id.* 26, 37, 6 *Capuae amissae Tarentum captum aequabant.* 'They set the capture of Tarentum against the loss of Capua.'

Cicero is the first to make a similar use of the present participle in the nominative: *Att.* 7, 11, 4 *fugiens Pompeius mirabiliter homines movet.* 'The flight of Pompeius is having a remarkable effect on people.'

This use of the future participle, like all other predicative uses of the future participle, begins with Livy: 1, 25, 3 *nec his nec illis obversatur animo futura ea patriae fortuna quam ipsi fecissent.* 'The fact that their country's fortune would be what they themselves had made it was not present to the mind of either the one side or the other' (*esse* is not to be understood here with *futura*); Tac. *Ann.* 1, 36 *augebat metum gnarus Romanae seditionis et, si omitteretur ripa, invasurus hostis.* 'The fact that the enemy were aware of the Roman mutiny, and the prospect of hostile invasion, if the river-bank were abandoned, increased their fear.'

For the similar predicative use of an adjective instead of a participle, cf. *gnarus* in the above example, and for an appositional noun, see Tac. *Ann.* 1, 19 *superbire miles quod filius legati orator satis ostenderet necessitate expressa quae per modestiam non obtinuissent.* 'The soldiery was arrogant because the fact that the legate's son was their ambassador showed clearly enough that they had extorted by compulsion what they had not obtained by good behaviour.'

A similar use of the gerundive begins with Livy: 2, 13, 2 *moverat eum subeunda dimicatio.* 'The necessity of submitting to the risk had unnerved him.'

The neatness and conciseness which this pregnant construction imported into Latin prose-style can be seen from the above examples.

96. *Further notes on the predicative participle in agreement*

(i) If an example like . . . *ne eum Lentulus et Cethegus deprehensi terrerent* were expressed passively, we should have: *ne Lentulo et Cethego deprehensis terreretur,* where the ablative may well be instrumental ('by the exposure of L. and C.'), though it is commonly regarded as Ablative Absolute. The insertion of *ab* before *Lentulo* would give quite another meaning ('by L. and C., who had been detected'). The idiom with which we have been dealing accounts for quite a number of examples of what appear at first sight to be Ablatives of the Agent without *ab*; e.g. Juv. 1, 13 *adsiduo ruptae lectore columnae,* 'columns shattered by the constant efforts of the declaimer' (= *adsiduitate lectoris*). Hor. *Od.* 1, 6, 1–2 *Scriberis Vario fortis et hostium/victor Maeonii carminis alite.* 'Your bravery and victories over the enemy shall be celebrated with Varius as your winged poet of Homeric song.' (There is no mss. justification for the editorial emendation *aliti.* Neither the dative nor the ablative of the agent would give Horace's meaning, which is: 'You are a fitter subject for Varian epic than for Horatian lyric'.)

(ii) The neuter singular of a perfect participle is occasionally used impersonally in the nominative or accusative in a manner corresponding to the impersonal Ablative Absolute noted in section 93, Note (2). The neuter participle by itself is then equivalent to an abstract verbal noun: Livy 7, 22, 1 *temptatum domi ut ambo patricii consules crearentur rem ad interregnum perduxit.* 'The attempt in home affairs to make both the elected consuls patricians brought matters to an interregnum'; *Ibid.* 8, 5 *diu non perlitatum tenuerat dictatorem.* 'The failure for a long time to obtain favourable omens had detained the dictator.'

Before Livy this usage is very rare.

(iii) The development of this noun and participle idiom accounts for the fact that from classical times onwards the Gerundive in agreement with a noun superseded the oblique cases of the Gerund governing an accusative object. *petendo pacem* was superseded by *pace petenda.* (See Section 206.)

97. *II. Adjectival Uses*

A participle may be used as an epithet-adjective: Cic. *Verr.* II, 1, 67 *aqua ferventi Philodamus perfunditur.* 'Philodamus was soused with boiling water'; *Id. Fam.* 5, 12, 7 *laudari se laetatur a laudato viro.* 'He rejoices that he is praised by a praised man' ('. . . by a man who has himself been praised').

The participle may also be used as a predicated adjective: Caes. *B. G.* 4, 3, 3 *fuit civitas florens.* 'The community was flourishing' (i.e. 'their community was a flourishing one', which is not the same as *florebat*).

Some present participles are so often used as epithets that they come to be regarded as ordinary adjectives, and lose their verbal characteristics when so used. For instance, if formed from a transitive verb, they cease to take an accusative object and require the objective genitive instead: *homo laborum patiens,* 'a man enduring of toil'; *semper appetentes gloriae fuistis,* 'you were always desirous of glory'. Also they become capable of degrees of comparison: *homo legum neglegentior,* 'a man more neglectful of the laws'; Cic. *Fam.* 16, 7 *ad nos amantissimos tui veni,* 'Come to us who are most fond of you'.

Up to the time of Cicero, the only future participle regularly used as an adjective is *futurus,* as Cic. *N. D.* 2, 12 *res futurae,* 'future things', 'things to come'. (See Section 104.)

98. Participles are occasionally used adjectivally without losing their verbal characteristics. They are then equivalent to a relative clause of either (*a*) the 'descriptive' type ('*A* man *who does this* is foolish') or (*b*) the determinative 'identifying' type ('*The* man *who lives here* is my uncle'):

(*a*) (Descriptive): Cic. *Off.* 3, 60 *omnes aliud agentes, aliud simulantes perfidi sunt.* 'All men aiming at one thing and pretending another are treacherous' (i.e. 'all *such as* aim at . . .'); *Id. T. D.* 3, 10 *immoderata laetitia est voluptas animi elata et gestiens.* 'Immoderate joy is mental pleasure that is transported and exulting'; *Id. Phil.* 11, 28 *est lex nihil aliud nisi recta ratio imperans honesta, prohibens contraria.* 'Law is nothing but a right principle that enjoins what is honourable and forbids the reverse.'

This use of the present participle is fairly common in Cicero, especially in the philosophical works, for the purpose of giving definitions. The perfect participle is rare, and the future participle is not so used (except for *futurus*) before Livy: Livy 2, 10, 11 *tranavit, rem ausus plus famae habituram apud posteros quam fidei.* 'He swam across, having dared a deed that was to have greater renown among posterity than credence.'

(*b*) (Determinative): Cat. 64, 8 *diva quibus retinens in summis urbibus arces/ ipsa levi fecit volitantem flamine currum,* 'for whom *the* goddess *who holds* the citadels on the heights of cities herself made *the* chariot *that flies* before the light breeze'.

This 'identifying' use of the participle is extremely rare in prose, but becomes fairly common in post-Augustan poetry. In the above passage from Catullus, which seems to be the earliest example, *diva retinens* = *ea diva quae retinet,* and the relative clause would be required in prose.

Note. A participle that is equivalent to a relative clause of the co-ordinating or parenthetic type is not to be counted as adjectival but as predicative, since it adds a new statement, e.g. Cic. *de Or.* 3, 137 *Pisistratus Homeri libros confusos antea sic disposuisse dicitur ut nunc habemus.* 'Pisistratus is said to have arranged the books of Homer, which were confused before, as we now have them.' The only difference between the use of *confusos* here and of *captam* in the sentence *urbem captam incendit* is that the agent who is understood with the passive *captam* is identical with the subject of the finite verb, whereas the agent with *confusos* is not identical with the subject of *dicitur*.

99. A participle can be predicated with part of *esse* without losing its verbal characteristics. It then forms with *esse* what is almost equivalent to a compound tense of the verb: Cic. *de Sen.* 26 *videtis ut senectus sit operosa et semper agens aliquid et moliens.* 'You see how old age is laborious and always doing and contriving something.' Here *agens* and *moliens*, although they are parallel to the adjective *operosa*, describe *senectus* with reference to an activity in which it is engaged as well as to a quality it possesses. Therefore there is enough of the verbal notion present to justify the accusative object *aliquid* instead of an objective genitive *alicuius rei.*

This use of the present participle is not very common, but the perfect participle is used with *esse* as an auxiliary for the perfect tenses of the passive, while the future participle with *esse* forms a periphrastic future tense.

100. *The Perfect Participle with* esse

The perfect participle in *-tus* originally denoted a *state*, so that *Hannibal victus est* meant firstly 'Hannibal is beaten' (of a present state). But this, for practical purposes, is equivalent to saying 'Hannibal has been beaten' (of an act completed). Thus *victus est* came to be used as the passive tense-equivalent of *vicit*, and in both senses of *vicit* (true perfect, and aorist). Nevertheless *victus* could still be used as a predicated adjective, so that Hannibal *victus est, erat, erit*, may mean either 'Hannibal is, was, will be, a beaten man', or 'Hannibal has been, had been, will have been, beaten', according to the context.

Notes. (i) The only forms of *esse* regularly used as auxiliaries with the perfect participle to form compound tenses of the passive are *esse, sum, eram, ero*. With the other tenses of *esse* (*fuisse, fui, fueram, fuero*) the participle is normally an adjective denoting a state. Thus *victus fui* means '(at a particular moment in the past) I was in a beaten state (but that state has since ended)'; *victus fueram*, '(up to a particular moment) I had been in a beaten state (but that state then ended)'; *victus fuero*, '(at a particular moment in the future) I shall have been (i.e. ceased to be) in a beaten state'.

In addition to this regular usage, the forms *fuisse, fueram*, and *fuero* are sometimes employed as follows:

(*a*) to express priority to the time of the action of another verb which is itself already in the perfect infinitive, pluperfect, or future perfect indicative: Livy 31, 19, 3 *tumultus qui exortus fuerat, brevi oppressus erat,* 'a revolt which had arisen had soon been put down'; Cic. *T. D.* 4, 35 (*impotentia*) *si quando adepta erit id quod ei fuerit concupitum* . . . 'if ever incontinence shall have acquired that for which it had conceived a desire . . .'. (*b*) Occasionally *victus fueram, fuero, fuerim, fuissem* are loosely used for *victus eram, ero, sim, essem,* particularly from Livy onwards. But *victus fui, fuisse* are never confused with *victus sum* and *victus esse.*

(ii) Under the heading of 'predicated participle' should be put the occasional use of the perfect participle after *habeo,* 'have', 'keep', and *facio, do, reddo* in the sense of 'consider', 'render', e.g. *hanc rem cognitam habeo,* 'this matter is known to me', 'I am aware of it' (lit. 'I have the matter known'); Cic. *de Or.* 1, 194 *domitas habere libidines,* 'to have (keep) the passions tamed'; Id. *Sest.* 138 *missos faciant honores,* 'let them consider office lost' ('give up all thought of it'). Here *habeo,* etc., are acting as factitive verbs, and the participle is an essential complement. The usage is mainly colloquial, but a few expressions are common and general, e.g. *cognitum habere, sollicitum habere aliquem,* 'to have someone worried', *missum facere,* 'give up', 'let go', etc. We can here see the beginning of the use of *habeo* as an auxiliary with the participle to form a compound perfect tense, but in literary Latin it did not degenerate so far.

101. *The Participle used as a Noun*

By an ellipse of the noun qualified, a participle may be used by itself as a noun-equivalent, just as the adjective *boni* may by itself mean 'good men', *bonae* 'good women', *bona* 'good things'. When a participle is so used, it retains its verbal characteristics: Caes. *B. G.* 7, 7, 4 *timentes confirmat.* 'He encourages *the fearful*'; Cic. *Div.* 1, 30 *iacet corpus dormientis ut mortui.* 'The body of a sleeping man (sleeper) lies like that of a dead man'; Livy 25, 11, 11 *propius inopiam erant obsidentes quam obsessi.* 'The besiegers were nearer to starvation than the besieged'; *Id.* 31, 36, 11 *plures ab obsidentibus vias quam ab emissis ad caedem interficiebantur.* 'More were being killed by *those besetting* the roads than by *those sent out* to kill.'

It is to be noted that this use of the participle is very rare in the nominative singular. The future participle is hardly ever so used, though there are isolated examples in the historians and in post-Augustan writers, e.g. Quint. 1, 4, 17 *admoneo docturos,* 'I advise those intending to teach'. In any case, the commoner method of expression is a relative clause. In the above examples *timentes* = *eos qui timebant, obsidentes* = *ei qui obsidebant,* etc.

It is to be observed that Latin does not add to a participle so used a demonstrative pronoun, as English does. A pronoun with the participle renders it predicative; e.g. *eos timentes confirmat* would mean '*when they were afraid*, he encouraged them'; *ei obsidentes* would mean 'they, *while conducting the siege . . .*', and so on.

The comparative rarity of the substantival use of the participle in Latin is due to the lack of a definite article. The article makes the usage easy in Greek, and even in the uninflected English, as 'the living', 'the vanquished', etc.

102. *Further notes on the participles*

The present participle in *-ans*, *-ens*, *-iens*, when used predicatively, regularly expresses incomplete action contemporaneous with that of the finite verb of its clause. Occasionally, it is used to express long-continued or conative action not completely contemporaneous, but prior to that of the main verb: Sall. *Jug.* 113, 1 *haec Maurus secum ipse diu volvens tandem promisit.* 'This the Moor, turning it over for a long time in his mind, at length promised'; Livy 27, 43, 3 *Numidae propraetorem primo incertis implicantes responsis, ut metus tormentorum fateri vera coegit, edocuerunt . . .* 'The Numidians, after trying at first to mislead the propraetor with evasive replies, when the fear of torture compelled them to confess the truth, revealed . . . etc.'. Cf. also the fairly common *roganti mihi respondit . . .* 'to my question he replied . . .'.

In these examples the present participle seems to be loosely used in the sense of a past participle active, much as in English. This is fairly common in the historians. It is not a complete violation of the Latin language, for, as already stated (88), the participles do not by themselves express time. Even if there were a perfect participle active, it would not convey the correct meaning in the last example from Livy. Only the present participle *implicantes* can convey the idea of long-continued or conative action which Livy requires. If he had written *cum implicuissent*, he would have indicated priority to *edocuerunt*, but not the conative action. Hence the priority is implied by the insertion of the adverb *primo*.

103. The perfect participle in *-tus*, *-sus*, was originally an adjectival formation denoting 'affected by' or 'full of', cf. *dentatus*, 'provided with teeth', 'toothed'; *scelestus*, 'criminal'. When the suffix was attached to verb-forms, it was not at first restricted to a passive sense, cf. *taci-tus*, 'silent', and the active sense of the perfect participles of deponents. A survival of this time-less adjectival use is to be seen in the common use of the perfect participles of many deponents to express an action, or state, contemporaneous with the time of the finite verb: Caes. *B. G.* 1, 20, 1 *Divitiacus, complexus Caesarem, obsecrare coepit.* 'Divitiacus, embracing Caesar, began to entreat him . . .' (= *complectens*). Often so used are *arbitratus*, *ratus* (*reor* actually has no present participle in use), *usus*, *secutus*, *veritus*, *confisus*, *diffisus*, *solatus*, *gavisus*, *admiratus*. As *ratus* originally meant 'thoughtful', *veritus* 'fearful', and so on, this need cause no surprise.

However, in extant Latin literature, this form, when connected with an active transitive verb, is always passive in sense, and normally denotes a completed state. Accordingly, when it is predicative, its tense is past in relation to that of the finite verb. Nevertheless, just as the lack of a perfect participle active sometimes caused the present participle to be used instead, so from the time of Livy onwards the perfect participle is sometimes used in the sense of a present participle passive: Livy 2, 36, 1 *servum sub furca caesum medio egerat foro.* 'He had driven a slave through the midst of the forum, scourged beneath a pillory.' Here the scourging accompanied the driving, and Cicero, in relating the same incident (*Div.* 1, 55), writes: *servus per circum, cum virgis caederetur, furcam ferens ductus est.* 'A slave, while he was being scourged with rods, and bearing a cross, was led through the circus.' See also Livy 23, 1, 6 *prae se actam praedam ostentantes* 'displaying the booty (being) driven before them'.

It was mainly Livy and Tacitus who, in search of terseness, sacrificed accuracy by disregarding the sense of 'prior completion' which is attached to the perfect participle passive in classical Latin. In Tacitus the perfect participle is frequently employed aoristically to express an event actually subsequent to the time of the main verb. This, too, was begun by Livy: 25, 25, 13 *post paucos dies rediit, multis donis donatus.* The context shows that this means 'He returned after a few days, being (subsequently) presented with many gifts'.

104. *The Future Participle*

The restrictions which have been noted in the use of the future participle would be explained, if its history were known with certainty. An examination of the usage of various authors shows that the form in *-urus* did not reach the full status of a participle till the time of Livy. Up to the time of Caesar and Cicero, its use was almost restricted to a combination with the verb *esse*, making a periphrastic future tense: *hoc facturus sum*, 'I am going to do this'; *dicit se hoc facturum esse*, 'he says that he is going to do this'.

The most likely explanation is that the form was originally an indeclinable neuter abstract verbal noun (i.e. a sort of infinitive), which came to end in *-urum.* Its form is comparable with the declinable feminine verbal nouns such as *pictura*, '(the art of) painting', *cultura*, 'cultivation'. If this is so, then *promittit daturum* should mean the same as *promittit dare* (see Section 30, Note iii), 'he promises a giving'. With the growth of the Acc. and Infin. construction, an accusative noun or pronoun would begin to be inserted. As this accusative noun or pronoun would very often be masculine singular, the feeling would arise that the form in *-urum* was in agreement with it. The form in *-urum* would then begin to be declined, as if it were a predicated adjective or participle, and *esse* would be added (or understood). We thus get this order of development: *promitto facturum—promitto me facturum—promitto me facturum esse.* The last implies *facturus* *sum*. This is as far as the development had gone by the time of Caesar and Cicero, but there was no logical reason why what was now a verbal adjective or participle should not be used as freely as the other participles.

This view is supported by the great number of examples in which not only *esse*, but the subject-accusative is omitted, as Cic. Verr. II, 1, 97 *descensuros pollicebantur*, 'they promised to descend'; Livy 21, 12, 4 *precibus aliquid moturum ratus*, 'thinking to achieve something by entreaties'. Such examples may be due to unconscious archaism. More concrete evidence is to be found in isolated examples that look like survivals of the original usage: Plaut. *Cas*. 670 *deieravit occisurum eum hac nocte*, (a woman speaks) 'she swore to slay him this night'; see also *Cas*. 693; *Merc*. 243; *Truc*. 400. Aulus Gellius, *Noctes Atticae* 1, 7, quotes a number of examples from pre-Ciceronian authors, and one from Cicero himself (*Verr*. 5, 167 *hanc sibi rem praesidio sperant futurum*). Gellius' explanation is that the form is an indeclinable infinitive. For once, the ancient grammarian's explanation is not to be scouted.

VIII

The Moods. The Subjunctive used independently

105. *The Moods of the Verb*

By 'mood' as a grammatical term is meant the form which a verb assumes in order to reflect the manner (*modus*) in which the speaker conceives the action. The Greek grammarians adopted ἔγκλισις, 'inclination', 'change of tone', as a term for this. Roman grammarians adopted *modus*, 'mode', 'manner', which has been Anglicized as 'Mood'.[1]

While the attitude of mind of a speaker or writer towards an action, event, or state about which he wishes to make a communication admits of almost infinite variety, there must obviously be a limit to the number of forms of the verb with which a language can be loaded. In Latin the mood-forms have been reduced to three: (1) *The Indicative*. This form of the verb is used when the speaker assumes the attitude of a detached observer who wishes to point out an observed fact to someone, without necessarily expressing his own feelings about it. The same form will naturally be used to ask a question about a matter of fact. (2) *The Imperative*. This form is used when the speaker assumes an authoritative attitude, and wishes to enforce on someone the action denoted by the verb. It expresses his *Will* about an action, event, or state. (3) *The Subjunctive*. This mood is used to express a variety of attitudes. Like

[1] The English word 'mood' meaning 'temper', 'frame of mind', is of Teutonic origin (cf. Germ 'Muth'), and has nothing to do with Latin *modus*.

the imperative, it can express the speaker's will, but it can also express an action, event, or state as something *wished for*, or as something that the speaker views as a *possibility*. In short, the use of the subjunctive mood in the main verb means that the speaker's or writer's attitude towards the action, event, or state, is not neutral or detached.

Note. The Infinitive is usually classed as a mood of the verb, but, with the exception of the idiomatic Historic Infinitive, the main verb of an independent sentence can never be in the infinitive. It is best to regard only the finite forms as expressing 'mood'.

106. *The Subjunctive Mood*

The name 'subjunctive' has been taken over from the Roman grammarians, who called the mood *modus subiunctivus* or *coniunctivus*. In adopting this term they were translating the Greek ἡ ὑποτακτικὴ ἔγκλισις. It means 'sub-joining', 'subordinating', or 'connective', and implies that the function of the mood is to mark subordination, and that it is used only in subordinate clauses.

There is no doubt that the subjunctive did come to be regarded as a distinguishing mark of subordination (cf. Section 179), but subordinate clauses are the result of a long process of development in syntax, and the use of the subjunctive in them must have developed out of its independent use in principal clauses. It follows that the use of the subjunctive in subordinate clauses will not be fully understood, unless the independent uses are studied first.

107. As indicated in Section 105, the use of the subjunctive mood makes an expression subjective. The speaker or writer is indicating that he himself has feelings or thoughts about the action, event, or state about which he is making a communication.

There are three main attitudes which may be expressed by the subjunctive, though there is no sharp dividing line between them:
I. *Will.* The speaker may express an action or event as something which he is concerned to bring about, as when he says : *hoc fiat*, 'let this be done'; *ne eat*, 'let him not go'. In such expressions the speaker implies that he has authority. The subjunctive is then called *Jussive* (sometimes *Volitive*). The negative is *ne*.
II. *Wish.* The speaker may express an action or event as something which he wishes to happen or which he prays for, implying that he has not the power or authority to enforce it, as when he says: *utinam (ne) hoc fiat!* 'O may this (not) be brought about!' In such expressions the subjunctive is called *Optative*. The negative is normally *ne*.
III. *Opinion as to possibility.* The speaker may express an action as something of which the possibility has occurred to him, as *aliquis hoc dicat*, 'someone *may* say this'; *hoc non fiat*, 'this would not happen'. The

subjunctive is then called *Potential.* It is used mostly to state what *would* happen, were such and such a condition fulfilled. The negative, as with indicative statements, is always *non.*

108. The three moods of Will, Wish, and Opinion as to possibility, seem never to have had a separate form of the verb for each. In early Sanskrit and in Greek there are two forms, one called subjunctive, the other optative, but each form has more than one duty. In early Sanskrit and in Homeric Greek, the subjunctive is used to make emphatic statements about the future, as well as to express will. The optative is used to make hesitant or conditional statements about the future, as well as to express wishes. In later Sanskrit the optative forms for the most part absorbed the functions of the subjunctive, which became obsolete. In Latin the subjunctive forms have absorbed the functions of the optative, and whatever originally optative forms survive are counted as subjunctive.

109. *The Jussive Subjunctive. Negative* ne

The *present tense* expresses what *is to be* done. The first person expresses self-exhortation or resolve, the second and third persons express commands or prohibitions (see further, Sections 126–30). Cic. *Sest.* 143 *amemus patriam, pareamus senatui, consulamus bonis, praesentis fructus neglegamus, posteritatis gloriae serviamus,* 'let us love our country, obey the senate, and consult the interests of good citizens; let us ignore present enjoyments, and serve the glory of posterity'; *Id. Verr.* 4, 15 *ne difficilia optemus,* 'let us not desire what is difficult'; *Id. Fam.* 16, 9, 4 *cautus sis, mi Tiro,* 'you must be careful, my dear Tiro'; Livy 3, 48, 4 *primum ignosce patrio dolori; deinde sinas (me) nutricem percontari,* 'firstly, forgive a father's grief; secondly, you must allow me to question the nurse'. (For the difference between the imperative and the jussive subjunctive in the second person, see Section 126, Note ii.) Cato *R. R.* 5, 1 *haec erunt vilici officia: alieno manum abstineat; sua servet diligenter; vilicus ne sit ambulator, sobrius sit semper,* 'these will be the duties of a farm-bailiff: he must keep his hands off others' goods; he must preserve his own carefully; a bailiff should not be a lounger, he should always be sober'.

Notes. (i) The first person singular is not common, since an individual normally expresses his resolve by the future indicative, but see Plaut. *Trin.* 1136 *sed maneam, opinor,* 'but I must wait, I think'; Ter. *H. T.* 273 *mane: hoc quod coepi primum enarrem,* 'stop: let me first finish the story I began'.

(ii) If a jussive subjunctive is made interrogative, it no longer expresses the will of the speaker, but enquires as to the will of someone else. The negative is then not *ne,* but *non . . .?* (rarely *nonne . . .?*). This type of question, with the verb in the subjunctive, is called Deliberative (see

Sections 172–5). Sometimes the reply is a statement of opinion as to duty or fitness, rather than an expression of will, and for this also the negative is sometimes *non* instead of *ne:* Ter. *Hec.* 342 *non visam uxorem Pamphili?—Non visas; ne mittas quidem visendi causa quemquam*, 'Must I not visit the wife of Pamphilus?' 'You should not visit her; you should not even send anyone to visit her.'

110. The *imperfect tense* of the jussive subjunctive expresses what *was to be* done, or what *ought to have been* done, in the past. Firstly it expresses what was the speaker's will in the past, and implies that his orders have not been obeyed. For instance, if I order someone to do something, and find out that he has not done it, I say to him later: *hoc faceres*, 'You were to do this (but you did not)'. But I might use the same words to him, if he had been ordered by someone else, and not by me. The imperfect subjunctive then expresses, not the speaker's will, but his opinion as to what was the past duty or obligation of the subject, and *hoc faceres* means the same as *hoc facere debebas.* This is the commonest meaning of the imperfect jussive subjunctive used independently. Though the negative is still sometimes *ne*, the feeling that a statement of opinion is being expressed sometimes causes *non* to be used instead, particularly in reply to a negative deliberative question, as in Plaut. *Trin.* 133 below.

Examples: Plaut. *Rud.* 841 *Pl. quin occidisti extemplo? Tr. gladius non erat. Pl. caperes aut fustem aut lapidem.* '*Pl.* Why didn't you slay him on the spot? *Tr.* I had no sword. *Pl.* You should have taken a club or a stone.' Ter. *H. T.* 332 *Quid faceret?—Rogas? aliquid reperiret, fingeret fallacias.* 'What was he to do?' 'Do you ask? He should have discovered something, he should have invented a falsehood'; Plaut. *Pseud.* 437 *tu ne faceres tale*, 'you should not have behaved so'; *Id. Trin.* 133 *non ego illi argentum red-derem?—non redderes*, 'should I not have paid him the money?'—'You should not have paid it'; Virg. *Aen.* 8, 643 *at tu dictis, Albane, maneres!* 'But thou, O man of Alba, should'st have abided by thy words'; Cic. *Verr.* 5, 59 *in tanta inopia navium, etiam si precario essent rogandi, tamen ab eis impetraretur*, 'amidst such a dearth of ships, even if you had to ask them on your knees, your requirements ought to have been obtained from them'. (Here *impetraretur* = *impetrandum erat*, or *impetrari debebat.*)

Note. It will be clear from the above examples that the imperfect subjunctive in this sense has the same force as a past tense of *debeo* or *oportet* with the infinitive, or as a gerundive with a past tense of *esse.* These alternative methods of expression tended to replace the imperfect subjunctive, which became rare after Cicero.

111. The *pluperfect subjunctive* is used in a jussive sense by Cicero and the poets, but by other authors rarely, in a manner indistinguishable from the imperfect. This was probably an attempt to make the reference

to the past unambiguous: Cic. *Verr.* 3, 195 *quid facere debuisti? pecuniam rettulisses, frumentum ne emisses*, 'what ought you to have done? You should have restored the money, you should not have bought the corn'; Luc. 7, 645 *post proelia natis/si dominum, Fortuna, dabas, et bella dedisses*, 'if thou had'st a tyrant in store, O Fortune, for those born after the fight, thou should'st have given them also a (chance to) fight'.

112. The *perfect subjunctive* in a jussive sense is used mainly (*a*) in the second person in prohibitions (for which see Sections 128–9), and (*b*) in all persons to grant concessions for the sake of argument: Livy 41, 24, 11 *fecerit aliquid Philippus cur adversus eum hoc decerneremus: quid Perseus, novus rex, meruit?* 'granted that Philip perpetrated some act to justify our making this decision against him, but what wrong has Perseus, the new king, committed?' (More lit. 'let Philip have perpetrated . . .'); *Id.* 31, 7, 8 *ne aequaveritis Hannibali Philippum; Pyrrho certe aequabitis*, 'granted that you have not put Philip on a level with Hannibal; you will certainly put him on a level with Pyrrhus' ('let it be that you have not . . .').

Notes. (i) The present tense also is commonly used in this concessive sense: Cic. *Verr.* 5, 4 *sit fur, sit sacrilegus; at est bonus imperator*, 'Let him be a thief, let him be a temple-robber; yet he is a good general'.
(ii) The perfect subjunctive in a concessive sense always refers to the past. The perfect subjunctive with *ne* in prohibitions is aoristic, i.e. it merely denotes that the action is viewed in its entirety, and has no reference to the past. It must, of necessity, refer to the future.
(iii) Verbs of perfect form with present meaning will naturally occur in the perfect subjunctive in a jussive sense: Accius 203 *oderint, dum metuant*, 'let them hate, provided that they fear'. The perfect passive also occurs in a jussive sense, when the participle is treated as an adjective: Cic. *Off.* 1, 121 *illud exceptum sit*, 'let that be excepted'.

113. *The Optative Subjunctive in Wishes*

The subjunctive used independently to express wishes came to be reinforced, particularly in tenses other than the present, by the particle *utinam*, 'O that . . .'. Occasionally, mostly in early Latin, an expression of wish is introduced by *ut* or *qui* ('how'), and in poetry *O si* . . . is found: Plaut. *Cas.* 279 *qui illum di perdant; Aul* 785 *ut illum di perduint!* 'how may the gods ruin him!'; Virg. *Aen.* 8, 560 *O mihi praeteritos referat si Iuppiter annos!* 'Oh if only Jupiter would bring back to me my past years!' Probably *qui* and *ut* (of which *utinam* is a reinforced form) were interrogative rather than indefinite adverbs in origin.

114. The tenses of the subjunctive in wishes are used as follows:

The *present* tense expresses a wish or a prayer that something may come to pass in the future: Cic. *Mil.* 93 *valeant cives mei! sint incolumes, sint florentes, sint beati! stet haec urbs praeclara!* 'May my fellow-citizens fare well! May they be safe, flourishing, and happy! May this city continue to stand in its glory!'; Gell. 10, 6, 2 *utinam reviviscat frater aliamque classem in Siciliam ducat!* 'Would that my brother might come back to life and lead another expedition against Sicily!'

Note. As the present subjunctive normally refers to the future, it does not necessarily imply impossibility of fulfilment. A wish that things were different from what they are in the present does imply unfulfilment. Early Latin does not yet clearly distinguish between wishes that are still capable of fulfilment and those which are not. Hence examples will be found in Plautus and Terence and in poetry of the present optative subjunctive referring to the present: Plaut. *Asin.* 418 *utinam nunc stimulus in manu mihi sit*! 'I wish I had a goad in my hand now!' But already in Plautus a tense-shift is taking place whereby the imperfect subjunctive is used to express unfulfilled wishes in the present, and the pluperfect to express past unfulfilled wishes. For examples, see below.

115. The *perfect* subjunctive expresses a wish that something may prove to have happened: Plaut. *Poen.* 799 '*quicum litigas abscessit*': '*utinam hinc abierit malam crucem!*' 'The man with whom you are at law has absconded' 'May he have gone to perdition!' (or 'I hope he has gone . . .!'); Cic. *Rep.* 4, 8 *utinam vere auguraverim*, 'May I have prophesied truly!' Pliny, *Ep.* 3, 18, 10 *utinam (dies) iam venerit*, 'I hope the day has already arrived!'

Notes. (i) The perfect subjunctive in wishes is not very common. In early Latin the commonest form is the sigmatic aorist (*faxim*, *servassim*, etc.), which refers to the future: Plaut. *Asin.* 654 *di te servassint semper*, 'May the gods preserve you always!'; Cic. *Fam.* 14, 3, 3 *dei faxint ut . . . liceat* . . . 'May the gods effect that it be allowed . . .'.
(ii) The English method of expressing a prayer that something may have happened, by means of 'I hope . . .!' is not paralleled in Latin. The Latin for 'I hope he has escaped!' would be *Utinam effugerit!* and not *Spero eum effugisse.* The latter would not be an emotional expression of wish, but would mean 'I have good hopes that he has escaped'.

116. The *imperfect* subjunctive in wishes is used in a sense parallel to that of the imperfect jussive. Firstly it expressed what was wished for in the past, implying that the wish has not been fulfilled. But the desire to distinguish between the possible and the impossible caused the tense-shift mentioned above, and the imperfect subjunctive usually refers to the present. Examples in which it refers to the past are found mostly in early Latin and in poetry, more rarely in classical prose: (*a*) (Referring to the past): Plaut. *Capt.* 537 *utinam te di prius perderent quam periisti e patria tua!* 'Would that the gods had made away with you, before you were lost to your country!'; Ovid *Met.* 8, 72 *di facerent sine patre forem!*

'Would that the gods had made me fatherless!' (Even here the sense is really 'would that I had no father now'); *Id. Her.* 10, 133 *di facerent ut me summa de puppe videres*, 'Would that the gods had allowed you to see me from your high stern'; Cic. *T. D.* 5, 63 *utinam ego tertius vobis amicus adscriberer!* 'Would that I had been enrolled as a third friend to you!' (But the sense is 'would that I were now one of your company'.) (*b*) (Referring to the present): Plaut. *Amph.* 575 '*homo hic ebrius est, ut opinor*' '*utinam ita essem*'*!* 'This man is drunk, I think!', 'I wish I were!'; Cic. *Fam.* 5, 17, 3 *illud utinam ne vere scriberem!* 'Would that what I am writing were not true!'

117. The *pluperfect* subjunctive in wishes, being a tense of completed action, expresses regret that something happened or did not happen in the past: Cic. *Off.* 2, 3 *utinam res publica stetisset nec in homines cupidos incidisset!* 'Would that the republic had stood, and had not fallen into the hands of greedy men!'; *Id. N. D.* 3, 75 *utinam istam calliditatem hominibus dei ne dedissent!* 'Would that the gods had not bestowed that cleverness on mankind!'; *Id. Att.* 11, 9, 3 *utinam susceptus non essem!* 'Would that I had not been reared!'

The Potential Subjunctive (*Negative* non)

118. The potential subjunctive represents the action denoted by the verb, not as an event which the speaker merely wishes to record, but as *something which he has thought of*, as being possible, likely, or even certain. The tone of the mood varies greatly, from diffidence to certainty, from expressions like *non facile dixerim*, 'I could not easily say . . .', to *ecquis id dixerit? certe nemo!* 'Would anyone say that? No one, for sure!' (Cic. *T. D.* 1, 87). Consequently any one of several different English auxiliaries may be required to represent it, according to the context: 'may', 'might', 'can', 'could', 'should', 'would'.

Most commonly, however, a speaker or writer, in stating his opinion as to future, present, or past possibility, has in view certain hypothetical conditions on the fulfilment of which such and such an event would, or would have, come to pass, as: 'He would go, if you were to ask him' (*eat, si roges*); 'He would be going, if it were not raining' (*iret, nisi plueret*); 'He would have gone, had you asked him' (*iisset, si rogasses*). English in such cases uses the auxiliaries 'should' or 'would', and these render the commonest meaning of the Latin potential subjunctive, since it is found most commonly in the main clauses of conditional sentences.

But as subordinate clauses are not original, neither is a use of the subjunctive which implies their existence. The 'should–would' potential which implies a condition must therefore be a development of the 'can–may' potential, which can stand alone.

The potential subjunctive in conditional sentences will be treated in Chapter XVI.

119. *The Tenses of the Potential Subjunctive*

In sentences in which no condition is expressed, there is usually no observable distinction in sense between the present and the perfect tenses. The latter is 'aoristic' and usually refers to the future. It is, however, occasionally used with reference to the past, to express what 'may have', 'could have', or 'would have' been the case.

Examples and notes: Plaut. *Most.* 266 *velim lapidem qui illi speculo dimminuam caput*, 'I should like a stone with which to smash that mirror's head'; *Id. Capt.* 942 *te nolim suscensere*, 'I should not like you to be angry'; Quint. 1, 3, 13 *caedi discipulos minime velim*, 'I should by no means like pupils to be caned'.

In the above examples the subjunctive differs from the indicative only in being milder and more deprecatory. This is commonest with *velim, nolim, malim, ausim, possim.*

Another very common use of the present and perfect is the 'generalizing' second person singular: Ter. *Andr.* 460 *fidelem haud ferme mulieri invenias virum*, 'you scarcely ever find a man faithful to a woman' (or 'one may scarcely find . . .'); Plaut. *Aul.* 520 *iam absolutos censeas, cum incedunt infectores*, 'you *may* think they are paid off, when in walk the dyers' (here *censeas* = *fortasse censes*); Other persons of the verb: Plaut. *Capt.* 237 *quod tibi suadeo, suadeam meo patri*, 'what I advise you, I would advise my own father'; Cic. *Off.* 1, 57 *pro patria quis bonus dubitet mortem oppetere?* 'what good man would hesitate to die for his country?' Livy 9, 4, 12 *quid habent quod morte sua servent? tecta urbis, dicat aliquis*, 'what have they to preserve by their deaths?—the roofs of the city, someone may say'. Here *dicat* = *fortasse dicet.* In this particular expression the perfect *dixerit* is commoner: Cic. *Off.* 3, 76 *'non igitur faciat' dixerit quis 'quod utile sit?'* 'Would he not be doing, someone may say, what is useful?' Other examples of the perfect: Cic. *T. D.* 1, 40 *ego ipse cum Platone non invitus erraverim*, 'I myself would not unwillingly go wrong in company with Plato'; Tac. *Ann.* 4, 11, 1 *haec prompte refutaveris*, 'this (account) one may readily refute'; Cic. *de Or.* 1, 36 *quis tibi hoc concesserit?* 'Who would grant you this?'

120. In the following examples the perfect subjunctive refers to the past and expresses the speaker's or writer's opinion as to what is likely to have been the case: Cic. *Off.* 1, 75 *Themistocles nihil dixerit in quo ipse Areopagum adiuverit at ille vere ab se adiutum Themistoclem*, 'Themistocles could not have cited any circumstance in which he himself had rendered assistance to the Areopagus, but that council might truly have said (*dixerit* again understood) that Themistocles had received assistance from itself'. Cicero is here citing historical examples, and *dixerit* appears to mean the same as *dicere potuit.* Had a condition been attached, e.g. 'had he

been asked', a pluperfect subjunctive would have been required, or else the modal equivalent *dicere potuit*. Livy, 21, 38, 7 *qui ambo saltus eum non in Taurinos sed . . . ad Libuos Gallos deduxerint*, 'both these passes would have brought him down, not amongst the Taurini, but to the Libuan Gauls'. Here again Livy is more concerned to assert his view of Hannibal's route against the accounts of other writers, rather than to state a conditional hypothesis. The passage is parallel to the previous example, but editors usually change *deduxerint* to *deduxissent*, without any manuscript authority. Lucan, 4, 298 *non se tam penitus . . . merserit Astyrici scrutator pallidus auri*, 'not so deep would the pale seeker of Asturian gold have buried himself' (sc. as the Pompeian soldiers did, digging for water). Here the metre prevents editors from changing to *mersisset*. A possible explanation is that what we have is *Repraesentatio*, i.e. the writer imagines himself contemporary with the events described, and uses the tenses appropriate to that point of view. Similarly in English, *dixerit, deduxerint, merserit*, could be translated 'could say', 'would bring him down', 'would bury'. That explanation, however, does not fit the following example: Pliny, *Ep*. 1, 23, 2 *ipse cum tribunus essem, erraverim fortasse, qui me aliquid putavi*, 'when I myself was tribune, I may perhaps have been wrong, but I thought I amounted to something'.

There are no examples cited from early Latin of the perfect potential subjunctive referring to the past in this way.

121. The *imperfect* potential subjunctive expresses the speaker's or writer's opinion as to what *was likely to happen* in the past, i.e. what *could have*, or *might have* happened. The imperfect tense implies that the opportunity for the event to take place has gone by, and that it can no longer be fulfilled, whereas the present and perfect tenses imply that the event may yet take place, or that something may yet prove to be the case. The range of expressions in which the imperfect potential is used without a condition being expressed or implied is very limited: Plaut. *Pseud.* 309 *ego te vivom salvomque vellem*, 'I could have wished you alive and safe'. Here *vellem* implies that the wish is unfulfilled, as is shown by the remark which follows: *eho! an iam mortuost?* 'Goodness! is he dead already?' This use of the imperfect subjunctive in the first person occurs mostly with verbs of wishing, e.g. *vellem, nollem, mallem, cuperem:* Cic. *Att.* 4, 16, 7 *cuperem vultum videre tuum, cum haec legeres*, 'I should have liked to see your face, when you read this'. Here too the impossibility of Cicero's being present is emphasized.

The second person singular is nearly always indefinite and generalizing, i.e. an imaginary 'you': Livy, 2, 43, 9 *crederes victos*, 'one would have thought them beaten'.

The third person is very common in questions, and is then sometimes difficult to distinguish from a deliberative: Cic. *Man.* 31 *quis unquam arbitraretur bellum ab uno confici posse?* 'who would ever have thought that the war could be brought to an end by one man?' (or 'who was to think . . .?'); Tac. *Ann.* 4, 11, 2 *quis filio exitium offerret? quin potius ministrum veneni excruciaret*, 'who would have offered a deadly poison to his son? Nay, he was more likely to put to the torture the agent who administered the poison'; Livy, 22, 24, 4 *ipse autem, quod minime quis crederet, tertiam partem militum frumentatum dimisit*, 'he himself, which one would hardly have believed, sent off a third of the soldiers to forage for corn'.

Notes. (i) In conditional sentences the imperfect potential came to refer mainly to the present, in the same way as did the imperfect optative (see above, 116). It then expresses what would be happening, were things other than they are (see Ch. XVI).
(ii) The pluperfect subjunctive in the potential sense occurs but rarely, except for its regular use in the apodosis of 'past unreal' conditions. There are a few examples in early Latin, e.g. Plaut. *Epid.* 628 *pedibus plumbeis qui perhibetur prius venisset quam tu*, 'the fellow who is supposed to have had feet of lead would have got here quicker than you'. There are no certain examples in classical Latin.

IX

Alternatives to the Subjunctive in Expressions of Duty, Necessity, Permission, Possibility: Direct Commands and Prohibitions

122. In English the ideas of duty, obligation, and necessity, are commonly expressed by the verbs 'ought', 'should', 'must'; the idea of permission by 'may', 'might'; and the idea of possibility by 'may', 'might', 'can', 'could'. These verbs are now necessary auxiliaries which in combination with the infinitive supply the meanings of the moods. They therefore have to be used to translate many examples of the subjunctive in Latin. Latin also has various 'modal' verbs which, with a prolative infinitive, can express similar ideas, though they were not necessary auxiliaries, so long as the subjunctive remained in use. Such verbs are *debeo*, 'I owe', 'I owe it as a duty', 'I ought', 'I should'; *oportet*, 'it is morally binding', 'it behoves'; *licet*, 'it is allowable'; *possum*, 'I am able', 'I can'. The indicative of these verbs, followed by an infinitive, tends to replace the subjunctive, whenever the speaker or writer was stating his opinion, rather than giving direct expression to his will or feelings (cf. the examples in 110 and note; 111). For instance, a man issuing orders as to

what he wants done would say *Hoc fiat*, rather than *Hoc fieri oportet*; in a burst of patriotism he would say *Amemus patriam* rather than *Patriam amare debemus*, etc. In short, the bare subjunctive is a much warmer method of expression than the indicative of a 'modal' verb with the infinitive.

123. *Duty, obligation, necessity*, are often expressed by:

(1) The gerundive with the indicative of *esse* (see Sections 203–4): *patria nobis amanda est; senatui a nobis parendum est*, 'We must love our country; we must obey the senate'. *argentum illi a te non reddendum erat* (or *fuit*), 'You ought not to have paid him the money'.
(2) The personal verb *debeo* with the infinitive: *debemus patriam amare, senatui parere*, 'We ought to love our country and obey the senate'. *argentum illi reddere non debebas* (or *debuisti*), 'You ought not to have paid him the money'.
(3) The impersonal verb *oportet*, with the accusative of the person, and the infinitive: *oportet nos patriam amare*, 'It behoves us (we ought) to love our country'. *non te oportebat* (*oportuit*) *illi argentum reddere*, 'You ought not to have paid him the money'. Livy, 5, 4, 9 *aut non suscipi bellum oportuit, aut geri pro dignitate populi Romani oportet*, 'Either the war should not have been undertaken, or else it ought to be waged in accordance with the dignity of the Roman people'.
(4) The impersonal phrase *necesse est*, 'it is necessary', with the dative of the person and the infinitive: *necesse est nobis senatui parere*, 'It is necessary for us to obey the senate'. *non tibi necesse erat* (*fuit*) *illi argentum reddere*, 'You need not have paid him the money'.

Notes. (i) It will be seen from the examples that *past* obligation or necessity is expressed by the tense of the finite verb only, and not by the tense of the infinitive. Thus *debebas, debuisti hoc facere* = 'it *was* your duty to do this', i.e. 'you ought *to have* done it'. So with *oportebat, oportuit*, and with *licebat, licuit; poteram, potui*, in Sections 124–5 below, though the imperfect tense did sometimes refer to the present, as explained in Section 125.
(ii) With *oportet* and *necesse est* (also with *licet*, see below) we get the construction *oportet hoc facias, necesse est hoc facias*, 'it behoves that you do this', 'it is necessary that you do this'. So with reference to the past, *oportebat* (*oportuit*) *hoc faceres*, etc. The subjunctives are semi-dependent jussives ('you *are to do* this: it behoves you'), and the subordinating conjunction *ut* is normally omitted.

124. *Permission*. Although the jussive subjunctive often has the force of 'you *may*, if you want', 'he *may*, so far as I am concerned', these ideas are more often expressed by the impersonal verb *licet*, followed by the infinitive. The person to whom the permission is given is expressed by the dative, and the person by whom it is given, if expressed, by *per* with the accusative: *tibi per me ire licet* (*licebat, licuit*), 'you may go (might

have gone), so far as I am (was) concerned'; Cic. *pro Flac.* 71 *cur his per te frui libertate sua, cur denique esse liberos non licet?* 'why do you not allow these men to enjoy their liberty? why, finally, do you not allow them liberty at all?'; *Id. Rep.* 1, 1, 1 *Catoni licuit Tusculi se in otio delectare*, 'Cato might have enjoyed himself in peace at Tusculum'.

Notes. (i) With *esse* after *licet*, a predicated noun or adjective is more often attracted into the dative of the person. By the time of Livy this usage has spread to other expressions, such as *necesse est*: Livy 21, 44, 6 *illis timidis et ignavis esse licet, qui respectum habent . . ., vobis necesse est fortibus viris esse*, 'those may be timid and cowardly, who can see a way of escape behind them . . ., but you must needs be brave men'.
(ii) Although the idea of 'permission' in *licet* is usually distinguished from the idea of 'possibility' in *possum*, we occasionally find *licet* used, where we should expect *possum*: Caes. *B. C.* 3, 27, 1 *hic subitam rerum commutationem videre licuit*, 'hereupon one might have seen a sudden change of fortune'.
(iii) As with *oportet* and *necesse est*, a subordinate subjunctive (normally without *ut*) is an alternative to the infinitive: Cic. *de Or.* 1, 195 *fremant omnes licet, dicam quod sentio*, 'let all cry out as they may, I will say what I think'. This construction of the subjunctive with *licet* is used mostly in a concessive or adversative sense, as above. See Sections 248–9.

125. *Possibility.* Except in the main clauses of conditional sentences (Sections 192, 197–9), the ideas of 'can', 'could', 'could have', 'may', 'might', 'might have', expressing possibility, are more often conveyed by the indicative of *possum* with the infinitive, than by the potential subjunctive. Even in the main clauses of 'ideal' and 'unreal' conditional sentences, *possum*, or an equivalent indicative expression, is often substituted (see Section 200).

To begin with, *possum hoc facere* means 'I am able to, I can do, this', but it came to mean 'I have it in my power to do this (but I will not)', or 'I *could*, I *might*, do this': Cic. *de Sen.* 55 *possum persequi permulta oblectamenta rerum rusticarum, sed ea ipsa quae dixi sentio fuisse longiora*, 'I might go on to speak of very many delights of rustic life, but I see that what I have actually said has been rather tedious'.

Similarly *poteram hoc facere*, 'I was able to do this (and did so)' came to mean 'It was in my power to do this (but I refrained)', i.e. 'I *might have* done this (but I did not)'. By classical times, however, just as the imperfect subjunctive expressing wish and possibility had come to indicate 'unreal' action in present time, so the imperfect indicative of 'modal' verbs commonly referred to the present. Accordingly, to make a clear reference to the past, it was now necessary to say *hoc facere potui*, *debui*, etc., and we even find *potueram*, *debueram*, etc., instead of the perfect.

Examples: Cic. *Att.* 13, 26, 2 *etsi poteram remanere, tamen proficiscar hinc*, 'although I might have stayed (= have been staying now) nevertheless I shall leave here'. It is difficult to see that *possum* instead of *poteram* here would have made any difference to the sense. *Id. Verr.* 4, 35–6 *ede mihi scriptum . . . quamquam non debebam abs te has litteras poscere; me enim tabulas tuas habere et proferre oportebat*, 'produce me the written evidence . . . although I ought not to have been demanding this document from you; for it behoved me to be in possession of your accounts and to be producing them (myself)'.

Referring to the past: Cic. *Fam.* 14, 16 *Volumnia debuit in te officiosior esse quam fuit, et id ipsum, quod fecit, potuit diligentius facere*, 'Volumnia should have been more attentive to you than she was, and what she actually did, she might have done with greater care'; *Id. Mur.* 51 *erupit e senatu triumphans gaudio, quem omnino vivum illinc exire non oportuerat*, 'he burst from the senate exulting joyfully—he who ought not to have left the place alive at all'.

Note. When the verbs *debeo, oportet, possum*, etc., with the infinitive, are doing duty for the jussive or potential subjunctive, they are very rarely themselves put into the subjunctive. When they are so, it is usually because they are being used as verbs with full sense, so that, to make the sense 'jussive' or 'potential', they must themselves be in the subjunctive, or else the subjunctive is required for some other reason. For instance, *potui hoc facere, si me rogasses*, would mean 'I might have done this, if you had asked me', but *potuissem hoc facere*, etc. would mean 'I should have been able to do this, etc.'. Similarly *quid facere debeat?* would mean 'What *would it be* his duty to do (under certain conditions)?'

Many examples of the subjunctive of these verbs which are quoted as being contrary to usage are in relative clauses, and the subjunctive is to be explained as generic or consecutive (cf. Sections 155–6): e.g. Cic. *Verr.* 5, 84 *est enim locus quem vel pauci possint defendere.* Here *possint* is not for the more usual *possunt*, for the sense is 'It is a place *such that* even a few could defend it'. Nevertheless there still remain a few examples where the subjunctive seems to be due to a sort of inner attraction of the form to the sense, e.g. we find in Cic. *Fin.* 2, 9 *quis istud possit negare?* 'Who could deny that?', and a little before, *dici nihil potest verius*, 'no truer statement could be made'. There seems to be no difference in sense here between *possit* and *potest*, and *possit negare* is probably due to conflation of *quis neget?* with *quis potest negare?* In most examples of inner attraction of this sort, the sentence is interrogative.

Direct Commands and Prohibitions

126. Although the use of the jussive subjunctive in issuing orders in the second and third persons has been already referred to in Sections 109 ff., it would be convenient here to give a summary of classical usage with regard to the use of the imperative and the subjunctive:

A direct positive command in the second person is expressed by the imperative: *Veni!* 'Come (thou)!'; *Venite!* 'Come (ye)!'.

Notes. (i) The above form of the imperative commands immediate obedience. The second or so-called 'future' imperative in *-to, -tote*, expresses an order that is not to be obeyed immediately, e.g. Cic. *Verr.* 5, 154 *cum testem produxero, refellito, si poteris*, 'when I have (shall have) produced my witness, refute him, if you can'. Accordingly this form is regularly found in the texts of laws, and in general precepts or proverbs. A few verbs are regularly used in this form in all circumstances, e.g. *scito, memento*, and often *habeto*.

(ii) The use of the second person of the present subjunctive instead of the imperative, e.g. *taceas* for *tace*, 'be silent', is common in early and colloquial Latin, but rare in classical prose. On the other hand it is regularly used, even in classical Latin, in addressing an *indefinite* second person, i.e. in giving general instructions or precepts. Similarly *ne* with the present subjunctive is used in general prohibitions: Cic. *de Sen.* 33 *isto bono utare, dum adsit; cum absit, ne requiras*, 'make use of that blessing, while you have it; when it is lacking, do not yearn for it'.

127. Positive instructions referring to a third person are expressed by the present subjunctive: *Veniat*, 'Let him come'; *Veniant*, 'Let them come'. (See Section 109.)

Note. The third person of the imperative in *-to, -nto*, is archaic and poetic. In prose, it is used chiefly in legal language: Cic. *Leg.* 3, 8 *regio imperio duo sunto; iique consules appellamino; nemini parento; ollis salus populi suprema lex esto*, 'let there be two officers with royal power, and let them be called consuls; they are to obey no one; to them the welfare of the people shall be the supreme law'. For poetry, cf. Virgil, *Aen.* 6, 153 *ea prima piacula sunto*, 'let those be the first offerings'.

128. A negative order or prohibition in the second person is regularly expressed by *ne* with the perfect subjunctive, or by the imperatives *noli, nolite*, with the infinitive: *Ne hoc feceris, feceritis*, or *noli, nolite, hoc facere*, 'Do not do this'. The latter form is less peremptory.

Notes. (i) With the negative *ne* must be included such negative words as are compounded with the negative *nĕ*, e.g. *nihil, nemo, nullus, nunquam, nusquam, nec.* These words are as common in prohibitions as *ne* with the corresponding positive indefinites, e.g. *nihil feceris* as *ne quid feceris*: Cic. *Mur.* 65 *nihil ignoveris . . . nihil gratiae concesseris . . . misericordia commotus ne sis . . . in sententia permaneto*, 'Forgive nothing . . . make no concession to favour . . . be not moved by pity . . . abide by thy decision'. (Cicero is quoting the precepts of the Stoics.) Livy, 2, 12, 11 *nullam aciem, nullum proelium timueris*, 'fear no battle-line, fear no battle'; *Id.* 21, 44, 6 *ne transieris Hiberum . . . nusquam te vestigio moveris*, 'Do not cross the Ebro . . . move nowhere from your position'; Id. 23, 3, 3 *clausos omnes in curiam accipite; nec quicquam temere egeritis,* 'Receive them all imprisoned in the senate-house, but do not make any rash move'.

(ii) The first form of the imperative is not used with *ne* in classical prose, but it is common enough in early and colloquial Latin, and in poetry: Ter. *Ph.* 664 *ne clama,* 'Do not shout'; Virg. *Aen.* 7, 202 *ne fugite hospitium neve ignorate Latinos/Saturni gentem* . . . 'shun not our hospitality, and be not ignorant that the Latins are the race of Saturn . . .'. There is an isolated example in Livy, 3, 2, 9 *erit copia pugnandi, ne timete,* 'There will be an opportunity of fighting, do not fear'.

The second, or future imperative is regularly used with *ne* in legal language and in general precepts, but that also is archaic: Cic. *Leg.* 2, 58 *hominem mortuum, inquit lex in XII tabulis, in urbe ne sepelito neve urito,* 'in the XII Tables the law says "Bury not nor burn a dead man within the city"'.

(iii) A negative command is regularly continued by *neve* (neu) and not by *nec,* but a negative command is regularly joined to a previous positive command by *nec* (cf. Livy 23, 3, 3 above).

129. A prohibition in the third person is regularly expressed by *ne* with the present subjunctive (109): *ne quis* (or *nemo*) *hoc faciat,* 'Let no one do this'; *ne veniant,* 'Let them not come'.

Note. The perfect (i.e. aorist) subjunctive also is sometimes used. Being a tense of complete or momentary action, it appears to be more peremptory than the present: Livy 9, 9, 9 *nec a me nunc quisquam quaesiverit* . . . 'and let no one ask me now . . .'; *Ibid.* 11, 13 *moratus sit nemo quo minus abeant,* 'let no one delay them from departing'.

130. Besides *noli, nolite,* with the infinitive, the following periphrases also are frequently employed for the sake of politeness: (i) For positive commands, *fac, facite,* with a quasi-subordinate subjunctive: *Fac mihi scribas; facite mihi scribatis,* 'See that you write to me'. The subordinating conjunction *ut* is usually omitted. Similarly *vide,* 'see that . . .', and *velim,* 'I should like . . .' are used with the subjunctive: Plaut. *Asin.* 755 *scribas vide plane et probe,* 'see that you write clearly and properly'; Cic. *Fam.* 9, 12, 2 *tu velim animo forti sis,* 'I should like you to be of brave heart'. (ii) For negative commands *fac ne* . . ., *facite ne* . . ., and *vide ne* . . ., are used. Rather more frequent are *cave* (sometimes *caveto*), and *cavete* with, or more often without, *ne*: Plaut. *Most.* 324 *cave ne cadas,* 'mind you don't fall'; Cic. *Att.* 3, 17, 3 *cave vereare,* 'mind you don't fear'.

X

The Subjunctive in Subordinate Clauses. Final Noun-clauses

131. Subordinate clauses originated in the placing side by side of two independent sentences, one of which came to be felt as dependent on the other, e.g. 'This is to be done: the master says (so)' became 'The master says (that) this is to be done'. The two sentences have become one, and the originally independent sentence 'This is to be done' is now a subordinate noun-clause standing as object to the verb 'says'. The placing of two independent sentences side by side is called *Parataxis* (co-ordination), and the subordinating of one to the other is called *Hypotaxis* (subordination).

A subordinate clause may be the equivalent of (*a*) a noun, (*b*) an adjective, (*c*) an adverb.

Note. To say that a clause is the equivalent of the sort of word that is usually classed as an adjective does not necessarily mean that it is performing the syntactical function of an adjective in the sentence. It may be used predicatively, and therefore perform an adverbial function (cf. Section 88).

132. When clauses became subordinate, it was felt that some connecting word was required to link them to the main clause. Such connecting words are the *Subordinating Conjunctions.* New words were not invented for the purpose, but old indefinite pronouns and adverbs were pressed into use. Their new function made them *relative.* Thus *qui,* instead of meaning 'someone' (cf. *quis, qui,* in *si quis, si qui*), now meant '(someone) who'; *uti* and *ut*, instead of meaning 'somehow', 'in some way', now meant 'in *which* way' or 'as'. Interrogative pronouns, adjectives, and adverbs could perform their new function without any change of meaning.

133. A clause which, as an independent sentence in parataxis, would have required one of the types of independent subjunctive indicated in Section 107, will also require the subjunctive, when it is subordinated. It is not possible to trace back every subordinate use of the subjunctive to a particular one of the three independent uses, for some subordinate subjunctives are composite in origin, while in some subordinate clauses (e.g. in indirect questions of fact) the subjunctive is not logically necessary, but is used because it had come to be regarded as the distinguishing mark of subordination.

134. *The Jussive Subjunctive subordinated*

A jussive subjunctive, when subordinated, expresses the will, purpose, intention, in the mind of the subject of the main or governing verb. In other words, it quotes or reports indirectly the will of someone other than the speaker or writer. It is then called a 'Final' subjunctive (from *finis*, 'end' or 'aim'). As with the independent jussive, the negative is *ne*.

Compare the following pairs of examples:

(*a*) Co-ordinate: *eat: pater imperat*, 'He is to go: his father orders it'. Subordinate: *pater imperat* (*ut*) *eat*, 'His father orders that he is to go' or 'orders him to go'. In the latter sentence the word *eat*, together with the conjunction *ut*, if expressed, forms a *noun-clause* standing as object to the governing verb *imperat*.

(*b*) Co-ordinate: *frater ei librum dedit: hunc* (*librum*) *legeret*, 'His brother gave him a book: he was to read it'. Subordinate: *frater ei librum dedit quem legeret*, 'His brother gave him a book which he was to read' or 'gave him a book to read'. Here the relative pronoun *quem* is the subordinating conjunction, and the words *quem legeret* form an adjective-clause describing the book as seen through the eyes of the brother. But the clause is predicative, and means 'his brother gave him the book *as a book to read*'. Therefore, though the equivalent of an adjective, the clause is performing the function of an adverb in the syntax of the sentence.

(*c*) Co-ordinate: *frater eum docet litteras: scribere discat*, 'His brother is teaching him letters: he must learn to write'. Subordinate: *frater eum docet litteras ut scribere discat*, 'His brother is teaching him letters *so that* he may learn to write'. Here the words *ut scribere discat* form an adverb-clause, modifying the verb *docet* by giving the brother's reason for the action.

135. *The Deliberative Subjunctive subordinated*

A deliberative question such as *Quid faciam?* 'What am I to do?' can be subordinated to a verb of asking, or its equivalent, without any change, since the interrogative word can act as the conjunction: *rogo te quid faciam*, 'I ask you what I am to do'. But the person and tense of the subordinated verb have to be adapted to the point of view of the narrator. In sentence-questions the particle *num* is used as the conjunction: *rogavit me num iret*, 'He asked me whether he was to go'. (*O. R. Eamne?*)

Such indirect questions are all noun-clauses, since they must be either the object or the subject of the governing verb.

136. *The Potential Subjunctive subordinated*

A statement of opinion as to possibility coming immediately next to a statement of fact implies that there is a connexion between the fact and the action or event which is expressed as a possibility. If I say 'He may escape: he is running so fast', I imply that the possibility of escape *results from* the fast running. All that is needed to make the sentence 'He may escape' subordinate in form, is a relative adverb of manner corresponding to 'so': 'He is running so fast *that* he may escape' (or 'so fast *as* to escape'): *tam celeriter currit ut effugiat.*

To begin with, the subordinate subjunctive can have indicated only a possible or hypothetical result. But the use of the subjunctive having become established *to mark a connexion of cause and effect,* the reality or unreality of the action denoted by the subjunctive verb came to be considered irrelevant. Thereafter the subjunctive was used in the subordinate clause merely to indicate the connexion between two events, even when the event expressed in the subjunctive was a real fact. Hence *tam celeriter currit ut effugiat* may mean either 'He runs fast enough to escape' or 'He runs so fast that he is (actually) escaping'.

Such subordinate clauses are called Consecutive, as showing what follows as a result. As with the independent potential subjunctive, the negative is *non.*

137. The consecutive clause used as an illustration in the previous section is adverbial, but the same sort of subjunctive may occur in a noun- or adjective-clause: Co-ordinate: *Qui homo id facere audeat? Nemo est,* 'What man would dare to do that? There is no one'. Subordinate: *Nemo est qui id facere audeat,* 'There is no one who would dare to do that'.

Note. As with adverbial consecutive clauses of fact, so also *nemo est qui audeat* may mean, according to the context, 'there is no one who dares'. For further discussion and examples, see Sections 155–7.

Consecutive noun-clauses may be supposed to have developed as follows: Co-ordinate: 'Someone may say this: it often happens', *aliquis hoc dicat: saepe fit.* Subordinate: 'It often happens that someone says this', *saepe fit ut aliquis hoc dicat.* (Consecutive noun-clause standing as subject to *fit.*)

138. *The Optative Subjunctive subordinated*

The type of subordinate subjunctive clause in which the subjunctive is most obviously optative in origin is the noun-clause which stands as object to a verb of fearing: Co-ordinate: 'May this not happen! I am afraid', (*utinam*) *ne hoc fiat: vereor.* In the Latin subordinate form the negative *ne* acts as a conjunction, and no change in the form of words is needed: *vereor ne hoc fiat,* 'I am afraid (lest) this may happen'. In conformity with this, *Ut* (*utinam*) *hoc fiat! Vereor,* 'Oh that this may happen! I am afraid (*sc.* that it will not)' produces in the subordinate form *Vereor ut hoc fiat,* 'I am afraid that this will *not* happen'. Presently *ne non* was substituted for *ut* to introduce a negative clause after a verb of fearing, but *ut* is still the commoner in early Latin.

The subjunctive which occurs in subordinate *si*-clauses is probably composite in origin. Sometimes the condition might be stated paratactically by means of a jussive subjunctive, sometimes by an optative: Co-ordinate: *modo hoc faciat: eum paeniteat*, 'Only let him do this! He would be sorry'. Subordinate: *si hoc faciat, eum paeniteat*, 'If he were to do this, he would be sorry'. Co-ordinate: *utinam hic adesset: laetarer*, 'O that he were present! I should be happy'. Subordinate: *si hic adesset, laetarer*, 'If he were present, I should be happy'.

139. *Final Noun-clauses* (*Indirect Commands*)

Final noun-clauses contain an indirect report of orders, requests, advice, resolutions, or of the end aimed at. They stand as objects or (when the governing verb is passive) as subjects, to verbs of commanding, requesting, advising, exhorting, resolving, contriving, or the like, e.g. *impero*, *rogo*, *peto*, *moneo*, *suadeo*, *persuadeo*, *hortor*, *statuo*, *constituo*, *decerno*, *efficio*, etc.

Positive indirect commands are normally introduced by the conjunction *ut* (*uti*), negative ones by *ut ne*, or, more usually, by *ne* alone, and additional negative ones by *neve* (*neu*).

If a negative indirect command follows a positive one, it may be introduced either by *neve* or by *nec* (*neque*). A positive following a negative is introduced by *et ut*, *atque ut*, or *-que ut*. (Cf. Section 128, note iii, on direct commands.)

Note. The use of the negative word *ne* by itself as a conjunction means that other negative words such as *nemo*, *nihil*, *nullus*, etc., are not normally used in indirect prohibitions. For them are substituted the corresponding positive indefinites preceded by *ne*. In final clauses, therefore, the normal Latin for:

'that no one' is *ne quis* (or *ne quisquam*),
'that no slave' is *ne ullus servus*,
'that never' is *ne unquam*, or *ne quando*,
'that nowhere' is *ne usquam*, or *necubi*,
'that from no place' is *necunde*; and so on.

When *ut non*, *ut nihil*, etc., occur in final clauses, *non* negatives a particular word, or the negative is very emphatic, e.g. *rogo te ut non hoc sed illud facias*, 'I ask you to do not this, but that'.

140. *Sequence of Tenses*. In final clauses the only tenses of the subjunctive normally required are the *present* and the *imperfect* (cf. Sections 109, 110), according to whether the tense of the governing verb is primary or

historic. Thus, if the tense of the governing verb is present, present-perfect, future, or future-perfect, the present subjunctive will be required in the subordinate clause. If the tense of the governing verb is imperfect, aorist-perfect, or pluperfect, the imperfect subjunctive will be required in the subordinate clause:

Dux imperat *imperavit* *imperabit* *imperaverit*	*ut milites procedant*	The general orders, has ordered, will order, will have ordered	that the soldiers *are* to advance.
Dux imperabat *imperavit* *imperaverat*	*ut milites procederent*	The general was ordering, ordered, had ordered,	that the soldiers *were* to advance.

Note. When the governing verb is in the present-perfect (English perfect with 'have'), historic sequence seems to be almost as common in final noun-clauses as primary sequence: Plaut. *Trin.* 591 *tandem impetravi abiret.* 'I have at last got him to go away'; Cic. *T. D.* 1, 14 *extorsisti ut faterer.* 'You have wrested a confession from me'; *Ibid.* 1, 15 *coegisti ut concederem.* 'You have compelled me to yield', and so fairly often. In final adverb-clauses historic sequence is far commoner. The reason is that to a Roman the present-perfect and the aorist-perfect were one and the same tense. This tense-form merely indicates that the action has been completed. Whether the completion is very recent or more remote, depends on the context. If it is thought of as very recent, then primary sequence is used, but often the completion of the action seemed to a Roman distant enough to justify historic sequence, even though English might still render the idea by the perfect with 'have'.

141. The verbs *iubeo, veto,* and *sino* are followed by the infinitive, rarely by a subjunctive clause: Caes. *B. G.* 1, 27, 2 *eos suum adventum exspectare iussit.* 'He ordered them to await his arrival'; *Ibid.* 2, 20, 3 *legatos Caesar discedere vetuerat.* 'Caesar had forbidden the envoys to depart'; Cic. *Rep.* 3, 16 *nos Transalpinas gentes oleam et vitem serere non sinimus.* 'We do not allow the Transalpine peoples to plant the olive and vine.'

In the passive, these verbs are always used personally: Livy, 3, 30, 3 *consules iubentur scribere exercitum.* 'The consuls are bidden to enrol an army'; *Id.* 23, 16, 9 *Nolani muros adire vetiti sunt.* 'The people of Nola were forbidden to approach the walls'; Cic. *Sest.* 95 *Sestius accusare Clodium non est situs.* 'Sestius was not allowed to prosecute Clodius.'

Notes. (i) In the above examples the infinitive is prolative, and the accusative of the person is alone the object of the active verb. When, however, a passive infinitive follows the active verb, as in Caes. *B. G.* 1, 7, 2 *Caesar pontem iubet rescindi*, 'Caesar orders the bridge to be broken down', we have an accusative and infinitive noun-phrase standing as object to the

verb. This accusative and passive infinitive is also fairly common after *impero*, instead of the more usual *ut*-clause: Cic. *Cat.* 1, 27 *nonne hunc in vincla duci imperabis?* 'Will you not order this man's imprisonment?'
(ii) In later Latin *iubeo* occasionally borrows the construction of *impero.* When *iubeo* is followed by an *ut*-clause in classical Latin, it means 'ordain', 'decree': Cic. *Verr.* 2, 161 *senatus decrevit populusque iussit ut statuas Verris quaestores demoliendas locarent.* 'The senate decreed and the people ordained that the quaestors should contract for the demolition of the statues of Verres.'

142. Examples of final noun-clauses: Caes. *B. G.* 4, 21, 8 *huic imperat quas possit adeat civitates.* 'He orders him to approach what states he can.' (The omission of the conjunction *ut* is not very common in literary Latin, except in indirect reports of speeches. It is commoner in the familiar or conversational style.) *Id. B. G.* 5, 22, 5 *imperat Cassivellauno ne Mandubracio neu Trinobantibus noceat.* 'He orders Cassivellaunus not to injure Mandubracius or the Trinobantes.' But historic sequence after a governing verb in the Historic Present is almost equally common: Cic. *Verr.* II, 1, 66 *servis suis Rubrius ut ianuam clauderent imperat.* 'Rubrius ordered his slaves to shut the door.' *Nep.* 4, 4 *Pausanias orare coepit ne enuntiaret neu se proderet.* 'Pausanias began to beg that he would not make the matter public nor betray him'; Cic. *in Caec.* 52 *suadebit tibi ut hinc discedas neque mihi respondeas.* 'He will urge you to depart hence and not to answer me.' (For *neque* following *ut*, see 139. *nec* or *neque* is the commoner, but *neve* is also found.) Livy, 35, 20, 4 *consuli permissum est ut duas legiones scriberet novas.* 'The consul was permitted to raise two new legions'; Caes. *B. G.* 5, 26, 4 *conclamaverunt uti aliquis ex nostris ad colloquium prodiret.* 'They shouted that someone of our men should come forward for a conference.' It is to be observed that many verbs of speaking, besides actual verbs of commanding, etc., may have a final noun-clause as object, e.g. Ter. *H. T.* 340 *dicam ut revortatur domum.* 'I will say that he is to return home' (or 'I will tell him to return . . .'); *Id. Hec.* 839 *me fecisse arbitror ne id merito mi eveniret.* 'I think I have managed that that should not deservedly happen to me.' The governing verb is here the perfect infin. *fecisse*, after which the imperfect subjunctive is required.

Verbs of contriving such as *facio*, *efficio*, *perficio*, etc., may also be followed by a consecutive clause, if the result rather than the intention is in mind. The negative would then be *ut non.* (See Section 168.)

143. The verbs of advising and persuading, *moneo*, *suadeo*, *persuadeo*, may be followed either by a subjunctive clause of indirect command, or, as being verbs of speaking, by an accusative and infinitive of indirect statement: (*a*) one may advise, warn, urge, persuade someone to do something, or that something should be done; (*b*) one may warn or convince someone about a matter of fact. The distinction in sense is to be observed in the following groups of examples:

(*a*) Caes. *B. G.* 1, 20, 6 *monet ut in reliquum tempus omnis suspiciones vitet.* 'He warns him to avoid all suspicion for the future'; Vell. 2, 63, 2 *suasit Lepido ne se cum Antonio iungeret.* 'He urged Lepidus not to join Antonius'; Nep. 2, 2, 2 *Themistocles persuasit populo ut classis aedificaretur.* 'Themistocles persuaded the people that a fleet should be built.'
(*b*) Caes. *B. C.* 3, 89, 4 *Caesar monuit victoriam in earum cohortium virtute constare.* 'Caesar warned them that victory depended on the valour of those cohorts'; Nep. 19, 2, 4 *Nicanorem insidiari Piraeo a Dercyllo monebatur.* 'He was being warned by Dercyllus that Nicanor had designs on the Piraeus'; Cic. *pro Caec.* 15 *suadebant amici Caesenniae nusquam posse pecuniam melius conlocari.* 'Caesennia's friends were advising her that the money could be nowhere better invested'; *Id. de Sen.* 80 *mihi nunquam persuaderi potuit animos emori.* 'I could never be persuaded that our spirits passed entirely away.'

Note. Instead of the subjunctive of indirect command, a prolative infinitive is occasionally used with these verbs (as after *iubeo*) even by authors of the classical period (though rarely, if ever, by Caesar). *Suadeo* meant originally 'to make pleasant' (cf. *suavis*), and *moneo* 'to put in mind', 'make to think'. The infinitive after them, as a verbal noun in either locative or accusative case, would not be an unnatural development. Thus *moneo te ire* would then mean originally 'I make you think in the matter of going', *suadeo tibi ire*, 'I make going pleasant to you' or 'I recommend going to you'. Rare in classical prose, this construction is common in poetry and in post-Augustan prose: Cic. *de Or.* 1, 251 *nemo suaserit adulescentibus in gestu discendo elaborare.* 'No one would urge young men to go to great pains in learning gestures'; *Id. Phil.* 13, 35 *an corrupti sunt quibus persuasum sit hostem persequi?* 'Were they corrupted who were persuaded to pursue the enemy?' *Id. Fin.* 1, 66 *monet ratio ipsa amicitias comparare.* 'Reason herself advises (us) to acquire friends'; Sall. *Cat.* 52, 3 *res monet cavere ab illis.* 'The facts warn (us) to be on our guard against them.'

With *suadeo* and *persuadeo* this construction cannot often cause ambiguity, because there is usually no accusative word which could be taken with the infinitive. After *moneo*, there would be ambiguity, if the object were expressed, for the accusative word might be taken as the 'subject' of the infinitive. In the above examples from Cicero and Sallust it will be noticed that the object of *moneo* is indefinite, and is left unexpressed. In the authors of the Silver Age ambiguity is not always avoided, and there are examples which depend for their correct interpretation on a careful reference to the context, as Tac. *Hist.* 5, 24 *Cerealis propinquos monebat fortunam belli opportuno erga populum Romanum merito mutare.* This does not mean 'Cerealis was giving warning that his kinsmen were changing the fortune of war . . .', but 'Cerealis was advising his kinsmen to change the fortune of war by a timely act of service towards the Roman people'.

144. The construction of the verbs of resolving, *statuo, constituo, decerno,* depends on the exact sense in which they are used and the idea they are to introduce. Briefly, the three commonest constructions are: (1) a final noun-clause: *constitui ut hoc fieret,* 'I resolved that this should be done'. (2) A prolative infinitive: *constitui hoc facere,* 'I decided to do this'. (3) An accusative and infinitive: *constitui haec vera esse,* 'I decided that these things were true'.

No hard-and-fast rules can be drawn up, but a classification of their senses and the ideas they can introduce should show what construction or constructions will be available in each case.

Statuo and its compound *constituo* mean firstly 'to set upright', 'fix in position', 'establish' (cf. *statua, status*). From this concrete physical sense developed the metaphorical sense of fixing on a course of action, deciding, arriving at a conclusion, whether about what should be done, or about a matter of fact. *Decerno,* or at least the uncompounded *cerno,* meant firstly to pass through a sieve and sort out, in the physical sense. Then it came to be used metaphorically of sorting out and deciding between various solutions of a problem, and so 'to decide', 'resolve', 'decree'. The first two verbs contain the idea of establishing, arranging, settling; *decerno* contains the idea of sorting out, or choosing between things. Therefore, although they have come to be synonymous in the sense of 'decide', 'resolve', their respective ranges of meaning will not be quite the same.

(1) The idea of arriving at a conclusion about *what should be done* can obviously be expressed by a final noun-clause introduced by *ut* or *ne,* or by a dependent deliberative question: *statui, constitui, decrevi, ut hoc fieret,* or *quid fieret,* 'I decided that this should be done', or 'what should be done'; *senatus decrevit uter consulum bellum gereret,* 'the senate decided which of the consuls should conduct the war'. Such clauses *must* be used if the subject of the verb of resolving is different from the subject of the subordinate clause. But they *may* also be used when the subject is the same: *constitui ut hoc facerem,* or *quid facerem,* 'I decided that I should (ought to) do this' or 'what I should do'. Generally Latin would use an *ut*-clause where English would use a *that*-clause.

(2) The idea of deciding on a course of action for oneself can be conveyed by the prolative infinitive, as in English: *statui, constitui, decrevi, hoc facere,* or *vir bonus esse,* 'I decided to do this' or 'to be a good man'. The infinitive here acts as if it were an accusative noun standing as object. This construction can be used only when the subject of the verb of resolving is to be the doer of the action denoted by the infinitive. It does not begin to be used with *statuo* till the time of Cicero. This may possibly be explained on the ground that the idea of 'making up one's mind' developed earlier in the compound *constituo* and in *decerno. Statuo* is more obviously a transitive verb calling for an accusative object. *Statuit procedere* ought to mean 'he established a proceeding'. But the feeling that the infinitive was not an

accusative noun may have lingered long after the accusative and infinitive *noun-phrase* had developed. The latter combination could stand as an accusative object, but not the bare infinitive, until all perception of its locative or dative sense had faded. The use of the infinitive standing as sole object of a verb that is etymologically transitive, though it occurs in Plautus, is a comparatively late development of syntax; e.g. *amo currere*, 'I love running', does not begin till the Augustan period.

(3) If used in the sense of arriving at a conclusion, or making up one's mind about *a matter of fact*, these verbs will come under the heading of verbs of thinking, and will need to be followed by an accusative and infinitive noun-phrase, or by a dependent indirect question of fact: *statui eum virum improbum esse.* 'I have come to the conclusion that he is a bad man'; *non possum constituere quae causa fuerit*, 'I cannot establish what the reason was'.

(4) If used in the sense of making an arrangement or compact with someone to do something, *constituo* may be followed by an accusative and future infinitive, such as follows verbs of promising and swearing. But if the person who is to fulfil the arrangement is different from the subject of the verb of arranging, an *ut*-clause or dependent deliberative question is called for, as under (1): *constitui tecum me non abiturum*, 'I arranged with you that I should not go away'; *constitui cum eis quo conveniremus*, 'I arranged with them where we should meet'. But it would also be possible to say: *constitui tecum ne abirem.* The omission of the person or persons with whom the arrangement is made may sometimes give the appearance of an exception and cause misinterpretation. E.g. in Livy 22, 22, 17 *cum se nocte iturum ut custodias hostium falleret constituisset* looks as if it means the same as *cum nocte ire constituisset*, but it means in fact 'having arranged (with Bostar) that he should go by night'.

145. Examples of verbs of resolving, classified as above:

(1) Caes. *B. G.* 7, 21, 2 *statuunt ut decem milia hominum in oppidum mittantur.* 'They decide that ten thousand men shall be sent into the town'; Cic. *Phil.* 2, 97 *nuper fixa tabula est qua statuitur ne sit Creta provincia.* 'A tablet has recently been posted by which it is determined that Crete shall not be a province.' Sall. *Cat.* 43, 1 *constituerant uti L. Bestia contione habita quereretur de actionibus Ciceronis.* 'They had arranged that L. Bestia should hold a public meeting and complain about Cicero's measures'; Cic. *Cat.* 1, 4 *decrevit senatus ut L. Opimius videret ne quid res publica detrimenti caperet.* 'The senate resolved that L. Opimius should see to it that the republic took no harm.'

In the following, the subjects of the governing verb and of the subordinate clause are the same: Cic. *Off.* 3, 48 *Athenienses statuerunt ut urbe relicta naves conscenderent.* 'The Athenians resolved that they should leave the city and go on board their ships'; *Id. Att.* 16, 10, 1 *constitueram ut Aquini manerem.* 'I had decided that I should stay at Aquinum'; *Id. T. D.*

3, 65 *hic decernit ut miser sit.* 'This man decides that he should be (i.e. ought to be) wretched.' (Here the idea of obligation is required by the context, otherwise *decernit miser esse* would be the more usual construction.) Indirect deliberative: Nep. 18, 11, 2 *nondum statuerat conservaret eum necne.* 'He had not yet decided whether to preserve him or not.'
(2) Cic. *Verr.* 1, 1 *statuerat ac deliberaverat non adesse.* 'He had resolved and determined not to be present.' (With *statuo* not before Cicero.) Ter. *Ph.* 676 *dotem constituerunt dare.* 'They have decided to give a dowry'; *Id. Andr.* 219 *quicquid peperisset decreverunt tollere.* 'They decided to raise whatever (child) she bore'; Caes. *B. G.* 4, 17, 1 *Caesar Rhenum transire decreverat.* 'Caesar had decided to cross the Rhine.'
(3) Cic. *Quinct.* 92 *nos nostram causam perfacile cuivis probaturos statuebamus.* 'We felt sure that we should make good our case in anyone's eyes'; *Id. Phil.* 12, 12 *leges statuimus per vim et contra auspicia latas iisque nec populum nec plebem teneri.* 'We have passed judgment that his laws were carried by violence and contrary to the auspices and that neither people nor plebs are bound by them'; *Id. Quinct.* 89 *bona possessa non esse constitui.* 'I have established that the goods were not held in possession'; *Id. Id. Off.* 2, 9 *consuetudo eo deducta est ut constitueret esse honestum aliquid quod non utile esset.* 'Usage has come to the point of establishing that honour is something which is not expedient'; Ter. *H. T.* 147 *decrevi me minus iniuriae meo gnato facere, dum fiam miser.* 'I have decided that I am doing my son less injury, so long as I am wretched'; Cic. *Fam.* 2, 6, 3 *in eo omnia mea posita esse decrevi.* 'I have decided that all my fortunes depend on him'; Id. *Cat.* 4, 5 *mea diligentia coniurationem patefactam esse decrevistis.* 'You passed a resolution that the conspiracy had been brought to light by my watchfulness.'

Indirect questions of fact: Cic. *Fam.* 12, 27, 1 *nondum satis constitui molestiaene plus an voluptatis attulerit mihi Trebatius noster.* 'I have not yet quite made up my mind whether our friend Trebatius has brought me more trouble or pleasure'; Plaut. *Amph. fr.* 18 *nequeo vostrorum uter sit Amphitruo decernere.* 'I cannot decide which of you is Amphitryo.'
(4) Ter. *Hec.* 195 *constitui cum quodam me esse illum conventuram.* 'I arranged with a certain person that I would meet him'; Cic. *Off.* 1, 32 *si constitueris cuipiam te advocatum esse venturum atque interim graviter aegrotare filius coeperit, non sit contra officium non facere quod dixeris.* 'If you have made an appointment with someone to be present to support him in court, and in the meantime your son falls seriously ill, it would not be a breach of duty to fail to do what you have said.' Obviously an indirect deliberative question-clause also will be a useful construction after *constituo* in this sense: Cic. Verr. 2, 65 *constitui cum hominibus quo die mihi Messanae praesto essent.* 'I arranged with the men on what day they should be present in Messana to meet me.'

The idea of making an appointment or arrangement with someone is inherent in *constituo*, but not necessarily in *statuo*, and still less in *decerno.*

There are no examples of the accusative and infinitive with *decerno* in this sense recorded from classical authors, but it is found in early and in post-Augustan Latin: Ter. *Andr.* 238 *uxorem decreverat dare sese mi hodie.* 'He had resolved on his giving me a wife today'; Val. Max. 6, 5, 4 *collegium tribunorum decrevit se creditoribus auxilio futurum.* 'The college of tribunes resolved that it would come to the aid of creditors.'

146. Final noun-clauses are to be regarded as internal or 'cognate' objects of the verb, i.e. *moneo te ut eas* is parallel to *illud te moneo.* When a transitive verb has both an external and an internal object, it is always the external object which becomes the subject of the passive verb, while the internal object is retained, as *moneris ut eas,* 'you are advised to go'.

When an intransitive governing verb such as *impero* or *suadeo* is turned passively, then the internal object, i.e. the final noun-clause, becomes the subject: *imperatur, suadetur, ut eas,* 'you are ordered, advised, to go' (lit. 'that you should go is ordered, advised', cf. Section 60).

XI

Final Relative and Adverb-clauses: Other Methods of expressing Purpose. The Supine

147. As already explained in Section 134, the jussive subjunctive, when subordinated, expresses the purpose or motive of the subject of the main verb. If the subordinate clause is introduced by the relative pronoun *qui* or its equivalent, the effect is to indicate the use to which someone or something, denoted by the antecedent, is being put by the subject of the main verb, e.g. *nuntios mittit qui haec nuntient,* 'he is sending messengers *who are to report* these things', or 'messengers to report . . .'.

If the subordinate clause is introduced by the relative adverb *ut* (negative *ne* or *ut ne*), the clause modifies the action as a whole, indicating the purpose with which the subject of the main verb performs it. *nuntios mittit ut haec nuntient* means in effect: 'he is sending the messengers so that (in order that) they may report these things'. The use of *ut* draws attention to the purpose in the mind of the subject of *mittit,* whereas *qui* draws attention to the means by which he achieves it. It will be clear, therefore, that *qui* as a conjunction is not completely interchangeable with *ut*.

The rule about the tenses of the subjunctive in final relative and adverb-clauses is the same as for final noun-clauses, except that a governing verb in the true perfect more often has historic sequence. The historic present may be followed either by the present or by the imperfect subjunctive.

148. The relative pronoun introducing a final clause may or may not be the subject of the subordinate clause; it may be in any case, or it may depend on a preposition: Livy 5, 35, 4 *Clusini legatos Romam, qui auxilium a senatu peterent, misere.* 'The people of Clusium sent envoys to Rome to seek help from the senate'; Caes. *B. G.* 7, 11, 2 *ea qui conficeret Trebonium legatum relinquit.* 'He leaves (i.e. 'left') his legate Trebonius to finish that business'; Cato *R. R.* 53 *faenum condito quod edint boves.* 'Store up hay for the oxen to eat'; Cic. *Brut.* 56 *scribebat Aelius orationes quas alii dicerent.* 'Aelius used to write speeches for others to deliver'; *Id. N. D.* 2, 34 *natura homini addidit rationem qua regerentur appetitus.* 'Nature has added Reason to man whereby the appetites might be governed'; *Id. de Or.* 3, 141 *Philippus Aristotelem Alexandro filio doctorem accivit, a quo eodem ille et agendi acciperet praecepta et eloquendi.* 'Philip summoned Aristotle as a teacher for his son Alexander, from whom the latter might receive instruction in management and eloquence alike.'

For *in quo*, *ex quo*, may be substituted the equivalent relative adverbs of place *ubi*, and *unde*: Plaut. *Epid.* 382 *homines aequom fuit sibi habere speculum ubi os contemplarent suom.* 'It would have been right for men to keep a mirror in which to look at their faces'; Livy 4, 2, 7 *locum petit unde hostem invadat.* 'He seeks a place from which to attack the enemy.'

Notes. (i) It will be clear that, if the main verb is active and transitive, the antecedent of *qui* cannot be the main subject. But in the passive, one may say: *legati missi sunt qui pacem peterent.* It would also be possible to substitute for *missi sunt* an intransitive verb such as *venerunt*, e.g. Caes. *B. G.* 5, 10, 2 *equites a Q. Atrio ad Caesarem venerunt qui nuntiarent . . .* 'Horsemen came from Q. Atrius to report . . .'.

The noun or pronoun to which the relative refers may be indefinite and unexpressed, as *misit qui nuntiarent*, 'he sent (men) to report'; *non habeo unde dem . . .* 'I have not (the resources) from which to give . . .'

(ii) Sometimes the idea of purpose expressed in the relative clause is vague and does not belong to the main subject, e.g. Tac. *Germ.* 29 . . . *Chattorum quondam populus in eas sedes transgressus in quibus pars Romani imperii fierent*, '. . . formerly a tribe of the Chatti, which had migrated into those territories in which they were (destined) to become part of the Roman empire'. Here the purpose, if any, which is expressed by *fierent* is that of Destiny. It is sometimes difficult to decide whether such clauses are final or consecutive.

149. Final adverb-clauses, like final noun-clauses, are introduced by *ut*, if the purpose is positive, by *ne* (sometimes *ut ne*), if it is negative. If several clauses are joined together, the same rules about the conjunctions

apply as for noun-clauses (section 139). Examples: Plaut. *Amph.* 195 *me praemisit ut haec nuntiem.* 'He has sent me in advance in order that I may announce these tidings.' With the sequence here, compare *Ibid.* 909 *revorti uti me purgarem.* 'I have returned in order to clear myself.' The latter sequence is the more common. Cic. *N. D.* 2, 129 *gallinae pullos pennis fovent, ne frigore laedantur.* 'Hens keep their chickens warm with their wings, that they may not be harmed by the cold'; *Id. T. D.* 5, 58 *Dionysius, ne collum tonsori committeret, tondere filias suas docuit.* 'Dionysius, in order not to entrust his neck to a barber, taught his daughters to shave him.'

Notes. (i) One occasionally finds apparent exceptions to the rules of sequence, but they can usually be justified on logical grounds. E.g. Cic. *pro Mil.* 11 *lex non modo hominem occidi, sed esse cum telo hominis occidendi causa vetat, ut, qui sui defendendi causa telo esset usus, non hominis occidendi causa habuisse telum iudicaretur.* 'The law not only *forbids* a man to be killed, but forbids the carrying of a weapon with intent to kill, in order that, when a man had used a weapon in self-defence, a verdict *might* be brought in that he had not been carrying the weapon with intent to kill.' Here the imperfect *iudicaretur* takes us back to the time when the law was enacted; the governing verb *vetat* is in the present tense because the law is still in force.
(ii) As the tenses of completed action, in subordinate clauses, indicate something that is completed before the time of the action of the main verb, it is obvious that neither the perfect nor the pluperfect subjunctive can normally be used in a final clause. A purpose is not achieved before it is formed. Nevertheless one may conceivably form the purpose of rendering permanent, of undoing, or of affecting in some way, an action or state already completed. In such rare circumstances Latin sometimes uses the perfect or pluperfect subjunctive in a final clause, e.g. Livy, 44, 22, 4 *illud adfirmare pro certo audeo, me omni ope adnisurum esse ne frustra vos hanc spem de me conceperitis.* 'I venture to state as certain that I will strive with all my might, in order that you may not *prove to have* conceived this hope of me in vain'; Ovid, *Met.* 4, 800 *neve hoc impune fuisset/Gorgoneum crinem turpes mutavit in hydros.* 'and that this might not prove to have gone unpunished, she changed the Gorgon's locks into loathsome snakes'.

150. With a comparative adjective or adverb, *quo* is used instead of *ut* in the sense of *ut eo*, 'that by so much (the more . . .)', or whereby', e.g. Ter. *Eun.* 150 *adiuta me, quo id fiat facilius.* 'Help me, in order that it may be done more easily'; Cic. *de Or.* 2, 131 *opus est agro non semel arato sed iterato, quo meliores fetus possit et grandiores edere.* 'There is need of land not ploughed once, but worked over again, that it may be able to produce better and larger crops'; Ter. *Andr.* 196 *si sensero quicquam in his te nuptiis fallaciae conari quo fiant minus, te in pistrinam, Dave, dedam.*

'If I find you attempting any deception in connection with this marriage, to prevent its taking place, I shall deliver you to the treadmill, Davus.'

Notes. (i) In the last example *quo . . . minus* is used in the sense of *ne* (cf. *minus* as a milder negative in *si minus*, 'if not'). After verbs of hindering and preventing and analogous expressions, which imply negative purpose, *quo* and *minus* are joined together to form what is virtually a new conjunction *quominus*, meaning 'that . . . not' ('by which the less'), and synonymous with and alternative to *ne*: Cic. *Sest.* 8 *impedior quominus exponam quam multa ad me detulerit.* 'I am hindered from making public how much he reported to me.' But when, as here, the main clause is not negatived, *ne* remains the commoner, as Cic. *Att.* 11, 13, 5 *plura ne scribam dolore impedior*, 'I am hindered by grief from writing more'. When the governing verb or expression is negatived, however, *quominus* is commoner than *ne*. (ii) When things, not persons, are the subjects of verbs of hindering, etc., or when the verb is passive, or when it is negatived, the idea of intention grows faint, and it is hard to determine whether *quominus* is introducing a final clause, or a consecutive clause of result. When the governing verb or expression is negatived, the conjunction *quin* may also be used. It seems best, therefore, to accord the conjunctions *quominus* and *quin* separate treatment. (See Sections 184 ff.)

151. *Alternative Methods of expressing Purpose*

Although the final clause, introduced by *ut*, *ne*, or the relative, is probably the commonest method of expressing purpose, the same idea can be conveyed in a number of other ways:
(1) By the Supine in the Accusative of the Goal, after verbs of motion. (See Sections 152–4 below.)
(2) By *ad* with the accusative of the Gerund or Gerundive: *legatos mittit ad pacem petendam*, 'he sends envoys to ask for peace'. This method is very common at all periods of Latin. See Section 207 (4).
(3) By the genitive of the Gerund or Gerundive with (very rarely without) *causa* or *gratia: legatos mittit pacis petendae causa.* This also is fairly common at all periods. See Section 207 (4).
(4) By the Gerund or Gerundive, or a verbal noun, in the Dative of Purpose: Livy 5, 54, 4 *urbi condendae locum elegerunt.* 'They chose out a site for founding a city.' Except in particular phrases e.g. *receptui canere*, this method is rare before Livy, but fairly common in Tacitus.
(5) By a Gerundive used predicatively in the accusative agreeing with the object of verbs of giving, receiving, sending, lending, hiring, undertaking, and the like: *pecuniam dedit mihi servandam.* 'He gave me the money to keep.' This is common at all periods. See Section 207 (3).
(6) The preposition *in* with the accusative may express either purpose or tendency. Expressing purpose, it means 'with a view to', or 'for',

e.g. *miles gladium strinxit in mortem eius*, 'the soldier drew a sword with a view to his death', i.e. 'to kill him'.

(7) In early and colloquial Latin and in poetry, the infinitive is often used to express purpose, but only after verbs implying motion. (See Section 28.)

152. *The Supine*

The supine, like the infinitive, is an abstract verbal noun. It is of the fourth declension, masculine, but only the accusative and dative-ablative forms were in use (e.g. *factum*, *factu*). The functions which its other cases might have performed are performed by the infinitive or by the gerund. The supine resembles the infinitive and the gerund in that the accusative supine of a transitive verb governs an accusative object, and is not qualified by an objective genitive.

The accusative form is used only as an Accusative of the Goal of Motion, without preposition (cf. *Romam ire*). It therefore expresses end, aim, or purpose, and is found only after verbs of motion or verbs implying motion: Caes. *B. G.* 1, 11, 2 *legatos ad Caesarem mittunt rogatum auxilium.* 'They send envoys to Caesar to ask for help'; Plaut. *Stich.* 139 *stultitia est, pater, venatum ducere invitas canes.* 'It is folly, father, to take hounds a-hunting against their will'; Cic. *de Or.* 3, 17 *admonitum venimus te, non flagitatum.* 'We have come to remind you, not to importune.'

Neither Caesar nor Cicero is very fond of the construction; more often they use a final clause, or one of the methods involving the use of the gerundive.

153. The supine in *-u*, although it was occasionally used by earlier writers as an Ablative of Source (e.g. Cato, *R. R.* 5, 5 *cubitu surgere*, 'to rise from bed'), was, in classical Latin, mostly used with a limited number of adjectives, e.g. *facile factu*, 'easy to do'; *mirabile dictu*, 'wonderful to relate'; etc. With these adjectives the form may be conceived either as a Dative of the End aimed at ('easy for doing'), or as a locatival ablative ('easy in the doing'). Livy seems generally to have felt it to be ablative, to judge from 40, 35, 13 *dictu quam re facilius est provinciam rebellatricem confecisse.* 'It is easier said than done to subjugate completely a rebel province.' With *dignus*, e.g. *dignus relatu*, 'worth telling', the form will obviously be an ablative of the type which normally goes with *dignus*.

Not all verbs form a supine in *-u*. The majority of those that do are verbs of saying and perceiving, e.g. *dictu*, *visu*.

154. The commonest use of the supine in *-um* is to supply, with the aid of the impersonal passive infinitive of *eo*, the sense of the missing future infinitive passive: e.g. *dixit urbem captum iri*, lit. 'he said that there was a movement towards capturing the city'. Here *urbem* is the object of the supine *captum*, and not the subject of an accusative and infinitive phrase.

Examples: Ter. *Hec.* 39 *rumor venit datum iri gladiatores.* 'A rumour has spread that gladiators are going to be shown'; Cic. *Att.* 7, 1, 1 *has litteras tibi redditum iri putabam.* 'I thought that this letter would be delivered to you.'

Notes. (i) This periphrasis was never, in fact, very popular. In Caesar's *Bellum Gallicum* there are only three examples, and in the *Bellum Civile* only two. In the whole of Livy there are less than a dozen examples, most of them in the first Decade. Generally the periphrasis *futurum (esse) ut*, or *fore ut*, with a consecutive subjunctive is preferred, but usage varies from author to author. Both methods sometimes appear in the same sentence: Sall. *Jug.* 112, 3 *nuntiat . . . fore uti foedus fieret, neque hominem nobilem in hostium potestate relictum iri.* 'He reported that a treaty would be concluded, and that a man of noble birth would not be left in the hands of the enemy.'

Another favourite periphrasis for the future infinitive passive was *posse* with a present infinitive passive: Sall. *Cat.* 40, 1 *existumans facile eos ad tale consilium adduci posse*, 'thinking that they might (*or* 'would') easily be won over to such a design'. Here *adduci posse* is almost equivalent to *adductum iri.* This method is very common even as early as Plautus, and the context does not always require that it should mean 'could be' or 'might be' as opposed to 'would be'.

(ii) That the Romans themselves came to regard *itur* with the supine as a compound form of verb is shown by the fact that in early and in Silver Latin it is occasionally found used personally in the passive. This would mean that the phrase *-um iri* came to be regarded as a future passive infinitive, and that it was no longer perceived that the accusative word was the object of the supine rather than the subject-accusative of an accusative and infinitive phrase. An example such as Ter. *H. T.* 315 *tu tibi laudem is quaesitum?* 'are you setting out to seek praise for yourself?' would normally be expressed in the passive by *itur a te laudem quaesitum?* Yet we find the equivalent of *laus itur quaesitum*, 'praise is-going-to-be-sought': Gell. 10, 14, 3 (quoting Cato) *in hac contumelia quae . . . mihi factum itur*, 'in this insult which is going to be put upon me'; Plaut. *Rud.* 1242 *mihi istaec videtur praeda praedatum irier.* 'That plunder of yours appears to me to be about to be plundered.' (Stolz-Schmalz, p. 601 claim an active sense for this, but in view of the existing parallels this is futile.) Quint. 9, 2, 88 *reus damnatum iri videbatur.* 'It looked as if the defendant was going to be condemned.' The last example is clear enough evidence that the original force of the construction was lost to sight. But this loss of perception did not cause the normal usage to be changed.

XII

Generic and Consecutive Clauses

155. We have seen in Sections 136–7 that the use of the potential subjunctive in a subordinate clause establishes a logical connexion between what is stated in the main clause and what is stated in the subordinate clause.

The effect of the potential subjunctive instead of the indicative in a relative clause is to make the clause descriptive instead of determinative, i.e. it no longer tells *what* person or thing is meant, but *what sort of*. For example, *odimus eos qui haec faciunt*, 'we hate the people who do these things', indicates which people we hate, and implies that they are real people who are behaving, or do behave, in a certain way. If the relative clause does contain the reason for our hatred, the hearer or reader has to make the connexion for himself. But *odimus eos qui haec faciant*, 'we hate people who *would do* these things', indicates what sort of people we hate. The subjunctive generalizes, and colours the sentence with the speaker's or writer's own views.

To begin with, the subjunctive can have been used in this way to describe a person or thing only with reference to his or its potentialities, not with reference to some real act committed or being committed: Cic. *Verr.* 3, 221 *absolvite eum qui fateatur.* 'Acquit a man who confesses' (i.e. 'such as may confess'); Ter. *Hec.* 756 *faciam quod alia haud faceret.* 'I will do what another woman would not have done'; Cic. *Mil.* 29 *fecerunt id servi Milonis quod suos quisque servos in tali re facere voluisset.* 'Milo's slaves did what everyone would have wished his slaves to do under such circumstances.'

But there was nothing to prevent the subjunctive from being used for its descriptive force alone, even when the antecedent of the relative was real and particular, and even when the action expressed by the subjunctive verb was a fact. This development had already taken place in early Latin: Ter. *Andr.* 973 *solus est quem di diligant.* 'He is the only one whom the gods love' (i.e. 'the only one *of such a character that* the gods love him'); Plaut. *Bacch.* 543 *nullus est cui non invideant.* 'There is no one whom they do not envy' ('none such that they do not envy him'); Id. *Curc.* 86 *quisnam istic fluvius quem non recipiat mare?* 'What river is that which the sea does not receive?' ('what sort of river is there which does not run into the sea?'). In these clauses the present subjunctive has clearly lost its potential force. This is still clearer when the tense is one of completed action: Ter. *Ph.* 917 *quo redibo ore ad eam quam contempserim?* 'With what countenance shall I return to her whom I have scorned?' (i.e. '. . . to her, *a woman whom* I have scorned'); Cic. *Verr.* 3, 221 *sunt alii complures qui idem fecerint.* 'There are several others who have done the same thing' ('. . . of the same *sort*'); *Id. Off.* 3, 114 *octo hominum milia tenebat Hannibal, non quos in acie cepisset, sed qui relicti in castris fuissent a consulibus.* 'Hannibal was holding prisoner 8,000 men, not *men whom* he had taken in battle, but *men who* had been left in the camp by the consuls.'

The subjunctive in these descriptive clauses is called *Generic*, because it indicates the sort or type (*genus*) of the person or thing qualified. It is not always easy to render the exact force of it in English, but as a rule the same effect can be obtained in the singular by using the indefinite instead of the definite article ('*a* man who . . .', instead of '*the* man who . . .').

Note. Although the potential origin of such clauses is fairly clear, there are some scholars who would trace them to a jussive or deliberative origin. There are indeed examples which could have been stated paratactically by other types of independent subjunctive, e.g. Plaut. *Rud.* 211 *aliquem velim qui mihi ex his locis viam monstret*, 'I should like someone who would show me the way out of this place', might well go back to either an optative (*utinam aliquis monstret!*) or a jussive origin (*monstret quis: velim*). It is necessary, therefore, to admit the possibility of a composite origin for generic and consecutive clauses, but to rule out the potential subjunctive as a source of subordinate developments is manifestly absurd.

156. In most contexts a 'generic' subjunctive in a relative clause is either explanatory, i.e. it suggests a reason for what is stated in the main clause; or else it is adversative, i.e. it expresses opposition – something *in spite of which* the statement in the main clause holds true; or else it expresses a *result* of something in the main clause. The subjunctive is then called Causal, Concessive, or Consecutive accordingly.

It will be found that, if the *qui*-clause is attributive, i.e. directly attached to an antecedent, expressed or understood, or if it is parenthetic, then the logical connexion expressed is usually causal, occasionally adversative: for example, *odimus eos qui haec faciant* suggests that we hate people *because* they do these things. When the antecedent is particular, the *qui*-clause is of the parenthetic type, but the subjunctive has the same effect: Plaut. *Aul* 769 *sanus tu non es, qui furem me voces.* 'You are not sane, who call me a thief', i.e. 'you are mad *because* you call me a thief'. The connexion is adversative, if the relative clause expresses something apparently inconsistent with the main clause: Plaut. *Poen.* 234 *miror te sic fabulari, quae tam callida sis.* 'I am surprised that you, (a woman) who are so clever, talk like this' (i.e. 'although you are so clever'). In a parenthetic *qui*-clause, the generic subjunctive also developed a limiting or restrictive sense: Cic. *Br.* 203 *fuit Sulpicius vel maxime omnium, quos quidem ego audiverim, grandis et tragicus orator.* 'Sulpicius was quite the most lofty and tragic pleader of all, at least *such as I have heard.*'

If, on the other hand, the descriptive *qui*-clause is predicated with the verb 'to be', or otherwise predicative, its relations with the main clause are reversed. Instead of suggesting cause, it suggests tendency or result: Cic. *T. D.* 3, 16 *est innocentia adfectio talis animi quae noceat nemini.* 'Innocence is that state of mind which harms no one' (i.e. 'such that it harms no one'); *Id. Fin.* 1, 3 *quis est tam invidus qui ab eo nos abducat?* 'Who is so envious that he would withhold us from it?' *Id. T. D.* 2, 43 *nec quisquam fuit qui eum non laudandum putaret.* 'Nor was there anyone who did not think him praiseworthy' (i.e. 'of such a kind that he did not . . .'). There is usually an intensifying word in the antecedent clause, or else the main clause is negative, or the antecedent is indefinite, as in the common *sunt qui putent,* 'there are people who think . . .' ('such as think').

Note. As already emphasized in Section 88, an adjective or its equivalent can be predicative without being predicated by the verb 'to be'. In an example like Cic. *Off.* 3, 40 *incidunt multae saepe causae quae conturbent animos,* 'There often befall many cases (of a nature) to perplex our minds', the clause *quae conturbent animos* does not qualify the main subject *causae* so as to tell us simply what sort of cases befall, but makes an added statement about them. They befall *with a perplexing effect,* and the relative clause is as much adverbial, i.e. predicative, in function as that adverbial phrase. Similarly, to take an example with a transitive verb, in the sentence *vitia habet quae eum odiosum reddant,* 'he has faults such as to render him hateful', the clause *quae eum odiosum reddant* is not performing the same syntactical function as in the sentence *vitia quae eum odiosum reddant corrigi debent,* 'faults such as render him hateful ought to be corrected'. In the former sentence the clause is predicative and adverbial in function, in the latter it is attributive and adjectival.

Of descriptive clauses introduced by the relative, only those which are predicative can express result. This holds true, whatever the antecedent.

157. Examples of generic and consecutive relative clauses:

(1) *Attributive or parenthetic:*

(*a*) Purely descriptive: Cic. *Q. fr.* 1, 1, 28 *est eius qui civibus praesit, eorum quibus praesit commodis servire.* 'It is the duty of a man who is in authority over citizens to serve the interests of such as he controls.' Cf. also *Off.* 3, 114 in 155 above.

(*b*) Causal: Plaut. *Mil.* 59 *te omnes amant mulieres, qui sis tam pulcher.* 'All the women love you, who are so handsome'; Cic. *Leg.* 3, 22 *vehementer Sullam probo, qui tribunis plebis potestatem ademerit.* 'I greatly approve of

Sulla for having deprived the tribunes of their power'; *Id. Off.* 3, 79 *Marius a fide discessit, qui optimum civem, cuius legatus esset, in invidiam falso crimine adduxerit.* 'Marius was guilty of bad faith, who (= in that he) brought a good citizen, whose lieutenant he was (= although he was his lieutenant), into odium by a false charge.' (Here we have both an adversative and a causal subjunctive in the same sentence. The imperfect *cuius . . . esset* is used of a state, the aorist-perfect *adduxerit* of the completed act.) Nep. 23, 12, 2 *patres conscripti, qui Hannibale vivo nunquam se sine insidiis futuros existimarent, legatos in Bithyniam miserunt.* 'The senators, who thought they would never be free from intrigues while Hannibal lived, sent envoys into Bithynia'; Cic. *Rep.* 6, 10 *me, qui ad multam noctem vigilassem, artior quam solebat somnus complexus est.* 'I, who (= as I . . .) had remained awake far into the night, was embraced by a deeper sleep than usual.'

Note. The relative introducing a causal clause is often reinforced by *quippe*, *ut*, or *utpote:* Cic. *Leg.* 3, 19 *tribunorum plebis potestas mihi quidem pestifera videtur, quippe quae in seditione et ad seditionem nata sit.* 'The power of the tribunes seems to me pernicious, inasmuch as it was born in and for sedition'; Livy 7, 14, 6 *dictator, ut qui magis animis quam viribus fretus ad certamen descenderet, omnia circumspicere coepit.* 'The dictator, as he was entering the contest relying more on courage than strength, began to make a comprehensive survey'; Curt. 1, 4, 13 *te etsi nihil a me impetrare oportebat, utpote qui ne belli quidem in me iura servaveris, tamen coniugem et liberos recepturum te promitto.* 'Although you have no right to obtain a request from me, inasmuch as you have not even observed the laws of war towards me, yet I promise that you shall recover your wife and children.' *Quippe* originated in an interjected question (= 'why? –'), *ut qui* = 'as (being one) who . . .', *utpote qui* = 'as is possible (in one) who . . .' *ut qui* is not found in early Latin, but is fairly common in Livy. *utpote* is the least common of the three.

(*c*) Adversative: Ter. *Ph.* 60 *cuius tu fidem in pecunia perspexeris, verere verba ei credere?* 'Do you fear to entrust words to a man whose good faith you have proved in money-matters?' Cic. *Verr.* 5, 136 *tu Mamertinis ex foedere quam deberent navem per triennium remisisti.* 'You excused the Mamertines for three years from providing a ship which they owed by treaty' (i.e. '*although* they were bound by treaty to provide it'); Caes. *B. C.* 3, 96, 2 *hi miserrimo ac patientissimo exercitui Caesaris luxuriem obiciebant, cui semper omnia ad necessarium usum defuissent.* 'These men reproached Caesar's wretched and long-suffering army with high living, an army which had always lacked every bare necessity.'

(2) *Predicated or predicative:*

Plaut. *Rud.* 645 *quis homo est tanta confidentia qui sacerdotem audeat violare?* 'Who is the man of such boldness that he dares to lay violent hands on a priestess?'; Caes. *B. G.* 5, 30, 2 *neque is sum qui mortis periculo terrear.*

'Nor am I the man to be frightened by the danger of death'; Cic. *Fam.* 5, 21, 2 *ego is sum qui nihil unquam mea potius quam meorum civium causa fecerim.* 'I am a man who has never done anything for my own sake rather than for that of my fellow-citizens'; *Id. T. D.* 1, 30 *nemo omnium tam est immanis cuius mentem non imbuerit deorum opinio.* 'There is no one in the world so monstrous that a belief about the gods has not penetrated his mind'; *Id. Verr.* 4, 95 *nemo Agrigenti fuit qui non illa nocte surrexerit.* 'There was no one at Agrigentum who did not rise that night'; *Id. Deiot.* 34 *solus es, C. Caesar, cuius in victoria ceciderit nemo.* 'You are the only one, C. Caesar, in whose victory no one fell'; *Id. Inv.* 2, 144 *sunt qui occidi puerum dicant oportere.* 'There are some who say that the boy ought to be put to death'; Caes. *B. G.* 4, 34, 4 *secutae sunt tempestates quae et nostros in castris continerent et hostem a pugna prohiberent.* 'There followed storms such as both kept our men within their camp and prevented the enemy from fighting'; Cic. *T. D.* 2, 28 *philosophi inventi sunt qui summum malum dolorem dicerent.* 'There have been found philosophers who maintained that pain was the greatest evil.'

158. When a relative clause with the subjunctive is predicative, it is sometimes difficult to decide whether the subjunctive is final or consecutive. For example, in Cic. *Fin.* 2, 45 *homines rationem habent a natura datam . . . quae et causas rerum et consecutiones videat,* there seems to be an underlying idea of *intention* on the part of nature to equip man with a reasoning power which shall perceive the causes of things. The subjunctive is then final. But in *Ac.* 2, 15 *tum exortus est Ti. Gracchus qui otium perturbaret.* 'Then arose Ti. Gracchus to disturb the peace', Cicero is not attributing purpose to Gracchus, but indicating his own view of the natural effect of Gracchus' policy. The subjunctive is therefore consecutive. (For *perturbaret* to be final, *ut* instead of *qui* would be required. Cf. 147 and 148, Note (i).)

After demonstrative antecedents such as *is, talis, eiusmodi, tam* with an adjective, or a comparative with *quam* (see Section 166), a subjunctive relative clause is clearly consecutive. After such antecedents as *est qui, sunt qui, solus est qui, multi* or *pauci sunt qui,* and after negatives such as *nemo est qui, non habeo quod,* etc., the subjunctive may be of either type, according to the context. Of indeterminate character and probably of composite origin are the clauses which follow *dignus, aptus, idoneus*: Cic. *Br.* 71 *Livianae fabulae non satis dignae quae iterum legantur.* 'The plays of Livius are not sufficiently worthy to be read a second time'; Caes. *B. C.* 3, 10, 2 *Caesar Rufum idoneum iudicaverat quem cum mandatis ad Pompeium mitteret.* 'Caesar had judged Rufus a suitable person to send with a message to Pompey.'

It will be seen that, as with the independent jussive and potential subjunctive, so with their subordinate developments, methods of expressing ideas that were originally distinct have extended until they touch. Such indeterminate constructions are not evidence for any original unity in the force of the subjunctive, but they do show how the optative-potential and the subjunctive may have come to be regarded as a single mood in Latin.

159. In an attributive or parenthetic relative clause the subjunctive is not absolutely necessary in order to imply cause or opposition. The difference between the subjunctive and the indicative is that the latter states the facts objectively, and leaves the reader to draw his own conclusions, while the subjunctive expresses the connexion subjectively, as an opinion of the writer. But in a predicative *qui*-clause the difference is more important.

Although there are plenty of examples of the subjunctive in a causal sense in early Latin, and a few in an adversative sense, the indicative is still the commoner mood. As time goes on, the subjunctive becomes more and more frequent, until, by Cicero's time, it is the rule. Nevertheless the indicative remained possible, whenever it was desired to emphasize the fact rather than the causal connexion: Plaut. *Men.* 309 *insanit hic quidem, qui ipse male dicit sibi.* 'This fellow is mad, who calls down curses on him-self'; Cic. *de Sen.* 46 *habeo senectuti gratiam, quae mihi sermonis aviditatem auxit, potionis et cibi sustulit.* 'I am grateful to old age, which has increased my appetite for conversation and removed my appetite for drink and food.' For both indicative and subjunctive in the same sentence, see Ter. *Eun.* 302 *ut illum . . . di perdant, qui hodie me remoratus est; meque adeo, qui restiterim.* 'May heaven confound him, who has delayed me today; and me, too, for stopping!'

For the mood in an adversative clause, with Cic. *Leg.* 3, 22 (in sect. 157 (*b*) above) compare: Cic. *Phil.* 1, 23 *ego, qui illa nunquam probavi, tamen conservanda arbitratus sum.* 'I, who never approved of those things, nevertheless thought that they should be preserved.'

In a predicated or predicative *qui*-clause, only the subjunctive can express the effect or result of something in the main clause. The following example is therefore instructive: Livy, 9, 3, 12 *ista sententia ea est quae neque amicos parat nec inimicos tollit: . . . ea est Romana gens quae victa quiescere nesciat*, 'that policy is *the* (*very*) *one* which neither gains friends nor removes enemies: . . . the Roman race is *such that* it does not know how to rest when beaten'. The indicative clause here can be only identifying or determinative; it cannot have the descriptive effect of the subjunctive.

XIII

Consecutive Adverb-clauses and Noun-clauses

160. As adverb-clauses are extensions of the predicate, i.e. predicative, the effect of a potential subjunctive in an adverbial clause of manner is the same as in a predicative *qui*-clause. A parataxis like *deam putes: ita pulchra est*, 'one would think her a goddess – she is so beautiful', would produce *ita pulchra est ut deam putes*, 'she is so beautiful that one would think her a goddess' ('she is beautiful *in a way in which* one would think . . .') and finally *ita pulchra est ut omnes deam putent*, 'she is so beautiful that all think her a goddess', where *putent* expresses not a tendency, but an actual result. The indicative after *ut* makes it mean 'in *the* (*very*) way in which', or 'just as'; the subjunctive makes it mean 'in *a* way in which', or 'in such a way that'. Thus *ita serit ut metit* means 'he sows in the very way in which he reaps', or 'he sows just as he reaps'; *ita serit ut metat* means 'he sows in a way in which he reaps', i.e. 'in such a way that, as a result, he reaps'. In conformity with the 'potential' origin of the construction is the fact that the negative is always *non*. Therefore, in a clause of result, 'that no one . . .' is *ut nemo*; 'that no slave . . .' is *ut nullus servus*; 'that never . . .' is *ut nunquam*; etc.

161. Grammarians of the German school prefer to derive all types of consecutive clause, whether relative, adverbial, or noun-clauses, from an original parataxis of the repudiating type of deliberative question with a negative answer.[1] Thus *nemo est qui possit* is derived from *Qui possit? Nemo est*. And *Quis est tam demens ut sua voluntate maereat?* 'Who is so mad as to grieve of his own accord?' will presumably be derived from *Ut* (*quis*) . . . *maereat? Quis est tam demens?* 'A man by any means grieve? – Who is so mad?' A noun-clause as in *non faciam ut hoc ei dem*, 'I will not allow myself to give him this' will come from a repudiating deliberative such as *Ego ut . . . dem? Non faciam!*

It will be seen that this explanation assumes that there is no original difference between the subjunctives in sentences like *quis dicere audeat?* 'Who would venture to say?', and *quis legatus mittatur?* 'Who is to be sent as envoy?', though the one expects in reply a negative expression of opinion, the other an expression of will. While allowing for borderline cases such as have been mentioned, it is hard to believe that the legally-minded Romans themselves ever confused willed or intentional result with

[1] See Kühner-Stegmann, II, p. 234; Stolz-Schmalz, pp. 708, 760; Kroll, *Wissenschaftliche Syntax*, pp. 85 ff.

unintentional result, so as to develop an expression of will into a means of expressing unpurposed result. It is safer to assume that the similarity between final and consecutive clauses (except for the negative, which is important) was accidental, and that they had a separate history. For the origin of consecutive clauses it is better to appeal to a parataxis such as Cic. *Verr.* 4, 31 *canes venaticos diceres – ita odorabantur omnia et pervestigabant*, 'one would have said they were hunting-dogs, – they so sniffed out and tracked down everything'.

As for consecutive noun-clauses, they were probably a secondary development from the adverbial, rather than developed from an original parataxis themselves.

162. The rule about the sequence of tenses which applies to final clauses does not apply to consecutive clauses, for an historic tense in the main clause need not be followed by an historic tense of the subjunctive in the subordinate clause. A past act or circumstance may have a present result, or even one that is still awaited: Cic. *Ac.* 2, 3 *in Lucullo tanta prudentia fuit ut hodie stet Asia Luculli institutis servandis.* 'In Lucullus there was such wisdom that Asia stands today by preserving the ordinances of Lucullus.' So also it is possible to say: *adeo victus est ut nunquam posthac pugnaturus sit*, 'he was beaten to such an extent that he will never fight again': Cic. *Q. fr.* 1, 1, 38 *in eam rationem vitae nos fortuna deduxit ut sempiternus sermo de nobis futurus sit.* 'Fortune has led us into such a path of life that we shall be an everlasting subject of men's conversation.' But a future result does not need the periphrastic subjunctive to express it, if the main clause itself refers to the future: Cic. *Or.* 137 *sic dicet ut verset saepe multis modis eadem.* 'He will so speak as often to vary the same theme in a number of ways'; Plaut. *Rud.* 730 *ita te ornatum amittam ut te non noveris.* 'I will send you away so decorated that you will not know yourself.'

163. Since a result cannot precede its cause, it will be clear that, in an adverbial clause of result, a past tense of the subjunctive cannot follow a present tense in the main clause, nor a pluperfect subjunctive follow a past tense, except in exceptional circumstances. Such circumstances arise when the main clause contains a general statement which held true also before the time to which the consecutive clause refers: Cic. *de Or.* 1, 196 *patriae tanta est vis ut Ithacam vir sapientissimus immortalitati anteponeret.* 'Such is the influence of one's native land that to immortality the hero, for all his wisdom, preferred Ithaca.' See also *Id. Phil.* 2, 60; *Verr.* 3, 23; 5, 158. So also it would be possible to say: *tam stultus est ut pecuniam amiserit*, 'He is so foolish that he has lost his money', without implying that the loss preceded the existence of the folly.

Of the tenses of completed action, the pluperfect subjunctive in consecutive clauses is necessarily rare. It may, however, follow a pluperfect indicative of the main clause, or an imperfect that denotes a long-continued state, without implying priority to the time of the main action: Cic. *Verr.* 4, 54 *tantam multitudinem collegerat emblematum ut ne unum quidem cuiquam reliquisset.* 'He had collected such a multitude of ornamented vessels that he had not left anyone in possession of a single one'; Livy, 1, 2, 5 *tanta opibus Etruria erat ut iam non terras solum, sed mare etiam fama nominis sui implesset.* 'Etruria was so great in resources that it had already extended the fame of its name over not only lands but seas.' Here *implesset* denotes priority to the time of which Livy is speaking, but *erat* implies a long-continued state which had existed before that. Cic. *de Or.* 1, 26 *quo in sermone multa divinitus a tribus illis consularibus Cotta deplorata et commemorata narrabat, ut nihil incidisset postea civitati mali, quod non impendere illi tanto ante vidissent.* 'Cotta told of many things which those three consulars had by divine inspiration deplored and called to notice in that conversation, so that no evil had fallen upon the state afterwards which they had not seen long before to be impending.' What Cotta said was: . . . *ut nihil inciderit*, so that here *incidisset* is due to *O. O.* and denotes priority to the time of Cotta's narration, but not to the time of the consulars' forecasts, of which it expresses the result.

164. The difference between the perfect and the imperfect consecutive subjunctive, in past narrative, is not always clearly understood. As already indicated, the tenses of incomplete action of the subjunctive lay stress on the logical connexion of cause and effect, leaving it to the context to decide whether the effect is a reality or a mere tendency. But the tenses of completed action cannot help but indicate a fact. Therefore, after a main clause referring to the past, the perfect subjunctive tends to be used, whenever the author wishes to stress that the result is a historical fact, whether the action was long-continued or not. The imperfect subjunctive may be used of the same factual result, if it is desired to stress the logical connexion. Therefore the following two passages, which relate to the same incident, are instructive: Cic. *Att.* 6, 1, 6 *inclusum in curia senatum obsederat, ut fame senatores quinque morerentur.* 'He had shut up and besieged the senate in the senate-house, so that five senators died of hunger *in consequence*'; *Ibid.* 2, 8 *inclusum in curia senatum habuerunt ita multos dies ut interierint nonnulli fame.* 'They kept the senate shut up in the senate-house for so many days that some of them *actually* perished of hunger.'

Note. In some contexts the imperfect subjunctive does seem to be used merely to express the progressive nature of the action, where the imperfect indicative would have been used in a co-ordinate sentence: Caes. *B. G.* 7, 17, 3 *summa difficultate rei frumentariae affecto exercitu . . . usque eo ut complures dies milites frumento caruerint, et pecore e longinquioribus vicis adacto extremam famem sustentarent, nulla tamen vox est ab eis audita populi Romani maiestate . . . indigna.* 'Though the army was labouring under the extreme difficulty of the corn-supply, to such an extent that for a number of days the soldiers were (*actually*) without corn, and *were supporting* their extreme hunger by bringing in cattle from outlying villages, yet no utterance was heard from them unworthy of the prestige of the Roman people.' In independent sentences we should here have had *itaque . . . caruerunt, et . . . sustentabant.* Yet even here the absence of corn is a historical fact, while the relieving of hunger by eating meat is a natural consequence. Cic. *Fin.* 2, 63 *erat ita non superstitiosus ut sacrificia et fana contemneret, ita non timidus ad mortem ut in acie sit interfectus.* 'He was so devoid of superstition as to despise sacrifices and shrines, so unafraid in face of death that he was killed in battle.' Although here, too, *contemneret* describes a habit, and *sit interfectus* an isolated historical event, yet the logical difference is present also. Freedom from superstition involves contempt for ritual as a natural consequence, but fearlessness does not necessarily entail death in battle. The latter is merely an incidental result.

165. The perfect subjunctive dealt with in the preceding section is aoristic, but the true perfect subjunctive (= English perfect with 'have') also may follow a main verb in a past tense, if the context shows that the result has been only just completed, or that it has effects remaining, at the time of writing: Cic. *Off.* 2, 76 *Paullus tantum in aerarium pecuniae invexit ut unius imperatoris praeda finem attulerit tributorum.* 'Paullus brought so much money into the treasury that the booty of a single general *has* put an end to imposts.' The context shows that the reference is to the fact that the citizens were still free from imposts at the time of writing. If *attulerit* were aorist-perfect, it would mean that Paullus put an end to imposts at the time, though they might have been re-instituted later. *afferret* would mean 'so as to put an end to imposts (at the time)'. Nep. 3, 1, 2 *adeo excellebat Aristides abstinentia ut unus post hominum memoriam . . . cognomine Iustus sit appellatus.* 'Aristides so excelled in moderation that he is the only historical figure to have been called by the name of "The Just".' (I.e. he is still so called. *appellaretur* would mean that his moderation was such as to gain him the nickname of 'The Just' at that time.)

166. In a sentence of comparison expressing difference in degree, a consecutive clause may follow *quam*, to indicate the result of the difference: *sapientior est quam ut hoc credat*, (lit.) 'he is wiser than so as to believe this', i.e. 'he is too wise to believe this'. The comparative has a negative implication and involves a denial of possibility, so that the tenses of completed action of the subjunctive, since they emphasize the actuality of a result, are not likely to be found in such sentences. The corresponding Greek construction is ἢ ὥστε with the infinitive, the indicative (which, in a past tense, after ὥστε, is the equivalent of *ut* with the perfect subjunctive) being ruled out.

From about the time of Livy onwards, such consecutive clauses began to be introduced sometimes by the relative pronoun, instead of *ut:*

sapientior est quam qui hoc credat, (lit.) 'he is wiser than (one) who would believe this'.

Examples: Cic. *Br.* 70 *quis non intelligit Canachi signa rigidiora esse quam ut imitentur veritatem?* 'Who does not perceive that the statues of Canachus are too stiff to be life-like?' Livy, 40, 56, 1 *Perseus potentior erat quam ut fugam necessariam duceret.* 'Perseus was too powerful to consider flight necessary'; Nep. 12, 3, 2 *Chabrias indulgebat sibi liberalius quam ut invidiam vulgi posset effugere.* 'Chabrias indulged himself too freely to be able to escape the envy of the mob.' With relative pronoun: Ov. *Met.* 6, 195 *maior sum quam cui possit Fortuna nocere.* 'I am too great for Fortune to be able to harm me'; Livy, 33, 5, 6 *maiores arbores caedebant quam quas ferre miles posset.* 'They were cutting trees too large for the soldiery to be able to carry them'; *Id.* 26, 12, 6 *maiora deliquerant quam quibus ignosci posset.* 'They had committed wrongs too great to be forgiven.'

167. An idiomatic twist is often given to a consecutive *ut*-clause by expressing in it, not a natural result, but something unexpected or contradictory. For example, if instead of 'He is so credulous as to believe everything', we say 'He is so credulous as *not* to believe everything'—*ita credulus est ut non omnia credat*—we can only mean 'He is credulous to this limited extent, that he does not believe everything'. In such contexts *ut non* can usually be translated by 'without' and the verbal noun in *-ing*: 'He is credulous, without believing everything'.

This restrictive or adversative use of the consecutive *ut*-clause was further developed, from Terence onwards, into a means of making emphatic concessions: *ut non omnia credat, tamen credulus est*, 'granting that he does not believe everything, nevertheless he is credulous'. This use is commonest in Cicero, Livy, and Tacitus. The demonstrative *ita* or its equivalent, is normally omitted.

Finally, a consecutive *ut*-clause was occasionally used to state the limiting conditions under which something holds true, e.g. *ita sapiens existimatur ut non omnia credat*, 'he is considered wise so long as (lit. 'in such a way that . . .', 'on such terms that') he does not believe everything'. In such contexts *ita . . . ut* appears to mean 'on condition that', 'provided that', or 'if'. This stipulative use, however, verges on the function of the final subjunctive, and whenever the limiting conditions are viewed as something willed or demanded, and not merely as connected facts whose significance is stated by the writer himself, then the subjunctive *is* final, and the negative is *ut ne*. From Plautus onwards the latter is commoner.

Examples: (*a*) Restrictive or concessive: Cic. *Div. in Caec.* 44 *cuius ego ingenium ita laudo ut non pertimescam, ita probo ut me ab eo delectari facilius quam decipi putem posse.* 'I admire his ability without being afraid of it; I approve of it, while believing that I am more likely to be amused than deceived by it'; *Id. Fin.* 2, 71 *malet existimari vir bonus ut non sit, quam esse ut non putetur.* 'He will prefer to be thought a good man without being one, rather than to be one, without being thought one'; *Id. T. D.* 1, 23 *si, ut ista non disserantur, liberari mortis metu possumus, id agamus.* 'If we can secure freedom from the fear of death without those things being discussed, let us do so'; *Ibid.* 1, 16 *ut enim non efficias quod vis, tamen mors ut malum non sit efficies.* 'Granted that you do not establish what you wish, you will still establish that death is not an evil.' (*b*) Conditional or stipulative: Cic. *Off.* 2, 33 *bonis viris ita fides habetur ut nulla sit in iis fraudis iniuriaeque suspicio.* 'Good men are trusted only so long as no suspicion of fraud or wrong-doing attaches to them.' But the subjunctive is more often final: Cic. *Rosc. Am.* 55 *hoc ita est utile ut ne plane illudamur ab accusatoribus.* 'This is expedient only provided that we are not clearly abused by the accusers.' An idea of will or obligation underlies this—'the bringing of accusations is not to become an abuse'.

Note. The development of consecutive clauses to grant concessions is not to be confused with the concessive use of the independent jussive, as in Cic. *T. D.* 2, 14 *ne sit sane summum malum dolor, malum certe est,* 'granted that pain is not the greatest evil, it is at least an evil'. The positive of this construction does not require the conjunction *ut*, see Section 112.

168. *Consecutive Noun-clauses*

A consecutive clause introduced by *ut* or *ut non* (*ut nullus* etc.) may perform the function of a noun by standing as object or subject to a verb, by being predicated, or by standing in apposition to a noun or pronoun to amplify and explain it.

Verbs which commonly have a consecutive *ut*-clause as object (or as subject, when they are passive) are verbs of effecting, such as *facio, efficio, perficio, committo.* But a clause which follows these is final, if the intention rather than the actual result is in mind.

A consecutive clause will naturally stand as subject to the passive of the above verbs, and also to intransitive verbs or expressions with an analogous meaning, such as verbs denoting existence, coming to pass, befalling: *est* (*futurum est*), *longe* (*multum, tantum*) *abest, fit, fieri potest, accidit, evenit, contingit, usu venit, sequitur, consequens est, qui probari potest?* ('how can it be accepted?'), *proximum est, extremum est, reliquum est, restat, accedit.* On the analogy of some of these expressions a consecutive clause is sometimes used with a few impersonal expressions which are normally followed by an accusative and infinitive, e.g. *veri simile non est, aequum est, iustum est.*

Examples: Cic. *Fin.* 2, 15 *rerum obscuritas facit ut non intellegatur oratio.* 'The obscurity of the subject causes the language not to be understood.' With this cp. *Id. Clu.* 168 *fecisti ut ne cui innocenti maeror tuus calamitatem adferret.* 'You saw to it that your grief should not bring disaster on any innocent man', where the subjunctive expresses intention on the part of the subject, and is therefore final. *Id. de Or.* 1, 260 *Demosthenes perfecit meditando ut nemo planius locutus esse putaretur.* 'Demosthenes achieved by practice the result that no one was thought to have spoken more clearly'; Nep. 7, 3, 2 *accidit ut una nocte omnes Hermae deicerentur.* 'It happened that all the statues of Hermes were cast down in a single night'; Cic. *de Or.* 2, 152 *est ut plerique philosophi nulla tradant praecepta dicendi.* 'It is the case that the majority of philosophers give no instruction in speaking.' In this use of *est ut* can be seen the origin of the common periphrasis *futurum esse (fore) ut* for the future infinitive passive, as Cic. *Div.* 1, 101 *exaudita vox est futurum esse ut Roma caperetur.* 'A voice was heard saying that it would come to pass that Rome should be captured.' Plaut. *Amph.* 567 *nec potest fieri homo idem duobus locis ut simul sit.* 'Nor is it possible for the same man to be in two places at once.'

Tantum abest, with a consecutive noun-clause as subject, has one or more adverbial consecutive clauses following it: Cic. *Or.* 104 *tantum abest ut nostra miremur ut usque eo difficiles simus ut nobis non satisfaciat ipse Demosthenes.* 'We are so far from admiring our own works that we are so hard to please that even Demosthenes himself does not satisfy us.'

Cic. *de Sen.* 16 *ad Appi Claudii senectutem accedebat ut etiam caecus esset.* 'To the old age of Appius Claudius was added that he was also blind'; *Id. Par.* 22 *si virtutes pares sunt inter se, sequitur ut etiam vitia sint paria.* 'If virtues are equal to one another, it follows that vices also are equal.'

In all the examples above the tense of the subjunctive is one of incomplete action. A tense of completed action is possible only where the *ut*-clause refers to something previous to the time of the governing verb or phrase: Cic. *Rosc. Am.* 77 *reliquum est ut per servos id admiserit.* 'It remains for him to have perpetrated it through the agency of his slaves', or 'the remaining possibility is that he perpetrated . . .'; *Id. de Or.* 2, 285 *potest fieri ut iratus dixerit.* 'It may be that he spoke in anger'; *Id. Sest.* 78 *an veri simile est ut civis Romanus cum gladio in forum descenderit?* 'Is it likely that a Roman citizen came down into the forum with a sword?' (The *ut*-clause here, instead of an accusative and infinitive, is probably on the analogy of *fieri non potest.* It is found only after a negative, or implied negative, as above.)

No examples of the pluperfect subjunctive seem to be recorded, but, theoretically, it should be possible to say: *reliquum erat ut hoc fecisset*, 'the remaining possibility was that he had done this'.

When a consecutive clause is explanatory of a noun or pronoun, it may either be equivalent to a nominative complement predicated with *est*, or it may stand in apposition: Cic. *Br.* 84 *est mos hominum ut nolint eundem pluribus rebus excellere.* 'It is the custom of men that they do not like the same person to excel in a number of things'; Plaut. *Capt.* 583 *est miserorum ut invideant bonis.* 'It is characteristic of beggars to envy the well-to-do'; Cic. *Rosc. Am.* 28 *consilium ceperunt plenum sceleris et audaciae, ut nomen huius de parricidio deferrent.* 'They formed a plan full of criminality and daring, namely to charge my client here with parricide'; Caes. *B. G.* 1, 13, 2 *cum id quod ipsi diebus viginti aegerrime confecerant, ut flumen transirent, illum uno die fecisse intellegerent, legatos ad eum mittunt.* 'When they learned that he had done in a single day what had cost them the greatest trouble to achieve in twenty days, namely the crossing of the river, they sent envoys to him.'

Note. When verbs of happening and befalling are modified by an adverb, such as *bene, male, opportune,* etc., they more often have a substantival *quod*-clause standing as subject, and sometimes an accus. and infin. noun-phrase. (See Section 211.)

XIV

Questions, Direct and Indirect

169. *The Indicative in Direct Questions*

The mood of the verb in a question conforms with that of the verb in the answer which is expected, so that an inquiry about a matter of fact will have the indicative, just as the statement of fact which will reply to it.

Questions may be divided into (*a*) word-questions, and (*b*) sentence-questions:

(*a*) Word-questions are such as are introduced by interrogative pronouns, adjectives, or adverbs: *quis?* 'who?', *ecquis?* 'is there anyone who . . .?', *qui?* 'what?' (adj.), *uter?* 'which of the two?', *qualis?* 'of what sort?', *quantus?* 'how large?', *quot?* 'how many?' *quotus?* 'which in order?' ('how-manieth?'), *quotiens?* 'how many times?', *quomodo?* 'how?' ('in what way?') *ut?* 'how?' (e.g. *ut vales?* 'How are you?'. But in classical Latin mostly exclamatory, e.g. *ut delirat!* 'How he raves!'), *quam . . .?* 'how . . .?' (adv., e.g. *quam bonus?* 'how good?'), *cur?* 'why?', *quando?* 'when?', *ubi?* 'where?', *unde?* 'whence?', *quo?* 'whither?'.

(*b*) Sentence-questions are those which, instead of inquiring about a detail, inquire about the truth of the whole predicate, e.g. 'Have you done this?'. Normally the order of words marks a sentence as interrogative in English, but the order cannot have that effect in Latin. Therefore, normally, interrogative particles are used as a sign of interrogation in Latin, though it was always possible, as in English, to turn a statement into a question simply by the tone of voice: Cic. *pro Mil.* 60 *Clodius insidias fecit Miloni?* 'Did Clodius waylay Milo?'

Usually, however, a sentence-question is introduced by one of the particles *-ne*, *nonne*, or *num*, and alternative questions by *utrum . . . an*, *-ne . . . an*, or *- . . . an*.

170. The particle *-ne* normally asks an open question, without presuming either an affirmative or negative answer. It is 'enclitic', i.e. it 'leans on' or is attached to another word. The word to which it is attached becomes the important word of the question, and is usually placed first: Cic. *Verr.* 3, 180 *omnisne pecunia dissoluta est?* 'was *all* the money paid out?'

Nonne, which is *-ne* attached to the negative *non*, presumes the answer 'yes', whatever answer is really expected: Plaut. *Amph.* 406 *nonne ego nunc sto ante aedes nostras?* 'am I not standing at this moment in front of our house?'

When a number of questions of this sort follow one another, the particle *-ne* is usually attached only to the first *non:* Cic. *Cat.* 1, 27 *nonne hunc in vincla duci, non ad mortem rapi, non summo supplicio mactari imperabis? quid tandem te impedit? mosne maiorum? . . . an leges . . .? an invidiam posteritatis times?* 'Will you not command this man to be arrested, will you not order him to be hurried to execution, will you not order him to be put to death by the supreme penalty? What is hindering you? Is it the tradition of our ancestors? or is it the laws? Or are you afraid of the hatred of posterity?'

Num originally meant 'now' (cf. *etiamnum*, 'even now'). When it acquired the sense of an interrogative particle, it retained its old meaning only in the strengthened form *num-ce* = *nunc. Num* normally presumes the answer 'no': Cic. *Cat.* 1, 13 *num dubitas id facere?* 'Surely you do not hesitate to do that?'; *Id. T. D.* 1, 77 *num non vis igitur audire . . .?* 'Surely, then, you are not unwilling to hear . . .?'

The presumption of a negative answer was not original in *num.* In Plautus it is often neutral. It does not necessarily presume a negative answer when it is used as a subordinating conjunction ('whether') to introduce indirect questions (Section 182), nor when it is joined to the indefinite pronoun *quis*: Ter. *Eun.* 549 *Numquis hinc me sequitur?—Nemo.* 'Is anyone following me hence?' 'No one.'

Utrum is the neuter singular of the pronoun *uter?* 'which of the two?', and is parallel both in sense and etymology to English 'whether'. It introduces questions asking which of two things is true, and the conjunction which joins the two alternatives is always *an:* Plaut. *Pers.* 341 *utrum pro ancilla me habes an pro filia?* 'Do you take me for a slave or for a daughter?' *-ne* may be used as well as or instead of *utrum*, or both may be omitted: Plaut. *Rud.* 104 *utrum tu masne an femina es?* 'Are you male or female?' *Id. Bacch.* 162 *tibi ego an tu mihi servus es?* 'Am I your slave or are you mine?' The Latin for 'or not?' is *an non?*: Ter. *Ph.* 147 *pater eius rediit an non?* 'Has his father returned, or not?'

Note. aut can, of course, occur in a question, if it joins, not alternative questions, but subdivisions of the same question, e.g. 'Did he live or work in Athens, or (was it) in Rome?' *utrum domicilium aut negotium Athenis habuit an Romae?*

171. Latin has no words exactly equivalent to our 'yes' and 'no', which are used only as sentence-substitutes, but *etiam*, *ita*, and occasionally *sic*, are used as affirmative replies, and *minime*, *non ita*, occasionally *non*, for negative. More often the important part of the question is repeated as a statement, often with corroborative particles such as *vero*, *enimvero*, *sane*, *immo*: *Rediitne pater eius? – Rediit* (*Non rediit*), 'Has his father returned?' 'He has (not)'; Cic. *T. D.* 1, 25 "*Dasne . . .?*" "*Do vero*", "Do you grant . . .?" "Certainly I do." Ter. *Eun.* 347 "*Numquid vis?*" "*Etiam, ut actutum venias.*" "Do you want anything?" "Yes! that you should come at once." Pliny *Ep.* 4, 13 *Huic ego "studes?" inquam; respondit "etiam"*. 'I said to him "Are you at school?" He replied "Yes".' Ter. *Andr.* 849 "*Quid istic tibi negoti est?*" "*Mihin?*" "*Ita.*" "What business have you there?" "I?" "Yes!" Plaut. *Amph.* 362 "*Quid, domum vestram?*" "*Ita enimvero!*" "What! Your house?" "Yes indeed!" (*Enimvero* is the strongest of the corroborative particles). Cic. *Ac.* 2, 104 *aut 'etiam' aut 'non' respondere*, 'to reply either "yes" or "no".' *Id. Att.* 8, 9, 2 "*Num igitur peccamus?*" "*Minime vos quidem.*" "We are not doing wrong, then?" "Not you, at least."

When the reply is the opposite of that expected, it is usually introduced by *immo* or *immo vero*, 'nay, on the contrary': Plaut. *Ps.* 495 "*Numquid, Simo, peccatum est?*" "*Immo maxime*". "Surely no harm has been done, Simo?" "On the contrary, very much so!" Sometimes, however, *immo* is strongly corroborative: Cic. *Att.* 9, 7, 4 *Causa igitur non bona est? immo optima!* 'Then is not our cause a good one? – Nay, it is excellent.'

172. *The Subjunctive in Direct Questions*

As was pointed out in Section 109, Note ii, if a jussive subjunctive is used interrogatively, an inquiry is made as to someone's will, to ask for orders, or to ask that a command already given may be repeated or amplified: e.g. "*Maneat*". "*Ubi maneat?*" Let him stay." "Where is he to stay?" This type of question, with the verb in the subjunctive, was the start of a wide range of uses in which the subjunctive is called *Deliberative*. These are most conveniently classified according to whether the question is evoked by a second party, or whether it is spontaneous. Only in the latter case is the subjunctive truly 'deliberative'.

(1) The question is evoked by a command, question, or remark, of someone else:

(*a*) The question is a genuine inquiry about a command, as Plaut. *Bacch.* 731 "*Scribe*" "*Quid scribam?*" "Write!" "Write what?"

(*b*) The question is rhetorical, and is used as a form of repudiation, to express indignation, expostulation, surprise, or denial: Plaut. *Pseud.* 1224 "*saltem Pseudolum mihi dedas.*" "*Pseudolum ego dedam tibi?*" "You should at least give up Pseudolus to me." "I – give up Pseudolus to you?" This type enjoyed a wide extension, and calls for separate treatment.

(2) The question is spontaneous:

(*a*) Addressed to a second party in consultation, requesting advice or opinion as to duty, obligation, or fitness: Cic. *Inv.* 1, 17 *utrum Karthago diruatur, an Karthaginiensibus reddatur, an eo colonia deducatur?* 'Should Carthage be razed, or restored to the Carthaginians, or should a colony be settled there?'

(*b*) Soliloquizing, indicating hesitation, doubt, or helplessness: Plaut. *Curc.* 589 *Quid ego faciam? maneam an abeam?* 'What shall I do? Shall I stay or go?'

Note. In questions that are truly deliberative, the indicative is almost as common as the subjunctive, from Plautus to Tacitus, e.g. Cic. *Att.* 13, 40, 2 *quid mi auctor es? advolone an maneo?* 'What do you advise me? Do I come flying, or do I stay?'

173. The negative in deliberative questions is regularly *non*, sometimes, particularly in early Latin, *ni*, which survives in classical Latin in the combinations *quidni?* 'why not?' and *nimirum*, 'of course' (lit. 'not wonderful'). *Ni* is a reinforced form of *ne* (archaic *nei*), which quite early came to be restricted to negative conditions. The negative in an independent deliberative question is never *ne.*[1]

The reason why the negative is normally *non* is probably that, when the use of the deliberative was extended, the original jussive nature of the subjunctive was obscured. The speaker does not often mean to inquire as to someone's will, but more often to ask for a *statement of opinion* as to duty, obligation, or fitness. This is particularly clear when the reference is to the past. *Quid facerem?* may mean, in effect, 'What do you think I ought to have done?' As the reply to this would be an expression of opinion rather than of will, we sometimes find *non hoc faceres* instead of *ne faceres*, 'you should not have done this.' The force of the subjunctive is obscured also in expressions such as *Quis hoc faceret?*, which may mean either 'Who *should* have done this?' or 'Who *would* have done this?' *The force of the subjunctive is so weakened that the Jussive is merging into the Potential.* If the volitive force can be so weakened in independent subjunctives, it is much more so when the subjunctive is dependent.

174. *Examples and Notes*

1 (a) (Inquiring after orders): Ter. *Ph.* 813 "*Illa maneat?*" "*Sic.*" "Is she to stay?" "Yes." Plaut. *M. G.* 1311 "*Quid modi flendo facies?*"

[1] In Cic. *Att.* 12, 40, 2 *ne doleam? qui potest? ne iaceam? quis unquam minus?*, which Draeger quotes among independent questions, the subjunctives are of indirect prohibition depending on the preceding words *quid homines postulent, nescio.*

"*Quid ego ni fleam?*" "What limit will you put to your weeping?" "Why should I not weep?" *Id. Ep.* 586 "*Cur me patrem vocabas?*" "*Non patrem te nominem?*" "Why did you keep calling me 'Father'?" "May I not call you 'Father'?" *Id. Rud.* 379 "*Quid faceret?*" "*Rogas quid faceret? adservaret dies noctesque.*" "What should he have done?" "Do you ask what he should have done? He should have watched her day and night." *Id. Tr.* 133 "*Non ego illi argentum redderem?*" "*Non redderes.*" "Ought I not to have paid him the money?" "You should not have paid it."

In some of the negative questions above, a note of surprise or indignation can be detected. It is often difficult to draw the line between genuine inquiries and the repudiating use of the subjunctive, of which examples are given in Section 175.

2 (a) (Genuine deliberatives): Ter. *Eun.* 811 "*Quid nunc agimus?*" "*Quin redeamus?*" "What do we do now?" "Why should we not go back?" (Note: In a deliberative question introduced by *quin?* the subjunctive is less common than the indicative.)

(b) (Expressing helplessness): Plaut. *Aul.* 713 *perii, interii, occidi, quo curram? quo non curram?* 'I'm done for, murdered, ruined! Which way must I run? Which way not run?' Ter. *Ad.* 614 *Quo modo me expediam?* 'How can I extricate myself?' *Id. H. T.* 317 *quid illo facias?* 'What is one to do with the fellow?' Cic. *Sest.* 43 *Haec cum viderem, quid agerem, iudices? . . . contenderem contra tribunum plebis privatus armis?* 'When I saw this, Gentlemen, what could I do? Was I, in my private capacity, to engage in armed opposition to a tribune of the plebs?'

175. *Repudiating Deliberatives*

These include both word- and sentence-questions. The sentence-questions may have no introductory particles, but they are often introduced by *-ne*, sometimes in combination with *ut*, and sometimes by *ut* alone. The presence of *-ne* shows that *ut* in such cases is not the interrogative 'how?', but the indefinite 'anyhow', 'by any means': Cic. *Verr.* II, 1, 40 *itane vero? tu repente relinquas, deseras, ad adversarios transeas?* 'Is that so, indeed? Are you suddenly to leave, desert, and go over to the enemy?' *Ibid.* 154 *te putet quisquam sociis temperasse?* 'Can anyone think that you spared the allies?' Plaut. *Amph.* 748 "*Audivistine tu me narrare haec hodie?*" "*Ubi ego audiverim?*" "Did you hear me telling this today?" "Where can I have heard you?" (i.e. 'where am I to have heard?'); Ter. *Ad.* 83 "*Quid fecit?*" "*Quid ille fecerit? quem neque pudet quicquam nec metuit quemquam.*" "What has he done?" "What has he done!—he who is ashamed of nothing and afraid of no one." Cic. *Mur.* 21 *apud exercitum mihi fueris tot annos? . . . afueris tam diu, et cum his de dignitate contendas?* 'Are you, pray, to have been with the army so many years, are you to have been absent so long, and presume to contest with these the question of personal merit?' *Id. Q. Fr.* 1, 3, 1 *ego tibi irascerer? tibi possem irasci? . . . ego te videre noluerim?* 'I be angry with you? I be capable of anger against you? Can you suppose I was unwilling to see you?' (The difference here between the imperfect and the perfect subjunctive is difficult to bring out in translation. Both repudiate something which is now past, but the imperfect takes a past point of view, looking forward, while the perfect takes a present point of view, looking back: i.e. *irascerer?* means '*was* I likely to be angry?', while *noluerim?* means '*is* it likely that I was unwilling?', or 'can you now suppose that I was unwilling?' Similarly, *afueris . . . contendas?* above mean '*Is* it fair that you should have been away, and now contest . . .?').

The pluperfect subjunctive is rare and occurs first in Cicero: *pro Sull.* 45 *mihi cuiusquam salus tanti fuisset ut meam neglegerem? per me ego veritatem contaminarem aliquo mendacio? quemquam denique ego iuvarem . . .?* 'Should anyone's safety have been so important to me as for me to neglect my own? Was I by my own act to obscure the truth by any falsehood? In short, was it right for me to aid anyone . . .?'

For *quidni?* and particles, cf. Cic. *de Or.* 2, 273 *cum rogaret Salinator ut meminisset opera sua se Tarentum recepisse, "Quidni" inquit "meminerim?"* 'When Salinator asked him to remember that it was by his aid that he had recovered Tarentum, he said "How should I not remember it?"' (i.e. 'how can I help remembering?'). Plaut. *Aul.* 690 *egone ut te advorsum mentiar?* 'The very idea of my lying to your face!' *Id. Capt.* 139 *egone illum non fleam? ego non defleam talem adulescentem?* 'Do you expect me not to weep for him? Can I help mourning for such a youth?' Cic. *Cat.* 1, 22 *te ut ulla res frangat? tu ut unquam te corrigas?* 'Anything break you down? You mend your ways?—Impossible!' Ter. *H. T.* 1090 *mea bona ut dem Bacchidi dono sciens? Non faciam.* 'I wittingly make a present of my goods to Bacchis? I will not do it!' Cic. *Phil.* 6, 5 *huic denuntiationi ille pareat? ille se fluvio Rubicone circumscriptum esse patiatur? non is est Antonius.* 'He obey this proclamation? He allow himself to be circumscribed by the river Rubicon? Antonius is not the man!'

Note. The last two examples above show how easy it would be for such subjunctives to become subordinate. The example from Terence looks like the paratactic original of the consecutive noun-clauses dealt with in Section 168, and the last resembles the consecutive relative clauses of which examples are given in 157 (2). Accordingly some grammarians trace back consecutive clauses of all types to this source. That the repudiating deliberative subjunctive may have contributed to the development of consecutive noun-clauses cannot be denied, but that all generic and consecutive clauses owe their existence to this particular type of negative expression is highly improbable. The moment a subjunctive becomes subordinate, its emotional force evaporates, and the subordinate subjunctive in a sentence like *Antonius non is est qui pareat* might as well be potential in origin as deliberative, e.g. *Antonius non pareat: non is est*, 'Antonius *would* not obey: he is not the type.' When there are countless examples of subjunctives in relative clauses that are clearly potential (cf. 155), are we to suppose that the potential subjunctive had no subordinate developments at all?

176. *The Potential Subjunctive in Questions*

The potential subjunctive is naturally very common in questions, since the apodosis of a conditional sentence may be couched in the form of a question: Plaut. *Tr.* 468 *si apposita cena sit, edisne an incenatus accubes?* 'If a dinner were set before you, would you eat, or would you recline at table unfed?' Cic. *Fin.* 1, 57 *quis bonus dubitet mortem oppetere, si patriae sit profuturus?* 'What good man would hesitiate to meet death, if he were going to benefit his country?' *Id. Phil.* 8, 14 *num eum, si tum esses, temerarium civem putares?* 'Would you have thought him a rash citizen, if you had lived in those days?'

When there is no conditional clause present, it is often difficult to draw the line between the potential subjunctive and the deliberative type treated in the preceding Sections: Cic. *Lael.* 64 *ubi istum invenias qui honorem amici anteponat suo?* 'Where would you (*or* 'are you to') find that man who would set his friend's honour above his own?' *Fam.* 2, 11, 1 *putaresne unquam accidere posse ut mihi verba deessent?* 'Would you ever have thought it could happen that words should fail me?' *Ibid.* 15, 15, 2 *quis istum Asiae terrorem inlaturum putaret?* 'Who would have thought (*or* was to think) that he would inspire Asia with terror?' *Id. Man.* 31 *hoc tantum bellum quis unquam arbitraretur ab uno imperatore confici posse?* 'Who would ever have thought that this great war could be brought to an end by one general?'

Indirect Questions

177. The development of indirect question noun-clauses from an original parataxis of a direct question with a verb of asking (or with any expression which implies the asking or answering of a question) has been anticipated in Section 135.

It is obvious that, if the verb of the original direct question was in the deliberative subjunctive, the mood must remain unchanged when the question is made dependent and indirect.[1] If the original tense of the subjunctive was imperfect, neither can that be changed, without altering the meaning, even if the governing verb is present: Plaut. *Rud.* 379 "*Quid faceret?*" "*Rogas quid faceret?*" " What was he to do?" "Do you ask what he was to do?" Changes of person are, however, required,

[1] The words *and indirect* are important, since a question can be 'dependent' without being 'indirect', as *He asked "What are you doing?"* Here *What are you doing?* is a dependent noun-clause standing as object to *asked*, but it is not an indirect question. The term *Dependent Question* as an alternative to *Indirect Question* should be dropped.

according to the point of view of the person reporting the question; and if the governing verb is in a historic tense, a present subjunctive of the original direct question will have to be changed to the imperfect in the subordinate clause. Thus *Quid faciam?* when made indirect and dependent on *Rogat*, becomes (*Rogat*) *quid faciat*, 'He asks what he is to do', and when dependent on *Rogavit*, becomes (*Rogavit*) *quid faceret*, 'He asked what he was to do'.

Indirect Questions of Fact

178. When a question of fact, with a verb in the indicative, is made dependent and indirect, there seems at first sight to be no logical reason why the verb in the subordinate clause should be changed to the subjunctive. Nevertheless, from about the time of Plautus onwards, it became the rule to change the mood to the subjunctive, whenever the question was felt to be dependent and indirect. Thus we find *Quid agis? Rogo te*, 'What are you doing? I ask you', but *Rogo te quid agas*, 'I ask you what you are doing'. In the indirect form, therefore, the difference between a deliberative question and a question of fact may be obliterated. But if the context did not make it clear that an indirect question was deliberative, some other way of expressing the idea of duty or necessity could easily be found, e.g. instead of *Scire volo quid agat*, it was possible to say *Scire volo quid agere debeat*, or . . . *quid ei agendum sit*, for 'I wish to know what he *should* do'.

179. There are many examples in early Latin (Plautus and Terence), and in the poets, where the indicative is retained in questions of fact which are clearly indirect, and many more in questions which may be construed either as dependent or paratactic. But where the indicative is found in classical prose, it is due to parataxis, as in Cic. *T. D.* 1, 10 *dic, quaeso, num te illa terrent?* 'Tell me, pray, do those things frighten you?'

The following are examples of the indicative in questions that are clearly indirect: Plaut. *Curc.* 543 *scire volo quoi reddidisti*, 'I want to know to whom you gave it back'; *Id. Aul.* 174 *scio quid dictura es*, 'I know what you are going to say'; *Id. Most.* 459 *non potest dici quam indignum facinus fecisti*, 'It cannot be said how unworthy a deed you have done'. Sometimes both the indicative and the subjunctive are found depending on the same verb: Plaut. *Amph.* 17 *cuius iussu venio et quam ob rem venerim dicam*, 'I will tell you at whose behest I come and for what purpose I have come'.

It is clear from the above examples that the subjunctive in indirect questions of fact was not original in Latin. The explanation of the change of usage, which was completed by about 200 B.C., is that the subjunctive had come to be a means whereby the speaker disclaimed responsibility for what he stated. Used independently, as we have seen, the subjunctive expressed an event as something *reflected upon* by the speaker himself, and, as a result, willed, or desired, or pronounced possible by him. *A fortiori* it had to be used to express an event as pronounced upon in any way by someone else. We have already seen how it came to be used in final clauses to report or quote someone's will indirectly. From this it was but a short step for the function of the subjunctive to be extended as a convenient way of showing that something stated or asked in other kinds of subordinate finite clause was part of an indirect quotation, and that it did not represent the speaker's own views or observation. Had a finite clause, instead of an accusative and infinitive phrase, been adopted as the regular method of making indirect statements, classical authors would have used the subjunctive in it (cf. examples in Section 35). As it was, the subjunctive became regular in any finite clauses which were indirect, including indirect question-clauses of fact.

The subjunctive having already acquired this secondary modal force, it is clear that its extension to indirect questions of fact and other subordinate clauses in *Oratio Obliqua* was not purely formal. Nevertheless such extensions of usage usually start from a particular type of expression, and we need hardly look further than the type of deliberative illustrated in Section 175, in which the original jussive force is lost. Cf. Ter. *Ad.* 83, cited there, and also the following: Plaut. *Most.* 556 "*Quid nunc faciendum censes?*" "*Ego quid censeam?*" "What do you think ought to be done now?" "What do I think?" Ter. *Ph.* 685 "*Quid ergo narras?*" "*Quid ego narrem?*" "What are you talking about, then?" "What am I talking about! . . ." In these examples it is almost possible, though not necessary, to understand a governing verb such as *Rogas* . . .?

180. *Tenses of the Subjunctive in Indirect Questions of Fact*

The tense of the subjunctive in an indirect question which, in the direct form, had its verb in the indicative, depends on two things: (1) the tense of the governing verb, (2) the tense of the indicative in the original direct question.

(1) *Sequence of Tenses.* A primary tense in the governing verb must be followed by a primary tense of the subjunctive in the subordinate clause; and a historic tense in the governing verb must be followed by a historic tense of the subjunctive in the subordinate clause.

(2) As there are only three primary tenses of the subjunctive (*faciam*, *facturus sim*, *fecerim*), and three historic tenses (*facerem*, *facturus essem*, *ecissem*), the various types of action (progressive or complete), which can be expressed by the indicative in a direct question, cannot all be reproduced in the indirect form. For example, it is impossible, without a periphrasis, to express in Latin: 'I want to know what he *was doing* yesterday'. The normal Latin for this would be: *Scire volo quid heri fecerit*, 'I want to know what he *did* yesterday'. Here the imperfect

subjunctive *faceret* would be deliberative, and would make the sentence mean 'I want to know what he *should have done* yesterday'.

The tense-usage can best be made clear by the following table:

Original Direct Question			*Indirect*	
1. *Quid facit?* 'What is he doing?'	*Rogant* *Rogaverunt* *Rogabunt*	*quid faciat.*	They ask They have asked They will ask	what he is doing
2. *Quid fecit? Quid faciebat? Quid fecerat?* 'What has he done, did he do, was he doing, had he done?'	*Rogant* *Rogaverunt* *Rogabunt*	*quid fecerit.*	They ask They have asked They will ask	what he has done, did, was doing, had done
3. *Quid faciet? Quid facturus est?* 'What will he do?' 'What is he going to do?'	*Rogant* *Rogaverunt* *Rogabunt*	*quid facturus sit.*	They ask They have asked They will ask	what he will do, what he is going to do

The same questions, when made dependent on *rogabant, rogaverunt* (they asked), or *rogaverant,* become:

1. . . . *quid faceret.* (. . . 'what he was doing'.)
2. . . . *quid fecisset.* (. . . 'what he had done' or 'had been doing'.)
3. . . . *quid facturus esset.* (. . . 'what he would do', 'was going to do'.)

181. In colloquial Latin, and occasionally in literary prose, especially from Livy onwards, the simple form of the present or imperfect subjunctive is sometimes used with reference to the future: Plaut. *Most.* 58 *Qui scis an tibi istuc eveniat prius quam mihi?* 'How do you know whether that will happen to you, before it happens to me?' Livy 2, 55, 9 *e foro in curiam compelluntur, incerti quatenus Volero exerceret victoriam.* 'They were driven out of the forum into the senate-house, not knowing how far Volero would push his victory'; Tac. *Ann.* 14, 13, 1 *quonam modo urbem ingrederetur, an obsequium senatus, an studia plebis reperiret anxius,* 'anxious as to the circumstances of his entry into the city, whether he would find the senate compliant, whether the people would acclaim him'.

When the simple tense is thus used in Cicero or Caesar, either the context allows the subjunctive to have some real modal force (e.g. deliberative), or else there is a *si*-clause, or other circumstance in the context, that makes clear the reference to the future: Caes. *B. G.* 1, 31, 15 *haec si enuntiata Ariovisto sint, non dubitare quin de omnibus supplicium sumat.* 'If this were reported to Ariovistus, they did not doubt but he would exact vengeance from them all'; Cic. *ad Quir.* 14 *neque, re publica exterminata, mihi locum in hac urbe esse duxi, nec, si illa restitueretur, dubitavi quin me secum ipsa reduceret.* 'When the republic was driven out, I did not think there was a place for me in this city, nor, if it should be restored, did I doubt that it would itself bring me back with it.'

The same applies to other types of subordinate clause in *O. O.* dealt with in Section 277 below.

Note. The periphrastic future subjunctive in *-urus sim* was the product of literary precision, but there is no method of representing accurately in an indirect question (or in any other kind of subordinate clause in *O. O.*, cf. Sect. 277) the future indicative passive, or the future of a verb which has no future participle in use. There are no examples recorded of the periphrasis *futurum sit ut.* If the passive form could not be avoided, the simple present or imperfect subjunctive would be used, and if the context did not show that the reference was to the future, then an adverb such as *mox, brevi, postea,* would be inserted. Thus the Latin for 'He asked how soon the city would be taken' would be: *Rogavit quam mox urbs caperetur.* 'He asked whether this would be done' would be: *Rogavit num illud postea fieret.*

182. If the original direct question was a word-question, the interrogative word itself acts as a subordinating conjunction to introduce the noun-clause in the indirect form, e.g. *Rogant unde veneris, quo eas, quando rediturus sis,* 'They ask where you came from, where you are going, and when you will return'.

Indirect sentence-questions are introduced by the same particles as direct questions, which particles are then equivalent in function to the English subordinating conjunction 'whether':

(1) *-ne* is usually attached to the first word in the subordinate clause, but not always. As in direct questions, the word to which it is attached is the important word in the question: Cic. *N. D.* 3, 65 *videamus deorumne providentia mundus regatur,* 'let us see whether it is by divine providence that the world is governed'; *Id. Verr.* 4, 150 *haec sum rogaturus: navem populo Romano debeantne. fatebuntur. praebuerintne praetore C. Verre. negabunt.* 'I am going to ask these questions: whether they owe a ship to the Roman people. They will admit it. Whether they provided one during the praetorship of C. Verres. They will say no.'

(2) *Num* is the commonest of the conjunctions for introducing an indirect sentence-question. As a subordinating conjunction, it does not always presume the answer 'no'; indeed, it can hardly do so, when the governing verb is not a verb of asking: Cic. *de Sen.* 22 *senex dicitur quaesisse num illud carmen desipientis videretur,* 'the old man is said to have asked whether that seemed a poem written by a man out of his wits'. (Here the answer 'no' is presumed.) Cic. *Att.* 11, 14, 3 *ad te scribam num quid egerim,* 'I will write and tell you whether I have done anything'; *Id. Verr.* 4, 11 *quaerendum est*

num aes alienum habuerit, num auctionem fecerit, 'the question must be asked whether he had debts, (and) whether he held an auction'. (Additional questions are not usually joined by *et* or *-que,* but the interrogative particle is repeated.)

(3) *Nonne* very rarely introduces an indirect question. There are a few examples in Cicero, always after *quaero*: *Ac.* 2, 76 *ex me quaesieras nonne putarem . . .,* 'you had inquired of me whether I did not think . . .'

(4) Alternative indirect questions are introduced by *utrum . . . an, -ne . . . an,* or - . . . *an.* But *necne* is used instead of *annon.* Occasionally, particularly when the first particle is omitted, *-ne* is used for *an:* Cic. *Att.* 16, 8, 2 *consultabat utrum Romam proficisceretur an Capuam teneret, an iret ad tres legiones Macedonicas,* 'he was deliberating whether to set out for Rome, or make for Capua, or go to the three Macedonian legions'; Caes. *B. G.* 4, 14, 2 *perturbabantur copiasne adversus hostem ducere an castra defendere praestaret,* 'they were in confusion as to whether it was better to lead their forces against the enemy or to defend the camp'. (Here *perturbabantur* can introduce an indirect question, because it implies 'they were in doubt whether . . .'.) Cic. *Inv.* 2, 30 *servus an liber, pecuniosus an pauper sit, consideratur,* 'it is under discussion whether he is slave or free, wealthy or poor'; *Id. Fam.* 2, 17, 3 *Parthi transierint necne, praeter te video dubitare neminem,* 'I see that no one but you doubts whether the Parthians have crossed or not'; *Id. Ph.* 2, 41 *albus aterne fuerit ignoras,* 'you are ignorant as to whether he was white or black.'

(5) *An* instead of *-ne* or *num,* to introduce a single indirect question, is not used by Caesar or Cicero, except in the formulae *haud scio an, nescio an, dubito an*; but it occurs in early Latin, and then again from Livy onwards: Livy 40, 14, 7 *te quaerere ex iis iubebat an ferrum habuisset,* 'he bade you ask them whether he had had a sword'.

(6) The use of *si,* 'if', in the sense of 'whether', to introduce indirect questions, is a feature of colloquial Latin, but there are also a few examples in literary prose: Cic. *de Inv.* 2, 122 *agnati ambigunt si filius, antequam in suam tutelam venerit, mortuus sit,* 'the relatives dispute as to whether the son died before he came of age'; Livy 40, 49, 6 *quaesivit si cum Romanis militare liceret,* 'he asked if it were permissible to serve with the Romans'; also after *percontor* in Livy 33, 35, 3.

183. *The Potential Subjunctive in Indirect Questions*

When a question with a verb in the potential subjunctive is made dependent and indirect, the same ambiguity arises as with the deliberative subjunctive. Sometimes the potential subjunctive is allowed to remain unchanged, but usually the idea of possibility or likelihood is brought out by means of a periphrasis. The common periphrases are the future participle with the appropriate tense of *sum,* and the infinitive with the appropriate tense of *possum.* Thus *Numquis homini tam mendaci crederet?*

or . . . *credidisset?* 'Would anyone have believed such a liar?', is near enough in sense to *Numquis . . . crediturus erat (fuit)?* or to *Numquis . . . credere poterat (potuit)?*, for these periphrases to be preferred, when the question is indirect.

Examples: Plaut. *Pers.* 296 *scis quid dicturus fuerim, ni linguae moderari queam.* 'You know what I should have said, were I not able to restrain my tongue'. (This seems to be the earliest example of *-urus fuerim.* Early Latin usually avoids the ambiguity by using parataxis.) Livy 9, 33, 7 *dic quidnam facturus fueris, si eo tempore censor fuisses.* 'Tell me what you would have done, if you had been censor at that time'. (Direct: *quidnam fecisses?*); Sen. *Ep.* 32, 2 *cogita quantum additurus celeritati fueris, si a tergo hostis instaret.* 'Consider how much speed you would put on, if an enemy were pursuing you behind' (Direct: *quantum adderes . . .?*); Cic. *Planc.* 60 *quaeris quid potuerit amplius adsequi Plancius, si Cn. Scipionis fuisset filius.* 'You ask what more Plancius could have attained, if he had been Cn. Scipio's son.' (Direct: either *quid adsecutus esset?* or *quid adsequi potuit?*).

Historic sequence: Cic. *Fam.* 1, 9, 13 (*malui*) *declarari quanta vis esse potuisset in consensu bonorum, si iis pro me pugnare licuisset.* 'I preferred it to be made clear what effective support there would have been in the unanimity of loyal citizens, had they been allowed to fight for me.' (Direct: *quanta vis fuisset?* or . . . *esse potuit?*); Livy 10, 45, 3 *subibat cogitatio animum quonam modo tolerabilis futura Etruria fuisset, si quid in Samnio adversi evenisset.* 'It occurred to them to wonder how it would have been possible to cope with Etruria, if any reverse had been suffered in Samnium.' (Direct: *quonam modo tolerabilis . . . fuisset?*).

When the passive form is required, or when the verb has no future participle, then the periphrasis with *possum* is used, if the sense required admits of 'could have' or 'might have' as opposed to 'would have'. Sometimes the context admits of the idea of necessity, in which case the gerundive with *fuerim* (*fuissem*) may be used. E.g. 'I wonder how the camp *would have been defended,* (had not reinforcements arrived)' admits of either *Miror quomodo castra defendi potuerint,* or *quomodo defendenda fuerint.* If neither *possum* with the infinitive nor the gerundive expresses quite the right shade of meaning, then the original pluperfect subjunctive is allowed to remain, as in Cic. *Sest.* 62 *quod ille si repudiasset, dubitatis quin ei vis esset adlata?* 'Had he rejected this, do you doubt but that violence would have been done to him?'.

Examples such as the following, where a periphrasis was readily available, are rare: Cic. *Inv.* 2, 120 *permultum proficiet demonstrare quemadmodum scripsisset, si id intellegi voluisset.* 'It will be of great advantage to show how he would have written, if he had wished that to be understood.' Here we should have expected *quemadmodum scripturus fuerit.*

Note. These periphrases for the past potential subjunctive are employed not only in indirect questions, but also in any clause which already requires the subjunctive for some other reason, e.g. in consecutive clauses, or in a *cum*-clause, or in a clause which is in *O. O.* In all except indirect questions and *cum*-clauses, the sequence of tenses is usually disregarded, the perfect subjunctive being used in the periphrasis (*-urus fuerim . . . potuerim*), whatever the tense of the governing verb.

XV

The Conjunctions Quominus *and* Quin. *Clauses after Verbs of Fearing*

184. *Quominus.* The origin of this conjunction has been explained in Section 150. Although *quominus* (or *quo . . . minus*) may introduce ordinary Final clauses, as in Ter. *Eun.* 150, quoted in Section 150, it is mostly used after verbs and expressions of hindering, opposing, and preventing, such as *impedio, prohibeo, teneo* (and compounds), *mihi non tempero; terreo* (and compounds), *obsto, recuso, repugno, resisto; excipio* (in sense of 'exempt from'); *causa est, per me stat:* Cic. *de Sen.* 60 *aetas non impedit quominus litterarum studia teneamus.* 'Age does not hinder us from maintaining this study of literature.' *Id. Fam.* 12, 5, 1 *hiemem credo adhuc prohibuisse quominus de te certum haberemus.* 'I think the winter-weather has so far prevented us from having sure news of you.' (But *prohibeo* is more often followed by an accusative and infinitive.) Caes. *B. G.* 4, 22, 4 *naves vento tenebantur quominus in portum venire possent.* 'The ships were held by the wind from being able to come into harbour' (*or* 'so that they could not . . .' Here the *quominus*-clause is consecutive rather than final). Val. Max. 8, 9, 2 *fertur non temperasse sibi quominus exclamaret . . .* 'He is said not to have restrained himself from crying out . . .' Cic. *T. D.* 1, 91 *non deterret sapientem mors quominus rei publicae consulat.* 'Death does not deter a wise man from consulting the interests of the state.' *Id. N. D.* 1, 95 *quid obstat quominus sit beatus?* 'What stands in the way of his happiness?' *Id. Fin.* 1, 7 *non recusabo quominus omnes mea legant.* 'I shall not object to everyone's reading my works.' *Id. Verr.* 2, 187 *lege excipiuntur tabulae publicanorum quominus Romam deportentur.* 'The accounts of the tax-farmers are exempted by law from being brought to Rome.' Sall. *Cat.* 51, 41 *hanc ego causam quominus novum consilium capiamus in primis magnam puto.* 'I think that this reason for not taking any new resolution is particularly strong.' Caes. *B. C.* 1, 41 *Caesar cognovit per Afranium stare quominus proelio dimicaretur.* 'Caesar realized that the responsibility for there being no battle rested with Afranius.'

Note. All the above verbs and expressions may be followed by *ne*, when they are not negatived, and by *quin*, when they are. It will be observed that *quominus* may be used in either case. There seems to be no fixed principle determining an author's choice between *ne* and *quominus*, on the one hand, and between *quominus* and *quin*, on the other. All the same, when *ne* is used, the idea of intention is usually clear; when *quin* is used after a negative, the clause is one of result rather than purpose.

185. *The Conjunction* Quin

Quin is the old instrumental case of the interrogative, indefinite, and relative stem *qui-* with the negative *-ne* attached. The original sense of 'how not?', 'why not?', can be seen in such independent sentences as *Quin venis?* 'Why don't you come?' Plaut. *Mil.* 426 *Quin ego hoc rogem?* 'Why should I not ask this?' Such independent questions, particularly of the repudiating deliberative type, would often be followed by a denial of any objection or hindrance, such as *Nulla causa est*, 'there is no reason'; *non dubito*, 'I do not doubt it'; or *non possum teneri*, 'I cannot be restrained'. Then the question became dependent on the negative statement, and *quin* became a subordinating conjunction, as in *Nulla causa est quin hoc rogem*, 'There is no reason why I should not ask this'; *Non possum teneri quin hoc faciam*, 'I cannot be restrained from doing this'. Similarly from *Quin hoc verum sit? Non dubito*, 'Why should not this be true? I do not doubt it', we get *Non dubito quin hoc verum sit*, 'I do not doubt but that this is true'.

This origin accounts for the fact that, up to the time of Tacitus, *quin* is used as a conjunction only when the clause on which it depends is negatived.

186. When the use of *quin* as a subordinating conjunction extended and became a formula, the deliberative origin of the subjunctive was obscured, and in some expressions *quin* acquired the force of a relative adverb equivalent to *quominus* or *ut non* (occasionally to *qui non*), in which the subjunctive must be regarded as consecutive. This development had already taken place in early Latin, e.g. Plaut. *Most.* 329 *non cades quin* (= *ut non*) *cadam tecum.* 'You will not fall without my falling with you'; *Id. Stich.* 208 *curiosus nemo est quin* (= *qui non* or *ut non*) *sit malevolus.* 'No one is inquisitive without being an ill-wisher.' Nevertheless, in classifying examples, it seems best to begin with those in which the interrogative origin of *quin* is tolerably clear, as after denials of doubt or hindrance. Having acquired the sense of 'but that' or 'that not' in these, *quin* probably spread to expressions denying possibility (*fieri non potest*), and finally to other negative expressions after which it is equivalent to *ut non.*

187. *Examples and Notes*

(*a*) After negative verbs and expressions denying objection, hindrance, prevention, or analogous extensions of these, either *quominus* or *quin* may be used. *Quominus* is the commoner, except after the following: *me non teneo; non possum teneri* (*contineri, retineri*)*; non deterreo; nullam moram interpono; non recuso:*

Plaut. *Rud.* 1172 *contineri quin complectar non queo.* 'I cannot be restrained from embracing her.' *Id. Amph.* 559 *quin loquar nunquam me potes deterrere.* 'You can never frighten me from speaking.' Cic. *Ac.* 1, 1 *nullam moram interponendam putavimus quin videremus hominem.* 'We thought that no delay ought to be allowed to intervene in seeing the man.' *Ibid.* 2, 7 *non possumus quin alii a nobis dissentiant recusare.* 'We cannot object to others disagreeing with us.'

Other verbs and expressions of similar meaning are followed occasionally by *quin*, when negatived: Caes. *B. G.* 3, 23, 7 *non cunctandum existimavit quin pugna decertaret.* 'He thought he ought not to delay in fighting an action.' *Ibid.* 1, 33, 4 *neque sibi homines feros temperaturos existimabat quin in Italiam contenderent.* 'He did not think the barbarians would restrain themselves from making for Italy.' Livy 26, 40, 4 *nec quin erumperet prohiberi poterat.* 'Nor could he be prevented from breaking out.'

Note i. When not negatived, these verbs usually imply purpose, and are naturally followed by a clause introduced by *ne* or *quominus*: Cic. *Off.* 3, 100 *sententiam ne diceret recusavit.* 'He objected to expressing his opinion.' *Id. in Caec.* 33 *potuisti prohibere ne fieret.* 'You could have prevented it from happening.' *Ne* is commoner than *quominus* in early Latin and in Caesar.

Note ii. As *non recuso* is practically equivalent in sense to *volo*, it is sometimes followed by a prolative infinitive instead of a subjunctive clause: Caes. *B. G.* 3, 22, 3 *neque repertus est quisquam qui mori recusaret.* 'Nor was there found anyone who refused to die.'

Note iii. With *prohibeo* neither Caesar nor Cicero uses *quin.* Its commonest construction, whether positive or negative, is an accusative and infinitive, as with *veto*: Cic. *T. D.* 5, 103 *num ignobilitas sapientem beatum esse prohibebit?* 'Surely ignoble birth will not prevent a wise man from being happy?' *Id. Verr.* 5, 117 *parentes prohibentur adire ad liberos.* 'Parents are prevented from approaching their children.'

Other verbs of preventing, such as *deterreo, impedio,* are only rarely found with the infinitive.

(*b*) *Quin* introduces an indirect question clause after negative expressions of doubting and reasoning, such as *nulla causa est, non dubito, dubitari non potest, dubium non est, controversia non est, non ambigitur,* and the like. From these it is even extended occasionally to negatived verbs of speaking and knowing, such as *non nego, non dico, non ignoro,* in place of the usual accusative and infinitive: Plaut. *Capt.* 353 *numquae causa est quin viginti minas mihi des?* 'Is there any reason why you should not give me twenty minae?' Cic. *Br.* 71 *non dubitari debet quin fuerint ante Homerum poetae.* 'It ought not to be doubted but that there were poets before Homer.' *Id. Cael.* 11 *controversia non erat quin verum dicerent.* 'There was no dispute but that they were telling the truth.' Caes. *B. G.* 1, 4, 4 *neque abest suspicio quin ipse sibi mortem consciverit.* 'Nor is there lacking a suspicion that he committed suicide.' Livy 40, 36, 1 *respondit se negare non posse quin rectius sit exercitum mitti.* 'He replied that he could not deny that it would be better for an army to be sent.' Cic. *Flacc.* 64 *quis ignorat quin tria Graecorum genera sint?* 'Who is unaware that there are three kinds of Greeks?' Caes. *B. C.* 3, 94, 3 *neque vero Caesarem fefellit quin initium victoriae oriretur.* 'Nor did it escape Caesar's detection that the dawn of victory was arising.'

Note. Dubito in the sense of 'hesitate' takes a prolative infinitive: Cic. *Fin.* 1, 62 *sapiens non dubitat migrare de vita.* 'A wise man does not hesitate to depart from life.' In the sense 'to be in doubt (whether)', it introduces an indirect question, which may be either a question of fact or deliberative, e.g. *dubito num venturus sit,* 'I doubt whether he will come', or *dubito num veniam,* 'I doubt whether I should (ought to) come'. Hence *non dubito* followed by *quin* with a deliberative sometimes appears to be used in the sense of 'not to hesitate': Cic. *Att.* 8, 11b, 3 *non dubito quin ad te statim veniam.* 'I do not doubt but that I must come to you at once.' Caes. *B. G.* 2, 2, 4 *tum vero dubitandum non existimavit quin ad eos proficisceretur.* 'Then in truth he did not think he ought to doubt but that he must set out to them.'

On the other hand *non dubito* in the sense 'not to doubt' is sometimes followed by an accusative and infinitive, on the analogy of verbs of knowing and perceiving: *Nep.* 17, 3, 1 *non dubitans hostes impetum facturos,* 'not doubting that the enemy would make an attack'. Nepos always uses the accusative and infinitive after *non dubito* in this sense, Livy quite often, other authors rarely.

(*c*) *Quin* is used after the impersonal expression *non multum abest* (or *nihil, non longe, non procul, paulum, minimum, quid abest*): Cic. *Att.* 13, 15, 3 *nihil abest quin sim miserrimus.* 'Nothing is wanting for me to be most wretched.' Caes. *B. C.* 2, 35, 4 *neque multum afuit quin castris expellerentur.* 'Nor were they far from being expelled from the camp.'

Quin here introduces a noun-clause standing as subject to *abest* or *afuit,* which is therefore impersonal. It is to be noted that the use of *quin* in some of these expressions is illogical, for, in the last example, what was not far away was 'their expulsion', and one would have expected *ut.*

(*d*) *Quin* is an alternative to *ut non* after *facere non possum*, 'I cannot help (but) . . .'; *fieri non potest*, 'It cannot be (but that . . .)': Cic. *Att.* 12, 27, 2 *facere non possum quin cotidie ad te mittam litteras.* 'I cannot help but send you a letter every day.' *Id. Verr.* 5, 104 *fieri nullo modo poterat quin Cleomeni parceretur.* 'It was quite impossible but that Cleomenes should be spared.' But cp. *Id. de l. agr.* 2, 7 *neque ullo modo facere possum ut non sim popularis.* 'Nor can I by any means avoid being democratic.' *Id. Fin.* 1, 27 *fieri nullo pacto potest ut non dicas* . . . 'It is quite impossible for you not to say . . .'

(*e*) *Quin* introduces a negative descriptive or consecutive clause after negative pronouns such as *nemo, nihil,* and after negative adverbs such as *nunquam, nusquam*: Cic. *Fin.* 5, 63 *nemo est quin probet.* 'There is no one but approves.' Caes. *B. G.* 6, 39, 3 *nemo est tam fortis quin perturbetur.* 'No one is so brave that he is not perturbed.' Plaut. *Pers.* 690 *nihil mihi tam parvi est quin me id pigeat perdere.* 'Nothing is of so little value to me, but it irks me to lose it.' Ter. *Eun.* 791 *nunquam accedo quin abeam doctior.* 'I never approach you without departing more learned.' Cic. *Verr.* 4, 95 *nunquam tam male est Siculis quin aliquid facete dicant.* 'Things never go so ill with the Sicilians, but they pass some witty remark.' Caes. *B. G.* 5, 55, 1 *nullum tempus intermiserunt quin legatos mitterent.* 'They left no interval without sending (in which they did not send) envoys.'

In the above sentences *quin* appears to be equivalent either to *ut non* or to an indeclinable relative pronoun. It will be noticed that it is often equivalent to that idiomatic use of *ut non* which is best translated by 'without' and a verbal noun in '-ing', e.g. Sen. *Dial.* 2, 7, 5 *possum pedes movere ut non curram: currere non possum ut pedes non moveam.* 'I can move my feet without running: I cannot run without moving my feet.' In the negative sentence *quin* could be substituted for *ut . . . non.*

In sentences like *nemo est quin probet, quin* appears to be equivalent to *qui non,* which might in fact be used. But it is doubtful whether *quin* was any longer felt to contain a pronoun, since it stands for any gender or case (*quae non, quod non, quo non,* etc.), and the demonstrative pronoun is often added: Caes. *B. C.* 2, 19, 2 *nulla fuit civitas quin* (= *quae non*) *Caesari pareret.* 'There was no community but was obedient to Caesar.' Cic. *N. D.* 3, 30 *nihil est quin* (= *quod non*) *intereat.* 'There is nothing that does not perish.' Nep. 18, 11, 5 *non cum quoquam arma contuli quin is mihi succubuerit.* 'I have not measured swords with anyone, but he has succumbed to me.'

188. *Verbs of Fearing*

The origin of the construction used with verbs and expressions of fearing has been explained in Section 138. That the subordinate clause developed out of the parataxis of an expression of Wish introduced by *ut* or *ne* is supported by the fact that in early Latin *ut*, to express a fear that something may *not* happen, is four times commoner than *ne non*, though by the time of Cicero these proportions are reversed.

Fears about the present or future are expressed by the present subjunctive, if the governing verb or expression is primary, and by the imperfect subjunctive, if the governing verb or expression is historic. Fears about the past are expressed by the perfect subjunctive, if the governing verb is primary, and by the pluperfect subjunctive, if the governing verb is historic: Plaut. *M. G.* 1348 *metuo et timeo ne hoc tandem propalam fiat.* 'I fear and dread that this may at length come out.' *Id. Curc.* 464 *ornamenta metuo ut possim recipere.* 'I fear I may not be able to recover the trinkets.' Ter. *Andr.* 349 *id paves, ne ducas tu illam; tu autem, ut ducas.* 'Your fear is lest you marry her, and yours, lest you do not.' Plaut. *Cas.* 575 *metuo ne non sit surda atque haec audiverit.* 'I fear that she may not be deaf and that she has heard this.' Cic. *Leg. Agr.* 2, 58 *hoc foedus veretur Hiempsal ut satis firmum sit.* 'Hiempsal fears that this treaty will not be sufficiently respected.' *Id. Att.* 6, 4, 2 *vereor ut satis diligenter actum sit de litteris meis.* 'I fear that not sufficiently careful consideration has been given to my despatch.' Ter. *Andr* 582 *veritus sum ne faceres idem quod volgus servorum solet.* 'I was afraid that you would do the same as the general run of slaves is wont to do.' Caes. *B. G.* 1, 39, 6 *rem frumentariam, ut satis commode supportari posset, timere dicebant.* 'They said they had fears about their corn-supply, that it might not be able to be brought up conveniently enough.' Plaut. *Pseud.* 912 *metuebam ne abiisses.* 'I was afraid that you had gone away.'

Note i. To express fear for the future in clauses after verbs and expressions of fearing, there is normally no need of the periphrastic subjunctive (*-urus sim, essem*), any more than in Final clauses. In the few examples that occur, either the context is such that the simple form would cause some ambiguity in the time-reference, or else the future participle appears to be there in its own right, to express intention or likelihood: Matius *ap. Cic. Fam.* 11, 28, 8 *non vereor ne meae vitae modestia parum valitura sit in posterum contra falsos rumores.* 'I am not afraid that the moderation of my life will prove ineffective for the future against false reports.' (The context would allow *valeat* to refer to the present, though the insertion of *in posterum* would have been sufficient.) Cic. *Verr.* 5, 163 *verebatur ne populus Romanus ab isto eas poenas vi repetisse videretur, quas veritus esset ne iste legibus et vestro iudicio non esset persoluturus.* 'He was afraid that the Roman people might be thought to have exacted by violence that penalty which it had feared the defendant was not *destined to pay* to the laws and to your court.' (Here *persolveret* would cause no ambiguity, but the participle *persoluturus* contains a subtle reminder that the senatorial courts had a popular reputation for acquitting senatorial offenders.)

Note ii. Additional clauses depending on the same verb of fearing are usually joined by *et* (*-que, atque*), or *aut*, or *aut ne*, or by *ne . . ., ne . . .*, in asyndeton: Cic. *Leg.* 1, 12 *vereor ne, dum minuere velim laborem, augeam, atque ad illam causarum operam adiungatur haec iuris interpretatio.* 'I am afraid that, while wishing to lessen my labour, I may increase it, and that to my service in the courts may be added this interpreting of the law.' Caes. *B. C.* 1, 66, 2 *veriti ne noctu confligere cogerentur aut ne ab equitatu Caesaris tenerentur.* 'Fearing that they might be compelled to fight by night, or that they might be held up by Caesar's cavalry.'

One might have expected the regular connexion to be *neve* (*neu*), as in Final clauses, but this appears to be confined to early Latin, and to come in again with Livy: Plaut. *M. G.* 996 *metuo ne obsint neve obstent.* 'I fear that they will hinder me and get in my way.' Livy 3, 16, 2, etc.

189. The subordinate clause expressing fear need not depend on an actual verb of fearing such as *metuo, timeo, vereor*, etc., but may be introduced by almost any expression that contains the idea of apprehension, anxiety, worry, or danger, such as *timor incessit, cura est, periculum est, religio est*, etc. After such expressions *ut* is not used to express a negative fear, but always *ne non*: Livy 24, 42, 2 *pavor ceperat milites ne mortiferum esset vulnus Scipionis.* 'Panic had seized the soldiers, lest Scipio's wound was mortal. *Id.* 25, 32, 6 *illa restabat cura, ne alter Hasdrubal et Mago bellum extraherent.* 'The following anxiety remained, lest the other Hasdrubal and Mago should prolong the war.' *Id.* 4, 31, 4 *cum religio obstaret, ne non posset nisi ab consule dici dictator, augures consulti eam religionem exemere.* 'When a religious scruple stood in their way, lest a dictator could not be appointed except by a consul, the augurs when consulted removed that scruple.'

Sometimes there is no directly governing verb or expression at all, but the clause of fearing, introduced by *ne*, modifies the whole sentence adverbially, and depends on a general idea of anxiety inherent in the context: Plaut. *Capt.* 127 *ad captivos meos visam, ne quippiam turbaverint.* 'I will go and see my prisoners, in case they have created some disturbance.' Cic. *Verr.* II, 1, 46 *verbum facere non audebant, ne forte ea res ad Dolabellam ipsum pertineret.* 'They did not dare to utter a word, in case the matter touched Dolabella himself.'

190. As has been indicated in Section 23, verbs of fearing such as *metuo, timeo, vereor*, may be followed by a prolative infinitive, in the sense of 'to fear to do something'. This is a regular construction.

On the other hand, these verbs and expressions are occasionally treated as verbs of thinking or perceiving, and are followed by the accusative and infinitive accordingly: Livy 10, 36, 3 *abiissent, ni cedenti instaturum alterum timuissent.* 'They would have departed, had they not feared that the other party would attack the one retreating.' (For *ne instaret.*) *Id.* 7, 39, 4 *haud dubius timor incessit animos consilia sua emanasse.* 'No uncertain fear assailed their minds that their plans had leaked out.' (For *ne emanassent.*) Also

23, 14, 8, and fairly often in Livy. The only certain example in Cicero is *de Or.* 2, 334 *vincit utilitas plerumque, cum subest ille timor, ea neglecta ne dignitatem quidem posse retineri.* 'Expediency usually gains the upper hand, when there is the underlying fear that, if it is neglected, neither can dignity be retained.'

XVI

Conditional Clauses

191. Conditional clauses are subordinate adverbial clauses which express a hypothesis or condition under which the statement (question, command, or wish) of the main clause holds good. They are usually introduced by the conjunctions 'if' and 'unless' in English, and by *si* and *nisi* in Latin. The main clause is called the 'Apodosis', and the subordinate or 'if'-clause the 'Protasis'.

Open Conditions: The protasis may suppose or concede a fact, without any implication of denial that the fact is true, as 'If he said this (which is uncertain), he made a mistake': *Si hoc dixit, erravit*; or 'If anyone did wrong, he used to be punished': *Si quis peccaverat, poenas dabat*; or 'Even if he said this (which he did), I still do not believe it': *Etiam si hoc dixit, tamen non credo.* Such conditions are called 'Open', and the verb of the protasis will be in the indicative in Latin, just as in English, whatever the mood of the apodosis. The verb of the apodosis need not be in the indicative, because it need not contain a statement, e.g. 'If he did this, may he be punished!': *Si hoc fecit, utinam poenas det!*

Note. Alternative protases leading to the same apodosis are joined by *sive* (*seu*), lit. 'or if', usually repeated, e.g. Cic. *Att.* 12, 12, 2 *sive habes quid, sive nihil habes, scribe tamen.* 'Whether you have something, or whether you have nothing, write all the same.' When two protases are opposed and lead to different results, the second is usually introduced by *sin* or *sin autem*: Sall. *Jug.* 10, 6 *vobis regnum trado firmum, si boni eritis, sin mali, imbecillum.* 'I bequeath you a kingdom that will be strong, if you behave well, but weak, if you behave ill.'

192. *Conditions implying Denial:* on the other hand, the protasis may suppose, not a fact, but an imaginary condition, with the implication that it has not, or not yet, been fulfilled. The main clause will then normally contain a potential statement of what *would happen*, *would be happening*, or *would have happened*, were the imaginary condition fulfilled: e.g. 'If he said this (which he has not done yet), he would make a mistake'; 'If he said this (which he does not), he would be making a

mistake'; 'If he had said this (which he did not), he would have made a mistake'. The meaning of the apodoses in these sentences is usually expressed by the tenses of the potential subjunctive dealt with in Sections 118 ff. The subjunctive is also required in the protases, though here it is probably of different origin. Imaginary conditions are called, for want of better terms, 'Ideal', if they refer to the future, so that they may yet be realized, and 'Unreal', if they refer to the present or past, so that they are no longer capable of fulfilment. The tenses of the subjunctive required, according to classical usage, are the present, the imperfect, and the pluperfect respectively, so that the Latin for the above sentences would be: *Si hoc dicat, erret. Si hoc diceret, erraret. Si hoc dixisset, erravisset.*

193. It will be seen from the simple examples in the preceding sections that the Latin idiom in conditional clauses is much clearer than the English. The Latin for 'If he said this' may be *Si hoc dixit, dicat*, or *diceret*, according to the context. Therefore it cannot be insisted too strongly that, in order to interpret a conditional clause correctly, it is necessary to consider the apodosis first. For learning classical Latin usage, the following summary of the eight normal types of conditional clause may be found useful:

Type	*Ordinary vague English*	*Exact Meaning*	*Latin*
1. Present Particular.	If he says this, he makes a mistake.	If he is now saying this (which is uncertain), he is making a mistake.	*Si hoc dicit, errat.*
2. Present General.	If he says this, he makes a mistake.	Every time that (whenever) he says this, he makes a mistake.	*Si hoc dicit, errat.*
	If he sees a rose, he thinks spring is beginning.	Whenever he sees a rose, he thinks spring is beginning.	*Si rosam vidit, putat ver incipere.*[1]
	If you say anything, it is believed.	Whenever one says anything, it is believed.	*Si quid dicas, creditur.*[2]
3. Present Unreal.	If he said this, he would make a mistake.	If he were now saying this (which he is not), he would be making a mistake.	*Sic hoc diceret, erraret.*[3]

[1] See Section 194. [2] Section 195. [3] See Section 197.

Type	*Ordinary vague English*	*Exact Meaning*	*Latin*
4. Past Particular.	If he said this, he made a mistake.	If he said (*or* was saying) this at (*or* during) a particular time in the past (but whether he did is uncertain), then he made (*or* was making) a mistake.	*Si hoc dixit (dicebat), erravit (errabat).*
5. Past General.	If he said this, he made a mistake.	Every time that (whenever) he said this, he was making a mistake.	*Si hoc dicebat, errabat.*
	If he did wrong, he was punished.	Whenever he had done wrong, he used to be punished.	*Si peccaverat, poenas dabat.*
	If he said anything, it was believed.	Whenever he had said anything, it used to be believed.	*Si quid dixisset, credebatur.* (Only from Livy on, see Section 196).
6. Past Unreal.	If he had said this, he would have made a mistake.		*Sic hoc dixisset, erravisset.*
7. Future 'Ideal'.	If he said this, he would make a mistake.	Should he, at some future time say this, (I suggest that) he would be making a mistake.	*Si hoc dicat, erret.*
8. Future, more vivid.	If he says this, he will make a mistake.	If he is going to say this, (I state emphatically that) he will be making a mistake.	*Si hoc dicet, errabit.*
	If he does this, he will be punished.	If he shall have done this, (I threaten that) he will be punished.	*Si hoc fecerit,* (fut. pf.), *poenas dabit.*

194. *Open Conditions, 'Particular' and 'General'*

From the examples in the above summary it will be seen that often only the context can determine whether a conditional clause and its apodosis have a particular or a general reference. So *Si hoc dicebat, errabat* can mean either 'If he was saying this on a particular occasion, he was making a mistake', or 'If he used to say this, he used to make a mistake'. In the generalizing type 'If anyone does (did) wrong, he is (used to be) punished', the idea of repetition obviously calls for a tense of incomplete action (present or imperfect) in the apodosis. But in the protasis, as the condition on which the repetition depends has first to be completed or fulfilled every time, then, in Latin, a tense of completed action (present-perfect or pluperfect) is normally used. Thus, from Plautus to Tacitus, the normal Latin for the above sentence would be: *Si quis peccavit (peccaverat), poenas dat (dabat).*

Examples: (*a*) *Particular:* Ter. *H. T.* 105 *erras, si id credis.* 'You are wrong, if you believe that.' Cic. *Cl.* 23 *redargue me, si mentior.* 'Refute me, if I am lying.' Ter. *H. T.* 631 *si peccavi, insciens feci.* 'If I did wrong, I did it unwittingly.' Cic. *Mil.* 30 *si id iure fieri non potuit, nihil habeo quod defendam.* 'If that could not be done justifiably, I have no defence to make.' *Id. Att.* 14, 1, 1 *Si ille exitum non reperiebat, quis nunc reperiet?* 'If he could not find a way out, who will find one now?' *Id. Sest.* 54 *Si meis incommodis laetabantur, urbis tamen periculo commoverentur.* 'If they were rejoicing at my discomfiture, yet they ought to have been moved by the danger to the city.'

It will be seen that it is not necessary for both the protasis and the apodosis to refer to the same time, but different tenses of the indicative may occur in each. Nor need the apodosis contain an indicative statement, for in the last example the apodosis contains a subjunctive of past obligation.

In colloquial Latin, as in English, a present indicative sometimes has a future reference: Ter. *Andr.* 210 *Si illum relinquo, eius vitae timeo.* 'If I leave him, I fear for his life.'

(*b*) *General:* Cato *pro Rh. si quis advorsus rem suam quid fieri arbitratur, summa vi contra nititur.* 'If (whenever) anyone thinks something is being done contrary to his interests, he opposes it with all his might.' Plaut. *As.* 143 *ea si erant, magnas habebas dis gratias.* 'If (whenever) you had those things, you used to be very thankful to heaven.' Cic. *T. D.* 2, 52 *si dens condoluit, ferre non possumus.* 'If we get the tooth-ache, we cannot bear it.' Ter. *Eun.* 403 *sicubi eum satietas hominum, aut negoti siquando odium ceperat, tum me convivam solum abducebat sibi.* 'If he became tired of people anywhere, or if ever a distaste for business seized him, then he would take me off with him as his sole companion.' Sall. *Jug.* 50, 6 *si ab persequendo hostes deterrere nequiverant, disiectos circumveniebant.* 'If they failed to deter the enemy from pursuing, they would surround them when they were scattered.'

Note. The tenses of the indicative are similarly used in generalizing relative or temporal clauses introduced by such relative pronouns and adverbs as *qui, quicumque, quisquis, cum, ubi, quoties, simul ac, ut quisque, etc.*: Cic. *Verr.* 5, 10 *cum rosam viderat, tum incipere ver arbitrabatur.* 'Whenever he saw a rose, he used to think spring was beginning.' Tac. *Ann.* 14, 35 *Boudicca, ut quamque nationem accesserat, solitum Britannis feminarum ductu bellare testabatur.* 'As she approached each tribe, Boudicca proclaimed that it was customary for the Britons to wage war under the leadership of women.'

195. *The Subjunctive in Generalizing Conditions*

In present 'general' *si*-clauses, and other clauses introduced by an indefinite relative word, the present subjunctive is used when the verb is in the generalizing or 'ideal' second person singular: Plaut. *Men.* 103 *standum est in lecto, si quid de summo petas.* 'It is necessary to stand on the couch, if you are seeking something from the top.' Cato *ap. Gell.* 11, 2, 6 *ferrum si exerceas conteritur; si non exerceas, rubigo interficit.* 'If you use iron, it is worn away; if you do not use it, rust destroys it.'

Although the indicative is occasionally found, this second singular subjunctive is the rule from Plautus to Tacitus.

This usage is probably connected with that attenuated use of the potential subjunctive which does not differ in sense from an indicative, except that it indicates that the speaker is reflecting on the matter. An English parallel is to be found in the use of the auxiliaries 'should', 'may', 'can', to express events that really take place and are not merely mental conceptions, as 'Should a ruler misgovern, he forfeits his authority', or 'Wherever you may go, you (may) see', meaning 'wherever you go, you *do* see'.: Plaut. *Aul.* 505 *nunc quoquo venias, plus plaustrorum in aedibus videas quam ruri.* 'Wherever you go nowadays you see more carts among the city-houses than in the country.' *Id. Cist.* 97 *si ames, extemplo melius illi quem ames consulas quam rei tuae.* 'If you are in love, you straightway consult the interests of him you love better than you do your own.'

It has been suggested that the subjunctive came into the subordinate clause originally by attraction from the main clause. It is noticeable, however, that when the person of the subordinate verb is not second singular, the indicative is retained: Plaut. *Bacch.* 914 *si non est, nolis esse neque desideres; si est, abstinere quin attingas non queas.* 'If you haven't one, you don't want one and don't miss it; if you have one, you cannot keep your hands off it.' *Id. Trin.* 671 *quom inopia est, cupias; quando eius copia est, tum non velis.* 'When something is scarce, you want it; when there is plenty of it, then you do not.' Conversely the indicative is used in the main clause, when the person is not second singular: Plaut. *Most.* 782 *quicquid imponas, vehunt.* 'Whatever you put on them, they carry.'

The importance of this idiom lies in the fact that it establishes a use of the subjunctive whereby it expresses facts, and not actions merely conceived. The mood here indicates, not that the actions expressed are hypothetical, but that the speaker is practising induction upon them and arguing from the particular to the general. The general conclusion is normally expressed in an indicative statement. This change in the modal force is also to be seen in descriptive clauses of fact (see Section 155).

196. The subjunctive in generalizing clauses containing an idea of repetition, whether introduced by *si* or other conjunctions, becomes common with other persons of the verb than the ideal second person only from Livy onwards. This development is commonest in historical narrative, and the normal tenses are the imperfect and pluperfect. The present and perfect remain rare throughout. The classical construction, with the indicative, by no means dies out, but by the Silver Age the indicative and the subjunctive seem to be employed indiscriminately: Livy 3, 38, 8 *si quis collegam appellasset, ab eo ad quem venerat ita discedebat ut paeniteret non prioris decreto stetisse.* 'If anyone appealed to another member of the board, he used to come away from the one he had approached regretting that he had not abided by the decree of the former.' *Id.* 21, 35, 2 *elephanti tutum ab hostibus, quacumque incederent, agmen praebebant.* 'The elephants kept the line of march safe from the enemy, wherever they advanced.' Tac. *Hist.* 2, 5 *Vespasianus, si res posceret, manu hostibus obniti.* 'Vespasian, if occasion demanded it, would struggle hand to hand with the enemy.'

Note. In generalizing temporal clauses this use of the subjunctive in a 'frequentative' sense is said to begin earlier with *cum* than with the other temporal conjunctions. For this reason it is usually regarded as due to the influence of 'narrative' *cum* with the subjunctive. But the evidence for this explanation seems to be derived from Cicero alone, in whom there are many examples of *cum* with the subjunctive in a frequentative sense, but no certain examples of other conjunctions. Yet the subjunctive in *si*-clauses, of which examples are given above, is obviously of the same kind, and it is found as early in *si*-clauses as in *cum*-clauses: Caes. *B. C.* 3, 110, 4 *si quis a domino prehenderetur, consensu militum eripiebatur.* 'If anyone was caught by his master, he would be rescued by the concerted action of the soldiers.' Also *B. C.* 2, 15, 2 *ubi imbecillitas materiae postulare videretur, pilae interponuntur.* 'Where(ever) the weakness of the material seemed to demand it, pillars were placed between.'

Neither can this development be attributed to an extension of the subjunctive in the generalizing second person, for the latter is used mainly in the present tense, while examples of the third person with reference to the present are extremely rare and do not occur before Caesar: *B. G.* 6, 11, 4 *suos opprimi non patitur, neque, aliter si faciat, ullam inter suos habet auctori-*

tatem. 'He does not suffer his dependents to be oppressed, nor has he any authority among his people, should he do otherwise.' (One example in Caesar and one in Sallust.) Tac. *Agr.* 13 *munera impigre obeunt, si iniuriae absint.* 'They zealously perform their duties, if injustices are not inflicted.' Sen. *Ep.* 5, 3 *nomen philosophiae, etiam si modeste tractetur, invidiosum est.* 'The name of philosophy is unpopular, even if it is handled with moderation.'

The most likely explanation is, not that the subjunctive in frequentative clauses is an extension of the subjunctive with narrative *cum*, but that both are an extension of the descriptive or generic subjunctive dealt with in Sections 155 ff.

197. *'Ideal' and 'Unreal' Conditions*

In early Latin, in the statement of hypothetical conditions, no clear distinction is made between what may yet happen and what is no longer capable of fulfilment. The present subjunctive is used both in the main clause and in the *si*-clause to express what would be the case, were certain conditions, not now in existence, to be fulfilled. It is left to the context to make clear whether future possibility is contemplated, or whether the thought is confined wholly to the present. In the following examples the reference is clearly to the present: Plaut. *Asin.* 188 *si nunc habeas quod des, alia verba praehibeas.* 'If you now had anything to give us, your language would be different.' *Id. Men.* 640 "*me rogas?*" "*haud rogem te, si sciam.*" 'Do you ask me?' 'I should not be asking you, if I knew.' Ennius *Tr.* 271 *deos non curare opinor quid agat humanum genus; nam, si curent, bene bonis sit, male malis, quod nunc abest.* 'I do not think the gods care how the human race is faring; for, if they cared, it would go well with the good and ill with the bad, which is not now the case.'

But just as often the reference is to the future, and it is implied that the content of the protasis is capable of realization. Quite often the context admits of either interpretation, as in Plaut. *Asin.* 458 *si sciat, suscenseat.* 'If he knew, he would be angry.'

When the action is thought of as completed in its entirety, the perfect subjunctive is used, whether in the protasis or apodosis: Plaut. *As.* 878 *possis, si conspexeris, cognoscere?* 'Would you be able to recognize him, if you had seen him?' *Id. Cas.* 424 *si nunc me suspendam, meis inimicis voluptatem creaverim.* 'If I were to hang myself now, I should find I had gratified my enemies.' Ter. *Hec.* 424 *aufugerim, si eo mihi redeundum sciam.* 'I should be off like a shot, if I knew I had to return thither.'

Nevertheless, the means to show that the thought was wholly confined to the present lay ready to hand in the inherent sense of the imperfect subjunctive, and was already being employed by Plautus: *Pseud.* 640 *si intus esset, evocarem.* 'If he were within, I should be calling him out.' However, the use of the imperfect subjunctive in 'present unreal' conditions is as yet less common in Plautus than the present subjunctive. By the time of Terence, the tense-shift has established itself, and the proportions are reversed. The imperfect subjunctive was able to have this reference to the present because it was a sort of 'future-in-the-past', expressing what *was to* happen, or what was bound to, destined to, or likely to happen. But that which was about to happen in the immediate past ought, in theory, to be in existence now. Hence the imperfect subjunctive could have reference to theoretical circumstances in the present, as in *Plaut. Cist.* 683 *si nemo hac praeteriit, cistella hic iaceret.* 'If no one has passed this way, the casket was bound to be, *or* should have been, *or* would be, lying here.'

The establishment of this new function of the imperfect subjunctive, to express present unreality, did not cause its old function of expressing past obligation, necessity, or likelihood, to become obsolete. Hence a new ambiguity arose, which caused a consequential tense-shift in the expression of past unfulfilled conditions. Henceforward the *pluperfect* subjunctive is normally employed in both members, to express what would have happened, had certain conditions been fulfilled in the past: Plaut. *Trin.* 927 *si appellasses, respondisset.* 'If you had called him, he would have replied.' But examples are not yet numerous in Plautus.

198. The use of the present (and perfect) subjunctive in conditions referring to the present, and of the imperfect subjunctive in conditions referring to the past, has not died out in classical Latin, but both become rarer as time goes on. The present subjunctive is still used with reference to the present, if the speaker or writer does not wish to rule out the idea of ultimate fulfilment: Cic. *Lael.* 38 *si rectum statuerimus concedere amicis quicquid velint . . ., perfecta quidem sapientia si simus, nihil habeat res vitii.* 'If we had decided it was right to yield friends whatever they wished, if we were of perfect wisdom, there would be no fault in the matter.' Here the argument is not yet concluded, and the decision is still in suspense. Livy 26, 49, 3 *ad sexaginta captos scripserim, si auctorem Graecum sequar.* 'I should have put the number captured at sixty, if I followed the Greek authority.' In the context Livy leaves the matter open, and makes no decision at all. The pluperfect and imperfect tenses here would imply that Livy had definitely rejected the Greek's version. It is also useful to compare the two following passages: Cic. *Cat.* 1, 19 *haec si tecum patria loquatur, nonne impetrare debeat?* 'If your country were to speak to you in this way, would it not be her due to gain her request?' *Id. in Caec.* 19 *Sicilia tota si una voce loqueretur, hoc diceret.* 'If the whole of Sicily spoke with one voice, she would say this.' In the former passage Cicero is suggesting the possibility that one's country may appeal to one, and is not excluding it. In the context of the latter passage he goes on to say that, since the whole province cannot speak for itself, it is necessary for it to choose a representative. Therefore he is careful to use the tense which does not admit the possibility.

As the present and the perfect subjunctive represent a hypothetical condition more vividly by not excluding the idea of fulfilment, they are found more frequently in poetry than in prose, in contexts where we should expect the imperfect and pluperfect, e.g. Virg. *Aen.* 2, 598–600 *quos omnes undique Graiae/circumerrant acies, et ni mea cura resistat,/iam flammae tulerint inimicus et hauserit ensis.* 'Round them all on every side the Grecian troops are roaming, and did not my care withstand them, the flames would have taken them off ere now, and the enemy sword devoured them.'

199. The use of the imperfect subjunctive in past unreal conditions, whether in protasis, apodosis, or both, continues to be common up to the time of Livy, but becomes less common thereafter. It is said that the imperfect is preferred to the pluperfect, when it is desired to express a supposed state, or continuous action, but the sense 'was destined to', 'was likely to', can usually still be seen: Ter. *H. T.* 230 *si mihi secundae res de amore meo essent, iam dudum, scio, venissent.* 'If I was destined to have any luck in my love-affair, it would have come long ago, I know.' *Id. Ad.* 103 *haec non sivit egestas facere nos, nam si esset unde id fieret, faceremus.* 'It was poverty that did not allow us to do these things, for if the means for doing them had existed, we should have done them' (*or* 'were like enough to do them'). Cic. *Clu.* 80 *at tum si dicerem, non audirer.* 'But if I had spoken then, I was not likely to be (should not have been) heard.' *Id. Ph.* 8, 14 *num igitur eum, si tum esses, temerarium civem aut crudelem putares?* 'Would you then, if you had been living in those days, have thought him a rash or cruel citizen?' (*or* 'were you likely to think . . .?'). *Id. Arch.* 16 *si nihil litteris adiuvarentur, nunquam se ad earum studium contulissent.* 'If they were likely to derive no benefit from literature, they would never have betaken themselves to the study of it.' Caes. *B. C.* 3, 111, 4 *quas si occupavissent, mare totum in sua potestate haberent.* 'If they had seized these (ships), they would have had (were likely to have) the whole sea in their power.' Livy 9, 19, 5 *Persas, Indos, aliasque Alexander si adiunxisset gentes, impedimentum maius quam auxilium traheret.* 'If Alexander had attached to him the Persians, Indians, and other nations, he was likely to be dragging about with him a greater hindrance than help.' *Livy* 21, 5, 11 *centum milia fuere, invicta acies, si aequo dimicaretur campo.* 'There were a hundred thousand of them, an invincible army, if the battle were to be fought on the level plain.'

From the above examples it will be seen that the imperfect subjunctive usually represents the past point of view of someone looking forward. Sometimes it comes near to being a subjunctive of virtual *oratio obliqua*, as in the last example. This is particularly clear when the place of the apodosis is taken by a future participle, as in at least half of the few examples quoted from Tacitus, e.g. *Hist.* 3, 54 *si liceret, vere narraturi*, 'likely to tell the truth, had they been allowed'. *Ibid.* 56 *si consulerentur, vera dicturis*, 'likely to tell the truth, had they been consulted'. (The centurions seem to be represented as saying to themselves: *si consulemur, vera dicemus.*) Examples are very few in which the imperfect does seem to be used to denote merely a longer-continued action than that which would be expressed by the pluperfect, as Sall. *Jug.* 59, 3 *neque diutius Numidae resistere quivissent, ni pedites . . . magnam cladem facerent.* 'Nor would the Numidians have been able to resist any longer, had not the infantry been wreaking great slaughter.'

200. *The Indicative in the Apodosis of 'Unreal' Conditions*

The indicative is often used in the apodosis of unreal conditions under the following circumstances:

(i) Modal verbs with the infinitive, such as those mentioned in Sections 122–5, express ideas analogous to those of the potential subjunctive. So also do the future participle and the gerundive participle with a past tense of the verb 'to be'. Such verbs and expressions in the apodosis of an unreal condition normally remain in the indicative: Plaut. *Curc.* 449 *in cavea si forent conclusi, . . . ita non potuere uno anno circumirier.* 'Had they been cooped up in a cage, even so it would not have been possible to go round them in a year.' Livy 7, 7, 9 *neque sustineri poterant, ni extraordinariae cohortes se obiecissent.* 'They could not have been withstood, had not the detached cohorts interposed themselves.' Tac. *Agr.* 31 *nisi felicitas in socordiam vertisset, exuere iugum potuere.* 'Had not their success turned to sloth, they might have cast off the yoke.' Cic. *Ph.* 2, 99 *eum contumeliis onerasti quem patris loco, si ulla in te pietas esset, colere debebas.* 'You loaded with insults him whom you should have reverenced as a father, had there been any natural feeling in you.' Plaut. *Cist.* 152 *si tacuisset, tamen ego eram dicturus.* 'If she had kept silent, nevertheless I should have told you.' Livy 2, 38, 5 *si unum diem morati essetis, moriendum omnibus fuit.* 'If you had delayed for a single day, you must all have perished.'

(ii) The imperfect tense is often used of a movement attempted or begun, but not finished, e.g. Cic. *Lig.* 24 *veniebatis in Africam . . . prohibiti estis in provincia pedem ponere.* 'You *were for coming* into Africa, but you were prevented from setting foot in the province.' Livy 7, 17, 12 *orta contentio est quod duo patricii consules creabantur.* 'A dispute arose because *a movement was afoot to* elect two patrician consuls.' In this conative or inceptive sense *faciebam* is almost equivalent to *facturus eram*, and accordingly the imperfect indicative, like *-urus eram*, is sometimes found in the apodoses of unreal conditions: Cic. *Leg.* 1, 52 *labebar longius, nisi me retinuissem.* 'I was slipping further, had I not caught myself up.' *Id. Verr.* 5, 129 *si per L. Metellum licitum esset, matres illorum miserorum sororesque veniebant.* 'If it had been allowed by L. Metellus, the mothers and sisters of those wretched men were for coming.' Tac. *Ann.* 1, 65 *Caecina delapsus circumvenieba-*

tur, ni prima legio sese opposuisset. 'Caecina fell and was in a way to be surrounded, had not the first legion interposed itself.'

As *labebar, veniebant, circumveniebatur,* in the above examples, express facts independent of the condition, the usual explanation of the idiom is that the real apodosis (*et lapsus essem,* etc.) is suppressed and understood. This explanation is supported by an example like Nep. 18, 2, 3 *eum interficere conatus est, et fecisset, nisi ille effugisset.* 'He tried to kill him, and would have done it, had not the man escaped.'

(iii) A pluperfect indicative in the apodosis is sometimes due to the suppression of the real apodosis, the indicative expressing an independent fact, but sometimes also to sheer rhetorical exaggeration, whereby what might have happened is vividly presented as a fact: Livy 2, 22, 1 *Volsci comparaverant auxilia quae mitterent Latinis, ni maturatum ab dictatore Romano esset.* 'The Volsci had made ready reinforcements to send to the Latins, had not hurried measures been taken by the Roman dictator.' (Understand *et misissent.*) Cic. *Fam.* 12, 10, 3 *praeclare viceramus, nisi fugientem Lepidus recepisset Antonium.* 'We had won a famous victory, had not Lepidus given asylum to the flying Antonius.' Livy 3, 19, 8 *nisi Latini arma sumpsissent, capti et deleti eramus.* 'Had not the Latins taken up arms, we had been captured and destroyed.' Hor. *Odes* 2, 17, 27 *me truncus illapsus cerebro/sustulerat, nisi Faunus ictum/dextra levasset.* 'A treetrunk falling on my head had made an end of me, had not Faunus lightened the blow with his right hand.'

(iv) The adverbs *paene* and *prope* give a quasi-potential sense to the indicative: Plaut. *Pers.* 594 *paene in foveam decidi, ni hic adesses.* 'I nearly fell into a pit, had not you been at hand.' Livy 2, 10, 2 *pons Sublicius iter paene hostibus dedit, ni unus vir fuisset.* 'The Sublician bridge nearly gave an entry to the enemy, had it not been for one man.'

(v) If the *si*-clause is granting a concession, the indicative in the apodosis may be quite natural: Cic. *Sull.* 68 *etiam si quis dubitasset antea, sustulisti hanc suspicionem.* 'Even if anyone would have doubted before, you have removed this suspicion.'

XVII

The Gerund and Gerundive

201. The gerund is a verbal noun which corresponds generally with the English verbal noun in *-ing*, as in *corpus currendo exercetur,* 'The body is exercised *by running*.' Like the infinitive and supine, it governs the same case as the verb from which it is formed, and is not qualified by an objective genitive: *petendo pacem,* 'by seeking peace'; *parendo parentibus,*

'by obeying parents'. It is always *active* in sense. It is *never* used in the nominative case, and in the accusative only when governed by a preposition. Its nominative, and also the accusative of the object, is supplied by the infinitive.

It will be seen that the Latin gerund is not parallel to that English verbal noun in *-ing*, which may be qualified by an adjective or the article, which may be used as a nominative subject, and which may be followed by an objective prepositional phrase with 'of', e.g. '*The taking of the town* ended the war.'

202. The gerundive is a verbal adjective, i.e. a kind of participle. It is *passive* in sense, and may be used either with reference to the future, as in *pax petenda est*, 'Peace is to-be-sought', *vir laudandus*, 'a man to-be-praised', or as a present participle passive, as in *pace petenda*, 'by peace *being sought*'. The latter usage, which is a development whereby the gerundive adjective replaced the gerund with an object, obscures the passive sense, for 'by peace being sought' is equivalent to 'by seeking peace'.

The agent with the passive gerundive is normally expressed by the dative: *pax nobis petenda est*, 'Peace is to be sought by us'. The dative denotes the person for whom the necessity exists, and a more literal rendering would be 'Peace is for us to seek'.

203. *The Gerundive expressing Necessity*

It is doubtful whether the passive sense of the gerundive was original, for the gerundival forms of some intransitive verbs survive, and these can be only active in sense, e.g. *secundus* (from *sequor*), 'following'; *oriundus*, 'originating'; *moribundus*, 'dying'; cf. also Livy 3, 3, 10 *consul per agrum populabundus ierat*. 'The consul had gone *ravaging* through the territory.' So, too, *volvendus* is used by Ennius and Virgil in the intransitive sense of 'rolling': *clamor volvendus per aethera*, 'a shout rolling through the heavens'.

However, the adjectival suffix in *-ndus*, when attached to the root of a transitive verb, had acquired a passive sense before extant Latin literature begins, so that, except for isolated survivals such as those mentioned above, only the gerundive of transitive verbs can be used in agreement with a noun. This then indicates that the person or thing qualified is capable of suffering or fit to suffer the action of the verb. *Vir laudandus* means 'a man fit-to-be-praised'. The implication is that the action of praising has not yet taken place, therefore *laudandus* is future in tense. When the gerundive is predicated with the verb 'to be', there develops from the idea of 'fitness' the sense of *necessity*, so that *vir laudandus est* means 'The man is to be (*or* must be) praised'.

When the gerundive is thus used in agreement with a noun, it is said to be used *personally*, or in the *personal construction*. Clearly the personal construction is confined to gerundives of transitive verbs.

204. *The Gerundive used Impersonally*

The gerundive of an intransitive verb can be used impersonally in the neuter. *Currendum est* means 'Running is to-be-done', or 'There is running to do', or 'One must run'. The noun of which the adjective *currendum* is predicated is the idea of 'running' contained in the root of the verb, and the construction is parallel to the impersonal passives *curritur, cursum est.*

Note i. This neuter gerundive used impersonally is not to be mistaken for a gerund, which may have had a different origin. The gerundive existed in other Italic dialects, but the gerund was a peculiarly Latin development said to have arisen from the attachment of the post-position *-do*, meaning 'towards' or 'at', to the accusative of the verbal root-noun. Thus *agen-do* or *agun-do* would mean 'towards acting' or 'in acting'. It looked like a dative or ablative noun, and so was given an accusative and genitive inflexion also, but some unconscious inhibition prevented it from being used as a nominative noun. However, its form was similar to that of the gerundive adjective, so that the Romans themselves were deceived, and the two forms influenced each other's constructions.

Note ii. In early Latin the impersonal construction is still found with the gerundive of transitive verbs, as Plaut. *Trin.* 869 *agitandum est vigilias.* 'One must keep watch.' Here the impersonal passive *agitandum* governs an accusative object ('action is to be taken *with regard to* watching'). By the time of Plautus this impersonal construction was already being replaced by the personal construction, and Plautus himself would normally say *agitandae sunt vigiliae.* When the construction occurs in later poets, such as Lucretius and Catullus, it is an archaism: Lucr. 1, 111 *aeternas quoniam poenas in morte timendum est.* 'Since one must fear after death eternal punishment.' There is an isolated example in Cicero: *de Sen.* 6 *viam quam nobis quoque ingrediendum sit,* 'the road which we, too, must tread, (for the more usual *viam quae . . . ingredienda sit*). Possibly Cicero is intentionally archaizing, since he is writing in the character of Laelius, who lived a century before his time. There are no examples in Caesar, Sallust, Livy, or Tacitus.

205. *The Uses of the Gerund*

The cases of the gerund of intransitive verbs are used freely in all periods of Latin. The gerund of a transitive verb governing an accusative object is rare in classical Latin, but common in early and colloquial Latin (see Section 206 and note ii below):

(*a*) Accusative (only after prepositions, mostly *ad* or *in*, occasionally *inter* or *ob*): Cic. *Br.* 92 *nulla res tantum ad dicendum proficit quantum scriptio.* 'Nothing gives so much help towards speaking as writing.' (Cicero probably uses the nominative verbal noun *scriptio* here to balance *nulla res.* Instead he might have used the infinitive *scribere,* but not the gerund *scribendum,* which is never nominative.)
(*b*) Genitive: Cic. *Fin.* 1, 42 *sapientia ars vivendi putanda est.* 'Wisdom is to be considered the art of living.' Ter. *Ph.* 885 *eludendi occasio est senes.* 'There is an opportunity of fooling the old men.'

The objective genitive after adjectives such as *cupidus, studiosus, peritus,* etc., is very common: Ter. *Hec.* 283 *cupidus redeundi,* 'desirous of returning'.
(*c*) Dative: (Rare, though it occurs after verbs and expressions requiring the dative, and there are a few examples of the 'dative of the end aimed at'): Plaut. *Ep.* 605 *Epidicum operam quaerendo dabo.* 'I will give my attention to looking for Epidicus.' Vitr. 2, 1, 3 *struebant parietes vitandoque imbres tegebant arundinibus.* 'They would construct walls, and for keeping out showers would cover them with reeds' Livy 21, 54, 1 *equites tegendo satis latebrosum locum,* 'a sufficiently shady spot for concealing horsemen'.

There are a few idiomatic phrases in which the dative of the gerund or gerundive is used predicatively, e.g. *esse solvendo,* 'to be solvent' (lit. 'to be for paying'); *adesse scribendo,* 'to be present at the signing of a contract', i.e. 'to witness a hand'; *esse censui censendo,* 'to come under assessment' (of goods); *esse oneri ferendo,* 'to be capable of bearing a burden'.
(*d*) Ablative: (Both the bare instrumental ablative and the ablative with prepositions such as *ab, ex, de, in,* are very common): Plaut. *Amph.* 1014 *sum defessus quaeritando.* 'I am tired with asking.' Cic. *Off.* 1, 105 *hominis mens discendo alitur et cogitando.* 'The mind of man is nourished by learning and thinking.' Plaut. *Trin.* 1048 *male fidem servando abrogant fidem.* 'By keeping faith ill they destroy confidence.' *B. Afr.* 82, 1 *in circumeundo exercitum animadvertit* . . . 'In reviewing the army he noticed . . .' Cic. *Fin.* 1, 5 *de bene beateque vivendo disputare,* 'to argue about living well and happily'.

A gerund in the instrumental ablative is sometimes used so vaguely that it is almost equivalent to a present participle in agreement with the subject: Livy 8, 17, 1 *consules populando usque ad moenia pervenerunt.* 'The consuls in plundering came right up to the walls', *or* 'came a-plundering'. Here *populando* almost = *populantes.*

206. *The Gerundive replacing the Gerund*

It will be noticed that the majority of the examples in Section 205 of a transitive gerund with an accusative object are from early authors, or from such as do not rank as strictly classical. Already by the time of Plautus it was becoming the custom to replace the gerund by the gerundive adjective in agreement with the noun. Instead of *fidem servando* one began to say *fide servanda*. It is impossible to dissociate this change from the development of the idiom described in Section 95, whereby a participle or adjective in agreement may have the force of a noun-phrase or noun-clause. Just as *fides servata* might mean 'the keeping of faith', or 'the fact of faith having been kept', so *fides servanda* might mean 'the (prospective) keeping of faith'. So *fide servanda* came to mean 'by the keeping of faith', which is indistinguishable in sense from *fidem servando*.

Once this stage had been reached, the accidental likeness in form of the gerund to the gerundive, together with the natural tendency of an inflected language towards agreement, made it inevitable that the gerundive should supersede the gerund in phrases of this sort. A careful and educated writer saying *ad fidem servandum* would feel uneasy, for the form *servandum* might be the accusative masculine of the gerundive as well as the accusative of the gerund, while *fides* is feminine. How, then, could he help preferring *ad fidem servandam*, if the meaning was the same in either case?

Hence it came about that, in the literary language, from about the time of Cicero onwards, the gerundive in agreement almost completely ousted the gerund with an accusative object, except under special circumstances (see Note ii, below). The gerund continued to be used, however, in the common language of the people and by less careful writers. This is shown by the fact that the gerund survived into the Romance languages (*en chantant* = *in cantando*), while the gerundive did not.

Note i. The adoption of this idiom caused the gerundive's sense of futurity or fitness to be obscured in this particular kind of phrase, and also its passive nature is obscured, since the phrase as a whole is equivalent to an active expression: *castris capiendis* means 'by the camp being taken' = 'by taking the camp'. The gerundive now includes the idea of progressive as well as prospective action, but not of action completed: Plaut. *Poen.* 224 *aggerunda aqua sunt defessi.* 'They are tired by (continually) bringing water.' It is not, therefore, synonymous with a past participle in agreement, e.g. it would not be used to express the idea 'He terrified the enemy *by capturing* their camp' (*captis castris terruit hostem*), if the action was viewed as a completed historic event. The gerundive is correct only when the action is (or was) in progress or repetitive or contemplated: Livy 28, 19, 2 *Iliturgitani prodendis qui ad eos perfugerant interficiendisque scelus etiam defectioni addiderant.* (I.e. they had betrayed *every* refugee and the action was repetitive.)

Note ii. The prevalence of the gerundive construction over the gerund with an object varies according to the author and period. In general it may be said that the gerund with an accusative object is archaic and post-classical, except under the following circumstances: (*a*) When the object is a neuter pronoun or adjective: Cic. *Inv.* 1, 36 *consilium est aliquid faciendi excogitata ratio.* 'A plan is a thought-out method of doing something.' *Id.*

de Or. 2, 289 *subabsurda dicendo et stulta reprehendendo risus moventur.* 'Laughs are raised by saying incongruous things and by castigating foolish things.' Livy 1, 46, 7 *initium turbandi omnia a femina ortum est.* 'The beginning of the throwing of all things into confusion came from a woman.'

In the above sentences *stultis reprehendendis, turbandorum omnium,* would obscure the gender and cause real ambiguity. When, however, a neuter adjective has come to be used as a noun, e.g. *verum,* 'the truth', *falsum,* 'a falsehood', the gerundive may be used: Cic. *Fin.* 2, 46 *veri videndi cupiditas,* 'desire for seeing the truth'. But there are isolated examples of the gerundive with neuter adjectives and pronouns, where no ambiguity is caused.

(*b*) Some authors, notably Caesar, seem sometimes to use the gerund in the genitive when the object is plural, in order to avoid the heavy *-orum . . . -orum* or *-arum . . . -arum* caused by the gerundive: Caes. *B. G.* 1, 52, 3 *ut spatium pila in hostes coniciendi non daretur,* 'so that space was not allowed for hurling their javelins against the enemy'. But this is by no means a rule, for cf. *B. G.* 3, 6, 2 *in spem potiundorum castrorum venerant.* 'They had conceived the hope of taking the camp.' So also *B. G.* 4, 24, 1, and fairly often. Cicero rarely avoids the genitive plural of the gerundive.

(*c*) Of the gerund with an object used in preference to the gerundive in other cases than the genitive there are only isolated examples in classical Latin. When the gerund is so used, it seems intended to stress the verbal notion: Cic. *in Caec.* 60 *iniurias ferendo maiorem laudem quam ulciscendo mererere.* 'You would have earned more credit by *bearing* your wrongs than by *avenging* them.' Here *iniuriis ferendis . . . ulciscendis* could not make the same point, because the gerundives, being adjectives, are not independent words, and cannot carry the same weight as the gerunds.

Note iii. In early Latin, during the period of transition, and more rarely in later authors, examples such as the following are found: Plaut. *Capt.* 852 *nominandi istorum tibi erit magis quam edundi copia.* 'You will have the privilege of naming those things rather than of eating them.' *Ibid.* 1008 *lucis das tuendi copiam.* 'You give me the privilege of seeing the light.' Cic. *Phil.* 5, 6 *facultas agrorum suis latronibus condonandi,* 'the opportunity of bestowing lands on his fellow-bandits'.

The explanation that *istorum, lucis, agrorum,* are objective genitives depending on the gerund treated as an ordinary verbal noun may be rejected at once, for there are no examples of the gerund with a genitive except when the gerund itself is in the genitive. An alternative suggestion is that each genitive depends separately on the nouns *copia, copiam, facultas,* since one could say either *das copiam lucis,* or *das copiam tuendi.* Furthermore it is urged that the assimilation of the genitive gerund to the other genitive in these particular expressions turned the gerund into a gerundive adjective, much as assimilation turned the old infinitive in *-urum* into the declinable future participle (Section 104), and that this was the beginning of this gerundive construction. Against this it must be pointed out that it could not have happened without the previous development of the *post urbem conditam* construction, which could itself account for the change independently of any particular case-usage. Finally, this explanation does not account for examples of confusion in other cases than the genitive: Cic. *de Dom.* 1, 1 *ut religionibus sapienter interpretando rem publicam conservarent*, 'that they might safeguard the commonwealth by wisely interpreting religious duties'. Livy 2, 60, 5 *patribus ex concilio submovendo*, 'by removing the patricians from the assembly'. (It is useless to look up these examples in an edition without an apparatus, because editors emend them away, though without mss. authority). Clearly the true explanation of all these examples is that they are due to ungrammatical conflation of the two constructions. The authors have fallen between two stools.

207. *Summary of the Uses of the Gerundive*

(1) Attributive: The use of the gerundive as an epithet is not very common and is mainly confined to verbs of emotion such as *amo*, *metuo*, *contemno*, etc. It is practically equivalent in sense to the adjectives in *-bilis*: Cic. *Har. Resp.* 62 *nuntiatur terrae motus cum multis metuendisque rebus.* 'An earthquake was reported accompanied by numerous and fearful phenomena.' *Id. Off.* 1, 153 *rerum expetendarum fugiendarumque scientia*, 'the knowledge of things to be sought and things to be shunned'.

(2) Predicated with *esse* (any tense): In this use the gerundive always expresses the idea of future necessity. But for the introduction of the idea of necessity, it would form a periphrastic future passive tense parallel to the periphrastic future active formed by the participle in *-urus* with *sum.* The agent is expressed by the dative, or, under circumstances indicated in the note below, by *ab* with the ablative: (*a*) Personal Construction: Cic. *Font.* 36 *si Galli bellum facere conabuntur, excitandus nobis erit ab inferis C. Marius.* 'If the Gauls try to make war, we shall have to rouse C. Marius from the dead.' (*b*) Impersonal Construction: (This alone is possible with intransitive verbs, e.g. *pugnandum nobis est pro patria*, 'We must fight for our country', including those whose meaning is completed by a dative, ablative, or genitive): Cic. *de Sen.* 36 *nec vero corpori soli subveniendum est, sed menti.* 'Nor is the body only, but the mind to be aided.' *Id. N. D.* 3, 1 *obliviscendum est nobis iniuriarum acceptarum.* 'We must forget injuries we have received.' *Id. Off.* 1, 91 *est utendum consilio amicorum iisque tribuenda auctoritas.* 'The advice of friends is to be used and authority attributed to them.' (On *utendum est* see note on (3) below.)

Note. A sentence such as *amico mihi subveniendum est* would be ambiguous, for it would not be clear which is to be the aider and which the aided. In such a case the agent is expressed by *ab* with the ablative: *amico a me subveniendum est:* Cic. *Planc.* 78 *ei ego a me referendam gratiam non putem?* 'Am I not to think that the favour ought to be returned to him by me?'

But when the second dative denotes a thing, not a person, so that no ambiguity can arise, or if the context leaves no doubt as to which dative denotes the agent, then the dative of the agent remains: Cic. *Verr.* 3, 103 *moderandum mihi est orationi meae.* 'I must moderate my speech.' *Id. de Or.* 1, 105 *gerendus est tibi mos adulescentibus.* 'Young men must be humoured by you.'

(3) Used predicatively in agreement with the object of verbs such as *do, peto, curo,* etc.: Plaut. *Bacch.* 338 *diviti homini id aurum servandum dedit.* 'He gave that gold to a rich man to keep.' (Lit. 'to be kept', but it is more natural to use the active form of the equivalent predicative infinitive in English.) Plautus uses the gerundive thus predicatively after the following verbs: *do, adduco, peto, rogo, conduco* ('hire'), *loco* ('let'). Terence adds *habeo* and *curo:* Ter. *Phorm.* 305 *ibi agrum de nostro patre colendum habebat.* 'He had there a piece of land from my father to farm.' Cicero and subsequent authors extend the usage to many other verbs, e.g. *concedo, defero, denoto, mitto, posco, me praebeo, relinquo, suscipio, trado,* etc.: Caes. *B. G.* 1, 13, 1 *Caesar pontem in Arare faciendum curat.* 'Caesar arranged for the building of a bridge over the Arar.' Nep. 18, 13, 4 *Antigonus Eumenem mortuum propinquis eius sepeliendum tradidit.* 'Antigonus handed over the dead Eumenes to his relations to bury.' *Id.* 15, 4, 1 *Epaminondam pecunia corrumpendum suscepit.* 'He undertook the bribing of Epaminondas with money.'

Note. The intransitive deponents *utor, fruor, fungor, potior, vescor,* whose sense in classical Latin is completed by an instrumental ablative, had in early Latin begun to be used transitively. Hence they had acquired a passive gerundive *utendus, fruendus,* etc., used personally in agreement. These can be used predicatively as above, but they are never predicated with *esse* to form the periphrastic conjugation. For the latter only the impersonal construction was used, i.e. one can say *ad hanc rem utendam,* 'for using this thing', or *hanc rem tibi utendam do,* 'I give you this thing to use', but NOT *haec res utenda est.* For the latter one must say *hac re utendum est.* (Cf. Cic. *Off.* 1, 91, in (2) (*b*) above.) The following are examples of the available uses: Plaut. *Mil.* 347 *meos oculos habeo nec rogo utendos foris.* 'I have my own eyes and do not ask for eyes from someone else to use.' Cic. *Off.* 1, 48 *ea quae utenda acceperis iubet reddere Hesiodus.* 'Hesiod bids one restore the things which one has received for use.' *Ibid.* 106 *tenendus est voluptatis fruendae modus.* 'Moderation must be kept in the enjoyment of pleasure.'

(4) Replacing the gerund with an object (as explained in Section 206): (*a*) Accusative (only after prepositions): Caes. *B. G.* 3, 19, 1 *ut quam minimum spatii ad se colligendos armandosque Romanis daretur,* 'in order that as little respite as possible might be allowed the Romans for recovering and arming themselves'. Plaut. *Cist.* 721 *inter rem agendam istam,* 'amidst the transacting of that business'. (But only the prepositions *ad* and *in,* ex-

pressing purpose, are common.) (*b*) Genitive: (The objective or quasi-objective is the commonest type, but see Note ii below): Cic. *T. D.* 4, 2 *ira est libido poeniendi eius qui videtur laesisse.* 'Anger is the lust for punishing him who is thought to have injured us.' The ablatives *causa* and *gratia* with the genitive gerundive are very common for expressing purpose: Caes. *B. G.* 4, 22, 1 *Caesar navium parandarum causa moratur.* 'Caesar delays for the purpose of preparing ships.' (*c*) Dative: (The dative is not so common as the other cases, but it will naturally be used after verbs or expressions requiring the dative, e.g. *operam dare, studere.* A dative of the 'end aimed at', from Livy onwards, is sometimes loosely attached to an adjective or noun, but is rare in classical Latin): Caes. *B. G.* 3, 4, 1 *ut rebus administrandis tempus daretur,* 'that time might be given to the administration of affairs.' *Ibid.* 5, 27, 3 (*dixit*) *omnibus hibernis Caesaris oppugnandis hunc esse dictum diem.* 'He said that this day had been appointed for attacking all Caesar's winter-camps.' (These are the only two examples in the *B. G.*) Livy 29, 21, 9 *mons pecori bonus alendo erat.* 'The mountain was good for nourishing a flock.'

Loose attachment of the dative gerundive to a noun, as in legal formulae like *duumviri sacris faciundis* is common in early Latin, rare in Caesar, Cicero, and Sallust, but fairly common in Livy and Tacitus.

(*d*) Ablative: (Both the instrumental ablative and the ablative with prepositions is common at all periods): Cic. *Off.* 2, 87 *de quaerenda, de collocanda pecunia, vellem etiam de utenda, a quibusdam optimis viris disputatur.* 'Discussion is held by certain excellent fellows on the acquiring and investing of money, and I could have wished also on the employment of it.' The gerundive equivalent of the vague ablative of the gerund which is equivalent to a present participle (Section 205 (*d*)) is rare, but does occur: Livy 3, 65, 4 *insectandis patribus tribunatum gessit.* 'He spent his tribunate in attacking the patricians.'

Note i. With personal pronouns, the genitives *mei, tui, sui, nostri, vestri,* with the gerundive in agreement, were commoner than the gerund with the accusative from the first. The gerundive always agrees with this neuter singular form, even when the sense is plural: Caes. *B. G.* 7, 43, 2 *legatos sui purgandi gratia mittunt.* 'They sent envoys for the purpose of clearing themselves.'

Note ii. A gerundive phrase in the 'Genitive of Description' (or 'Quality'), of the type mentioned in Sections 84, 85 (*c*), developed a sense of 'purpose' in some such way as follows. If for the adjective in a phrase like *res magni laboris,* 'a thing of great toil', i.e. 'involving great toil', a gerundive is substituted: *res evitandi laboris,* the sense is 'a thing involving, or connected with, the avoiding of labour', or 'a device *for* avoiding labour', with the implication of purpose. The sense of the genitive in such a phrase comes very close to that of the dative of 'the end aimed at': Livy 36, 27, 2 *pacis petendae oratores miserunt.* 'They sent spokesmen for the begging of peace', i.e. 'to beg for peace'. Sall. *Or. Phil.* 11 *arma cepit libertatis subvortundae.* 'He has taken arms for the overthrowing of liberty.'

These adjectival gerundive-phrases are predicative. Therefore, as explained in Section 88, they do not qualify *oratores, arma,* directly, but appositionally, cf. 'They sent envoys *as peace-makers*', 'He took up arms *as subversive weapons*'. These phrases, therefore, though they are in the genitive case as being grammatically adjective-equivalents, are adverbial in function and express the purpose of the action. It is not, therefore, surprising that, in the end, we find such genitive gerundive phrases used adverbially to qualify the action of the verb, without there being any noun or noun-equivalent expressed to which they can be grammatically attached: Tac. *Ann.* 2, 59 *Germanicus Aegyptum proficiscitur cognoscendae antiquitatis.* 'Germanicus set out for Egypt for the purpose of learning its antiquities.' There is no need to postulate the influence of the Greek *τοῦ* with the infinitive, to account for it (cf. Thuc. 1, 4 *τὸ ληστικὸν καθῄρει τοῦ τὰς προσόδους μᾶλλον ἰέναι αὐτῷ*), but it is noticeable that the usage is commonest in Sallust and Tacitus, who were undoubtedly students of Thucydides.

XVIII

Impersonal Verbs

208. Impersonal verbs are those which have no person-ending except the third singular. This does not mean that they have no 'subject', for the activity denoted by the third-personal verbal inflexion must be performed by someone or something, even if the speaker does not know what it is. As was suggested in Section 60, with reference to the impersonal passive of intransitive verbs, the subject may be assumed to be the noun implied in the root of the verb. With those impersonal verbs of active form which denote the activities of natural phenomena, such as *tonat,* 'it thunders'; *pluit,* 'it rains'; *ningit,* 'it snows'; *vesperascit,* 'the shades of evening fall'; etc., the subjects are 'thunder', 'rain', 'snow', 'evening', etc. If the augur takes it upon himself to attribute the activity to the deity, and says *Iuppiter tonat,* he is using the verb as a regular personal intransitive verb.

With impersonal verbs denoting the activity of the emotions, the sphere in which the emotion is exerting itself (i.e. the cause of the emotion) is expressed by the genitive, and the person affected by the emotion is expressed by the accusative (*piget me laboris,* 'the irksomeness of work affects me'). With some of these verbs, instead of the genitive, the cause of the emotion may be expressed by an infinitive, or other noun-equivalent, standing as subject: *pudet me mentiri*, 'it shames me to lie'.

Also classed as 'impersonal' are verbs which, though they are used only in the third singular, regularly have a subject expressed in the form of an infinitive, accusative and infinitive, or clause. With some of these the person concerned is expressed by the accusative (*oportet me ire*, 'It behoves me to go'), with others by the dative (*licet mihi ire*, 'It is permissible for me to go'). Examples of all these are given in the following sections.

209. The verbs which are constructed with the genitive of the thing causing the emotion, and the accusative of the person affected, are: *piget*, *pudet*, *paenitet*, *taedet*, *miseret*. As these verbs really mean 'fretfulness is at work', 'shame is at work', 'remorse is at work', 'weariness comes on', 'pity is at work', they obviously cannot be translated literally. With the exception of *paenitet*, all have, in addition to the perfect active form (*piguit*, *puduit*, *taeduit*, etc.), a deponent or impersonal passive form of the perfect. Cicero prefers *puditum est* to *puduit*, *pertaesum est* is commoner than *taeduit*, and *miseritum est* much commoner than *miseruit*. Besides the impersonal *miseret*, there is the personal form *misereor*, and also an impersonal passive *miseretur*. Examples: Cic. *de Dom.* 29 *me non solum piget stultitiae meae sed etiam pudet.* 'I am not only fretted by my stupidity, but actually ashamed of it.' *Id. Verr.* I, 1, 35 *sunt homines quos libidinis infamiaeque suae neque pudeat neque taedeat.* 'There are men who are neither ashamed nor tire of their licentiousness and infamy.' Sen. *Benef.* 6, 23, 1 *nunquam primi consilii deum paenitet.* 'God never repents of his first design.' Nep. 25, 15, 2 *nunquam suscepti negotii eum pertaesum est.* 'He never wearied of a business he had undertaken.' Plaut. *Tr.* 430 *me eius miseritum est.* 'I pitied him.' Cic. *Mil.* 92 *eorum nos miseret.* 'We pity them.' But the personal *misereor* is equally common: Cic. *Verr.* 1, 72 *aliquando miseremini sociorum.* 'Take pity some day on the allies.'

Note. The impersonal construction is very ancient. The impersonal third singular was the earliest form of the passive conjugation. Once transitive verbs and the personal forms of the passive had evolved, there was a natural tendency to bring all verbs into line by analogy. These impersonal verbs, therefore, are relics, and Vulgar Latin tended to suppress them. This tendency can be seen at work in examples like Ter. *Ad.* 754 *non te haec pudent?* 'Do not these things shame you?' Cicero only goes so far as to use a neuter pronoun occasionally as the subject: *T. D.* 5, 80 *sapientis est nihil quod paenitere possit facere.* 'It is the characteristic of a wise man to do nothing that can cause remorse.' (*paenitet me* can also mean 'I am dissatisfied with'; see Fraenkel's *Horace*, p. 5, footnote 6.)

210. *Impersonal Verbs with an Infinitive, Noun-phrase, or Noun-clause as Subject*

Of the verbs in the previous section which express emotion, *piget*, *pudet*, and *paenitet* are used with an infinitive, accusative and infinitive, or sometimes even an indicative *quod*-clause or indirect question-clause standing as subject: Cic. *de Sen.* 84 *neque me vixisse paenitet.* 'Nor do I repent of having lived.' *Id. T. D.* 1, 60 *nec me pudet fateri nescire quod nesciam.* 'Nor am I ashamed to confess that I do not know what I do not know.' Tac. *Ann.* 1, 73 *non piget referre . . .* 'It is not irksome to relate . . .' Cic. *Att.* 11, 13, 2 *ait se paenitere quod animum tuum offenderit.* 'He says he is sorry that he offended you.' (His words were: *Me paenitet quod . . . offendi*, 'The fact that I have offended you causes me remorse', though it would be possible to construe the *quod*-clause as causal and adverbial – 'I am sorry because I offended'). *Id. Off.* 1, 2 *te quantum proficias non paenitebit.* 'You will be satisfied with the extent of your improvement.'

Other impersonal verbs which take an infinitive, or accusative and infinitive, as subject, and the accusative of the person affected, are: *oportet*, 'it behoves'; *decet*, 'it becomes', 'befits' (and *dedecet*); *delectat*, 'it delights'; *iuvat*, 'it pleases': Cic. *T. D.* 4, 25 *oratorem irasci minime decet.* 'It is not at all becoming for a speaker to lose his temper.' (But *deceo* is also used personally, cf. Plaut. *Most.* 172 *contempla ut haec (vestis) me deceat.* 'See how this dress suits me.'). Cic. *Lael.* 49 *quam delectabat eum defectiones solis praedicere.* 'How it delighted him to foretell eclipses of the sun!'

In addition to their personal use, the following also are used impersonally in the third singular: *constat*, 'it is agreed'; *praestat*, 'it is preferable'; *apparet*, 'it is apparent'; *liquet*, 'it is clear'; *patet*, 'it is obvious': Caes. *B. G.* 1, 17, 3 *dicunt praestare Gallorum quam Romanorum imperia perferre.* 'They say it is better to endure the rule of the Gauls than of the Romans.' Ov. *Tr.* 1, 1, 62 *te liquet esse meum.* 'It is clear that you are mine.' *constat inter omnes hoc verum esse.* 'It is agreed among (by) all that this is true.'

Note i. Taedet does not seem to be used with the infinitive in classical prose, but there is an example in Terence, *Phorm.* 487 *taedet iam audire eadem miliens.* 'I am tired of hearing the same things a thousand times over.' But it is found in classical poetry and later prose.

Note ii. Many impersonal phrases consisting of a neuter adjective with *est* give a similar meaning and require the same construction as some of the above impersonal verbs, e.g. *manifestum est*, 'it is clear'; *veri simile est*, 'it is likely' or 'probable'. The latter can often be rendered by the English idiomatic use of the adverb, e.g. *veri simile est eum abiisse.* 'He has probably gone away.'

11. *Impersonal Verbs and Expressions with the Dative of the Person concerned*

The following impersonal verbs are followed by the dative of the person concerned, and have an infinitive or accusative and infinitive as subject: *licet* (*mihi ire*), 'it is allowable (for me to go)'; *libet* (*mihi ire*), 'it is agreeable (to me to go)' or 'it is my whim'; *placet* (*mihi ire*), 'it pleases (me to go)' or 'it seems good . . .', or 'I decide . . .'; *displicet*, 'it displeases'; *conducit*, 'it is advantageous'; *expedit*, 'it is expedient'; *prodest*, 'it benefits'; *obest*, 'it is disadvantageous'; *videtur*, 'it seems good', 'is one's decision' (cf. *placet*).

The verbs *accidit*, 'it happens'; *evenit*, 'it turns out'; *contingit*, 'it falls to one's lot', are followed by a dative of the person to whom the thing happens, but normally have a consecutive *ut*-clause standing as subject (see Section 168). An infinitive or accusative and infinitive is very rare with these verbs, unless they are modified by an adverb, e.g. Plaut. *Cist.* 309 *opportune mi evenit redisse Alcesimarchum.* 'It has happened luckily for me that Alcesimarchus has returned.' Also Cic. *pro Caec.* 8. More often, when an adverb is present, an indicative *quod*-clause stands as subject: Cic. *Att.* 1, 17, 2 *accidit perincommode quod eum nusquam vidisti.* 'It happens very inconveniently that you have seen him nowhere.' With *contingit* the infinitive is found in poetry: Hor. *Ep.* 1, 17, 36 *non cuivis homini contingit adire Corinthum.* 'It does not fall to every man's lot to reach Corinth.'

To impersonal verbs followed by the dative may be added many expressions consisting of a neuter adjective with *est*, e.g. *necesse est* (*mihi ire*), 'it is necessary (for me to go)'; *opus est*, 'there is need'; *consilium est* (*mihi ire*), 'it is (my) plan (to go)' (cf. *statuo*); *tempus est* (*mihi ire*), 'it is time (for me to go)'.

Examples: Cic. *Att.* 14, 19, 4 *Caerelliae facile persuasi mihi id, quod rogaret, ne licere quidem, non modo non libere.* 'I easily persuaded Caerellia that what she asked was not even permissible for me, much less agreeable.' (A neuter pronoun such as *id, hoc, illud*, may take the place of the infinitive as subject.) *Id. Ac.* 2, 99 *duo placet esse Carneadi genera visorum.* 'It is Carneades' theory that there are two types of phenomena.' Tac. *Ann.* 4, 19 *hos corripi placitum.* 'It was decided that these should be arrested.' (The dative of the person may be omitted or understood.) With *placet* also an *ut*-clause may stand as subject (cf. *constituo*): Caes. *B. G.* 1, 34, 1 *placuit ei ut ad Ariovistum legatos mitteret.* 'He decided to send envoys to Ariovistus.' Cic. *Phil.* 13, 8, 16 *omnibus bonis expedit salvam esse rem publicam.* 'It is expedient for (to the interest of) all loyal men that the republic should be safe.'

212. Notes on *licet:* (i) When a noun or adjective is predicated with the infinitive after *licet*, it is normally attracted into the dative of the person concerned. One does not normally find *licet mihi virum bonum esse*, but . . . *viro bono esse*, 'It is allowable for me to be a good man': Cic. *T. D.* 1, 33

licuit esse otioso Themistocli. 'It was allowable for Themistocles to be at leisure' (i.e. 'Themistocles might have been a private citizen'). Caes. *B. G.* 5, 41, 6 (*dicunt*) *licere illis incolumibus discedere.* 'They said they might depart unharmed.'

This 'dative attraction' with *licet* is regular at all periods of Latin. In poetry, and in prose from Livy onwards, it spreads to analogous expressions like *necesse est, dare,* 'grant', etc.: Livy 21, 44, 8, *vobis necesse est fortibus viris esse.* 'It is necessary for you to be brave men.' Hor. *Ep.* 1, 16, 61 *da mihi fallere, da iusto sanctoque videri.* 'Grant that I may deceive, grant that I may seem a just and pious man.'

(ii) An accusative and infinitive may stand as subject to *licet,* with or without the dative of the person for whom the thing is permissible. But *licet me ire* does not mean quite the same as *licet mihi ire.* The latter is more particular, and means 'I am permitted to go'. The former means 'My going is permissible', and the person to whom permission is granted for the event to take place is not stated: Cic. *Verr.* 5, 154 *non licet me isto tanto bono uti.* 'My use of that great advantage is not allowable.' Here *mihi* would give the wrong sense, for permission to do something is not being withheld from Cicero personally. He means that he cannot take advantage of a blunder on the part of the defence, because his own witnesses will refute their claim. The effect of the accusative and infinitive, instead of dative attraction, is similar, even when the dative of the person is expressed: Caes. *B. C.* 3, 1, 1 *is erat annus quo per leges ei consulem fieri liceret.* 'That was the year in which election to the consulship was permissible for him by law.' Here the reference is to the law permitting re-election to *anyone* after a certain interval, whereas *ei consuli fieri* would imply a special dispensation for Caesar personally. Cf. also Cic. *Balb.* 29 *civi Romano licet esse Gaditanum.* 'The acquisition of the citizenship of Cadiz is permissible for a citizen of Rome.' Here again the statement is general, and does not mean that Balbus in particular was permitted to become a citizen of Cadiz.

213. Refert *and* Interest

The impersonals *refert* and *interest,* 'It is important,' may have as subject: (*a*) a neuter pronoun, e.g. *id. hoc, illud, quid?* (*b*) an infinitive or accusative and infinitive; (*c*) a final *ut-* or *ne-*clause; (*d*) an indirect question clause. The person to whom the thing is important is, if expressed, denoted by the ablative singular feminine of the possessives *mea, tua, sua, nostra, vestra.* Only with *interest* the person may also be expressed by the possessive genitive of a noun or pronoun (*eius interest, Caesaris interest*). A thing concerned is expressed by *ad* with the accusative (*refert ad communem salutem,* 'It is of importance for the common safety'), though with *interest* the genitive is sometimes used of things also. The degree of importance is expressed either by an adverb, e.g. *magnopere, magis, maxime, vehementer*; or by adverbial neuter singulars such as *multum, parvum, plurimum, tantum,* *quantum, aliquantum, nihil, quid?* etc.; or by the genitives of value such as *magni, parvi, tanti, quanti, pluris, minoris.*

Examples: Plaut. *Cas.* 330 *quid id refert tua?* 'Of what importance is that to you?' Ter. *H. T.* 467 *illud permagni referre arbitror, ut ne scientem sentiat te id sibi dare.* 'I think that is of great importance, that he should not perceive that you are knowingly giving it to him.' Varr. *R. R.* 1, 16, 6 *refert ad fundi fructus quemadmodum vicinus consitum agrum habeat.* 'It is of importance to the produce of the estate how your neighbour has his field sown.' Cic. *Fin.* 2, 72 *interest omnium recte facere.* 'It is to the interest of all to do right.' Livy 24, 8, 17 *magis nullius interest quam tua, Tite Otacili, non imponi cervicibus tuis onus.* 'It concerns no one more than you, T. Otacilius, that the burden should not be placed on your shoulders.' Cic. *Fam.* 16, 1, 1 *magni ad honorem nostrum interest me venire.* 'It greatly concerns our honour that I should come.' *Id. Br.* 210 *magni interest quos quisque audiat cotidie.* 'It is of the greatest importance whom each man listens to every day.' *Id. Mur.* 4 *ostendam quantum salutis communis intersit duos consules in re publica Kalendis Ianuariis esse.* 'I will show how important it is for the common safety for there to be two consuls in the state on January 1st.' *Tac. Hist.* 1, 30 *vestra interest ne imperatorem pessimi faciant.* 'It is to your interest that the worst elements should not appoint the emperor.'

Sallust seems to be the first to use a genitive of the person with *refert: Jug.* 111, 1 *faciundum aliquid quod illorum magis quam sua retulisse videretur.* '(He said) something must be done which might seem to have been more to their interest than to his own.' There are a few examples in Livy, but it is mostly Silver Latin.

Note. The most reasonable explanation of this strange construction is that it began with *mea res fert*, 'my interest involves'. By the apocope of final *s* in early Latin, this came to be pronounced *rēfert.* The first syllable was then thought to represent an ablative, and the last syllable of *mea* (or *tua, sua,* etc.) was lengthened to agree with it. Hence, to indicate the person concerned, with *refert,* there was no precedent for any forms other than *mea, tua,* etc. The genitive of the person came to be used only later, on the analogy of the construction of *interest,* since the verbs were now synonymous in the sense of 'it matters'.

Interest, to begin with, meant 'there is between', i.e. 'there is a difference between (e.g. whether you do this or that)'. So *interest* came to mean 'it makes a difference', 'it is important', and thus becoming synonymous with *refert,* it borrowed *mea, tua,* etc., from the latter. But with *interest* the construction was further extended by the introduction of the genitive of nouns and pronouns to express the concern of a third person. By the period of Silver Latin, *refert* has in turn borrowed this extension from *interest.* With both the use of *ad,* to indicate a thing concerned, is borrowed from *attinet.*

Caesar uses only *interest,* and Cicero prefers it.

XIX

Temporal Clauses

214. Temporal clauses are adverbial clauses which answer the questions 'when?' or 'for how long?' or 'up to what point of time?' or 'since when?' They fix the time of the action of the main verb by indicating another action, event, or state *after* which, *at the same time as* which, or *before* which the action of the main verb takes, took, or will take place.

The subordinating conjunctions which introduce temporal clauses are relative adverbs, or adverbial phrases, of Time, of which the antecedents are often omitted. As temporal clauses have the effect of *comparing* the time of two events, they have some affinity with Comparative Clauses (Chapter XXII), and this accounts for the fact that some of the conjunctions dealt with below are compounded with the comparative conjunction *quam*, 'than'. Again, a temporal clause may suggest circumstances because of which, or even in spite of which, the main action took place; e.g. 'He did this when I asked him' implies '*because* I asked him', and 'He did this when he knew it was wrong' implies '*although* he knew it was wrong'. It was chiefly the conjunction *cum* which developed the latter two senses, but they are sometimes latent in temporal clauses introduced by other conjunctions.

215. *Temporal Clauses indicating 'Time after which'*

The conjunctions which introduce clauses indicating an event *after* which the action of the main verb takes place are the following: *postquam* (or *posteaquam*, or *post . . . quam*, or *postea . . . quam*), 'after (that)'; *ubi*, 'when'; *ut*, 'as', 'when'; *simulac* (*simul atque*), 'as soon as'; *cum*, 'when'. To these may be added the phrases *cum primum*, *ut primum*, 'at the first moment that', and *quotiens*, 'as often as'.

The commonest of all is *cum*, but this requires separate treatment (see Chapter XX). Of the rest, *postquam* is probably the next commonest.

The verb in clauses introduced by all these conjunctions except *cum* is regularly in the *indicative* mood. This is natural, since the action is usually one which has really taken place before the action of the main clause, and it is difficult for any other idea than that of time-relation to enter in.

All tenses of the indicative are found with one or other of these conjunctions, but not all with all. For example, *postquam* is never used with either the future or the future perfect, nor is it used to introduce generalizing clauses of repeated action. The commonest tense found with all these conjunctions is the aorist-perfect. This is probably due to the fact that the great bulk of prose literature is historical narrative.

It is to be observed that the aorist-perfect in the subordinate clause denotes an act already completed before the action of the main verb. The pluperfect indicative is used only when it is necessary to emphasize the priority (see Section 217 (2)).

216. *Postquam*, like *ante-* and *priusquam*, is a compound conjunction consisting of the adverb *post*, 'after' or 'later', and the conjunction *quam*, 'than'. Very often it is written as two words, with *post* modifying the main verb, while *quam* is the conjunction that introduces the temporal clause: *hoc post fecit quam advenit*, 'he did this after (later than) he arrived'. This division usually occurs when *post* is qualified by an Ablative of the Measure of Difference, or when there is an Ablative of Time present, marking the interval between two events: *tribus post diebus mortuus est quam domum pervenerat*, 'he died three days after he had arrived home' (lit. 'he died later by three days than he had arrived'. For the pluperfect here, see Section 217 (2)). Cf. Caes. *B. G.* 1, 27, 3 *eo postquam Caesar pervenit, obsides poposcit.* 'After Caesar had arrived there, he demanded hostages.'

It is perhaps worth noting that the subject of the main verb is not often placed after the conjunction, i.e. inside the temporal clause, as in this example and so often in English. The more usual Latin order would be: *Caesar, postquam eo pervenit . . .*

Ubi was first an adverb of place. It still refers to place, when it is used as an interrogative or indefinite, i.e. *ubi?* = 'where?' and *sicubi* = 'if anywhere'. But as a relative adverb it normally means 'when', not 'where': Caes. *B. G.* 1, 7, 3 *ubi de eius adventu Helvetii certiores facti sunt, legatos ad eum mittunt.* 'When the Helvetii had been told of his arrival, they sent envoys to him.'

Ut is really an adverb of manner, cf. *ut?* = 'how?'. Even as a relative adverb, it usually refers to manner, i.e. *ut* normally means 'as' (= 'in the way in which'). Its temporal sense developed out of this, cf. Eng. 'He sang *as* he came' = 'while he came'. But as a temporal conjunction it was never so common as the rest: Caes. *B. C.* 3, 94, 5 *Pompeius, ut equitatum suum pulsum vidit, acie excessit.* 'When (as) Pompey saw his cavalry beaten, he left the line of battle.'

Simulac means literally 'at the same time . . . and'. The sense 'as soon as' developed out of a coordination such as *simul abiit atque hoc fecit*, 'he went away and did this at the same time', i.e. 'he went away as soon as, or the moment that, he had done this'. In a similar way *atque* came to be used as a subordinating, instead of a coordinating, conjunction in expressions of comparison, e.g. *idem atque*, 'the same *as*', *aliter atque*, 'otherwise *than*':

simulac domum pervenero, scribam ad te. 'As soon as I reach home, I will write to you.'

Sometimes *atque* is dropped and *simul* used by itself, as if it were a conjunction (cf. the parallel English use of 'after' and 'before' as conjunctions): Caes. *B. G.* 4, 26, 5 *nostri simul in arido constiterunt, in hostes impetum fecerunt.* 'Our men, as soon as they stood on dry land, charged the enemy.'

217. *Examples and Notes on the Tenses*

(1) Aorist-perfect: As indicated above, this is the commonest tense. The main verb itself must obviously be in a historic tense: Plaut. *Bacch.* 277 *postquam aurum abstulimus, in navem conscendimus.* 'After we had carried off the gold, we went on board ship.' Caes. *B. G.* 7, 82, 1 *Galli, postea quam propius successerunt, in scrobes delati transfodiebantur.* 'After the Gauls had approached nearer, they began to fall into the trenches and be impaled.' *Id. B. G.* 4, 12, 1 *ubi primum nostros equites conspexerunt, impetu facto celeriter nostros perturbaverunt.* 'The moment they caught sight of our cavalry, they charged and quickly threw our men into confusion.' Sall. *Jug.* 25, 6 *ille ubi accepit homines claros venisse, metu agitabatur.* 'When he heard that important personages had come, he began to be agitated with alarm.' Cic. *Fam.* 3, 10, 1 *ut me collegi, cetera mi facillima videbantur.* 'When I had gathered my wits, the rest seemed to me very easy.' Nep. 16, 5, 3 *Pelopidas non dubitavit, simul ac conspexit hostem, confligere.* 'Pelopidas, as soon as he had caught sight of the enemy, did not hesitate to engage him.'

(2) Pluperfect: (*a*) With *postquam* the pluperfect is regular, when a definite interval of time is expressed by the ablative: Cic. *Div.* 2, 46 *signum Iovis biennio post, quam erat locatum, in Capitolio conlocabatur.* 'The statue of Jupiter was being erected on the Capitol two years after it had been contracted for.' *Id. Att.* 12, 1, 1 *undecimo die postquam a te discesseram, hoc litterularum exaravi.* 'I scribbled this bit of a note on the eleventh day after I had left you.'

When an interval of time is thus mentioned, the aorist-perfect is rare, though it does occur.

(*b*) If the main verb is itself pluperfect, the use of the pluperfect in the temporal clause is the only way of expressing the priority: Livy 24, 35, 4 *postquam ab Hippocrate occupatae Syracusae erant, facile perpulerat ut copiae in Siciliam traicerentur.* 'After Syracuse had been seized by Hippocrates, he had easily obtained that forces should be sent across to Sicily.' This would also apply to clauses introduced by *ubi, ut,* or *simulac.*

(*c*) In generalizing clauses of repeated action, i.e. when *ubi,* etc. means 'whenever', the pluperfect will be regular, as indicated in Section 194, Note. It is to be noted that *postquam* is not found in clauses of repeated action, but mostly *ubi* and *simulac* (and, of course, *cum*). *Ut* is only so used in combination with *quisque* or *quisquis*: Sall. *Jug.* 60, 3 *illi qui moenia de-*

fensabant, ubi hostes pugnam remiserant, intenti proelium equestre prospectabant. 'Whenever the enemy slackened the fight, those who were defending the walls eagerly watched the cavalry-battle.' Cic. *Verr.* 4, 47 *simulatque in oppidum quodpiam venerat, inmittebantur illi canes.* 'As soon as he came to any town, those hounds used to be let loose.' *Ibid.* 5, 143 *ut quisque istum offenderat, in lautumias statim coniciebatur.* 'Whenever anyone had offended the defendant, he used to be straightway cast into the stone-quarries.'

Similarly, for generalizing clauses in the present, the perfect indicative is the usual tense: Plaut. *Aul.* 198 *istos novi polypos qui, ubi quicquid tetigerunt, tenent.* 'I know those octopuses, who, when they touch anything, stick to it.' Cic. *ad Her.* 4, 24 *simulac fortuna dilapsa est, devolant omnes amici.* 'As soon as one's fortune has slipped away, all friends fly away.' But the present and imperfect tenses are used, if the action in the temporal clause is continuous, i.e. co-extensive and contemporaneous with that of the main clause: Plaut. *Pers.* 312 *vomica est, pressare parce; nam ubi qui mala tangit manu, dolores cooriuntur.* 'It's a boil, refrain from touching it, for whenever anyone is touching it with ungentle hand, pains arise.' Sall. *Jug.* 55, 4 *ubi frumento opus erat, exercitus partem Marius ducebat.* 'Whenever there was need of corn, Marius used to lead out part of the army.'

Note i. In present generalizing clauses, the present or perfect subjunctive is used of the 'ideal' second person (cf. Section 195): Sall. *Jug.* 31, 28 *bonus segnior fit, ubi neglegas.* 'A keen man becomes more apathetic, when you neglect him.' *Id. Cat.* 1, 6 *ubi consulueris, mature facto opus est.* 'When you have taken counsel, there is need of quick action.'

Note ii. The subjunctive of other persons began to be used in this generalizing sense from Livy on (see Section 196): Livy 1, 32, 13 (*Fetialis*) *id ubi dixisset, hastam in fines eorum emittebat.* 'When the fetial priest had said this, he used to hurl his spear into their territory.'

(*d*) The pluperfect indicative is sometimes used in the historians (Sallust, Livy, Tacitus) without any of the reasons given above, where one would normally expect the aorist-perfect: Sall. *Jug.* 11, 2 *postquam illi iusta magnifice fecerant, reguli in unum convenerunt.* 'After they had performed for him the proper obsequies in a magnificent manner, the chieftains met together.' All the same, the pluperfect does seem intended in such cases to stress the prior completion of the act in the temporal clause; e.g. in the above example, the princes would not think of conducting business, before the old king's funeral was properly over.

(3) Historic Present: This is rare, except in the historians, and then mostly with *ubi*. The verb in the subordinate clause is usually one of perceiving. The main verb may be in a historic tense, or itself in the Historic Present: Livy 21, 32, 2 *ubi deserta munimenta videt, ad naves rediit.* 'When he saw the fortifications deserted, he returned to the ships.' Sall. *Jug.* 76, 6 *postquam murum arietibus feriri vident, aurum atque argentum domum regiam*

comportant. 'When they saw the wall was being battered by the rams, they carried their gold and silver to the king's palace.'

(4) True Present, and Perfect with 'have': Neither of these tenses is very common, except in generalizing clauses (2) (*c*). Used of a 'particular' action, they seem always to make the conjunction mean 'now that', or 'since', either in the causal sense, or in the sense of 'time since when': Plaut. *Truc.* 919 *iamne abis, postquam aurum habes?* 'Are you going away, now that you have the gold?' *Id. Men.* 234 *hic annus sextus est, postquam ei rei operam damus.* 'This is the sixth year since we have been paying attention to that matter.' (Or, 'We have been paying attention for five years'). Tac. *Ann.* 14, 53 *octavus annus est ut imperium obtines.* 'This is the eighth year that (since) you have been holding the empire.'

(5) Imperfect: This tense is common only in the historians. It is rare both in early Latin and in Caesar and Cicero. It describes a continuing situation which accounted for the action of the main clause, i.e. it gives a quasi-causal sense. The main verb will normally be aorist-perfect or historic present: Caes. *B. G.* 7, 87, 5 *Labienus, postquam neque aggeres neque fossae vim hostium sustinere poterant, Caesarem facit certiorem.* 'Labienus, when neither mounds nor trenches were able to withstand the might of the enemy, informed Caesar.' There are no examples of the imperfect with *ubi* in Caesar, but see Livy 9, 45, 14 *ubi nemo obvius ibat, ad castra hostium tendunt.* 'When (as) no one was coming out to meet them, they proceeded to the camp of the enemy.' Cic. *Verr.* I, 1, 18 *ut Hortensius domum reducebatur e campo, fit obviam ei C. Curio.* 'As Hortensius was being escorted home from the campus, he was met by C. Curio.'

The imperfect tense denotes overlapping, and therefore contemporaneous rather than prior action. This is usually expressed by *dum* with the present indicative (Section 221), and may account for the imperfect being rare with *postquam, ubi, ut.* Not even Livy uses it with *simulac.*

(6) Future and Future Perfect: Neither of these tenses is used by classical authors with *postquam,* though there are examples of the future perfect in technical writers: Cato *R. R.* 65, 1 *post diem tertium quam lecta erit, facito.* 'Make (the oil) three days after (the olive) has been picked.' Varro, *R. R.* 1, 63 *aliquanto post promere quam aperueris oportet.* 'You should remove (the grain) some time after you have opened (the pit).' In other authors both tenses occur occasionally with *ubi* and *simulac,* more rarely with *ut.* They naturally involve a future tense in the main verb, or an expression that refers to the future, such as an imperative, or an expression of necessity. They are obviously more likely to occur in dialogue, letters, or speeches, rather than in narrative. Perhaps this is the only reason for their comparative rarity: Plaut. *Bacch.* 688 *ubi me aspiciet, ad carnuficem rapiet continuo senex.* 'When he sees me, the old man will hale me straight off to the hangman.' Cic. *Att.* 12, 40, 5 *simulac constituero, ad te scribam.* 'As soon as I have made up my mind, I will write to you'. *Id. Rab. Post.* 36 *ubi semel quis peieraverit, ei credi postea non oportet.* 'When once a man has perjured

himself, he ought not to be trusted thereafter.' *Id. Att.* 8, 8A, 4 *ubi nihil erit quod scribas, id ipsum scribito.* 'When there is nothing for you to write, write just that.'

218. *Temporal Clauses expressing Contemporaneous Action*

There are three types of contemporaneous action that a temporal clause may express: (1) The action of the temporal clause is co-extensive with that of the main clause: 'While (as long as) he lived here, he was happy': *dum hic vivebat, felix erat.* (2) The temporal clause may express partial co-extension, denoting a longer progressive action in the course of which the action of the main clause takes place: 'While he was awaiting reinforcements, the enemy attacked': *dum novas copias exspectat, hostes impetum fecerunt.* (3) The temporal clause may express an action that marks the limit of the action of the main verb: 'Until the enemy attacked, he remained within the camp': *dum hostes impetum fecerunt, in castris mansit.*

The conjunctions which are used in these senses are: *dum, donec, quoad,* 'while' or 'until'; *quamdiu,* 'as long as'. In the sense 'while yet', i.e. in the second type of clause, only *dum* is used. *Dum* is by far the commonest of these conjunctions. *Donec* is avoided entirely by Caesar and Sallust, and Cicero has few examples, but it is common enough in other writers.

Dum was originally a demonstrative adverb of time meaning 'during that time', or 'the while', which came to be used in the relative and subordinating sense of 'while'. Cf. *agedum!* 'Come, then!' and *interdum,* 'between whiles'. A sentence like Plaut. *Bacch.* 737 *mane dum scribit* might almost be construed paratactically: *mane dum: scribit,* 'Wait the while: he is writing'. The sense of 'until' developed out of that of 'during the time that', or 'as long as', cf. 'Wait while he comes' and 'Wait until he comes'.

Donec originally meant 'up to the time that' (= *quoad*), but from about 100 B.C. onwards it borrowed the sense of 'while' or 'as long as' from *dum,* with which it became interchangeable. It is normally used in the sense of 'until'. The sense 'while' does not appear before Lucretius, and was rare in prose before Livy.

Quoad also, from the classical period onwards, borrows the sense of 'as long as', in addition to its original sense of 'up to the point that'.

219. (1) '*While*' = '*As long as*'

Dum, donec, quoad, or *quamdiu* in this sense take the indicative, so long as there is no other intention than to compare the times of two events. As complete coextension is indicated, the temporal clause normally has the same tense as the main clause, but it is possible to have the imperfect in the one, and the aorist-perfect in the other: Cic. *Phil.* 2, 90 *dum timor abest, a te non discedit audacia.* 'So long as fear is absent, boldness does not desert you.' *Id. Att.* 9, 10, 3 *ut aegroto, dum anima est, spes esse dicitur, sic ego, quoad Pompeius in Italia fuit, sperare non destiti.* 'Just as for a sick man, while there is life there is said to be hope, so I, so long as Pompey was in Italy, did not cease to hope.' Caes. *B. C.* 1, 51, 5 *ii, dum pari certamine res geri potuit, magnum hostium numerum pauci sustinuere.* 'So long as it was possible to fight on equal terms, they, few as they were, withstood a great number of the enemy.' *Id. B. G.* 7, 82, 1 *dum longius ab munitione aberant Galli, plus multitudine telorum proficiebant.* 'So long as the Gauls were at a distance from the fortifications, they produced greater effect with their superior number of weapons.' Cic. *Off.* 2, 43 *Gracchus tam diu laudabitur, dum memoria rerum Romanarum manebit.* 'Gracchus will be praised as long as the memory of Rome shall last.'

For different tenses, cf. Cic. *T. D.* 1, 101 *fuit Lacedaemoniorum gens fortis, dum Lycurgi leges vigebant.* 'The race of Spartans was brave, so long as the laws of Lycurgus continued in force.' (The tense of complete action *fuit* implies that the period of their bravery is now over, but that does not prevent the period's having lasted as long as that indicated by the imperfect *vigebant.*) Livy 30, 25, 7 *quinqueremis defendebatur egregie, quoad tela suppeditarunt.* 'The quinquereme was (continued to be) defended with distinction, so long as (up to the point that) the ammunition lasted.' Livy 27, 27, 7 *non tamen omisere pugnam Fregellani, donec integri consules rem sustinebant.* 'Nevertheless the men of Fregellae did not abandon the fight, so long as the consuls, unwounded, kept things going.'

Note. The pluperfect and future perfect, being tenses that denote previously completed action, are ruled out by the sense.

220. *'So long as' = 'Provided that'*

If a clause introduced by *dum*, 'so long as', instead of indicating objectively an event that goes on at the same time as the action of the main verb, indicates what the speaker (or subject of the main verb) *wills* or *wishes* to happen at the same time as the action of the main verb, then the subjunctive is used: *adsit, dum ne nos interpellet*, 'Let him be present, so long as (provided that) he does not interrupt us'.

The subjunctive here is clearly a subordinated jussive, as may easily be seen by reference to the original demonstrative sense of *dum:* 'Let him be present, (but) let him not interrupt us the while.' *Dum* in this sense is often reinforced by *modo* ('provided only that . . .'), and *modo* is often used by itself, the subjunctive being then virtually independent. *Dummodo* is common in Plautus, Terence, Cicero, Livy, and later writers, but for some reason Caesar and Sallust avoid it, saying *dum tamen* instead.

Examples: Acc. *Tr.* 203 *oderint, dum metuant.* 'Let them hate, provided that they fear.' Cic. *Off.* 3, 82 *omnia recta et honesta neglegunt, dummodo potentiam consequantur.* 'They neglect all rectitude and decency, provided only that they acquire power.' *Id. Att.* 8, 11B, 3 *si cui videor segnior fuisse, dum ne tibi videar, non laboro.* 'If anyone thinks I have been rather lazy, I am not distressed, provided that I do not seem so to you.' *Id. Fam.* 16, 21, 6 *omnia postposui, dummodo praeceptis patris parerem.* 'I considered all of secondary importance, so long as I obeyed the instructions of my father.' *Id. Off.* 1, 89 *Mediocritas placet Peripateticis et recte placet, modo ne laudarent iracundiam et dicerent utiliter a natura datam.* 'Moderation pleases the Peripatetics, and rightly so, *if only* they had not praised quickness of temper and said that it was a useful gift of nature.' (Here the jussive origin is clear: 'only they *should not have, ought not to have,* praised . . .' The imperfect subjunctive may follow *placet,* because the Peripatetic doctrines were in fact formulated long before.)

Note. It will be observed that the negative is *ne,* a sure sign of jussive (or possibly optative) origin. As this subjunctive is a type of final, only the present and imperfect tenses are likely to be found.

221. Dum = *'while yet'* or *'during the time that'*

When the *dum*-clause denotes a longer period in the course of which the action of the main verb takes place, it was the custom from the earliest Latin to use the present indicative in the *dum*-clause, even when the main verb was in a past tense. Only *dum* is used in this sense, *quoad* and *quamdiu* being ruled out by their sense. The main verb is usually aorist-perfect, historic present, or imperfect, the pluperfect and future being rare: Cic. *Fin.* 5, 50 *Archimedes, dum in pulvere quaedam describit attentius, ne patriam quidem captam esse sensit.* 'Archimedes, while he was over-intently drawing certain diagrams in the dust, did not even perceive that his native city had been captured.' Caes. *B. G.* 5, 37, 2 *interim, dum de condicionibus inter se agunt, paulatim circumventus interficitur.* 'In the meantime, while they were negotiating with one another about terms, he was gradually surrounded and slain.' Livy 21, 7, 1 *dum ea Romani parant consultantque, iam Saguntum summa vi oppugnabatur.* 'While the Romans were making these preparations and deliberating, Saguntum was already being vigorously attacked.' Cic. *Verr.* 5, 91 *haec dum aguntur, interea Cleomenes iam ad Pelori litus pervenerat.* 'While this was going on, Cleomenes had in the meantime already reached the shore of Pelorus.' (But the pluperfect in the main clause is rare.) *Id. Fam.* 3, 5, 4 *perpaucos dies, dum pecunia accipitur, commorabor.* 'I shall delay a few days, while the money is being received.' (But the future in the main clause is rare.)

Note i. Other tenses than the present indicative in the *dum*-clause, when it means 'during the time that', are very rare. One might have expected the imperfect, but there is only one example of this in Cicero: *Rosc. Am.* 91 *dum is in aliis rebus erat occupatus, erant interea qui suis vulneribus mederentur.* 'While he was engaged in other matters, there were in the meantime men who were recouping their own losses.' (But even here, in spite of *interea*, there is nothing to prevent *dum* meaning 'so long as', implying complete coextension.) There are a few examples in Livy, e.g. 5, 47, 1 *dum haec Veiis agebantur, interim arx Romana in ingenti periculo fuit.* 'While this was going on at Veii, in the meantime the citadel at Rome was in great danger.' But in Livy, and in colloquial Latin, *dum* is apt to be confused in construction with *cum* (cf. Note iii below), which, in the sense 'during the time that', or 'at the time when', takes the indicative. There are more examples of the perfect indicative than of the imperfect in such *dum*-clauses, but then there seems to be a latent causal or concessive sense: Cic. *Br.* 282 *dum Cyri et Alexandri similis esse voluit, multorum Crassorum inventus est dissimillimus.* 'While he wanted to be like Cyrus and Alexander, he was found to be most unlike many of the Crassi.'

Note ii. If the *dum*-clause denotes a longer period in the course of which something happens, it is clear that a tense of complete or instantaneous action is logically impossible in it. Therefore the normal present indicative is not the 'historic present', as is so often asserted, because this is equivalent in sense to the aorist-perfect, though more vivid. It is therefore the true 'present continuous', though it is used to refer to the past by the same sort of *Repraesentatio* as causes the historic present to be used of completed past events.

Note iii. Dum in this sense means practically the same as *cum* with the imperfect subjunctive in narrative (see Section 235). In colloquial Latin, in poetry, and in prose from Livy on, the construction of the two is apt to be confused, and *dum* is found with the imperfect subjunctive in contexts where there is no idea of 'proviso' or 'intention' to account for it: Livy 1, 40, 7 *dum intentus in eum se rex totus averteret, alter elatam securim in caput deiecit.* 'While the king, attending to him, was completely turning his back, the other raised his axe and brought it down on his head.' Cf. Virg. *Geor.* 4, 457–9 *illa quidem, dum te fugeret per flumina praeceps, . . . hydrum non vidit in herba.* 'She, while flying from thee headlong along the river, did not see a snake in the grass.' Here, however, it is just possible to read the idea of intention into the adjective *praeceps.*

Note iv. It is often stated that the present indicative with *dum* generally resists transference into the subjunctive even in *Oratio Obliqua.* On the contrary, this retention of the indicative is extremely rare in classical Latin, and rare even in Livy. It is only in Silver Latin, particularly in Tacitus, that it becomes at all common. For the regular construction, see Sall. *Cat.* 7, 6 *se quisque conspici, dum tale facinus faceret, properabat.* 'Each was eager to be observed, while he was performing such an exploit.' Livy 25, 20, 6 *legati nuntiabant Cn. Fulvium, dum urbes quasdam oppugnaret, intentius rem egisse.* 'The envoys reported that Cn. Fulvius, while he was attacking certain towns, had acted with more zeal.' Suet. *Ner.* 35, 5 *Rufium Crispinum mergendum mari, dum piscaretur, servis ipsius demandavit.* 'He handed over Rufius Crispinus to his own slaves to be drowned in the sea, while he was fishing.'

When a thing is reported indirectly, the vividness is gone, so that, when the governing verb is past, the present indicative of the *dum*-clause normally goes into the imperfect, not the present, subjunctive. For the less usual retention of *repraesentatio*, see Tac. *Ann.* 1, 46 *civitas incusare Tiberium quod, dum patres et plebem ludificetur, dissideat miles.* 'The public reproached Tiberius because, while he was deluding the senate and people, the soldiers were mutinying.'

For the retention of the present indicative, which certainly is common in Tacitus, see *Ann.* 14, 58, 3 *(mandata attulit) si sexaginta milites propulisset, dum refertur nuntius Neroni, multa secutura . . .* 'He brought a message that, if he fought off the sixty soldiers, while the news was being brought to Nero, many things would supervene.'

222. '*Until*'

When *dum, donec,* or *quoad* introduce a clause in which there is no other intention than to indicate the time-limit of the action of the main verb, the indicative is used, e.g. *mansit ibi dum ego redii,* 'He remained there until I returned'. Here *redii* marks the limit of the action of *mansit,* and the indicative indicates something that really took place.

But it is very easy for the idea of intention, design, or anticipation to enter into these clauses, and then a final subjunctive is used: *mansit ibi dum ego redirem,* 'He waited there until I *should* return', i.e. 'He waited for me to return.' Here the *dum*-clause expresses the intention in the mind of the subject of tne main verb, and it does not matter whether the action of the subordinate verb really took place, or not. If the temporal clause expresses something that did not really happen, but was anticipated and prevented by the subject of the main verb, then the subjunctive is essential, e.g. *non mansit dum caperetur,* 'He did not wait to be captured'.

This habit of reading intention, or interpreting the mind of the subject of the main verb, grew to such an extent that, from Cicero onwards, the subjunctive became commoner than the indicative in such clauses, and ended by being used by Livy and Silver Latin writers, even where the context seems to demand the indicative. (See Section 224, and cf. the similar use of the subjunctive with *ante-* and *prius-quam.*)

223. Dum, donec, quoad = '*until*', *with indicative*

The chief tenses found are the present, aorist-perfect, and future perfect. The future simple is very rare and occurs only in early Latin and in poetry. The pluperfect is ruled out, because an action that marks the limit of another action cannot very well have finished before it. Neither does the imperfect seem to occur.

(*a*) Present: When the main verb is future, imperative, or an expression that refers to the future, *and is not negatived*, the present indicative (*not* the future simple) is used in the temporal clause: Ter. *Ad.* 196 *delibera hoc, dum ego redeo.* 'Deliberate on this, until I return.' *Id. Eun.* 206 *concedam hinc intro atque exspectabo dum venit.* 'I will go in and wait until he comes.'

This use of the present indicative occurs mostly in early and colloquial Latin, and is less usual in prose than the present subjunctive. For an example of both in the same sentence, see Cic. *Fam.* 9, 2, 4 *latendum tantisper ibidem, dum effervescit haec gratulatio, et simul dum audiamus quemadmodum negotium confectum sit.* 'We must lie low meanwhile in the same spot, until this enthusiastic reception dies down, and at the same time until we hear how the business has been settled.'

(*b*) Future perfect: This tense is fairly common. It indicates objectively the limit that will be set to the action of the main verb. The main verb is usually negatived, but not always: Ter. *Phorm.* 420 *haud desinam, donec perfecero hoc.* 'I shall not stop, until I have finished this.' Cic. *Fam.* 12, 19, 3 *mihi usque curae erit quid agas, dum quid egeris sciero.* 'It will be a source of worry to me how you are faring, until I have knowledge how you have fared.'

The indicative states how long the action of the main verb will go on, not what is the intention behind it. As the subjunctive kills both birds with one stone, as it were, it tends to become commoner: cp. Cato *R. R.* 86 *ubi coctum erit, lacte addat paulatim usque adeo donec cremor crassus erit factus.* 'When it is cooked, let him add milk gradually, until a thick gruel has been produced.' and *Ibid.* 95, 1 *igni leni coquito, usque adeo dum fiat tam crassum quam mel.* 'Cook it on a gentle fire, until it becomes as thick as honey.'

(*c*) Aorist-perfect: This is the commonest tense: Livy 23, 31, 9 *de comitiis, donec rediit Marcellus, silentium fuit.* 'There was silence about the elections, until Marcellus returned.' Caes. *B. G.* 5, 17, 3 *nostri non finem sequendi fecerunt, quoad praecipites hostes egerunt.* 'Our men did not put an end to their pursuit, until they had driven the enemy in headlong rout.' (Once more, English is apt to use the pluperfect in the temporal clause, where Latin uses the aorist-perfect.)

224. Dum, donec, quoad = *'until', with the Subjunctive*

When the temporal clause marks the limit which it is the aim of the subject of the main verb to reach (or avoid reaching, if the main verb is negatived), the final subjunctive is used. The temporal clause is then merely a type of final clause: Plaut. *Pseud.* 1234 *ne exspectetis dum hac domum redeam via.* 'Do not expect me to return home by this road.' (This is the normal construction after *exspecto*, or a verb or expression of equivalent sense. Sometimes *ut* is the conjunction, instead of *dum*. The accusative and infinitive is rare.) *Id. Trin.* 170 *lupus observavit dum dormitarent canes.* 'The wolf watched until the dogs dozed.' (or 'watched for them to doze'). *Id.*

Truc. 843 *haud mansisti dum ego darem illam: tute sumpsisti tibi.* 'You did not wait for me to give her; you took her for yourself.' Livy 32, 9, 8 *paucos moratus est dies, dum se copiae ab Corcyra adsequerentur.* 'He delayed a few days, for the forces from Corcyra to catch him up.' *Id.* 38, 40, 9 *Thraces nihil se moverunt, donec Romani transirent.* 'The Thracians made no movement until the Romans crossed.' (I.e. 'waiting for them to cross', but it is often easier, in translating, to neglect the nuance of the subjunctive.)

Note i. As this use of the subjunctive is 'final', tenses other than the present and imperfect are rare. If the pluperfect occurs in classical Latin, it is usually due to virtual *O. O.*: Caes. *B. G.* 5, 24, 8 *ipse interea, quoad munita hiberna cognovisset, in Gallia morari constituit.* 'He himself meanwhile decided to stay in Gaul until he had learned that the winter-quarters had been fortified.' The subjunctive here is not of the same type as in the examples above, for it reports Caesar's thought: *morabor quoad cognovero,* 'I will stay till I have learned . . .', and in the indirect report *cognovero* becomes *cognovisset,* according to the rule of sequence.

From Livy on, however, the pluperfect subjunctive seems to be used sometimes to denote repeated action (cf. Section 217 (2) Note ii): Livy 21, 28, 11 *elephanti trepidationis aliquantum edebant, donec quietem ipse timor fecisset.* 'The elephants would show some signs of panic, until their very fear had made them quiet.'

Note ii. The fondness for this use of the subjunctive caused its nuance to become outworn, and in Silver Latin writers it is sometimes used for the indicative in contexts where the idea of 'intention' would be absurd: Tac. *Ann.* 2, 6 *Rhenus servat nomen donec Oceano misceatur.* 'The Rhine preserves its name until it reaches the North Sea.' *Ibid.* 5, 11 *consules mansere infensi ac minitantes, donec magistratu abirent.* 'The consuls remained hostile and threatening, until they left office.' In these examples the idea of 'intention' is most unlikely.

225. *Temporal Clauses expressing 'Time before which'*

The conjunctions which introduce a clause indicating an action *before* which the action of the main verb takes, took, or will take place, are *priusquam* and *antequam,* 'before' (lit. 'earlier *than*', cf. formation of *postquam*). *Priusquam* is the older form, and is still commoner in classical Latin than *antequam.* Caesar, Sallust, and Livy prefer *priusquam;* Cicero and Tacitus prefer *antequam.*

As with the conjunctions already dealt with, the indicative is used, if there is no intention but to indicate the time-relation of two events. But if the idea of design, anticipation, or prevention, comes in, the subjunctive is used. With *priusquam* and *antequam* the subjunctive is even commoner than with *dum.* Even classical writers use it with little justification; Livy and Silver Latin writers with no justification at all.

226. Antequam *and* priusquam *referring to the Present*

The present indicative referring to the present, whether the clause is generalizing or particular, is rare, but does occur: Varro, *L. L.* 7, 58 *ante rorat quam pluit.* 'It drizzles before it rains' (generalizing). Cic. *Att.* 8, 7, 2 *ante fugit quam scit quem fugiat aut quo.* 'He is running away before he knows from whom he is running, or whither' (particular).

In generalizing clauses referring to the present, the perfect indicative is the normal mood and tense, as already indicated: Cic. *Fin.* 3, 66 *membris utimur priusquam didicimus cuius ea utilitatis causa habeamus.* 'We use our limbs before we have learnt for the sake of what employment we have them.' With the 'ideal' second person, the present subjunctive is used, as usual: Sall. *Cat.* 1, 6 *priusquam incipias consulto, et ubi consulueris, mature facto opus est.* 'Before one begins, there is need of deliberation, and when one has deliberated, there is need of quick action.'

227. Antequam *and* priusquam *referring to the Future*

When the main verb refers to the future, the future simple after *antequam* or *priusquam* is extremely rare. There are isolated examples in early and later Latin, but apparently none in classical Latin. Instead, when the main clause is positive, either the present indicative or the present subjunctive is used. When the main clause is negative, i.e. when *priusquam* or *antequam* may be translated by 'until', the future perfect indicative is used.

Examples: (*a*) Positive: Plaut. *Trin.* 198 *numquid prius, quam abeo, me rogaturus es?* 'Are you going to ask me anything, before I go?'

This is the regular construction in early Latin, the subjunctive being used only when the main clause is an expression of will or wish, so that the idea of purpose is clear: Plaut. *Merc.* 559 *hunc vicinum prius conveniam, quam domum redeam.* 'I must meet this neighbour of mine, before I return home.' Cato *R. R.* 143, 2 *vilica focum purum cotidie, priusquam cubitum eat, habeat.* 'Let your housekeeper have the hearth clean every day, before she goes to bed.'

As the *priusquam*-clause indicates the desired end, to which the action of the main clause is an indispensable preliminary, the subjunctive is clearly a type of 'final'. But it spreads to contexts where the idea of purpose on the part of the subject of the main clause is not so clear. In classical Latin the indicative and the subjunctive are equally common: Cic. *Cat.* 4, 20 *nunc, antequam ad sententiam redeo, de me pauca dicam.* 'Now, before I return to my theme, I will say a few words about myself.' *Id. Leg. agr.* 2, 53 *is videlicet, antequam veniat in Pontum, litteras ad Cn. Pompeium mittet.* 'Of course, before coming to Pontus, he will send a letter to Pompey.' (The subjunctive sarcastically credits Rullus with the *intention* of preparing Pompey for his arrival.)

In classical Latin the idea of purpose in the subjunctive is usually fairly clear. But the subjunctive became obligatory also when the action of the main clause must of necessity, for any reason, precede that of the temporal clause: Sall. *Cat.* 4, 5 *pauca prius explananda sunt quam initium narrandi faciam.* 'A few things have to be made clear, before I (can) begin my narrative.' Cf. Sen. *N. Q.* 2, 12, 6 *ante videmus fulgorem quam sonum audiamus.* 'We see the flash before we hear the sound.' Here the force of the subjunctive can hardly be translated.

(*b*) Negative: The future perfect indicative is regular: Cic. *de Or.* 3, 145 *non defatigabor antequam illorum rationes percepero.* 'I shall not weary until I have understood their methods.' *Id. Flacc.* 51 *nihil contra disputabo priusquam dixerit.* 'I shall urge no counter arguments, until he has spoken.'

Note. There are only isolated examples of the future perfect, when the main clause is positive. It will naturally be used on the rare occasions when it is desired to emphasize the time-relation only, without suggesting any idea of anticipation or prevention: Cic. *Mil.* 99 *praeclare vixero, si quid mihi acciderit priusquam hoc tantum mali videro.* 'I shall have lived famously, if something happens to me before I have seen so much evil as this.' Even here Cicero might have suggested the desire to forestall the sight by using *videam* instead of *videro. Id. Phil.* 11, 24 *ante provinciam sibi decretam audiet, quam potuerit tempus ei rei datum suspicari.* 'He will hear that the province has been decreed him, before he will have been able to suspect that time has been given to the matter.' Here the priority in time is emphasized. But if Cicero had not used *potuerit,* he would undoubtedly have said *antequam . . . suspicetur,* 'before he *can* suspect'.

228. Antequam *and* priusquam *referring to the Past*

(*a*) When the main clause refers to the past and is *negative,* i.e. when *priusquam* = 'until', the temporal clause normally has the aorist-perfect indicative (not the pluperfect, cf. on *postquam, ubi,* etc.), and occasionally the historic present: Cic. *de Or.* 2, 195 *non prius sum conatus misericordiam aliis commovere, quam misericordia sum ipse captus.* 'I did not try to move others to pity before (*or* until) I myself had been seized by pity.' Caes. *B. G.* 1, 53, 1 *hostes terga verterunt, neque prius fugere destiterunt quam ad flumen Rhenum pervenerunt.* 'The enemy turned their backs, and did not stop running until they (had) reached the river Rhine.'

This is the regular usage. The use of the indicative means that the action expressed in the *priusquam*-clause really did take place, but even so, it is possible for the author to read purpose into the mind of the subject of the main clause, even when it is negative, and then the subordinate clause has the subjunctive: Caes. *B. C.* 1, 22, 2 *neque ab eo prius Domitiani milites discedunt, quam in conspectum Caesaris deducatur.* 'Nor did the soldiers of Domitius leave him, until he was brought into Caesar's presence.' (Historic present, with primary sequence. It was the soldiers' purpose to watch him until they had escorted him to his destination.)

(*b*) When the main verb is *positive*, the usage is as follows:

The indicative occurs frequently in early and colloquial Latin, in Cicero's Letters, and in his earlier speeches, but is very rare thereafter. It does not occur at all in Caesar. Its place is taken by the imperfect (occasionally the pluperfect) subjunctive. The idea of purpose is still usually visible in classical authors, but it began to wear very thin, and occasionally in Livy, more frequently in later authors, the subjunctive seems simply to have replaced the indicative for no logical reason.

Examples of the indicative: Plaut. *Aul.* 208 *priusquam intro redii, exanimatus fui.* 'Before I got back indoors, I was exhausted.' Cic. *Att.* 2, 7, 2 *antequam tuas legi litteras, hominem ire cupiebam.* 'Before I read your letter, I was wishing the man to go.' Livy 9, 32, 6 *prius sol meridie se inclinavit quam telum hinc aut illinc emissum est.* 'The sun at mid-day began to sink, before a weapon was discharged from either side.' (There are only three examples of the indicative in Livy.)

Examples of the subjunctive: Caes. *B. G.* 1, 19, 3 *priusquam quicquam conaretur, Divitiacum ad se vocari iubet.* 'Before attempting anything, he ordered Divitiacus to be summoned to him.' Sall. *Jug.* 54, 10 *Numidae, priusquam ex castris subveniretur, in proximos colles discedunt.* 'The Numidians, before help could be brought from the camp, made off into the nearest hills.' In these examples the idea of purpose is fairly clear, but it is often enough that the action of the main clause forestalls and prevents the action of the *priusquam*-clause, without any intention on the part of the main subject: Cic. *Div.* 1, 55 *antequam ludi fierent, servus per circum, cum virgis caederetur, furcam ferens ductus est.* 'Before the games took place, a slave, being scourged with rods and bearing a cross, was led through the circus.' A reason can be found for the subjunctive here in that the ritual was a necessary preliminary. In the following, the idea of purpose is very faint, if it exists at all: Cic. *T. D.* 4, 49 *hi conlocuti inter se, priusquam manum consererent, nihil iracunde fecerunt.* 'They, after talking together before engaging in combat, did nothing in anger.' Caes. *B. G.* 3, 26, 3 *prius in hostium castris constiterunt, quam plane ab his quid rei ageretur cognosci posset.* 'They stood in the enemies' camp before it could well be perceived by the latter what was afoot.'

Cicero sometimes uses the pluperfect subjunctive of *possum: Planc.* 98 *qui antequam de meo adventu audire potuissent, in Măcedoniam perrexi.* 'Before these could have heard of my arrival, I went on into Macedonia.' Here the subjunctive is probably potential or generic-consecutive: 'at a time such that they had been unable . . .'

In the following, the pluperfect subj. is due to the pluperfect tense of the main verb: Cic. *Verr.* 2, 171 *Carpinatius, antequam in istius familiaritatem tantam pervenisset, aliquotiens ad socios litteras de istius iniuriis miserat.* 'Carpinatius, before he had become so very intimate with the defendant, had written a number of times to his partners about the latter's injustices.'

For the subjunctive plainly replacing the indicative, see Livy 25, 31, 12 *paucis ante diebus quam Syracusae caperentur, T. Otacilius Uticam transmisit.* 'A few days before Syracuse was captured, T. Otacilius crossed to Utica.'

Note. The imperfect and pluperfect indicative after *priusquam* and *antequam* are very rare: Livy 23, 48, 1 *nec ante consul violavit agrum Campanum quam herbae pabulum praebere poterant.* 'Nor did the consul violate Campanian territory before the herbage was able to provide fodder.'

XX

Relative Clauses and the Constructions of Cum (Quom)

229. Up to about the time of Cicero the conjunction *cum* was spelt *quom.* The spelling *quum,* which is found in some grammars, was a device of grammarians to distinguish it from the preposition *cum,* and was never in regular use. *Quom* or *cum* was the accusative singular masculine of the relative stem, which persisted only as a relative adverb (subordinating conjunction) of time, meaning '(at the time) when'. Its demonstrative co-relative is *tum.*

The most reasonable explanation of the use of the moods with *cum* is that which refers to the parallel development of the descriptive and generic subjunctive in *qui*-clauses. Therefore it may be of advantage to begin with a recapitulation of the various types of relative clause.

230. *Types of* Qui-*clause*

Qui-clauses may be classified as follows:

(1) Determinative: The *qui*-clause identifies, telling 'what' person or thing is referred to, not 'what sort of': Cic. *de Sen.* 10 *Ego Q. Maximum, eum qui Tarentum recepit, dilexi.* 'I was fond of Q. Maximus, *the one who* recovered Tarentum.' Livy 22, 54, 1 *Eo tempore quo haec Canusii agebantur, Venusiam ad consulem ad quattuor milia et quingenti pedites equitesque pervenere.* '*At the time at which* these things were going on at Canusium, about 4,500 infantry and cavalry reached the consul at Venusia.'

When the relative clause identifies in this way, the indicative is obligatory.

(2) Generalizing: In generalizing relative clauses *qui* means 'whoever', and *quicumque* is commoner. For moods and tenses, cf. 194 (*b*) and Note: Cic. *T. D.* 3, 14 *qui fortis est, idem est fidens.* 'He who (= 'whoever') is brave, is at the same time confident.' *Ibid.* 2, 54 *qui restiterunt, discedunt saepissime superiores.* 'Those who resist (have resisted) most often come off the victors.' *Id. Verr.* 3, 94 *quemcumque equitem Romanum in provincia viderant,*

beneficiis ac liberalitate prosequebantur. 'Whatever Roman knight they saw in the province, they used to treat with kindness and generosity.'

(3) Descriptive: For the development whereby the potential subjunctive came to be used in these clauses, even of facts, see Section 155:

(*a*) Purely 'generic' or characterizing: Cic. *Phil.* 2, 64 *mea sententia, qui rei publicae sit hostis, felix esse nemo potest.* 'In my opinion, no man who is (such as is) an enemy of his country can be fortunate.'

(*b*) Consecutive: *non is sum qui terrear.* 'I am not the man to be frightened.'

The generic subjunctive obtrudes the speaker's or writer's personality into the sentence and makes the clause subjective and explanatory. The subjunctive does not leave the reader to draw his own conclusions, as the indicative does. This type of subjunctive can equally well convey an idea in the speaker's mind that the fact stated in the relative clause accounts for, or that it is in opposition to, the action stated in the main clause. Hence the generic clause developed a causal and a concessive sense.

(4) Causal: Plaut. *Mil.* 59 *te omnes amant mulieres, qui sis tam pulcher.* 'All the women love you, who are (i.e. 'a man who is' or 'because you are') so handsome.' Cic. *Leg.* 3, 22 *vehementer Sullam probo, qui tribunis potestatem ademerit.* 'I greatly approve of Sulla for having deprived the tribunes of their power.'

All tenses of the subjunctive are possible in this sense.

(5) Concessive (or 'adversative'): Caes. *B. C.* 3, 96, 2 *exercitui Caesaris luxuriem obiciebant, cui semper omnia ad necessarium usum defuissent.* 'They reproached Caesar's army with luxurious living, (an army) which had always lacked everything for necessary needs.' (i.e. 'although it had lacked . . .').

But in early Latin usually, and sometimes still in classical Latin, the indicative is used, even though a causal or an adversative sense is clear. For examples, see Section 159.

(6) The relative serves as a connexion: The relative pronoun is often used, especially from the classical period onwards, instead of a coordinating conjunction or particle, to serve as a connexion between two independent sentences. The *qui*-clause is not then adjectival and subordinate, but *qui = et is, sed is, is autem, is enim, is igitur*, etc.: Cic. *Mil.* 53 *res loquitur ipsa, iudices; quae (= et ea) semper valet plurimum.* 'The fact speaks for itself, Gentlemen; and that always has the greatest weight.' *Id. N. D.* 2, 75 *ratio docet esse deos: quo concesso (= et eo concesso) confitendum est eorum consilio mundum administrari.* 'Reason teaches us that there are gods: which being granted, we must confess that the world is governed by their design.' Caes. *B. G.* 5, 43, 6 *centuriones hostes vocare coeperunt: quorum (= sed eorum) progredi ausus est nemo.* 'The centurions began to call the enemy: but none of them dared to come forward.' Cic. *Div.* 1, 105 *Appius Claudius augur nuntiavit bellum domesticum fore. quem (= sed eum) irridebant collegae tui . . .: quibus (= nam eis) nulla videbatur in auguriis scientia veritatis futurae.* 'Appius Claudius, the augur, announced that there would be a

civil war. But your colleagues mocked him . . .; for there seemed to them to be no knowledge of future truth in auguries.'

It will be observed that the relative thus used contains within itself the sense of whatever connecting particle is needed, and these particles (*et, sed, enim, igitur*, etc.) are not added to the relative. The only exception is *tamen*, but that can also be added to *sed* or *at*.

This connecting use, therefore, is to be distinguished from the following, where *qui* = *is qui*, and refers, not to what goes before, but to what comes after: Cic. *Fin.* 3, 27 *quod est bonum, omne laudabile est; quod autem* (= *id autem quod*) *laudabile est, omne honestum est. bonum igitur quod est* (= *id igitur quod*) *honestum est.* 'What is good is always praiseworthy; but what is praiseworthy, is always honourable. Therefore what is good is honourable.'

Note. The feeling that the clause introduced by this connecting relative is a new main clause, and not subordinate, is shown by the fact that in *O. O.* the relative (or the word which it qualifies, if the relative is in an oblique case) goes into the accusative, and the verb into the infinitive. Thus, the first and third examples above, if reported indirectly, would run: (*dicunt*) *rem loqui ipsam; quam semper valere plurimum.* (*nuntiatum est*) *centuriones hostes vocare coepisse: quorum progredi ausum esse neminem.*

231. *The parallel Constructions of* Cum

In early Latin, just as the indicative is still often used in *qui*-clauses, where classical Latin would use the subjunctive, so in *quom*-clauses the indicative is the regular mood, whatever the sense of *quom*: Ter. *Andr.* 517 *quom intellexeras* (*eos*) *id consilium capere, quor non dixti Pamphilo?* 'When you had learned that they were entertaining this design, why did you not tell Pamphilus?' Here there is an adversative idea ('although you had learned . . .'), and the subjunctive would have been obligatory in classical Latin. In early Latin the indicative is also regular when *quom* has a causal sense: Plaut. *Cas.* 417 *quom nos di iuvere, gaudeo.* 'Since the gods have aided us, I rejoice.'

But the development of the subjunctive in *cum*-clauses ran parallel to that in *qui*-clauses, and even went beyond it, in that, in the narrative use of *cum* with the imperfect or pluperfect subjunctive, the characterizing or descriptive idea is very faint, and these clauses have to be classed as purely temporal.

In the following sections the uses of *cum* follow the order of the corresponding *qui*-clauses in Section 230.

232. Determinative: When the *cum*-clause 'identifies' the time at which the action of the main clause took place, giving the date, as it were, the indicative is required at all periods: Cic. *Rosc. Am.* 50 *tu, Eruci, accusator esses ridiculus, si illis temporibus natus esses, cum ab aratro arcessebantur qui*

consules fierent. 'You, Erucius, would have been a ridiculous accuser, if you had been born in the times when men were summoned from the plough to be consuls.' Here the antecedent *illis temporibus* is expressed, but just as often the antecedent is omitted: Caes. *B. G.* 6, 12, 1 *cum Caesar in Galliam venit, alterius factionis principes erant Haedui, alterius Sequani*. 'When Caesar came to Gaul, the Haedui were the leaders of one faction, the Sequani of the other.' Here the subjunctive *venisset* would give quite a different meaning, for it would imply that the division into factions did not take place till after Caesar's arrival. The distinction is therefore very important.

A determinative *cum*-clause, instead of indicating at what time an action took place, may sometimes identify it by indicating another action to which it is equivalent: Cic. *Cat.* 1, 21 *cum quiescunt, probant; cum patiuntur, decernunt; cum tacent, clamant*. 'Their acquiescence is equivalent to approval; when they allow it, they make their decision clear; their silence is as good as shouting.' *Id. Phil.* 14, 28 *cui cum imperium dabamus, eodem tempore etiam spem eius nominis deferebamus*. 'When we were giving him (= 'in giving him') the command, we were at the same time offering him the hope of bearing that title.'

The subjunctive in the above examples would be subtly different. It would introduce a quasi-causal idea. *cum quiescant . . . patiantur . . . taceant . . .* would mean 'Since they acquiesce, etc.' or 'They show their approval *by* (not 'in') acquiescing.' The subjunctive would make the clause subordinate to, and not equivalent to, the main clause.

233. Generalizing: When *cum* = 'whenever', the indicative is regular up to the time of Livy: Cic. *T. D.* 1, 24 *dum lego, adsentior, cum posui librum et coepi cogitare, adsensio omnis illa elabitur*. 'While I am reading, I agree, but when I have put the book down and begun to think, all that agreement slips from me.' *Id. Or.* 41 *cum a nostro Catone laudabar, reprehendi me a ceteris facile patiebar*. 'When (= 'whenever') I was praised by our friend Cato, I easily suffered my being censured by the rest.' *Id. Cat.* 3, 16 *neque vero, cum aliquid mandarat, confectum putabat*. 'Nor, whenever he had assigned some commission, did he think it accomplished.'

But the subjunctive (originally generic) is sometimes (not always) used of repeated action in past tenses from Livy onwards (cf. 196): Livy 2, 27, 8 *cum in ius duci debitorem vidissent, undique convolabant*. 'Whenever they saw a debtor being haled to court, they used to flock together from all sides.' But for the retention of the classical indicative, compare *Id.* 38, 21, 2 *cum comminus venerant, gladiis a velitibus trucidabantur*. 'Whenever they came to close quarters, they were cut down by the swords of the light-armed.'

For the imperfect subjunctive of repeated action, see Tac. *Ann.* 1, 7, 8 *nusquam cunctabundus, nisi cum in senatu loqueretur*, 'never hesitant, except when he was speaking in the senate'.

234. Descriptive or characterizing: When *cum* means 'at *a* time when', i.e. 'a time *such that*', the subjunctive is required, just as in *qui*-clauses: Cic. *Off.* 3, 50 *incidunt saepe causae cum repugnare utilitas honestati videatur.* 'Cases often happen when expediency seems to clash with honour.' (I.e. 'cases such that . . .'.) *Id. Mil.* 69 *erit illud profecto tempus cum tu amicissimi benevolentiam desideres.* 'That time will surely come when you will long for the services of a great friend.' (i.e. the time will be 'such as for you to long for . . .'). *Id. Rosc. Am.* 33 *accepit enim agrum temporibus eis cum iacerent pretia praediorum.* 'He received the farm in times when the prices of estates were low.' (Here the indicative *iacebant* would mean 'at *the* time when'. The subjunctive does more than indicate the time when the action took place; it *describes* it as well.) Caes. *B. G.* 6, 24, 1 *fuit tempus cum Germanos Galli virtute superarent.* 'There was *a* time when the Gauls surpassed the Germans in courage.'

235. *The Extension of the Generic Subjunctive to Temporal* Cum *in Narrative*

In the examples in the previous section, the 'descriptive' force of the subjunctive in the *cum*-clauses can be seen, because the antecedent is expressed. When the antecedent is not expressed, it is sometimes difficult to decide whether the subjunctive is used for its descriptive force or not: Cic. *de Sen.* 16 *is, cum sententia senatus inclinaret ad pacem cum Pyrrho foedusque faciendum, non dubitavit dicere illa* . . . 'He, when the opinion of the senate was inclining towards making peace and a treaty with Pyrrhus, did not hesitate to say those things . . .' Here the descriptive force is fairly clear, for the circumstances indicated in the *cum*-clause might be said to account for the action of Claudius, and *cum* might mean 'as' or 'since'. Similarly in *T. D.* 4, 74 *Alexander, cum interemisset Clitum, familiarem suum, vix a se manus abstinuit.* 'Alexander, when he had slain his friend Clitus, scarcely refrained from laying hands on himself.' Here again, the action of the *cum*-clause accounts for that of the main clause, and there is something more than a mere time-relation.

But when the action or circumstances indicated in the *cum*-clause give the background, or set the stage for the action of the main clause, this subjunctive continues to be used, even when the descriptive, causal, or concessive force is so doubtful that it is difficult to see anything but a mere time-relation between the actions expressed in the *cum*-clause and the main clause: Cic. *de Or.* 1, 160 *haec cum Crassus dixisset, silentium est consecutum.* 'When Crassus had said this, silence followed.' *Id. Ac. Pr.* 2, 13 *quae cum dixisset, sic rursus exorsus est.* 'When he had said this, he began again as follows.'

So, finally, *cum* came to be used with the imperfect or pluperfect subjunctive (not with any other tense) merely to show how things were at the time of the action of the main verb, or to show what had preceded and led up to it. This use of *cum* with the subjunctive, to set the stage, as it were, for the next step in the story or argument, had, by the time of Cicero, become the commonest of all its uses. The generic, causal, or concessive force of the subjunctive has faded away, and the clause must be classed as purely temporal. This is called the 'Narrative' use of *cum*. With the imperfect subjunctive it denotes something going on or present at the time of the main action, and is practically indistinguishable in sense from *dum* with the present indicative. That the Romans themselves saw no distinction is shown by the fact that the construction of *cum* began to affect that of *dum* in colloquial Latin and poetry (see 221, Note iii). With the pluperfect subjunctive, the sense became indistinguishable from that of *postquam* or *ubi* with the aorist-perfect indicative.

Note i. As participles can contain the sense of temporal clauses, it will be found that *cum* with the imperfect subjunctive is equivalent in sense to a present participle, since the tense of incomplete action denotes something still in progress at the time of the main action, while *cum* with the pluperfect subjunctive can be substituted for a past participle, since the tense of complete action indicates something completed before the time of the main action. Compare the following: Caes. *B. G.* 5, 37, 5 *pro castris fortissime pugnans occiditur.* 'He was killed (while) fighting bravely in front of the camp.' Nep. 8, 2, 7 *in secundo proelio cecidit Critias cum fortissime pugnaret.* 'Critias fell in the second battle, while fighting bravely.' Cat. 67, 41 *saepe illam audivi furtiva voce loquentem.* 'I often heard her speaking in a low voice.' Cic. *Div.* 1, 104 *L. Flaccum audivi cum diceret . . .* 'I heard L. Flaccus saying . . .' (where *cum dicebat* would mean 'I heard him on that occasion when he was saying').

Similarly *hoc facto abiit* is equivalent to *cum hoc fecisset, abiit.*

Note ii. Conversely, when an English temporal clause is to be translated into Latin, it is always possible to decide whether *cum* should have the subjunctive by considering whether a participle or participial phrase could be substituted for the temporal clause without altering the sense. An indicative determinative *cum*-clause can never be rendered by a participle, because it answers too important a question. Take, for example, the sentence 'When I was in London, I saw the Queen.' If this is in answer to the question 'When did you see the Queen?', it will be seen that the temporal clause is the more important part of the sentence, and the Latin will be: *cum Londini eram, reginam vidi.* If, on the other hand, the question was 'What did you do, when you were in London?' the temporal clause in the answer is more subordinate, and less important. A participle could be substituted: 'Being in London, I saw the Queen'. The Latin will then be: *cum Londini essem reginam vidi.*

236. Cum *in a causal or concessive Sense*

Both the causal and the concessive (adversative) uses of *cum* are really branches of the generic or descriptive use. Any tense of the subjunctive is possible in both: Cic. *Cat.* 1, 5 *quae cum ita sint, Catilina, perge quo coepisti.* 'Since these things are so, Catiline, proceed on the course you have begun.' Nep. 25, 17, 1 *quid plura commemorem, cum hoc ipsum gloriantem audierim?* 'Why should I quote further instances, when (seeing that) I have heard him himself making this boast?' *Id.* 23, 10, 4 *dolo erat pugnandum, cum par non esset armis.* 'It was necessary to fight by guile, since he was not a match in arms.' Cic. *Leg. agr.* 2, 30 *non intellego quare Rullus quemquam intercessurum putet, cum intercessio stultitiam intercessoris significatura sit, non rem impeditura.* 'I do not understand why Rullus thinks anyone will interpose a veto, seeing that a veto would ('is likely to' or 'will') reveal the stupidity of him who vetoes, and not hinder the business.'

Concessive: Livy 21, 31, 10 *Druentia flumen, cum aquae vim vehat ingentem, non tamen navium patiens est.* 'The river Druentia, though it carries a great volume of water, nevertheless does not admit of navigation.' Nep. 19, 1, 2 *fuit perpetuo pauper, cum divitissimus esse posset.* 'He was always poor, when (although) he might have been very rich.' Cic. *de Or.* 3, 60 *Socratis ingenium immortalitati scriptis suis Plato tradidit, cum ipse litteram Socrates nullam reliquisset.* 'Plato handed down the character of Socrates to immortality in his writings, though Socrates himself had left no writing at all.'

237. Cum *as a Connection* (Cum Inversum)

Cum sometimes serves as a connexion between two independent sentences (cf. the corresponding use of *qui*, Section 230 (6)), i.e. *cum* = *et tum*. The sentence introduced by *cum* is always the more important, so that it looks as if the *cum*-clause and the main clause have changed places. Hence this is usually called the 'Inverted' *cum*-clause, or *Cum Inversum*. As *cum* introduces what is really a new main verb, the mood must be indicative, if it makes a statement. The preceding sentence usually has its verb in the imperfect: Livy 29, 7, 8 *Hannibal iam subibat muros, cum repente in eum erumpunt Romani.* 'Hannibal was already approaching the walls, when the Romans suddenly sallied out against him.' In the *cum*-clause any other tense than the aorist-perfect or historic present is rare, except in the combination *cum interea* or *cum interim*, with which the imperfect is fairly common: Cic. *Verr.* 5, 162 *caedebatur virgis civis Romanus, cum interea nulla vox alia illius miseri audiebatur nisi haec: 'Civis Romanus sum'.* 'He was being scourged with rods—a Roman citizen, and meanwhile no other utterance was heard from the wretched man except this: "I am a Roman citizen".'

Note. Possibly there remained some feeling that *cum*, even here, was subordinating, for this type of *cum*-clause in *Oratio Obliqua* does not go so regularly into the accusative and infinitive as does the corresponding *qui*-clause. However, this does happen from Livy on: Livy 4, 51, 4 (*dixerunt*) *fugere senatum tabulas publicas, cum interim obaeratam plebem obiectari aliis atque aliis hostibus.* 'They said that the senate was evading a publication of accounts, while in the meantime the plebs, loaded with debt, was being exposed to one enemy after another.'

238. Cum *answering the question 'How long?' or 'How long since?'*

In the foregoing uses, *cum* is equivalent to an ablative expression of time, = *quo tempore.* The following determinative uses are peculiar, wherein *cum* is equivalent to a relative expression of time in the Accusative of Duration, = *per quod tempus.* In these *cum* indicates either how long an action has lasted, or the length of time which has elapsed since it happened. In English it then has to be rendered by the relative pronoun ('time *that*' or 'during which') or by 'since', in the temporal sense. The indicative mood is required, if the clause is determinative, as in the following: Cic. *Fam.* 15, 14, 1 *multi anni sunt cum (= per quos) ille in aere meo est.* 'It is many years that he has been in my debt.' (= *multos iam annos in aere meo est*). *Id. Phil.* 12, 24 *vicesimus annus est cum me petunt.* 'It is the twentieth year that they have been attacking me.' (= *vicesimum iam annum me petunt.*) Livy 9, 33, 3 *permulti anni iam erant cum inter patricios magistratus tribunosque nulla certamina fuerant, cum ex ea familia certamen oritur.* 'It was now many years since there had been any quarrels between patrician magistrates and the tribunes, when a quarrel arose from that household.' (Even here the first *cum = per quos*, and for *fuerant*, *erant* would have been possible. The second *cum* is a '*cum inversum*'.)

When the verb in this type of *cum*-clause is aorist-perfect, *cum = ex quo tempore*: Cic. *Off.* 2, 75 *nondum centum et decem anni sunt cum de pecuniis repetundis lata lex est.* 'It is not yet a hundred and ten years since the law about extortion was proposed.'

239. *Summary of the uses of Tenses and Moods with Temporal* Cum

(1) Present: When the *cum*-clause refers to the present, it cannot help being either of the determinative type (Section 232) or of the generalizing type (Section 233), i.e. *cum* = either 'now that', or 'whenever': Cic. *de Sen.* 18 *cessare nunc videor, cum bella non gero.* 'I seem to be shirking, now that I do not wage wars.' *Ibid.* 80 *animus, nec cum adest nec cum discedit, apparet.* 'The mind is not visible either when it is present or when it departs.' In either case the mood in classical Latin will always be indicative.
(2) True perfect: The same applies to this as to the present. The mood will always be indicative: *nunc, cum vidi eum, agnosco.* 'Now that I have seen him, I recognize him.' *cum rosam vidit, putat ver incipere.* 'When he has seen a rose, he thinks spring is beginning.'
(3) Future: It has been seen in Section 234 (Cic. *pro Mil.* 69) that the present tense of the consecutive subjunctive may be used to characterize a future time; but when it is intended to indicate nothing but a time-rela-

tion, the future (or future perfect) indicative is used. With Cic. *pro Mil.* 69 compare *Id. Att.* 12, 18, 1 *longum illud tempus cum non ero magis me movet quam hoc exiguum.* 'That long time when I shall not exist has more effect on me than this short span.' When no antecedent is expressed, the construction does not differ from that of *ubi* or *simulac*: Cic. *Fam.* 13, 1, 1 *non dubitabo operam dare, cum id facere potero.* 'I shall not hesitate to give my attention to it, when I can.' Livy 35, 19, 6 *cum de bello Romano cogitabis, inter primos amicos Hannibalem habeto.* 'When you think about the war with Rome, consider Hannibal among your foremost friends.'

If the action of the *cum*-clause is to be completed before that of the main clause takes place, the future perfect is required: Cic. *Verr.* 5, 154 *cum testem produxero, refellito, si poteris.* 'When I have produced my witness, refute him, if you can.'

(4) Imperfect:

(*a*) *Indicative*, if the clause is determinative or generalizing (Sections 232–3): Livy 29, 31, 1 *Hasdrubal tum forte, cum haec gerebantur, apud Syphacem erat.* 'Hasdrubal happened to be with Syphax, when this was going on.'

(*b*) *Subjunctive*, if the *cum*-clause gives the background for the main action, and if a participial phrase (whether in Latin or English) can be substituted for it (Section 235): Nep. 17, 8, 6 *Agesilaus, cum ex Aegypto reverteretur* (= *revertens*), *venissetque in portum, in morbum implicitus decessit.* 'Agesilaus, when he was returning from Egypt, and had entered the harbour, fell ill and died.'

(5) Aorist-perfect: Indicative, when the clause is determinative or 'date-giving', i.e. when it refers backwards, not forwards (Section 232): Livy 21, 39, 4 *cum Placentiam consul venit, iam ex stativis moverat Hannibal.* '(At the time) when the consul came to Placentia, Hannibal had already moved out of permanent quarters.' (*cum . . . venisset* here would make nonsense, for it would try to say '*after* the consul had come, Hannibal had *previously* moved'.)

(6) Pluperfect:

(*a*) *Indicative*, mostly in generalizing clauses of repeated action, but it occurs occasionally also when the clause is determinative or 'date-giving'. In the latter sense, it will naturally be used, when the main verb is itself pluperfect: Cic. *Verr.* 4, 30 *Verrem artificii sui cupidum cognoverant tum, cum iste Cibyram venerat.* 'They had discovered that Verres was keen on their work at the time when he had come to Cibyra.'

(*b*) *Subjunctive*, if the *cum*-clause leads up to (without necessarily accounting for) the main action. i.e. *cum* with the pluperfect subjunctive = a past participle, or *postquam* or *ubi* with the aorist perfect indicative (235): Caes. *B. G.* 1, 7, 1 *Caesari cum id nuntiatum esset, maturat ub urbe proficisci.* 'When that had been reported to Caesar he hastened to set out from the city.'

XXI

Causal and Concessive Clauses

240. *Causal Clauses*

How relative clauses and *cum*-clauses with the subjunctive developed a causal sense we have seen in Sections 156–7, 230, and 236. The other causal conjunctions are *quod, quia,* 'because', and *quoniam, quando, quandoquidem, siquidem,* 'now that', 'since', 'seeing that'. These are followed by the indicative, if the reason is one assigned by the speaker or writer. But if the reason is a quoted one, i.e. not the speaker's or writer's own, but one which he is putting into the mouth of someone else, the subjunctive is required, as in all subordinate clauses in *Oratio Obliqua.* The reason may be a quoted one, even when the main clause is not in formal *O. O.* E.g. in the sentence *aufugit, quod timebat,* 'He ran away, because he was afraid', *quod timebat* gives the writer's reason for the action. But in *aufugit, quod timeret,* 'He ran away, "because he was afraid" ', *quod timeret* gives the reason alleged by the subject of *aufugit* himself for his action, just as if *dixit se aufugisse, quod timeret* had been written. When the main clause is formally direct, the subjunctive in the subordinate clause is said to be due to 'Virtual *Oratio Obliqua*'. The force of the subjunctive in such clauses cannot be rendered in English without putting in a parenthesis, e.g. (as he said), (as was alleged).

The tense of the subjunctive follows the ordinary rules of sequence which were given for Indirect Questions in Section 180.

Quod, quia, etc., are often preceded by corresponding demonstrative adverbs such as *eo, ideo,* 'for that reason', *propterea, idcirco,* 'on that account'.

241. *The Causal Conjunctions*

Quod: Quod is firstly the neuter of the relative pronoun = 'that which'. Its use as a subordinating conjunction to introduce (*a*) a noun-clause, when it means 'the fact that', and (*b*) an adverbial clause, when it means 'because', arose out of its use in the accusative of the 'internal object' (see Section 13, iv). Just as *id gaudeo* means 'I rejoice (with) that rejoicing' or 'I feel that joy', so (*id*) *quod gaudeo* means 'the rejoicing (with) which I rejoice' or 'the joy which I feel'. This expression is a noun-equivalent and may stand as the subject or object of another verb, e.g. *quod gaudeo nihil ad te attinet,* 'The joy which I feel has nothing to do with you', or *adde quod gaudeo,* 'Add the joy which I feel'. But the necessity for translating the pronoun that is an 'internal' object by a noun in English obscures the fact that *quod gaudeo* really means '(the fact) that I rejoice'. In this particular example *quod*, though performing the function of a subordinating conjunction, is still a pronoun. But if for *gaudeo* there is substituted a verb or expression which would not normally have an internal or cognate object, then *quod* has no other function than that of a conjunction, e.g. *adde quod caecus erat*, 'Add the fact that he was blind'. This was the probable order of development.

The *quod*-clause itself came to be used also adverbially in the same way that a number of neuter pronouns or adjectives, originally 'accusatives of the internal object', became adverbs: e.g. *multum*, 'much', *parum*, 'little', *nihil*, 'not at all', 'in no respect', and even *id*, *hoc*, *illud*, *quid*, etc., 'in that respect', etc. So *id gaudeo* came to mean 'I rejoice on that account', or 'with respect to that'. Similarly *quod* came to mean 'with reference to the fact that', the main clause containing no verb to which its antecedent could stand as internal object: Ter. *Hec.* 368 *laetae exclamant 'Venit', id quod me repente aspexerant.* 'They joyfully exclaimed "He has come", with reference to the fact that they had suddenly caught sight of me.' Thus the *quod*-clause has become explanatory, and *quod* may be translated 'because'.

It is sometimes difficult to decide whether a *quod*-clause is a noun-clause or an adverbial clause, e.g. after verbs expressing emotion: *miror*, *laetor*, *gaudeo*, *doleo*, *irascor*, etc., *quod venisti*, 'I am surprised, rejoice, grieve, am angry, etc., that you have come'. Here it is difficult to know whether *quod venisti* is a noun-clause standing as internal object to these verbs, or whether *quod* means 'because'. (Similarly the interrogative pronoun *quid?* came to be used adverbially in the sense of *cur?*, and it is often difficult to decide whether it is a pronoun or an adverb. In Cic. *Rosc. Am.* 33 *cum ab eo quaereretur quid tandem accusaturus esset eum*, 'when he was asked *what accusation* he was going to bring against him', *quid* is an internal object to *accusaturus esset*. But in Plaut. *Amph.* 377 *loquere: quid venisti?* 'Speak: why have you come?', *quid* is an adverbial accusative meaning 'with reference to what?', i.e. 'why?'.)

Quia: This was originally a neuter plural interrogative pronoun of the same stem as *quis?*, *quid?* It became relative, replying to a *quid?* or *cur?*, and so came to mean 'because': Plaut. *Amph.* 687 '*Cur negas?*' '*Quia vera didici dicere.*' 'Why do you deny it?' 'Because I have learned to speak the truth.' *Quod* and *quia* are therefore synonymous. In early Latin *quia* is the commoner, but by classical times *quod* has become the more popular.

Quoniam: This is a combination of *quom* and *iam*, and was originally temporal in sense ('now that'). From this it developed the causal sense of 'since', 'seeing that', which is its normal meaning in classical Latin. From its sense it is clear that it must introduce a reason consisting of something that is true and evident: Cic. *Cat.* 3, 29 *quoniam iam nox est, in vestra tecta discedite.* 'Seeing that it is now night, depart to your homes.' The same applies to *quando*.

Quando: This is only occasionally used as a relative conjunction in a causal sense (= *quoniam*) and is then usually reinforced by *quidem* (*quandoquidem*). In classical Latin it is normally used as an interrogative adverb of time ('when?'), or else as an indefinite, e.g. *si quando*, 'if ever'. Its use as a relative adverb of time (= *ubi* or *cum*) is archaic (Plautus, Terence, Cato) and vulgar. In the common speech it continued to be so used throughout, and accounts for *quand* in French and *quando* in Italian. There are isolated examples of its relative use in Cicero, but mostly in his earlier works, or when he is quoting from an earlier author, e.g. *Off.* 2, 75 '*Utinam' inquit C. Pontius Samnis 'tum essem natus quando Romani dona accipere coepissent'.* 'Would that I had been born', says C. Pontius the Samnite, 'at the time when the Romans began to accept bribes.'

Si quidem, or siquidem, means literally 'if indeed', and is sometimes used in the sense of 'since', 'seeing that': Cic. *T. D.* 1, 3 *siquidem Homerus fuit ante Romam conditam, serius poeticam nos accepimus.* 'Seeing that Homer lived before the foundation of Rome, we were rather late in adopting the art of poetry.'

242. Examples: (*a*) Indicative: (The reason is the writer's own): Sall. *Cat.* 52, 30 *T. Manlius Torquatus filium suum, quod is contra imperium in hostem pugnaverat, necari iussit.* 'T. Manlius Torquatus ordered his own son to be put to death, because he had fought against the enemy contrary to orders.' Cic. *Lael.* 32 *quia natura mutari non potest, idcirco verae amicitiae sempiternae sunt.* 'Because nature cannot be changed, for that reason true friendships are everlasting.' *Id. de Sen.* 84 *neque me vixisse paenitet, quoniam ita vixi ut non frustra me natum existumem.* 'Nor do I regret having lived, seeing that I have so lived that I do not think I was born in vain.' *Id. T. D.* 4, 34 *quando virtus est affectio animi constans, ex ea proficiscuntur honestae voluntates.* 'Since virtue is a consistent state of mind, honourable impulses have their origin in it.' (There are about ten examples of *quando* in this sense in Cicero, but in the speeches he uses it only when reinforced with *quidem.*) *Id. Phil.* 2, 31 *sequitur ut liberatores sint tuo iudicio, quandoquidem tertium nihil potest esse.* 'It follows that they are liberators in your opinion, since there can be no third possibility.' Livy 8, 33, 7 *quandoquidem apud te nec auctoritas senatus nec aetas mea valet, tribunos plebis appello.* 'Since neither the authority of the senate nor my age weighs with you, I appeal to the tribunes of the people.'

(*b*) Subjunctive: (The clause is virtually oblique, and the reason is not the writer's own): Cic. *Off.* 2, 76 *laudat Africanum Panaetius quod fuerit abstinens.* 'Panaetius praises Africanus because he was ('for having been') temperate.' (Panaetius is represented as saying *laudo eum quod fuit* (or *erat*) *abstinens.*) Id. *Cat.* 3, 15 *supplicatio decreta est, quod Italiam bello liberassem.* 'A thanksgiving was decreed, because I had freed Italy from war.' (The decree is quoted, which presumably said: *supplicatio sit, quod Cicero . . . liberavit.*) Caes. *B. C.* 3, 25, 3 *crebris Pompei litteris castigabantur, quoniam primo venientem Caesarem non prohibuissent.* 'They were being reprimanded in frequent letters from Pompey, on the ground that they had not barred the way to Caesar on his first arrival.'

Note i. The speaker or writer may quote himself, or his own thoughts at another time: Cic. *Fam.* 1, 9, 18 *laetatus sum quod mihi liceret recta defendere.* 'I rejoiced that I was free to defend the right.' (*liceret* represents Cicero's feelings at the time: *laetor quod . . . licet. licebat* would represent his thoughts at the time of writing: 'I rejoiced because, (as I am now telling you) I was permitted to defend . . .').

Note ii. By a sort of attraction, or confusion of constructions, when a verb of speaking or thinking is introduced to quote a reason, it is itself usually put into the subjunctive, which would have been required, had not the verb of speaking been used: Cic. *Off.* 1, 40 *rediit quod se oblitum nescioquid diceret.* 'He came back, because he said he had forgotten something.' This is probably a mixture of *rediit quod nescioquid oblitus esset*, and *rediit; dixit enim se nescioquid oblitum esse.* This particular confusion arises in other kinds of subordinate clause also. Cf. Cic. *Verr.* 5, 17 *Verres nominat servum quem magistrum pecoris esse diceret.* 'Verres named a slave, who, he said, was the keeper of a herd.'

243. The person whose reason is quoted may be purely imaginary, and the subjunctive may be used simply to show that the writer rejects the suggestion. Such repudiated reasons are usually introduced, in classical Latin, by *non quod* or *non quo* (Cicero prefers *non quo*). *non quia* is commoner in early Latin, and comes into favour again with Livy. If an alternative and accepted reason is given, it is usually introduced by *sed* (*tamen*), or *sed quod*, or *sed quia*, with the indicative: Cic. *de Or.* 2, 74 *me exspectatio tenet quibus praeceptis ea tanta vis comparetur; non quo mea quidem iam intersit, sed tamen cognoscendi studio adductus requiro.* 'I am interested to hear by what precepts such great forcefulness is acquired; not that it concerns me any longer, to be sure, but nevertheless I am led to enquire by eagerness to know.' *Id. Fam.* 9, 1, 2 *non idcirco eorum* (sc. *librorum*) *usum dimiseram quod iis succenserem, sed quod eorum me suppudebat.* 'I had not laid aside my use of them (my books) for the reason that I was out of patience with them, but because they gave me a slight sense of shame.' Varr. *R. R.* 1, 5, 2 *neque eo dico, quo non habeant utilia quaedam,* 'Nor do I say it for the reason that they do not have some usefulness.'

But instead of *non quo non*, 'not that not', *non quin*, 'not but what', is often used: Cic. *Att.* 7, 26, 2 *ego me ducem in civili bello nolui esse; non quin rectum esset, sed quia, quod multo rectius fuit, id mihi fraudem tulit.* 'I did not wish myself to be a leader in the civil war; not that it was not righteous, but because the course which was much more righteous brought ruin upon me.' *Id. Mil.* 59 *maiores nostri in dominum quaeri* (sc. *de servis*) *noluerunt; non quin posset verum inveniri, sed quia videbatur indignum.* 'Our ancestors were unwilling for the evidence of slaves to be taken against their masters; not that it was not possible for the truth to be discovered, but because it seemed degrading.'

Note. If *non quod* (*quia*) introduces a reason which is factual and valid, but does not happen to be the one acted upon, the indicative is required: Cic. *Leg*. 2, 31 *neque vero hoc, quia sum ipse augur, ita sentio, sed quia sic existimare nos est necesse*. 'Nor do I think so because I am myself an augur, but because it is inevitable for us to hold this view.' (Cicero really is an augur, whereas *quia sim* would imply that he was not.)

On the other hand, from Livy onwards, and in poetry, *non quia* (though not *non quod*) is sometimes followed by the indicative, even when the reason seems to be merely a suggested one: Livy 8, 19, 3 *valuitque ea legatio, non tam quia pacem volebant Samnites quam quia nondum parati erant ad bellum*. 'And that embassy won its point, not so much because the Samnites wanted peace as because they were not yet prepared for war.' This ought to mean that the Samnites really did want peace, though the other reason was the more weighty one. But the context suggests that they wanted war and were biding their time. Sallust, Caesar, or Cicero would accordingly have written *non tam quia . . . vellent*.

244. *Concessive Clauses introduced by* etsi, etiamsi, tametsi

How the 'generic' subjunctive in a relative clause may have a concessive sense has been explained in Sections 156, 157(*c*), and for *cum* introducing a concessive clause, see Section 236.

A *si*-clause also may express a concession, as was pointed out in Section 191: e.g. *si miliens dicit, tamen non credo*. 'If he says it a thousand times, I still do not believe it.' *si rex ipse esset, tamen ei non parerem*. 'If he were the king himself, I still should not obey him.' However, when a *si*-clause is concessive, *et* or *etiam*, 'even', or *tamen*, 'still', 'yet', are usually added, to fix the concessive idea, and these were combined with *si* to produce the concessive conjunctions *etsi, etiamsi, tametsi*, 'even if', 'although'.

The mood in clauses introduced by these conjunctions follows the rules laid down for Conditional Clauses (192–3). If that 'in spite of which' the main action takes place is conceded as a fact, the indicative is required: *etsi bonus est, non amo eum*. 'Although he is a good man, I do not like him.' If the concession is a suppositional one, made for the sake of argument, the same tense of the subjunctive is required as would be required in an ordinary conditional clause: *etsi vera diceret, nemo ei crederet*. 'Even if (though) he were telling the truth, no one would believe him.'

But of these conjunctions, *etsi* is more often used to concede facts (i.e. with the indicative) than to make 'unreal' concessions. For the latter, *etiamsi* is more often used. *Etsi* came to be synonymous with *quamquam*.

245. Quamquam

Quamquam is a reduplicated *quam* (cf. *quisquis*, 'whoever', *quotquot*, 'however many'). Its literal meaning is therefore 'however', or rather 'however much', 'to whatever degree'; i.e. like *quam*, it originally modified adjectives and adverbs, rather than verbs, e.g. *quamquam malus est, amo eum* means 'However bad he is, I like him', and hence '*Although* he is bad, I like him.' *Quamquam* underlines a fact, whereas *etsi* assumes it; i.e. *etsi malus est, amo eum* means 'Even assuming that he is bad, I like him'. However, the distinction, at any rate between *etsi* and *quamquam*, was lost by classical times. *Quamquam*, as underlining an acknowledged fact, will naturally be followed by the indicative.

Note. Though *quamquam* is normally followed by the indicative, it is still possible to have a *potential* subjunctive in the *quamquam*-clause, e.g. Sall. *Jug.* 3, 2 *vi regere patriam, quamquam et possis et delicta corrigas, tamen importunum est.* 'To govern one's country by force, although one might be able to do so and one might correct faults, is nevertheless uncivil.' If the potential subjunctive is thus used, it is usually of the 'ideal' second person.

The subjunctive of a *fact* after *quamquam* is unclassical, but occurs from Livy onwards, probably on the analogy of the subjunctive in generalizing clauses after *quisquis*, etc. (Section 196). By the time of Tacitus, the subjunctive has become regular.

246. Quamvis

Quamvis is a combination of *quam* and *vis*, 'how you wish', or 'however much you please'. In classical Latin it is always followed by what was originally a jussive subjunctive: *quamvis bonus sit, tamen non amo eum*, 'Let him be as good as you please, I still do not like him', i.e. '*Although* he is good . . .' *quamvis mala fecerit, tamen ei ignoscam.* 'Although he has done evil, I shall still forgive him' (lit. 'Let him have done things as evil as you please . . .'). By the time of Cicero *quamvis* has become a conjunction of fixed form, and the fact that *-vis* is a finite verb that can be conjugated is forgotten. Any tense of the subjunctive may be used: *quamvis malus esset, tamen omnes eum amabant.* 'However bad he was, everyone still liked him.'

247. The development of *quamvis* as a subordinating concessive conjunction proceeded as follows. Originally, like *quamquam*, it modified adjectives and adverbs: *quam vis bonus erat*, 'he was as good as you please', or 'ever so good'; *quam vis celeriter currit*, 'he runs ever so quickly': Catullus 12, 5 *quam vis sordida res et invenusta est.* 'It is a thing ever so mean and disgusting.' But these, with an indicative verb, are independent sentences, not subordinate clauses. It is only *vis* that is subordinated by *quam*; i.e. the

last sentence stands for *res tam sordida est quam vis*. But if any of these independent sentences are followed by another one introduced by an adversative conjunction like *sed* or *tamen*, the sentence containing *quam vis* makes a concession, and is ready to become a subordinate clause: *quam vis bonus est: sed non amo eum*. 'He is ever so good: but I do not like him.' So far, *quam* and *vis* are not yet amalgamated into one word, and there is nothing to prevent *vis* being conjugated in the ordinary way: Cic. *Verr*. 2, 5, 11 *exspectate facinus quam voltis improbum: vincam tamen exspectationem omnium*. 'Expect a deed as wicked as you please, yet I shall surpass all your expectations.' But just as *tam – quam* sometimes modify a verb (= *ita – ut*), so may *quam vis*: Ter. *Hec*. 634 *turbent porro quam velint*. 'Let them create confusion (as much) as they wish.'

We have seen in Section 112, Note i, how the independent jussive subjunctive could be used to grant a concession, even without a phrase like *quam vis* to reinforce it. Such subjunctives with *quam vis*, being regularly opposed to another sentence, usually a statement, were soon felt to be subordinate, and *quamvis*, written as one word, became a mere conjunction with a similar sense to *quamquam*: Cic. *T. D*. 2, 61 *dolor, quamvis sis molestus, nunquam te esse confitebor malum*. 'Pain, you may be as troublesome as you please, I shall never confess that you are an evil.' (= 'however troublesome you may be . . .' = 'although you *are* troublesome.') In this way *quamvis* with the subjunctive, having developed the sense of 'although' (though in classical Latin it can usually still be translated by 'however') came to be used to make concessions of fact, as well as hypothetical ones. The nature of the subjunctive is obscured, and the negative ceases to be *ne* and becomes *non*: Cic. *Verr*. 3, 209 *quamvis res mihi non placeat, tamen contra hominum auctoritatem pugnare non potero*. 'Although the matter does not please me, I shall not be able to contend against their influence.'

It is observable that *quamvis* does not become a complete conjunction with the sense of 'although' until the time of Cicero. Caesar and Sallust, and even Livy, do not yet use it so. They use it only in the sense 'to whatever degree you please', with adjectives and adverbs: Caes. *B. G*. 4, 2, 5 *ad quemvis numerum ephippiatorum equitum quamvis pauci adire audent*. 'However few, they dare to approach any number of saddled cavalry.'

248. Licet

We have seen, in Section 123, Note ii, that *licet*, like *oportet*, etc., may be used with the jussive subjunctive in the sense 'It is permitted that . . .'. Hence, like *quamvis*, *licet* came to introduce clauses which were, in effect, subordinate concessive clauses: Cic. *de Or*. 1, 195 *fremant omnes licet, dicam quod sentio*. 'Though all may raise an outcry, I will say what I think.' But grammatically *fremant licet* is still an independent sentence, and *licet* never degenerated (not, at least, till later Latin) into a mere conjunction like *quamvis*. As its verbal force is still felt, the sequence of tenses allows only the present or perfect subjunctive to be used with it. The historic tenses (imperfect and pluperfect) begin to be used with it by the time of Juvenal, on the analogy of *quamvis* or *cum*.

249. *Examples and Notes*

(*a*) *Etsi, etiamsi, tametsi:* Caes. *B. G.* 4, 31, 1 *Caesar, etsi nondum hostium consilium cognoverat, tamen fore id quod accidit suspicabatur.* 'Caesar, although he had not yet discovered the enemies' plans, suspected that that would happen which did.' This is the normal use of *etsi*. With the subjunctive, it still means 'even if', and is less common than *etiamsi*: Livy 3, 68, 9 *me vera pro gratis loqui, etsi meum ingenium non moneret, necessitas cogit.* 'Necessity compels me to speak what is true instead of what is pleasing, even if my own nature did not urge me to do so.' Cic. *Off.* 2, 69 *inops ille, etiamsi referre gratiam non potest, habere certe potest.* 'The needy man we speak of, even if he cannot return a favour, can certainly feel gratitude.' *Id. Mil.* 79 *etiamsi propter amicitiam vellet illum ab inferis evocare, propter rem publicam non fecisset.* 'Even if on account of friendship he had been willing to call him from the dead, for the sake of the common weal he would not have done so.' Caes. *B. G.* 5, 34, 2 *tametsi ab duce et a fortuna deserebantur, tamen omnem spem salutis in virtute ponebant.* 'Although they were being deserted by their leader and by fortune, nevertheless they placed all their hopes of safety in their courage.'

(*b*) *Quamquam* (not used by Caesar; common in Cicero and other authors): Cic. *Div.* 2, 54 *medici, quamquam intellegunt saepe, tamen nunquam aegris dicunt illo morbo eos esse morituros.* 'Doctors, though they often know, nevertheless never tell their patients that they are going to die from their disease.' The indicative, as here, is the normal construction, but the potential subjunctive occurs occasionally: Livy 6, 9, 8 *quamquam exercitum qui in Volscis erat mallet, nihil recusavit.* 'Although he would have preferred the army which was in Volscian territory, he made no objection.'

But from Livy onwards the subjunctive begins to be used without any potential sense, where Cicero would have used the indicative. Juvenal always uses the subjunctive, Pliny the Younger and Tacitus nearly always: Tac. *Ann.* 14, 36 *quamquam confideret virtuti, tamen exhortationes et preces miscebat.* 'Although he trusted their valour, yet he mingled exhortations and entreaties.'

(*c*) *Quamvis:* (Usually means 'however'. Always subjunctive when the clause is subordinate. Normally primary tenses, when the main clause is primary, but the perfect subjunctive may be aorist-perfect. Normally imperfect or pluperfect subjunctive, when the main clause is historic. Makes both 'real' and 'unreal' concessions): Cic. *Phil.* 2, 68 *quamvis enim sine mente, sine sensu sis, ut es, tamen et te et tua et tuos nosti.* 'However senseless and insensitive you may be, as indeed you are, yet you know yourself and your interests and your kin.' *Id. Off.* 1, 35 *ii qui armis positis ad imperatorum fidem confugient, quamvis murum aries percusserit, recipiendi sunt.* 'Those who lay down their arms and throw themselves on the mercy of commanders, must, although the ram has battered their walls, be given quarter.' Here the concession is hypothetical, and the perfect subjunctive is true perfect: 'let the ram have battered the wall as much as you please . . .' *Id. Att.* 16, 7, 2 *etsi, quamvis non fueris suasor profectionis meae, approbator certe fuisti.* 'However, although you were not the adviser of my departure, you certainly approved of it.' Here *fueris* refers to the past and cannot be rendered by the perfect with 'have', but it arises out of the sense: 'however much you *may not have been* my adviser . . .'. For *etsi* in this sentence, see Note iii. *Id. de Or.* 3, 162 *quamvis sphaeram in scaenam attulerit Ennius, tamen in sphaera fornicis similitudo inesse non potest.* 'Although Ennius introduced the word "globe" into his plays, nevertheless there cannot be in a globe any similarity to an arch.' Here again *attulerit* has to be rendered as aorist-perfect, but the idea is: 'let the word have been introduced by Ennius as much as you please, even so the metaphor does not fit'. *Id. Lael.* 35 *quod qui recusarent, quamvis honeste id facerent, ius amicitiae deserere arguerentur.* 'Those who refused this, however honourable the motives from which they did so, would be convicted of breaking the laws of friendship.' (This is a hypothetical concession, but the imperfect subjunctive is probably due to the influence of the surrounding *O. O.* One would have expected the infin. *argui* rather than *arguerentur.*) *Id. Fam.* 7, 32, 3 *illa quamvis ridicula essent, sicut erant, mihi tamen risum non moverunt.* 'However ridiculous those things were, as they were, nevertheless they did not make me laugh.' Here the imperfect subjunctive after *quamvis* does seem to concede a real fact. However, the majority of examples of the imperfect and pluperfect subjunctive are due either to 'unreality', or to the sequence of tenses in *O. O.*, as in the following: Cic. *Lig.* 26 *constantiam Tuberonis, quamvis ipse probarem, ut probo, tamen non commemorarem, nisi a te cognovissem eam virtutem solere laudari.* 'I should not mention Tubero's firmness, however much I approved of it myself, as indeed I do, did I not know that that courage was wont to be praised by you.' Pliny *ad Tr.* 10, 1 *cognovi te Harpocrati Alexandrinam civitatem tribuisse, quamvis non temere eam dare proposuisses.* 'I learned that you had bestowed the citizenship of Alexandria on Harpocrates, although you had made it your policy not to give it rashly.'

Note. In poetry and post-Augustan prose *quamvis* is occasionally used with the indicative, on the analogy of *quamquam.*

(*d*) *Licet:* (Primary tenses of the subjunctive only): Cic. *Att.* 14, 4, 2 *sed omnia licet concurrant, Idus Martiae consolantur.* 'But though all things clash together, the Ides of March console me.' Ov. *Tr.* 4, 9, 9 *sim licet extremum, sicut sum, missus in orbem . . .* 'Though I have been sent to the end of the world, as I have . . .'

Note i. The use of these various conjunctions seems to have been a matter of personal choice on the part of the author. Thus Cicero employs *quamquam, etsi,* and *quamvis.* Caesar nowhere uses *quamquam,* but prefers *etsi.* Sallust avoids *etsi,* preferring first *tametsi,* and then *quamquam.* Tacitus avoids *tametsi.*

Note ii. Etsi, quamquam, and *quamvis* may qualify a single adjective or adverb, e.g. Livy 25, 6, 2 *etsi non iniquum, certe triste senatus consultum factum est.* 'A senatorial decree, though not unjust, certainly severe, was passed.'

With a participle or participial phrase (e.g. abl. abs.), *etsi* and *quamquam* begin to be used in classical Latin, but not *quamvis* till later: Caes. *B. C.* 1, 67, 5 (*dixit*) *etsi aliquo accepto detrimento, tamen locum capi posse.* 'He said the place might be taken, though with the suffering of some loss.' (But this is the only example in Caesar.) Suet. *Caes.* 70 *quamvis recusantem ultro in Africam sunt secuti.* 'They followed him of their own accord to Africa, in spite of his objections.'

Note iii. Etsi, quamquam, and *tametsi* are often used in the sense of the English 'However . . .', 'And yet . . .', to introduce a new main sentence which is opposed to, or corrects, what has gone before: Cic. *T. D.* 1, 89 *carere sentientis est, nec sensus in mortuo . . . . Quamquam quid opus est in hoc philosophari?* 'To feel a lack is the part of a sentient being, and the dead have no feeling. . . . Although, what need is there of philosophic argument in this matter?'

Quamvis is used in this way only in post-classical Latin.

XXII

Clauses of Comparison

250. Clauses of Comparison, or 'Comparative' clauses, are adverbial clauses which indicate something, real or imaginary, which is like or unlike that which is expressed in the main clause, either in degree or manner. They answer the questions 'To what extent?' or 'In what manner?' In the sentences: *Meus equus tam bonus est quam tuus* (*est*), 'My horse is as good *as* yours is', and *Meus equus melior est quam tuus* (*est*), 'My horse is better *than* yours is', the clauses '*as* yours is' and '*than* yours is' answer the question 'To what extent is my horse good?'. In the sentence: *Ut seris, ita metes,* '*As* you sow, so shall you reap', the clause 'as you sow' answers the question 'How' or 'In what manner shall you reap?' Clauses of Comparison can therefore be divided into 'Adverbial Clauses of Degree', and 'Adverbial Clauses of Manner'.

Again, in the sentence: *Ita facit ut iubetur,* 'He does as he is told', the clause 'as he is told' contains a real fact, and therefore requires the indicative mood. But in the sentence: *Ambulat quasi claudus sit,* 'He walks as if he were lame', the clause 'as if he were lame' compares the manner of walking with an imaginary condition, and therefore requires the subjunctive mood, just as in 'ideal' or 'unreal' conditions. Clauses of Comparison therefore fall into a further two classes, the 'real' and the 'unreal'. The latter are sometimes called 'Conditional Clauses of Comparison'.

251. *The Comparative Conjunctions*

The Latin relative adverbs which introduce clauses of comparison are: *quam,* 'as' or 'than'; *ut,* 'as'; *atque (ac),* 'as' or 'than'; together with various compounds of them such as *tanquam* (= *tam* and *quam* joined in one word); *sicut* (= *sic* + *ut*); *velut; quasi* (= *quam* + *si,* 'as if'). *Tanquam* and *quasi* are mostly used in 'conditional' or 'unreal' comparisons, but sometimes in the sense of *ut,* 'as'. *Ut,* 'as', i.e. 'in the way in which', is equivalent to *quem ad modum* (or *quemadmodum*) or *quomodo,* which phrases may be substituted.

The English relative adverb 'as' serves as a conjunction to introduce either clauses of degree or clauses of manner. In the former case, along with its correlative demonstrative 'so' or 'as', it means '*to that degree or extent to which*', and the corresponding Latin conjunction is *quam,* answering to *tam.* In the latter case it means 'in the *manner* in which', and the corresponding Latin conjunction is *ut,* answering to the correlative demonstratives *ita* or *sic.*

It has already been pointed out, in Section 80, how *quam,* 'as', also came to be used in the sense of 'than', to introduce clauses expressing unlikeness, after comparatives.

In Section 216, in connexion with *simulac,* it was shown how the co-ordinating conjunction *atque* came to be used in a subordinating function in the sense of 'as' or 'than'. *Atque* is only so used after adjectives or adverbs which directly express likeness or unlikeness, such as *idem,* 'the same'; *alius,* 'different', 'other'; *aliter,* 'differently', 'otherwise'; *par* and *pariter,* 'equal', 'equally'; *similis,* 'similar' (cf. *simul*); *perinde,* lit. 'continuing thence throughout', and so 'along the same lines', 'in like manner'; *pro eo,* 'in conformity with that', and so 'just as', 'in proportion as', etc. The co-ordinate origin of this use can easily be seen in sentences such as the following: *Hoc aliud est atque illud,* lit. 'This is different *and* (so is) that', i.e. 'This is *other than* that' or 'different *from* that'. *Perinde egit ac iussus est,* lit. 'He acted in such a manner *and* he was ordered (to act in such a manner)', i.e. 'He acted *just as* he was ordered (to act)'.

But while English always has to use the adverb 'as' (whether demonstrative or relative) with all adjectives and adverbs, to indicate comparative intensity ('as big as'), Latin has several separate demonstrative adjectives and adverbs with their relatives which are normally used instead of *tam . . . quam: tantus . . . quantus*, 'as big as' (= *tam magnus quam*); *talis . . . qualis*, 'such as'; *tot . . . quot*, 'as many as' (= *tam multa quam*); *tantopere . . . quantopere*, 'as much as' (with verbs, for which *tam . . . quam* are also sometimes used). (*Totiens . . . quotiens, tamdiu . . . quamdiu*, as also *postquam, antequam* and *priusquam*, are counted as temporal conjunctions, since they introduce comparative clauses of time.)

After *idem* the pronoun *qui* is as common as the conjunction *atque*.

Note. The circumstances under which the ablative case can perform the function of an adverbial clause of comparison are indicated in Sections 78–81. The ablative is restricted mostly to difference of degree, normally in the degree of some quality possessed by the persons or things denoted by two nouns or pronouns: *nemo sapientior est Socrate*. In a few stereotyped expressions only is the ablative used in expressing a difference of *manner*, in comparing two actions. This can happen only when a verbal noun is used to express the action with which the main action is compared: *Revenit celerius exspectatione omnium*, 'He came back more quickly than everyone expected'.

252. *Comparative Clauses of Degree*

In the following examples the words representing the compared things are italicized in the English:

(*a*) Likeness: *Hic vir tam clarus est quam ille* (*est*). '*This man* is as famous as *that* (one is).' (Two nouns compared.) *Hic ager tam latus est quam longus* (*est*). 'This field is as *broad* as it is *long*.' (Two qualities compared.) *Scribit tam plane quam* (*scribit*) *celeriter*. 'He writes as *clearly* as (he writes) *quickly*.' (Two manners of action compared.) *Haec urbs tanta est quanta illa* (*est*). '*This city* is as large as *that* (one is).' *Nunquam urbem tantam vidi quanta haec* (*est*). 'I have never seen so large *a city* as *this*.' *Haec res talis est qualis illa*. '*This thing* is of the same character as *that*.' *Tot sententiae sunt quot* (*sunt*) *homines*. 'There are as many *opinions* as there are *men*.' (= *tam multae . . . quam multi . . .*) *Idem est qui* (or *atque*) *semper fuit*. '*He* is the same as *he* always was.' *Hoc idem est quod* (or *atque*) *illud*. '*This* is the same as *that*.'

(*b*) Unlikeness: *Hic vir clarior est quam ille*. '*This man* is more famous than *that*.' *Hic ager longior est quam latior* (*est*). 'This field is *longer* than it is *broad*.' (See note i). *Scribit celerius quam planius*. 'He writes more *quickly* than *clearly*.' (Note i). *Hoc aliud est atque illud* (*est*). '*This* is different from (other than) *that*.'

Note i. When a difference of degree is expressed between two qualities, or between two manners of action, the second adjective or adverb is illogically attracted into the comparative. This, however, is not a really common method of expression till the time of Livy. The normal classical method is to use *magis* in the main clause, and to retain the positive after *quam* in the subordinate clause: *Hic ager magis longus est quam latus*, 'This field is rather long than broad'. *Scribit celeriter magis quam plane*, 'He writes quickly rather than clearly'.

Note ii. Except after *idem* and *alius*, and their equivalents (e.g. *similis*, *dissimilis*, etc.), and except for *quantus*, *quot*, etc., the conjunction in clauses of degree is always *quam*.

Note iii. A quality or manner of action may be compared with a possible result, i.e. *quam* may introduce a consecutive clause: *sapientior est quam ut hoc credat*. 'He is wiser than (so as) to believe this.' *lentius cucurrit quam ut aufugeret*. 'He ran too slowly to escape.' See Section 166.

Note iv. Quam may be followed by a prepositional phrase consisting of *pro* with the ablative in the sense of 'in conformity with', 'in accordance with', 'in proportion to': *cautius se gessit quam pro nota illa audacia eius*, 'He acted more cautiously than (was) in accordance with his well-known audacity' (i.e. 'than one would have expected from his well-known audacity').

253. *Comparative Clauses of Manner*

(*a*) Likeness: (*Sic*) *facit ut iubetur; perinde ac iubetur, sic facit; ut iubetur, ita facit; facit sicut iubetur;* etc. '*He does* as *he is told*.' *revenit tam celeriter quam ivit*. '*He returned* as quickly as *he went*.' (See Note i.)
(*b*) Unlikeness: *Aliter facit ac iubetur*. '*He does* otherwise than *he is told*.' This construction originates in the co-ordination: *Aliter facit atque aliter iubetur* (*facere*). 'He acts in one way, *and* he is ordered (to act) in another.' There are several ways of expressing the same idea, e.g. *aliter facit, aliter iubetur*. Cf. *aliud dicit, aliud sentit*. 'He says one thing, (and) he thinks another.' (= *aliud dicit ac sentit; aliter dicit ac sentit; aliter dicit, aliter sentit*.) *celerius revenit quam ivit*. '*He returned* more quickly than *he went*.' (See Note i, below.)

Note i. In the last examples in (*a*) and (*b*) above, two *actions* are compared, in respect of their manner, and not two *manners of action*, as in the third examples in Section 252 (*a*) and (*b*). Therefore *quam ivit* is an adverbial clause of manner, not of degree. Nevertheless, with an adverb other than *aliter*, etc., the conjunction is *quam*.

Note ii. It is possible for the verb of one or both of two compared actions to be in the subjunctive, whether of Will, Wish, or Potentiality. This often happens after *potius quam, citius quam, prius quam, libentius quam*, or the equivalent. The effect of the moods in the following sentences may be compared: *reprehendo eum potius quam laudo*. 'I am censuring rather than praising him.' (Indicative of objective fact—'my words amount to censure rather than praise'.) *reprehendam eum potius quam laudem.* 'I *would* censure him rather than (I would) praise him.' (Both potential). *moriatur potius quam cedat.* 'Let him die rather than yield' (= 'He *is to die* rather than *he is to yield*'. Here both subjunctives are jussive, of Will). *Utinam moriar potius quam serviam.* 'May I die rather than be a slave.' (Both optative.) But the subjunctive of jussive or optative origin in the above *quam*-clauses comes under the heading of the 'final' subjunctive, and cannot be differentiated from the final subjunctive after *antequam* and *priusquam* dealt with in Sections 227–8. It is required after *quam* in comparative clauses whenever the compared action is one that is to be, or was, *purposely rejected.* It is possible for the main clause to be an indicative statement, but it will be such as to imply purpose: *Animam amisit potius quam cederet.* 'He laid down his life rather than yield.'

The use of *ut* to introduce this subjunctive after *quam* is obviously unnecessary, and is, in fact, unclassical. It is used occasionally by Livy, and more frequently from then on, usually when the main clause is in the accusative and infinitive of *O. O.*: Livy 4, 2, 8 (*dicunt*) *se miliens morituros potius quam ut tantum dedecoris admitti patiantur.* 'They said they would die a thousand deaths rather than (that they should) suffer such a disgrace to be incurred.'

When the compared action is expressed in an infinitive depending on the main verb, the infinitive is usually retained after *quam*: Cic. *Fam.* 8, 13, 3 *Curio omnia potius subire constituit quam id pati.* 'Curio decided to suffer all things rather than to allow that.' (Here, too, *pateretur* would be possible, though less usual in classical Latin.)

Note iii. An *ut*-clause of manner can frequently express: (*a*) an adversative or concessive idea, (*b*) an explanatory or causal sense, (*c*) a restrictive or limiting sense, as follows: (*a*) Concessive: *ut via brevis est, ita ardua.* 'As the road is short, so it is steep' = '*Though* the road is short, *yet* it is steep.' This use of *ut . . . ita* is not to be confused with that of *ita* followed by a consecutive *ut*-clause (Section 167), which also may produce an adversative effect, e.g. Cic. *Scaur.* 5 *mortem ita laudant ut fugere vitam vetent.* 'They so praise death as to forbid the shunning of life' = '*Though* they praise death, *yet* they forbid etc.' Here it will be observed that it is the main clause (*ita laudant*) that makes the concession, whereas, in the indicative clause of comparison above, it is the subordinate *ut*-clause (*ut brevis est*) that makes the concession. (*b*) Causal: *ille, ut erat stultus, nihil profecit.* 'He, *in accordance with the fact that* he was foolish, made no headway' or 'Foolish *as he was*, he made no headway'. Frequently the verb is omitted in such clauses: *ille, ut stultus, nihil profecit.* 'He, as (being) foolish, etc.' (*c*) Limiting: In the above causal sense, *ut* implies 'as was to be expected, considering the circumstances'. It can also imply '*as much as could be expected*, considering the circumstances', in an apologetic or restrictive sense. So one might say: *multum profecit, ut stultus.* 'He made great headway, *considering his folly*', or '. . . , *for a fool*'. In this restrictive sense, the *ut*-clause is always abbreviated, the verb being omitted.

Note iv. Although the conjunction after adjectives and adverbs expressing unlikeness (*alius, contrarius, aliter, contra, secus,* etc.) is generally *atque,* nevertheless *quam* is also found, less commonly in classical Latin, more commonly from Livy on. In classical Latin *quam* is found as follows: (*a*) after *contra: res evenit contra quam exspectaverat.* 'The affair turned out oppositely from what he had expected.' But *atque* is regular; (*b*) after *alius, aliter, secus,* but only when negatived, e.g. *nullus alius quam . . .* 'no other than'. In classical Latin there are only isolated examples of *quam* after these words, when not negatived, but it is common enough in Livy and later authors. (*c*) For 'no other than' in the sense 'no one *but*', or 'nothing else but', Cicero always says *nihil aliud nisi.*

254. *Conditional or 'Unreal' Comparative Clauses*

When the idea expressed in the main clause is compared with something hypothetical ('He walks *as if* he *were* lame'), the comparative clause contains the protasis of an 'ideal' or 'unreal' conditional sentence, of which the apodosis is suppressed. The above example stands for 'He walks as (he would walk), if he were lame'. The Latin for 'He would walk so, if he were lame' would be *sic ambulet, si claudus sit.* The subjunctive is required in the comparative clause for the same reason, and is of the same type as in the protasis of ideal or unreal conditions.

The conjunctions are the same as for clauses of manner, with the addition of *si: ut si* (or *velut si*), *ac si, quasi* (from *quam si,* which remain uncompounded rarely, except after comparatives), *tanquam si. Tanquam* and *velut* are sometimes used with the subjunctive without *si.*

255. *Tenses of the Subjunctive in Unreal Comparisons*

Clauses of 'ideal' or 'unreal' comparison differ from Conditional clauses to the extent that the imperfect and pluperfect subjunctive found in present and past 'unreal' conditions is not used, if the main clause refers to the present or future, unless it is particularly desired to stress the unreality. In other words, the sequence of tenses is usually observed. This means that, if the tense of the main verb is primary, the verb of the 'unreal' comparative clause is generally present, perfect, or future periphrastic subjunctive. If the main verb is historic, the verb of the comparative clause is imperfect, pluperfect, or future-in-the-past periphrastic subjunctive (*-urus essem*):

(*a*) Primary: *ambulat tanquam si* (*quasi, velut si, perinde ac si, etc.*) *claudus sit.* 'He is walking as if he were lame.' *celerius currit quam si fugiat hostem.* 'He is running faster than if he were flying from an enemy.' *perinde dolet ac si omnem pecuniam perdiderit.* 'He is as grieved as if he had lost all his money.' *perinde terretur ac si moriturus sit.* 'He is as frightened as if he were going to die.'

If, in the above sentences, it were a known fact that the man was not really lame, that he had not really lost his money, etc., and if it were wished to make this clear, we should find: . . . *tanquam si claudus esset . . . perinde ac si perdidisset, . . . celerius quam si fugeret, . . . moriturus esset.*

(*b*) Historic: *ambulabat tanquam si claudus esset.* 'He was walking as if he was lame.' *celerius currebat quam si fugeret hostem.* 'He was running faster than if he had been flying from an enemy.' *perinde dolebat ac si omnem pecuniam perdidisset.* 'He was as grieved as if he had lost all his money.' *perinde terrebatur ac si moriturus esset.* 'He was as frightened as if he was going to die.'

256. *Further Examples and Notes*

(Cf. Section 252 (*a*)): Plaut. *Capt.* 310 *tam ego fui ante liber quam natus tuus; tam mihi quam illi libertatem hostilis eripuit manus; tam ille apud nos servit, quam ego nunc apud te servio.* 'I was formerly as free as your son; I as much as he lost my liberty at the hands of the enemy; he is as much a slave among us as I am now with you.' (Though *tam . . . quam* normally qualify adjectives or adverbs, they are sometimes used, as above, to qualify verbs directly, in the sense of *tantum . . . quantum* or *tantopere . . . quantopere.*) Cic. *Br.* 140 *non tam praeclarum est scire Latine quam turpe nescire.* 'It is not so famous to know Latin, as it is disgraceful not to know it.' Vell. 2, 89, 5 *dictaturam, quam pertinaciter ei deferebat populus, tam constanter reppulit.* 'He rejected the dictatorship as firmly as the people offered it him persistently.' Cic. *Verr.* 3, 194 *frumentum tanti fuit quanti iste aestimavit.* 'Corn was worth as much as (the amount at which) he valued it.' *Id. Lael.* 82 *plerique habere amicum talem volunt, quales ipsi esse non possunt.* 'Most people want to have a friend of such a character as they themselves cannot be.' Ter. *Phorm.* 454 *quot homines, tot sententiae.* 'As many men, as many minds.' Cic. *Fin.* 4, 7 *nihil commutantur animo, et idem abeunt qui venerant.* 'They are nothing changed in mind, and go away the same as they came.' *Id. Leg.* 1, 25 *virtus eadem in homine ac deo est.* 'Virtue is the same in man as in God.' Plaut. *Mil.* 1251 *parem hic sapientiam habet ac formam.* 'He has a wisdom equal to his beauty.'

257. (Cf. 252 (*b*)): Cic. *Inv.* 1, 51 *si vicinus tuus equum meliorem habeat quam tuus est, tuumne equum malis, an illius? . . . quid si fundum meliorem habeat quam tu habes, utrum tandem fundum habere malis?* 'If your neighbour had a better horse than yours is, would you prefer your horse or his? . . . Again, if he had a better farm than you have, which farm would you prefer to have?'

From the above correct expression it is to be observed that *quam*, like

English 'than', introduces a *clause*, which requires a finite verb, whether expressed or understood ('than yours *is*'), and therefore requires the nominative case after it. Nevertheless Latin has the ungrammatical equivalent of the English 'I have seen no one wiser than *him*', (where 'than' is apparently mistaken for a preposition = 'besides'): Ter. *Phorm.* 591 *ego hominem callidiorem vidi neminem quam Phormionem.* 'I have seen no shrewder man than Phormio' (for . . . *quam Phormio est.*) But this happens only after an accusative in the main clause. It is also worth observing that . . . *fundum meliorem quam tu habes* stands for . . . *quam quem tu habes*, 'than that which you have', i.e. the object *quem* of *habes* is understood. This omission of the relative pronoun is regular, but *quem* may be inserted, and other relative words, e.g. *quantum*, *quot*, etc., usually are: Cic. *Verr.* 2, 70 *ait accusatores eius multo maiorem pecuniam praetori polliceri quam quantam hic dedisset.* 'He said that his accusers were promising the praetor a much greater sum than (the amount which) he had given.' (But . . . *quam hic dedisset* would also be correct.) Livy 35, 12, 14 *plures occiderat quam quot supererant.* 'He had slain more than (the number which) survived.' (*quam supererant* also correct.) *Id.* 22, 38, 8 *Paulli contio fuit verior quam gratior populo.* 'Paullus' speech was more truthful than pleasing to the people.' *Id.* 41, 10, 3 *exercitus acrius quam perseverantius pugnavit.* 'The army fought with more keenness than perseverance.' Cf. also Cic. *Mil.* 78, but for the commoner classical method of expression, cf. Cic. *Att.* 10, 1, 4 *Celer tuus disertus magis est quam sapiens.* 'Your friend Celer is more eloquent than wise.' *Id. T. D.* 1, 41 *quod subtiliter magis quam dilucide dicitur.* 'This is spoken with greater subtlety than clarity.'

Tacitus frequently leaves *magis* to be understood from *quam*, and sometimes uses a positive after a comparative: *Hist.* 1, 83 *nimia pietas vestra acrius quam considerate excitavit.* 'Your excessive affection has roused you with greater zeal than prudence.'

258. (Cf. notes to 252): Plaut. *Pseud.* 1133 *alio sunt illi ingenio atque tu.* 'They are of different character from you.' Ter. *Phorm.* 31 *ne simili utamur fortuna atque usi sumus*, 'that we may not suffer a similar fortune to that which we have (in the past)'. Livy 1, 56, 6 *iuvenis longe alius ingenio quam cuius simulationem induerat*, 'a youth far different in character from that of which he had put on the pretence' (253, Note iv).

For *pro* with the ablative = 'in proportion to', replacing a clause after *quam*, cf. Livy 10, 14, 21 *minor caedes quam pro tanta victoria fuit.* 'The slaughter was less than in proportion to the greatness of the victory', or '. . . less than one would have expected in so great a victory'. Tac. *Germ.* 45 *patientius quam pro solita Germanorum inertia laborant.* 'They labour more patiently than one would expect from the usual laziness of the Germans.'

259. (Cf. 253 (*a*)): Cic. *de Or.* 2, 261 *ut sementem feceris, ita metes.* 'As you have made your sowing, so will you reap.' *Id. Mil.* 30 *haec, sicut exposui,*

ita gesta sunt. 'These things took place just as I have explained.' *Id. Lael.* 16 *pergratum mihi feceris si, quemadmodum soles de ceteris rebus, sic de amicitia disputaris.* 'You would do me a great favour if, in the manner in which you are wont to discuss other matters, you would so discourse on friendship.' *Id. Att.* 16, 5, 3 *(id) non perinde, atque ego putaram, arripere visus est.* 'He did not seem to seize on it quite as I had expected.' *Id. Br.* 188 *haec perinde accidunt, ut eorum qui adsunt mentes verbis et sententiis tractantur.* 'These things befall according as the minds of those present are handled by your words and arguments.' (After *perinde, proinde,* etc., *atque* and *ut* are about equally common.) Cic. *Cat.* 4, 3 *debeo sperare deos pro eo mihi ac mereor relaturos esse gratiam.* 'I have a right to hope that the gods will repay me according as I deserve.' (or '. . . in proportion to my deserts'). *Id. Fam.* 10, 31, 2 *eum nequaquam proinde ac dignus est oderunt homines.* 'Men do not by any means hate him in proportion as he deserves.' Livy 38, 50, 5 *id, prout cuiusque ingenium erat, interpretabantur.* 'They interpreted it according to their several natures.' (*prout* = *pro ut* = *pro eo ac* or *pro eo ut.*) *Id.* 38, 40, 14 *prout locus iniquus aequusve his aut illis, prout animus pugnantium est, prout numerus, varia fortuna est.* 'The fortune of battle varied according to whether the ground was unfavourable or favourable to one side or the other, according to the courage of the combatants, and according to their number.'

With reference to 253, Note ii, cf. Cic. *de Dom.* 56 *cur me flentes potius prosecuti sunt, quam irati reliquerunt?* 'Why did they escort me tearfully, rather than forsake me in anger?' (= '. . . and not forsake me in anger?' I.e. the question is an objective one put by Cicero from his own point of view. Had he been thinking of the forsaking as something considered and *consciously rejected* by the subject of *prosecuti sunt,* he would have said . . . *potius quam relinquerent.* Cf. the following example.) *Id. T. D.* 2, 52 *Zeno perpessus est omnia potius quam conscios indicaret.* 'Zeno suffered all things rather than give away his accomplices.'

With reference to 253, Note iii, cf. Nep. 4, 1, 1 *Pausanias, ut virtutibus eluxit, sic vitiis est obrutus.* 'Pausanias, though he shone with virtues, yet he was burdened with vices.' Cic. *Rosc. Am.* 33 *aiunt hominem, ut erat furiosus, respondisse . . .* 'They say that the fellow, like the madman he was, replied . . .' *Id. Off.* 3, 58 *Pythius, ut argentarius, apud omnes ordines gratiosus,* 'Pythius, welcomed by all classes, as being a banker . . .' ('as one might have expected, as he was a banker'). Livy 4, 13, 1 *Maelius, ut illis temporibus, praedives,* 'Maelius, a very rich man for those times . . .'.

260. (Cf. 253 (*b*)): Cic. *Off.* 1, 30 *aliter de illis ac de nobis iudicamus.* 'We judge them differently from ourselves.' Nep. 2, 6, 3 *hoc longe alio spectabat atque videri volebant.* 'This aimed in a far different direction from what they wished to appear.' Cic. *N. D.* 2, 23 *coepi secus agere atque initio dixeram.* 'I have begun to argue otherwise than I had said at the beginning.' *Id. Cat.* 3, 20 *iusserunt simulacrum Iovis, contra atque antea fuerat, ad orientem*

convertere. 'They ordered them to turn the statue of Jupiter towards the east, opposite to what it had been before.' *Id. de Dom.* 122 *quid de vestro iure, contra quam proposueram, disputo?* 'Why do I argue about your rights, contrary to what I had intended?' (On *contra quam*, see 253, Note iv.)

261. (Cf. 254–5): Plaut. *Asin.* 427 *tamquam si claudus sim, est ambulandum.* 'I must walk as if I were lame.' Cic. *Fin.* 5, 42 *parvi sic iacent, tanquam omnino sine animo sint.* 'Infants lie just as if they had no mind at all.' For imperfect subj., cf. *Id. Fam.* 13, 43, 2 *Egnatii rem ut tueare aeque a te peto ac si mea negotia essent.* 'I beg you to protect Egnatius' interests equally as if it were my business.' (That Egnatius' interests are not really Cicero's, i.e. that the condition is truly 'unreal', is clear.) *Id. Inv.* 1, 104 *rem verbis ante oculos eius ponimus, ut id, quod indignum est, perinde illi videatur indignum, ac si ipse interfuerit ac praesens viderit.* 'In our verbal description we set the matter before his eyes so that what is unworthy seems just as unworthy to him, as if he himself had been present and seen it in person.' Livy 31, 1, 1 *me quoque iuvat, velut ipse in parte laboris ac periculi fuerim, ad finem belli Punici pervenisse.* 'I, too, am pleased to have reached the end of the Punic War, just as if I myself had shared its toil and danger.' Cf. Cic. *Att.* 3, 13, 1 *quoniam nihil ad me scribis, proinde habebo ac si scripsisses nihil esse.* 'Since you write me nothing, I shall take it as if you had written that there was nothing (to write about).' (The 'unreality' is stressed, since Atticus has actually written nothing.) Sall. *Jug.* 46, 6 *Metellus pariter ac si hostes adessent, munito agmine incedere.* 'Metellus, just as if the enemy had been present, proceeded to advance with a guarded column.' (*incedere* is historic inf. = a historic tense). Livy 9, 25, 9 *deleta est Ausonum gens perinde ac si internecivo bello certasset.* 'The Ausonian people was wiped out just as if it had fought a war to the death.' (I.e. though it had actually been captured without a fight.)

XXIII

Remarks on Reported Speech

262. It will be convenient in this chapter to recapitulate the various forms of reported speech: (1) The words or thoughts of another may be quoted unchanged (in *Oratio Recta, O. R.*), either with an inserted parenthesis, to show that they are not the speaker's or writer's own, as Cic. *T. D.* 3, 5 *Animus aeger, ut ait Ennius, semper errat.* 'A sick mind, as Ennius says, always errs.' (*aio* is the commonest verb in such parentheses); or else they may be turned into a noun-equivalent standing as object of a verb of speaking: "*Animus aeger,*" *inquit Ennius,* "*semper errat.*" "A sick

mind," says Ennius, "always errs." (2) The words may be reported indirectly, being adapted to the point of view, with regard to person, tense, or mood, of the reporter (*Oratio Obliqua, O. O.*): *Ennius dicit animum aegrum semper errare.*

263. (1): The only verb which is regularly used to introduce direct quotation is the defective verb *inquam*. The following are examples of the regular formula and order of words: Caes. *B. G.* 7, 38, 7 "*Quasi vero,*" *inquit ille,* "*non necesse sit nobis Gergoviam contendere.*" "As if," said he, "it were not necessary for us to march to Gergovia." Cic. *N. D.* 1, 17 "*Mihi vero,*" *inquit Cotta,* "*videtur.*" "That indeed," said Cotta, "is my opinion."

The subject of *inquit*, when expressed, normally follows it, as in the above examples. But when *inquit* has adverbial modifications, the subject is placed first along with them, and *inquit* is sandwiched between the quoted words, as before: Cic. *de Or.* 1, 134 *tum Crassus arridens,* "*Quid censes,*" *inquit,* "*Cotta?*" 'Then Crassus said, smiling, "What do you think, Cotta?"'

The dative of the person to whom the words are addressed sometimes comes first (*Cui ille arridens:* "...), but sometimes follows *inquit*: Cic. *Att.* 5, 1, 3 *at illa, audientibus nobis,* "*Ego sum,*" *inquit,* "*hic hospita.*" *Tum Quintus,* "*En,*" *inquit mihi,* "*haec ego patior quotidie.*" 'But she, within our hearing, said "I am only a stranger here." Then Quintus said to me: "See! This is what I put up with every day."'

Inquit, not *respondet*, is normally used, even in quoting the reply to a question: Livy 22, 22, 12 *miranti Bostari percontantique . . .* "*Obsides,*" *inquit,* "*in civitates remitte.*" 'To Bostar's wondering question he replied: "Send back the hostages to their communities."'

264. *Dico* and *loquor* do not normally introduce direct quotation, but may have a pronoun (e.g. *haec, talia*) as object, to which quoted words may stand in apposition, and with *loquor* we frequently find *hunc in modum, sic,* or *ita*: Livy 22, 60, 5 *tum T. Manlius Torquatus ita locutus fertur*: ". . . 'Then T. Manlius Torquatus is said to have spoken as follows: ". . .'

But *dico* has to be used, when a form of the verb is required in which *inquam* is deficient, and there are occasional examples of *respondeo, aio,* and *exclamo* introducing direct speech: Cic. *Planc.* 33 *Granius M. Druso multa in rem publicam molienti, cum ille eum salutasset, ut fit, dixissetque* "*Quid agis, Grani?*", *respondit* "*Immo vero tu, Druse, quid agis?*" 'When M. Drusus, who had many unconstitutional schemes in hand, greeted him in the usual way, and said "How are you, Granius?", Granius replied "Nay, what are *you* contriving, Drusus?"' (The play on the double meaning of *quid agis?* cannot be reproduced.) Livy 21, 54, 2 "*Hic erit locus,*" *Magoni fratri ait,* "*quem teneas.*" '"This," said he to his brother Mago, "will be the place for you to hold."' Plaut. *Amph.* 1063 *ibi nescioquis maxima voce exclamat:* "*Alcumena, adest auxilium.*" 'Thereupon someone cried out in a loud voice: "Alcmena, help is at hand."' Livy 3, 2, 8 *unus ex statione hostium exclamat: "Ostentare hoc est, Romani, non gerere bellum."* 'Someone from the enemy outpost cried out: "This is to make a show of war, Romans, not to wage it."'

265. (2): Two kinds of indirect speech should be distinguished: (*a*) that which is dependent upon a verb of speaking or its equivalent which is expressed, as: *Dixit tempus venisse, libertatis, quam diu sperassent, potiundae.* 'He said that the time had come for gaining the liberty for which they had long hoped'; (*b*) that which arises naturally in the course of a long narrative, when the author, without introducing any verb of speaking or thinking, begins to represent the words, thoughts, or motives of the characters: Livy 23, 32, 7–9 *erant qui Magonem cum classe copiisque, omissa Italia, in Hispaniam averterent; cum Sardiniae recipiendae repentina spes adfulsit. 'Parvum ibi exercitum Romanum esse; veterem praetorem inde A. Cornelium provinciae peritum decedere, novum exspectari. ad hoc fessos iam animos Sardorum esse diurnitate imperii; et proximo iis anno acerbe atque avare imperatum. gravi tributo et conlatione iniqua frumenti pressos. nihil deesse aliud quam auctorem ad quem deficerent.'* 'There were some who were for passing Italy by and diverting Mago with his fleet and forces to Spain, when the sudden hope shone forth of recovering Sardinia. "The Roman army there was small: the old praetor, Aulus Cornelius, who knew the province, was on the point of leaving it, and a new governor was awaited. In addition the spirited Sardinians were weary of their long discipline, and in the last year the Roman rule had been harsh and greedy. They were oppressed by the weight of their tribute and an unjust contribution of corn. Nothing was wanting but a leader to whom they might desert."'

Such unheralded transitions to *Oratio Obliqua* are common in Latin historical prose, and also in English from the eighteenth century onwards: 'Her resentment of such behaviour, her indignation at having been its dupe, for a short time made her feel only for herself; but other ideas, other considerations, soon arose. *Had Edward been intentionally deceiving her? Had he feigned a regard for her which he did not feel? Was his engagement to Lucy an engagement of the heart? No; whatever it might once have been, she could not believe it such at present. His affection was all her own. She could not be deceived in that. . . . He certainly loved her.*' (Jane Austen.)

The life that is added to English by the introduction of this Latin trick of style hardly needs to be pointed out. This unheralded type of *oratio obliqua*, subject to the usual changes of tense, mood, and person, can retain the order of words and much more of the emotion of the original *oratio recta* than is possible in the more formal dependent type. Therefore a separate grammatical term has been sought for it, and 'Represented Speech' has been suggested.[1] It is to be observed, however, that such transitions are not always so clearly marked in English as they are in

[1] By Professor Otto Jespersen.

Latin. In Latin the accusative and infinitive leaves no doubt that the author is reporting the thoughts of someone else. Even the rhetorical questions in the above passage from *Sense and Sensibility* would be expressed in Latin by the accusative and infinitive (see Section 267).

266. *Main Clauses in* Oratio Obliqua

The rules for converting main clauses to *oratio obliqua* have been given in Sections 29 ff., 139 ff., and 178 ff. They may be summarized as follows: (1) An indicative statement becomes a dependent noun-phrase, of which the subject is in the accusative and the verb is in the appropriate tense of the infinitive: *O. R. Aliquis hoc dicit. O. O.* (*Dicunt*) *aliquem illud dicere.* (2) Potential statements, of which the verb in *O. R.* was in the present, imperfect, or pluperfect subjunctive, are also reported indirectly by means of the accusative and infinitive. A present subjunctive is represented by the future infinitive (*-urum esse*), and a past subjunctive by the periphrastic 'future-in-the past' infinitive (*-urum fuisse*). The latter is chiefly of importance for the understanding of Conditional Sentences in *O. O.* (see Sections 280 ff.). As it does not occur in Plautus or Terence, it was clearly a literary development of classical times. (3) Commands, prohibitions, and wishes, become dependent noun-clauses with the verb in the subjunctive: *O. R. Nolite desperare. O. O.* (*Hortatus est*) *ne desperarent.* (4) Real questions, whether deliberative or of the factual type, become dependent noun-clauses with the verb in the subjunctive. The rules of sequence are explained in Ch. XIV, Sections 177, 180. (5) Rhetorical questions, not directly dependent on a verb of asking or speaking, are sometimes represented by the accusative and infinitive, sometimes by a subjunctive clause.

267. *Rhetorical Questions in* Oratio Obliqua

The construction of questions that occur in the course of a long indirect report, or in any 'represented' speech or thought, normally depends on the notion conceived to have lain behind the original direct question:
(*a*) If the question was a real one, expecting an answer, an ordinary indirect question-clause is used in *O. O.*, just as after a governing verb of asking: Livy 37, 39, 1 *consul . . . in consilium advocavit, quid sibi faciendum esset, si Antiochus pugnandi copiam non faceret? instare hiemem, etc.* 'The consul called a council of war. What was he to do, if Antiochus afforded no opportunity of battle? The winter was approaching, etc.' (*O. R. quid mihi faciendum est?*).
(*b*) If the question did not expect an answer, but was merely a lively way of bringing home facts to an audience, or, in soliloquy, of marshalling facts in the mind, then the accusative and infinitive is used, as in ordinary indirect statements: *O. R. Quid est turpius?* (meaning *Nihil est turpius*): *O. O. Quid esse turpius?*

(*c*) If, on the other hand, the direct question was not a disguised statement, but a disguised exhortation or remonstrance, or if it contained a deliberative subjunctive, or implied an expression of opinion as to duty, necessity, or possibility – any of the notions able to be expressed by the independent subjunctive – then it is expressed in *O. O.* by means of a subjunctive clause: *O. R. Num putatis hoc verum esse?* (meaning *Nolite putare hoc verum esse*): *O. O. Num putarent id verum esse?* 'Did they think this was true?' *O. R. Cur hoc fecit?* (meaning *Non debuit hoc facere*, or *Hoc ne fecisset*): O. O. *Cur id fecisset?* 'Why should he have done that?'

It will be seen that the person of the verb in the original question has nothing to do with the form of the indirect question. Nevertheless, a rhetorical question that is a disguised exhortation will naturally be addressed directly to an audience in the second person. Questions that are disguised expressions of opinion as to duty, etc., and therefore likely to be couched in the first or third person, are less numerous. Hence most grammars give it as a rule that, if the person of the verb in the original question was first or third, the accusative and infinitive is used in *O. O.*; if the original verb was in the second person, the subjunctive is used in *O. O.* According to this rule:

Quo fugimus? becomes *Quo se fugere?*
Quo fugitis? ,, *Quo fugerent?*
Quo fugiunt? ,, *Quo eos fugere?*

This rule is based only on rough statistics. Possibly it is useful as a rule of thumb for Latin prose composition, but it is useless for the interpretation of Latin texts.

268. *Examples and Notes*

Usage is complicated by the formal influence of the ordinary indirect question-clause, which sometimes causes a subjunctive clause to be used where we should expect an accusative and infinitive, particularly when a governing verb can easily be understood from the immediate context. Such examples are often difficult to distinguish from those in which the subjunctive is present in its own right, because of a notion of deliberation, exhortation, etc. However, although there are many indeterminate examples, most can be ranged under the heads indicated in the previous section.

(*a*) (The question is a real one, the answer not being implied, or else a governing verb of asking can be understood from the context): Livy 5, 20, 2 *litteras ad senatum misit: Veios iam fore in potestate populi Romani; quid de praeda faciendum censerent?* 'He sent a letter to the senate saying that Veii would soon be in the power of the Roman people. What did they think should be done with the booty?' (*O. R. quid . . . censetis?*) *Id.* 3. 38, 8 *nova res mirabundam plebem convertit, quidnam incidisset cur ex tanto intervallo rem desuetam usurparent?* 'The unexpected action drew the wondering attention of the people. What had happened, to make them resort, after so long an interval, to a procedure which had been abandoned?' (*O. R. quidnam incidit cur . . . usurpent?* The use of the subjunctive here, instead of *quidnam incidisse . . .?* is probably due to the fact that the introductory words are equivalent to a governing verb of asking). *Id.* 4, 44, 3 *furere omnes tribuni plebis repulsa suorum incensi. quidnam id rei esset?* 'All the tribunes were in a rage, angered by the rejection of their kinsmen. What was the meaning of this?' (*O. R. quidnam id rei est?* The accusative and infinitive is not used, either because the tribunes are really puzzled, or else because the expression is a disguised remonstrance). *Id.* 6, 36, 10 *primores patrum interrogando de singulis fatigabant: auderentne postulare ut ipsis plus quingenta iugera habere liceret?* 'They beset the leading senators with harassing questions about details. Did they dare to claim that they themselves should be allowed to hold more than five hundred acres?' (*O. R. audetisne . . .?* The subjunctive is used, not because of the second person, but because *interrogando* acts as a governing verb.)

When the question is remote from any words out of which a governing verb can be understood, the accusative and infinitive is sometimes found; e.g. *quid attinere . . .?* and *quid attineret . . .?* are found without any obvious distinction of sense. Nevertheless the following passages suggest that the choice of construction is not entirely arbitrary: Livy 38, 59, 3 *an non praeter omnium oculos tantum auri argentique in triumpho L. Scipionis, quantum non decem aliis triumphis, sit latum? . . . Id ubi ergo esse regium aurum?* 'Had not more gold and silver been carried past everyone's eyes in the triumph of L. Scipio than in ten other triumphs? . . . Where, then, was this royal gold?' (*O. R. an non . . . est latum? . . . Id ubi ergo est . . . aurum?* Here the subjunctive clause *an non . . . sit latum?* contains an argument of L. Scipio's enemies which is a real question demanding an answer. The accusative and infinitive *id ubi . . . esse . . .?* contains Nasica's denial of possession of the gold, by way of answer, and is equivalent to a statement. Therefore editors who emend *sit latum* to *esse latum* are wrong.) *Id.* 39, 4, 8–11 *quid ab eo quemquam posse aequi exspectare . . .? iam de deorum templis, spoliatis in capta urbe, qualem calumniam ad pontifices adtulerit?* 'What justice could anyone expect of him . . . ? . . . Further, what groundless charge had he brought before the pontiffs about the temples of the gods despoiled in the captured city?' *O. R. quid quisquam . . . potest . . .? . . . qualem calumniam . . . adtulit?* Here again *quid . . . posse* is equivalent to a negative statement, while *qualem . . . adtulerit?* is a real question calling for an answer.)

269. (*b*) (The question is a disguised statement, and does not expect an answer): Caes. *B. G.* 5, 28, 6 *docebant . . . conventura subsidia; postremo quid esse levius aut turpius quam auctore hoste capere consilium?* 'They pointed out that reinforcements would gather; lastly, what was more

silly or disgraceful than to take decisions under the guidance of the enemy?' (*O. R. quid est levius . . .? = nihil est levius*). *Ibid.* 1, 14, 3 *Caesar ita respondit: si veteris contumeliae oblivisci vellet, num etiam recentium iniuriarum memoriam deponere posse?* 'Caesar replied as follows: "If he was willing to forget the ancient insult, could he lay aside the memory of recent injuries also?" ' (*O. R. num possum? = non possum.* For a question to be reported in the accusative and infinitive immediately after a governing verb, as *respondit* here, is rare.) Livy 25, 28, 8 *Karthaginiensibus pulsis, quam superesse causam Romanis cur non incolumes Syracusas esse velint?* 'With the Carthaginians expelled, what reason remained to the Romans for not wishing Syracuse to be unharmed?' (*O. R. quae superest causa? = nulla superest causa.*) *Id.* 3, 62, 1 *quando autem se, si tum non sint, pares hostibus fore?* 'When would they be equal to the enemy, if they were not then?' (*O. R. quando pares hostibus erimus, si nunc non sumus?*) *Id.* 3, 39, 9 (M. Horatius Barbatus is denouncing the Decemvirs to their face – *decem Tarquinios appellantem admonentemque . . .*): *cuius illi partis essent rogitare: – populares? – quid enim eos per populum egisse? – optimates? – qui anno iam prope senatum non habuerint?* 'He kept asking them which party they belonged to. Were they democrats? What measures had they carried through by popular vote? Were they aristocrats? – When they had held no meeting of the senate for nearly a year?' (*O. R. quid per populum egistis? = nihil . . . egistis.*) *Id* 4, 43, 9 *an bello intestino bellum externum propulsaturos?* 'Would they ward off a foreign war by fighting amongst themselves?' (*O. R. an . . . propulsabitis?*) *Id.* 6, 17, 2 *quem prope caelestem fecerint . . ., eum pati vinctum in carcere . . . ducere animam?* 'Did they suffer to drag out his life in prison a man of whom they had almost made a god?' (*O. R. quem . . . fecistis, eum patimini . . .?*) *Id.* 6, 39, 7 *quae munera quando tandem satis grato animo aestimaturos, si spem honoris latoribus incidant?* 'When would they value these boons with sufficient gratitude, if they cut off the proposers from hope of office?' (*O. R. quando . . . aestimabitis . . .?*)

As will be seen from several of the above examples, the use of the accusative and infinitive to report a question in the second person is not so rare as is usually made out. The following example is of particular interest: Livy 22, 50, 5 *cur enim illos, qui se arcessant, ipsos non venire? quia, videlicet, plena hostium omnia in medio essent.* 'Why did not they, who sent the summons to them, come themselves? – Obviously because all the middle ground was full of the enemy.' (*O. R. cur enim vos, qui nos arcessitis, ipsi non venitis?* The two bodies of Roman survivors after Cannae are exchanging messages with a view to effecting a junction. The above reply, which Livy thus reports, is an attempt by the recipients of the first message to excuse themselves by pointing out an awkward *fact*. It is, in effect, a comment on the situation. Had Livy conceived it as a *remonstrance* to the other side, for not making the attempt themselves, or as an attempt to *instigate* them to do so, he would have written: *cur ipsi . . . non venirent,* or *venissent?* 'Why *should* they not (have) come themselves?')

The above examples are all indirect reports of speeches or messages. For rhetorical questions in represented *thought*, cf. Livy 25, 35, 4 *imperator ipse, praeterquam quod hostium auctas copias sentiebat, coniectura etiam ad suspicionem acceptae cladis pronior erat: quonam modo enim Hasdrubalem ac Magonem nisi defunctos suo bello, sine certamine adducere exercitum potuisse? quomodo autem non obstitisse, aut ab tergo secutum fratrem?* 'The general himself, apart from the fact that he perceived that the enemy's forces were increased, was still more inclined to suspect that a reverse had been suffered, when he put two and two together. How had Hasdrubal and Mago been able to bring up their army without a struggle, unless they had successfully concluded their own campaign? And why had not his brother obstructed their passage, or pursued them from behind?' (*O. R. quonam modo . . . potuerunt? quomodo . . . non obstitit aut . . . secutus est frater?* The accusative and infinitive is used because these are not real questions, but awkward *facts* – data which Cn. Scipio is putting together in his mind.)

270. (*c*) (The question contains a notion of deliberation, exhortation, remonstrance, etc.): Caes *B. C.* 1, 72, 1 *Caesar in spem venerat se sine pugna rem conficere posse: cur etiam secundo proelio aliquos ex suis amitteret? cur vulnerari pateretur optime de se meritos milites?* 'Caesar had conceived the hope of being able to bring matters to a conclusion without a battle. Why should he lose any of his men even in a successful battle? Why should he suffer the soldiers who had deserved so well of him to be wounded?' (*O. R. cur . . . amittam? cur . . . patiar . . .?* The retention of the deliberative subjunctive in *O. O.* is obligatory). *Id. B. G.* 5, 29, 5 *quis sibi persuaderet Ambiorigem ad eiusmodi consilium descendisse?* 'Who could persuade himself that Ambiorix had resorted to a measure of that sort?' (*O. R. quis sibi persuadeat . . .?*, which may be either deliberative or potential.) Livy 7, 20, 5 *eane meritos crederet quisquam hostes repente sine causa factos?* 'Could anyone believe that people who had done such services had suddenly turned hostile without cause?' (*O. R. credat quisquam . . .?* – deliberative or potential). Caes. *B. C.* 1, 32, 3 *latum (esse) ut sui ratio absentis haberetur, ipso consule Pompeio; qui si improbasset, cur ferri passus esset? si probasset, cur se uti populi beneficio prohibuisset?* 'It was proposed that account should be taken of him in his absence when Pompey himself was consul. If Pompey had disapproved, why had he allowed the proposal to be carried? If he had approved, why had he prevented him from taking advantage of the favour conferred by the people?' (Here *passus esset* and *prohibuisset* probably represent indicatives of the *O. R.: cur ferri passus est? . . . cur me . . . prohibuit?* But the notion is one of remonstrance, and Caesar was passing an opinion on past unfulfilled obligation, meaning, in effect, *non debuit pati, non debuit prohibere*, – or *ne passus esset, ne prohibuisset*. This accounts for the use of the subjunctive instead of the accusative and infinitive, and the passage is not parallel to the examples under (*a*) above). Livy 3, 7, 2 *totis passim castris fremitu orto:*

quid in deserto agro desides sine praeda tempus tererent? 'Grumbling arose throughout the camp. Why were they idly wasting time in deserted territory without booty?' (*O. R. quid tempus terimus?* Possibly *fremitu orto* may count as a governing verb, in which case the example comes under the heading of (*a*) above. All the same, the underlying notion is one of remonstrance, and the meaning, in effect, is *ne tempus teramus.* Therefore the subjunctive, instead of *quid se tempus terere?*, would have been used in any case.) *Id.* 10, 24, 6 *quid se id aetatis sollicitassent, si alio duce gesturi bellum essent?* 'Why had they solicited him at his age, if they were intending to wage the war under another leader?' (*O. R. quid me sollicitavistis?* Here there is no governing verb in the vicinity, but the sense is 'you *should not have* importuned me . . .'.)

When a rhetorical question is addressed directly to an audience in the second person, it usually contains either a reproach, as in the last example above, or, more often, a veiled exhortation or prohibition: Caes. *B. G.* 1, 40, 4 *si Ariovistus bellum intulisset, quid tandem vererentur?* 'If Ariovistus should make war, what, after all, were they afraid of?' (*O. R. si A. bellum intulerit, quid veremini?* = *nolite vereri.*) Livy 10, 13, 5 *hic terror omnes in Q. Fabium Maximum etiam recusantem convertit: quid se iam senem sollicitarent?* 'This terror made everyone turn to Q. Fabius Maximus, in spite of his reluctance. Why did they solicit him, who was now an old man?' (*O. R. quid me sollicitatis?* = *nolite me sollicitare.*)

271. It will be clear from the examples in the previous sections that the usual grammar-book rule, that rhetorical questions in the first and third persons go into the accusative and infinitive, and questions in the second person into the subjunctive, is without real foundation. The real principles governing the choice of construction are as stated. Nevertheless, the interaction upon one another of habitual methods of expression causes exceptions to any rule that can be drawn up. Regular formulae are used more and more thoughtlessly as time goes on, until fine distinctions are finally blurred, and new methods of making them have to be found. It is difficult to account in any other way for the exchanges of notions between the subjunctive and the infinitive in passages such as the following: Livy 34, 11, 6 *orant ne se deserat: quo enim se, repulsos ab Romanis, ituros?* 'They begged him not to desert them. Where would they go, rejected by the Romans?' Here one might have expected the deliberative notion to be rendered by *quo . . . irent?*, but the accusative and infinitive is used from force of habit. *Id.* 45, 19, 10–15 (Attalus is being dissuaded by Stratius from intriguing against his brother Eumenes): *regnum eorum fraterna stare concordia. Attalum vero, quia aetate proximus sit, quis non pro rege habeat? . . . quid adtineret vim adferre rei sua sponte mox ad eum venturae? . . . sed enimvero quid ad deliberationem dubii superesse? utrum enim partem regni petiturum esse, an totum erepturum?* 'Their kingdom depended on harmony between the brothers. But as Attalus was next in age, who did not consider him as

good as king? What was the point of using violence to secure what would soon come to him of its own accord? Of a truth, what doubt remained to call for deliberation? Would he seek part of the kingdom, or steal the whole?' For *quis non . . . habeat?* one would have expected *quem non . . . habere?* But then there would be ambiguity between the two accusatives – *Attalum . . . quem non . . . habere?*, and this is avoided by using a subjunctive clause. For *quid adtineret?* one would have expected *quid adtinere?*, and there seems no reason for this at all. Finally, *utrum partem petiturum esse, an totum erepturum?*, although it stands for *O. R. utrum . . . petes, an . . . eripies?*, contains a deliberative notion, which would normally be rendered in *O. O.* by *utrum . . . peteret, an . . . eriperet?* It is clear that Livy did not always keep these fine distinctions in mind.

XXIV

Subordinate Clauses in Oratio Obliqua

272. The verb of a clause which was subordinate in the direct form is regularly put in the subjunctive in *O. O.*, whether it was already in the subjunctive, or not. The normal rules about the tenses of the subjunctive in subordinate clauses in *O. O.* are as follows:

(1) An original primary tense of the subjunctive remains unchanged, if the governing verb is primary, but is changed to the corresponding historic tense of the subjunctive, if the governing verb is historic: *O. R. Milites se recipiunt, ne ab hostibus capiantur.* 'The soldiers are retreating, in order that they may not be captured by the enemy.' *O. O.* (*Nuntiatur*) *milites se recipere, ne ab hostibus capiantur.* '(It is reported that) the soldiers are retreating, in order that they may not be captured by the enemy.'

(*Nuntiatum est*) *milites se recipere, ne ab hostibus caperentur.* '(It was reported that) the soldiers were retreating, in order that they might not be captured by the enemy.'

(2) An original historic tense of the subjunctive remains unchanged, whatever the tense of the governing verb:

O. R. Haec cum videret (*vidisset*), *Caesar constituit progredi.* 'When he saw (had seen) this, Caesar decided to advance.'

O. O. Dicunt / *Dixerunt* } *Caesarem, cum illa videret* (*vidisset*), *progredi constituisse.*

(3) An original indicative, whatever its tense, is represented by a primary tense of the subjunctive, if the governing verb is primary, and by a historic tense of the subjunctive, if the governing verb is historic. As this

sequence of tenses is regularly observed, when an original subordinate indicative is being represented, the various aspects of complete or progressive action cannot always be distinguished in *O. O.:*

(*a*) A present indicative is always represented by the present or by the imperfect subjunctive, according to sequence:

O. R. Librum quem lego tibi dabo. 'I will give you the book which I am reading.'

O. O. Dicit se librum quem legat tibi daturum.
Dixit ” ” ” *legeret* ” ” .

N.B. The present and the imperfect subjunctive, when representing a present indicative in the subordinate clause, always denote action contemporaneous with that of the governing verb.

(*b*) Any past tense of the indicative, whether imperfect, perfect, aorist-perfect, or pluperfect, is represented by the perfect or by the pluperfect subjunctive, according to sequence:

O. R. Librum quem heri legebam (legi, iam legeram), tibi dabo. 'I will give you the book which I was reading (read, had already read) yesterday.'

O. O. Dicit se librum quem heri (iam) legerit tibi daturum.
Dixit ” ” ” *pridie (iam) legisset* ” ” .

N.B. The perfect and the pluperfect subjunctive, when representing a past tense of the indicative in the subordinate clause, denote action prior to that of the governing verb, and tense-aspect cannot be differentiated.

(*c*) The future indicative is represented by the periphrastic subjunctive in *-urus sim, -urus essem,* according to sequence, except in subordinate clauses in which the reference to the future is determined by the context. In the latter the future indicative is represented by the simple present or imperfect subjunctive:

O. R. Pecunia quam accipiam iam tibi debetur. 'The money which I shall receive is already owed to you.'

O. O. Dicit pecuniam quam accepturus sit iam tibi deberi.
Dixit ” ” *esset* ” ”
O. R. Si hoc facies, poenas dabis. 'If you do this, you will be punished.'
O. O. Dicit te, si hoc facias, poenas daturum.
Dixit ” *id faceres* ” ”

(*d*) The future-perfect indicative is represented by the perfect or by the pluperfect subjunctive, according to sequence:

O. R. Ubi advenero, scribam ad te. 'When I arrive, I will write to you.'
O. O. Dicit se, ubi advenerit, ad te scripturum.
Dixit ” *advenisset,* ” ”

273. *Examples and Notes*

(1) (Original primary tense of subjunctive in subordinate clause): Caes. *B. G.* 1, 2, 2 *persuasit ut . . . exirent: perfacile esse, cum virtute omnibus praestarent, totius Galliae imperio potiri.* 'He persuaded them to migrate, (saying) that it was easy for them, since they surpassed all in courage, to gain command of all Gaul.' (*O. R. cum . . . praestetis.*) Livy 40, 35, 7 (*dixerunt*) *ita obstinatos esse milites ut non ultra retineri posse in provincia viderentur, iniussuque inde abituri essent, si non dimitterentur.* '(They said that) the soldiers were so fixed in their resolve that it seemed no longer possible to keep them in the province, and that they were likely to depart without orders, if they were not dismissed.' (*O. R. ita obstinati sunt ut . . . videantur, iniussuque inde abituri sint, si non dimittantur.*) Caes. *B. G.* 1, 11, 3 (*legatos mittunt*): *ita se meritos esse ut liberi eorum in servitutem abduci non debuerint.* '. . . such are their services that their children ought not to have been led off into slavery.' (*O. R. ita meriti sumus ut liberi . . . non debuerint.*)

Note. The perfect subjunctive of a consecutive clause, such as that in the last example, is usually retained, even after a historic governing verb: Livy 38, 58, 7 (*Nasica orationem habuit . . .*): *cum illorum gloriam tueri posteris satis esset, P. Africanum tantum paternas superiecisse laudes ut fidem fecerit non sanguine humano sed stirpe divina satum se esse.* '(Nasica said that) though it was enough to maintain for posterity their standard of glory, P. Africanus had so far surpassed his father's renown that he had given rise to the belief that he was born, not of human blood, but of divine descent.' *Id.* 41, 22, 7 *legatos misit petens ne diutius simultatum, quae cum patre suo fuissent, meminissent; nec enim tam atroces fuisse eas ut non cum ipso potuerint ac debuerint finiri.* 'He sent envoys, asking that they should no longer remember the quarrels in which they had engaged with his father; for they had not been so serious that they could not and should not be ended with him.'

In the above examples strict sequence demands *ut fidem fecisset, ut non potuissent ac debuissent.* There is an isolated example of the substitution of the pluperfect in Cic. *de Or.* 1, 26, quoted in Section 163.

274. (2) (Retention of original imperfect or pluperfect subjunctive after primary governing verb): Cic. *Cl.* 32 *memoria teneo Milesiam quandam mulierem, cum essem in Asia, rei capitalis esse damnatam.* 'I remember that, when I was in Asia, a certain Milesian woman was condemned on a capital charge.' (*O. R. mulier, cum in Asia essem, damnata est.*) *Ibid.* 119 *exempli causa ponam illud: C. Getam, cum a censoribus ex senatu eiectus esset, censorem esse ipsum postea factum.* 'I will cite the following as an example, that C. Geta, after being expelled from the senate by the censors, was later made censor himself.' (*O. R. C. Geta, cum . . . eiectus esset, censor . . . factus est.*) Cf. also Cic. *Cl.* 168, 183, etc. The retention of these historic

tenses of the subjunctive is regular in *cum*-clauses, *si*-clauses, final and consecutive clauses, and in any subordinate clause that requires an imperfect or pluperfect subjunctive in the *O. R.*

275. (3) (The subjunctive represents an original indicative): Primary: Caes. *B. G.* 1, 17, 2 (*Dicit*) *hos multitudinem deterrere ne frumentum conferant quod debeant.* 'He says that these are preventing the common people from contributing the corn which they owe.' (*O. R. . . . quod debent.*) Cic. *Cl.* 175 *cecidisse de equo dicitur et, postea quam ad urbem cum febri venerit, paucis diebus esse mortuus.* 'He is said to have fallen from his horse and to have died a few days after he had reached the city in a feverish condition.' (*O. R. postea quam . . . venit.*) Livy 36, 40, 3 (*Dicit*) *se de Gallis postulare triumphum, quos acie vicerit.* 'He says that he claims a triumph over the Gauls whom he has defeated in battle.' (*O. R. . . . quos acie vici.*) *Id.* 39, 54, 10 . . . *neque illos recte fecisse cum in Italiam venerint.* '. . . nor had they done right in coming to Italy.' (*O. R. non recte fecistis cum in Italiam venistis.*) Cic. *Cl.* 64 *non argumentabor eum corrupisse qui in periculo fuerit, eum qui metuerit, eum qui spem salutis in alia ratione non habuerit, eum qui semper singulari fuerit audacia.* 'I will not argue that the bribing was done by him who was liable to prosecution, by him who was in fear, by him who had no hope of safety in any other course, by him who was always of outstanding audacity.' (*O. R. . . . qui in periculo erat . . . metuebat . . . habebat . . . semper erat.*) Livy 42, 52, 14 (*Dicit*) *animos habendos esse quos habuerint maiores eorum.* 'He says that they must display the spirit which their ancestors had.' (*O. R. quos habebant maiores vestri.*) Tac. *H.* 3, 2 *quanto ferocius ante se egerint, tanto cupidius insolitas voluptates hausisse.* 'The more savage had been their former mode of life, the more eagerly they have plunged into unwonted pleasures.' (*O. R. quanto ferocius ante se egerant* (or *agebant*), *tanto cupidius . . . hauserunt.*) Livy 24, 13, 3 *Ii referunt . . ., si signa eius, si castra conspecta a Tarento sint, haud ullam intercessuram moram quin urbs dedatur.* 'They report that, if his standards and if his camp should be seen from Tarentum, there will be no delay in surrendering the city.' (*O. R. si signa tua . . . conspecta erunt, haud ulla intercedet. . . .*)

Note: For a discussion of the representation of the imperfect and pluperfect indicative by the perfect subjunctive, see Section 279.

276. (3) (continued): Historic: Livy 39, 19, 6 (*Senatus consultum factum est*) *uti consules praetoresque, qui nunc essent, quive postea futuri essent, curarent ne quid ei mulieri iniuriae fieret.* '(A senatorial decree was passed) that the consuls and praetors who were now in office, or who would be in office thereafter, should see to it that no harm was done to the woman.' (*O. R. . . . qui nunc sunt, quive postea erunt . . . .*) Livy 35, 5, 11 *consul obtestabatur milites ut paulum adniterentur: victoriam in manibus esse; dum turbatos et trepidantes viderent, instarent; si restitui ordines sivissent, integro*

rursus eos proelio . . . dimicaturos. 'The consul besought the troops to extend their efforts for a little while: victory was in their grasp; let them press on while they saw the enemy in confusion and panic; if they allowed the ranks to be reformed, they would be fighting again in a restored battle.' (*O. R. . . . dum . . . videtis, instate; si . . . siveritis . . . rursus . . . dimicabitis.*) (The retention in *O. O.* of a present indicative after *dum* is rare before the time of Tacitus.) Caes. *B. G.* 1, 34, 4 (*Dixit*) *sibi mirum videri quid in sua Gallia quam bello vicisset Caesari negoti esset.* 'He said it was a matter of wonder to him what business Caesar had in his part of Gaul, which he had conquered in war.' (*O.R . . . . quam bello vici . . . .*) Livy 42, 33, 3 (*Dixit eos*) *id tantum deprecari, ne inferiores iis ordines quam quos, cum militassent, habuissent, adtribuerentur.* 'He said their only request was that there should not be assigned to them ranks inferior to those which they had had, when they had been on service.' (*O. R. deprecamur ne inferiores nobis ordines quam quos, cum militabamus, habebamus, adtribuantur.* This example is instructive, as showing that not even in historic sequence can a subordinate imperfect indicative of the *O. R.* be represented by an imperfect subjunctive, when the priority in time, which it denotes in relation to the main verb, is important. Here *militarent, haberent,* would refer to the time of speaking, and would mean 'that they should not be assigned ranks inferior to those which they *now* held, now that they were on service.' With this compare Livy 42, 25, 10 *id* (*foedus*) *se renovari, non quia probaret, sed quia in nova possessione regni patienda omnia essent, passum.* 'He had allowed the treaty to be renewed, not because he approved of it, but because immediately on assuming the kingship, he had to endure anything.' (Here it is just possible that *essent*, as well as *probarem,* was already in the impf. subj. in the *O. R.*, being virtual *O. O.* – '. . . because, *as I realized*, all was to be endured' – However, one would normally expect the *O. R.* to be: *passus sum, non quia probarem, sed quia omnia patienda erant.* Since *erant* refers to a time prior to that at which Perseus made the statement, it would normally be represented by *fuissent.* If, therefore, *essent* does represent *erant,* it is because the reason holds good even up to the time of speaking, and the priority to the time of the verb of speaking is not important.) *Id.* 35, 44, 6 (*Dixit se*) *nec labori nec periculo parsurum, donec liberam vere Graeciam fecisset.* 'He said that he would spare neither toil nor danger, until he had made Greece truly free.' (*O. R. donec . . . fecero.*) *Id.* 40, 34, 11 *ad consules irent et quae ab iis imperata essent, facerent.* 'They should go to the consuls and do whatever was ordered by them.' (*O. R. ad consules ite, et quae ab iis imperata erunt, facite*). For historic sequence when the verb of speaking is in the Historic Present, cf. Cic. *Cl.* 23 *se nomen Oppianici, si interfectum M. Aurium esse comperisset, delaturum esse testatur.* 'He avowed that he would prosecute Oppianicus, if he found that M. Aurius had been killed.' (*O. R. nomen . . . deferam, si . . . comperero.*) Livy 24, 15, 8 *pronuntiat Gracchus esse nihil quod de libertate sperarent, nisi eo die fusi fugatique hostes essent.* 'Gracchus proclaimed that they had nothing to hope for, as far as liberty was concerned, unless the enemy were routed and put to flight that day.' (*O. R. nihil est quod . . . speretis, nisi hodie hostes fusi . . . erunt.*)

277. *The Representation in* O. O. *of a subordinate Future Indicative of the* O. R.

Although the present subjunctive by nature expresses what *is to be*, and the imperfect subjunctive what *was to be*, this reference to the future, or the future-in-the-past, was obscured, when the subjunctive came to replace the indicative in subordinate clauses as a mere grammatical sign of indirectness. Just as in indirect questions of fact, so in relative and adverbial clauses, it became necessary to employ the periphrasis *-urus sim* (*essem*), when the context did not make it clear that the subordinate clause referred to the future. But the periphrastic subjunctive was a particular feature of literary prose, and was developed as a means to express precise time-relations. Apart from indirect questions of fact, the need for it arises mostly in indirectly reported causal clauses and in relative clauses of the 'determinative' and 'parenthetic' type, whereas in temporal and conditional clauses the time-reference is fixed by the main clause. E.g. in a sentence like 'As you approach, you will see . . .', it is clear that the temporal clause must refer to the future: *ubi, ut, simulac, cum, appropinquabis, videbis . . .: O. O. dixit eum, ubi* (*ut, simulac, cum,*) *appropinquaret, visurum esse . . .* Here no ambiguity arises, and it would be quite unnecessary to say . . . *ubi appropinquaturus esset . . .* But the time to which a causal or a relative clause refers need have no connection with the time of the main clause. One can say: 'Because he used to act, acts, or will act so, he will be miserable in the future.': *Quoniam ita se gerebat, gerit, geret, miser erit.* As *gerit* is represented in *O. O.* by *gerat* or *gereret*, according to sequence, *geret* cannot also be represented by the same forms without ambiguity, and so we get: *Dicit eum, quoniam ita se gesserit, gerat, gesturus sit, miserum fore. Dixit eum, quoniam ita se gessisset, gereret, gesturus esset, miserum fore.*

Similarly, in relative clauses of the parenthetic type, one can say: 'Cicero, who was consul last year, who is a good man, and who will save the state, is my friend.' Again the periphrastic is needed in *O. O.: Dixit Ciceronem, qui priore anno consul fuisset, qui vir bonus esset, quique rem publicam conservaturus esset, suum amicum esse.*

In relative clauses of the descriptive (generic), or generalizing type, on the other hand, the time-relation with the main clause is not so precise or important, and the periphrastic is usually not needed: '*Anyone who* behaves so, will be wretched.' *O. R. Is qui* (*quicumque, si quis*) *ita se geret, miser erit. O. O. Dixit eum qui ita se gereret, miserum fore.*

Although the above are the guiding principles which determine whether the future indicative shall be represented in *O. O.* by the simple or by the periphrastic form of the subjunctive, many exceptions will be found. Colloquial Latin (e.g. Plautus, Terence) tends to prefer the less precise simple form, and even in literary Latin precision has to be neglected, when the verb is passive or when it has no future participle in use. Grammars sometimes give as the passive equivalent of *-urus sim (essem)* the cumbrous periphrasis *futurum sit (esset) ut* . . . but it is doubtful whether this was ever used. It often happens that ambiguity can be avoided by the addition of an adverb such as *mox* or *postea*. Again, the context often admits of the subordinate subjunctive having some real modal force (of deliberation, or necessity), e.g. Ter. *H. T.* 715 *quid me fiat parvi pendis*. Here *fiat* probably represents *fiat* of the *O. R.*: 'You reck little of what *is to become* of me.'

Conversely, examples of the periphrastic will be found in temporal and other clauses, where the simple form normally causes no ambiguity. In these, however, the context usually suggests that it is not a simple future indicative of the *O. R.* that is being represented, but the periphrastic future *-urus sum, eram*, and that the future participle is there in its own right.

Most of these points are illustrated by the examples below.

278. *Examples and notes on the future indicative represented in* O. O.

(*a*) The context fixes the time-reference of the subordinate clause: Livy 35, 35, 8 (*Dicit*) *Aetolos paratos esse venire Lacedaemonem, cum res poscat*. 'He says that the Aetolians are prepared to come to Lacedaemon, when the situation demands it.' (*O. R. cum res poscet.*) Cic. *Cl.* 33 *ab ea petivit ut apud Dinaeam, quoad pareret, habitaret*. 'He begged her to live with Dinaea, until she bore her child.' (*O. R. . . . quoad paries.*) Livy 44, 14, 6 (*Dixit*) *et ad id tempus se cum Romanis stetisse et, quoad bellum foret, staturum*. 'He said he had stood by the Romans up to that time, and would do so, as long as the war lasted.' (*O. R. . . . quoad bellum erit.*) *Id.* 45, 18, 5 *ubi in medio praeda administrantibus esset, ibi nunquam causas seditionum et certaminis defore*. 'Where plunder lay open to the administrators, there would never lack causes of sedition and strife.' (*O. R. ubi . . . erit . . . .*) *Id.* 39, 25, 7 *querelae Thessalorum adiectae, quod ea oppida, si iam redderentur sibi, spoliata ac deserta (rex) redditurus esset*. 'There were added the complaints of the Thessalians that, if the towns were now restored to them, the king would hand them back despoiled and deserted.' (*O. R. (querimur) quod ea oppida, si iam reddentur nobis, rex spoliata ac deserta reddet*. Here the future reference of *si redderentur* in relation to *querelae adiectae sunt* is fixed by *redditurus esset*. But the periphrastic is needed in the *quod*-clause in order to show that it, too, refers to the future in relation to the governing phrase. *quod . . . rex redderet* would mean that the king was actually restoring them at the time at which the complaint was being made.)

(*b*) The context does not fix the time-reference of the sub. clause: Caes. *B. G.* 1, 3, 6 *perfacile factu esse illis probat conata perficere, propterea quod ipse suae civitatis imperium obtenturus esset*. 'He proved to them that it was easy to carry out their designs, because he himself would hold the sovereignty of his own state.' (*O. R. . . . quod ego ipse . . . obtinebo.* Here *obtineret* could only represent *obtineo.*) Livy 39, 13, 5 *magnum sibi metum deorum, quorum occulta initia enuntiaret, maiorem multo, dixit, hominum esse, qui se indicem manibus suis discerpturi essent.* 'She said she had a great fear of the gods whose secret initiatory rites she was to divulge, but a much greater fear of the men who would tear her to pieces with their hands as an informer.' (*O. R. magnus mihi metus est deorum, quorum occulta initia enuntiem, maior multo hominum, qui me . . . discerpent* – or *discerpturi sunt.*) *Id.* 37, 10, 10 *paucas (naves) ante portum Ephesi in salo habiturum, quas, si exire res cogeret, obiecturus certamini foret.* 'He would keep a few ships in front of the harbour at Ephesus in deep water, which he would expose to battle, if circumstances compelled him to come out.' (*O. R. paucas . . . habebo, quas, si exire res coget, obiciam certamini.*)

But in most examples in which the periphrastic subjunctive is used, it may well stand for a periphrastic future indicative in the *O. R.*, i.e. the future participle may be there in its own right, conveying the notion of likelihood or intention: Livy 39, 5, 8 *petere ut ex ea pecunia, quam in aerario positurus esset, id aurum secerni iuberent.* 'He requested that out of the money which *he was intending* to place in the treasury, they would order that gold to be set aside.' (*O. R. . . . quam positurus sum.*) This is always the explanation, when the periphrastic occurs in clauses which do not normally require it: Cic. *Cl.* 158 *non enim debeo dubitare, iudices, quin . . . etiam si inviti absoluturi sitis, tamen absolvatis.* 'I ought not to doubt, gentlemen, that you would acquit him, even if you were likely to be doing so unwillingly.' Here the simple form and the periphrastic appear to have changed places, but the translation shows the reason: *absolvatis* is potential, and would still be *absolvatis*, even if not dependent on *non dubito quin. absoluturi sitis* is used in the *si*-clause, because the reinforcing sense of the future participle would have been required also in the non-dependent form of the sentence, which would be: *etiam si eum inviti absoluturi sitis, tamen absolvatis.*

(*c*) The subordinate clause has a general reference, so that no particular time-relation with the main clause needs to be expressed:

Caes. *B. G.* 7, 90, 2 *legati ab Arvernis missi quae imperaret se facturos pollicentur.* 'Envoys sent by the Arverni promised to do what he ordered.' (Here it does not matter whether *imperaret* stands for *imperabis* or *imperas.*) Livy 39, 39, 8 *respondit Flaccus nihil quod se indignum esset facturum.* 'Flaccus replied that he would do nothing that was unworthy of him.' (*O. R. . . . nihil quod me indignum sit . . .* i.e. the clause was probably generic in *O. R.*) *Id.* 37, 49, 8 (*denuntiatum est*) *si qua deinde legatio ex Aetolis, nisi permissu imperatoris qui eam provinciam obtineret, venisset Romam, pro hostibus omnes futuros.* 'If any embassy from the Aetolians subsequently came to Rome, except by the permission of the general who was holding (i.e. who would be holding) that province, they would all be treated as enemies.' (*O. R. si . . . legatio, nisi permissu imperatoris qui eam provinciam obtinebit, venerit Romam, pro hostibus omnes erunt.* Here, if a particular general and a particular time were referred to, *qui . . . obtenturus esset* would be required. Cf. Livy 39, 26, 13 *nec enim ullius rei minus diuturnam esse gratiam quam libertatis, praesertim apud eos qui male utendo eam corrupturi sint.* 'Nor was gratitude for anything shorter-lived than for liberty, especially with those who would defile it by making an ill use of it.' Here the relative clause is not generalizing, because Philip is referring directly to the Perrhaebi and Athamanes, and *corrupturi sint* stands for either *corrumpent* or *corrupturi sunt* of the *O. R.*)

(*d*) The simple form of the subjunctive is used, because the verb is in the passive, or has no future participle in use:

Cic. *Cl.* 45 *intellegebat Habito mortuo bona eius omnia ad matrem esse ventura, quae postea orbata filio minore periculo necaretur.* 'He saw that, when Habitus was dead, his property would all come to his mother, who would later on be murdered with less danger, if deprived of her son.' (*necaretur* can scarcely stand for anything except *necabitur* of the *O. R.*, but it is to be noticed that ambiguity is avoided by the presence of *postea.*) Tac. *Ann.* 14, 61 *ducem tantum defuisse, qui motis rebus facile reperiretur.* 'Only a leader had been wanting, who would easily be found, once disturbances had started.' (*O. R. qui . . . reperietur.*) *Ibid.* 58 *multa secutura quae adusque bellum evalescerent.* 'Many results would follow, which might strengthen into civil war.' (*O. R.* perhaps *quae . . . evalescent*, but possibly generic-consecutive *evalescant.*)

Rather more examples are found in indirect question-clauses than in subordinate clauses of other types. See Section 181.

279. *Excursus on apparent exceptions to rules of sequence*

Examples of the perfect subjunctive representing what must have been subordinate imperfect or pluperfect indicatives in the *O. R.* are numerous enough to show that Roman authors clearly felt themselves restricted by a rule about the sequence of tenses, even when this obscured the exact time-relation between the subordinate verb and the main verb of the *O. R.*, or the particular nuances expressed by the imperfect tense. This restriction, brought about by the analogical extension of the subjunctive to clauses in which it need no longer retain any of its original modal notions, must have been so irksome that it would be surprising if no exceptions were to be found. Examples of historic tenses of the subjunctive which appear to depend on a primary governing verb are in fact so numerous that it has actually been stated as a rule that, after a primary governing verb, the subordinate indicatives of the *O. R.* are reproduced in the subjunctive with their tenses unchanged.[1] But an examination

[1] Handford, *The Latin Subjunctive*, § 166. Cf. Leumann-Hofmann, P. 704: 'Für Caesar gilt das Gesetz: in der orat. obliq. darf überall der Konj. desjenigen Tempus stehen, welches in unabhängiger Rede gesetzt würde.' (This statement does not appear to be restricted to original subordinate subjunctives.)

of the examples will show that, in most of them, the imperfect or pluperfect subjunctive can be accounted for on other grounds, and only a small residue of possible exceptions remains. The following are the circumstances under which a historic tense of the subjunctive may be used after a primary governing verb:

(*a*) It frequently happens that the main verb of a reported sentence was in a past tense, which is represented in the *O. O.* by a perfect infinitive. This perfect infinitive, and not the governing verb of speaking or its equivalent, may account for the tense of the subjunctive in a subordinate clause: *O. R. Aufugit ne caperetur: O. O. Dicisne eum aufugisse ne caperetur?* In a sentence such as the following: *Scipio triumphum postulavit de Gallis quos vicerat*: the pluperfect indicative *vicerat* expresses a time-relation with *postulavit* – the conquering took place before the request for a triumph – but it is the historian recording the event who points out the relation. If the sentence is made dependent on *Blaesus dicit* . . . a new relation is introduced. Both *postulavit* and *vicerat* have to be represented as prior to *dicit*, and it is impossible at the same time to express their relation to one another. The sentence becomes: *Blaesus dicit Scipionem triumphum postulavisse de Gallis quos vicerit.* Here *postulavisse* and *vicerit* express priority to *dicit* independently or absolutely. On the other hand, the subordinate clause could have been in virtual *O. O.* in the original sentence, representing part of what Scipio himself said in requesting a triumph: *Scipio triumphum postulavit de Gallis quos vicisset.* 'Scipio demanded a triumph over the Gauls, whom (as he said) he had conquered.' According to Rule 2 in Section 272, this pluperfect subjunctive is retained when the sentence is made dependent on *Blaesus dicit.* To a careless interpreter this may appear to be a violation of the rules of sequence, but in fact *vicisset* instead of *vicerit* makes a very important difference to the sense.

It is possible that the influence of the perfect infinitive accounts for the tenses of the subjunctive in the following passage: Cic. *Cl.* 79 *confiteor, quod Oppianici nomen ante illud tempus populo ignotum fuisset, indignissimum porro videretur circumventum esse innocentem pecunia, hanc deinde suspicionem augeret Staieni improbitas, causam autem ageret L. Quinctius, summam illi iudicio invidiam infamiamque esse conflatam.* When this is compared with the sentence quoted from Cic. *Cl.* 64 in Section 275 above, it seems unlikely that *fuisset, videretur, augeret, ageret*, represent what would have been pluperfect and imperfect indicatives, if the sentence had not depended on *confiteor.* The non-dependent form would probably be: *summa invidia conflata est quod . . . fuisset . . . videretur . . .* etc., the past tenses of the subjunctive representing the reasons of the people in whom the disgust was aroused. When the sentence is made dependent on *confiteor*, these are retained according to rule. The sense then is: 'I confess that *the popular feeling that* the name of Oppianicus had been unknown to the public before that time, that it seemed outrageous for an innocent man to have been ruined through bribery, a suspicion which was increased by the (known) dishonesty of Staienus, and the fact that L. Quinctius was conducting the case, caused that court to incur the utmost unpopularity and ill repute.'

(*b*) A subordinate clause may contain, not only a pluperfect or imperfect subjunctive of virtual *O. O.* in a sentence which is otherwise independent, but also a past potential, or 'unreal', or a 'generic' subjunctive. When the whole sentence is in *O. O.*, such subjunctives may give the appearance of a violation of sequence. This is undoubtedly the explanation of *dedissent* in Livy 30, 30, 4: *tibi quoque non in ultimis laudum hoc fuerit* (fut. pf.), *Hannibalem, cui tot de Romanis ducibus victorias di dedissent, tibi cessisse.* 'This, too, will prove to have been not the least part of your renown, that Hannibal, *a man to whom* the gods had granted so many victories over Roman generals (*or* '*though* the gods had granted' . . .), yielded to you.' If Livy had imagined Hannibal's independent thought to have been . . . *cui . . . di dederant* . . ., he would have represented it by *dederint* in primary sequence after *fuerit*.

(*c*) The governing verb may be in the Historic Present, after which either primary or historic sequence is possible, even within the same sentence: Cic. *Cl.* 71 *quadraginta milia, si esset absolutus Oppianicus, pollicetur, et eum, ut ceteros appellet, quibuscum loqui consuesset, rogat.*

(*d*) Generalizing presents such as *aiunt, dicunt, ferunt, traditur*, and the like, do not represent a statement as being made at the present particular moment, and are therefore followed as often by historic tenses of the subjunctive as by primary: Cic. *de Sen.* 4 *obrepere aiunt senectutem citius quam putassent.* (*O. R. obrepit citius quam putaveramus.* As the foolish have always been making this complaint, in the past as well as in the present, *putassent* is logically justified.) *Id. T. D.* 5, 19 *nam quid profitetur* (*philosophia*)? *perfecturam se, qui legibus suis paruisset, ut esset . . . semper beatus.* 'What are the claims of philosophy? – that she will make anyone who has obeyed her laws be always happy.' (*O. R. perficiam ut, qui meis legibus paruerit, sit semper beatus.* But philosophy's claim is not new and is not represented as being made at the present particular moment. *profitetur* means in effect *iamdiu professa est.*) *Id. Verr.* 2, 191 *laudantur oratores veteres . . . quod . . . causas defendere solerent.* Here again *laudantur* is generalizing, and does not mean that anyone is praising the ancient orators at this particular moment, for then Cicero would have said *quod . . . soliti sint.* In view of the numerous other examples, editors are quite wrong who change *laudantur* to *laudabantur* against the unanimity of the mss.

Similar may be the explanation of Cic. *de Or.* 1, 124 *si quando aliquid minus bene fecerunt quam solent, aut noluisse aut valetudine impediti non potuisse consequi id quod scirent putantur.* 'Whenever their performance has been worse than usual, it is thought that either they were not trying, or that they were unable to do justice to the skill which they had, because they were hindered by ill health.' Here it is a wonder that editors have not changed *scirent* to *scirint*. But there is no need, because, again, *putantur* is generalizing.

The following example also has been adduced in favour of the theory that the tenses of the indicative of *O. R.* are retained in the subjunctive of *O. O.*: Cic. *Off.* 3, 103 *addunt etiam, quicquid valde utile sit, id fieri honestum, etiam si antea non videretur.* If this stands for *O. R. quicquid valde utile est, id fit honestum, etiam si antea non videbatur,* it cannot be classed, as an example of mixed sequence, with the examples above, because *videretur* in historic sequence would stand for *O. R. videtur,* so that *visum esset* would have been required. Therefore *videretur,* as usual, is retained from the *O. R.*, and the meaning is: 'Whatever is greatly expedient, becomes honourable, even if we had not thought so before (which we did)'. The objectors to the conduct of Regulus have been maintaining all along that what is expedient is honourable.

If Latin authors had not felt it impossible to represent the imperfect indicative by the imperfect subjunctive in *O. O.*, they would not have resorted to a periphrasis, when the idea of continuance or repetition was important, as Cicero does in *Verr.* 3, 45 *quanti conventus . . . fieri soliti sint, quis ignorat?* 'Who does not know what large meetings were repeatedly held?' (*O. R. quanti conventus fiebant?*)

There remain isolated examples which it is more difficult to explain on the above lines, e.g. Cic. *de Rep.* 2, 30 *multa intelleges etiam aliunde sumpta meliora apud nos multo esse facta, quam ibi fuissent, unde huc tralata essent.* One would naturally suppose that *fuissent* and *tralata essent* stand for *O. R. fuerant* and *tralata sunt.* If so, it must be confessed that even Cicero could be inconsistent in his syntax, for how then would he have expressed the idea: 'You will see that many institutions imported from abroad have been much improved by us on what they *would have been,* (had they remained) in the country of their origin'? It is just possible that *fuissent* is a retained past potential, equivalent to the more normal *futura fuerint* (see Section 183, and Note), and attracting *tralata essent* into the pluperfect along with it.

XXV

Conditional Clauses in O. O. Repraesentatio, *etc.*

280. Although sentences containing a conditional clause are converted into *O. O.* according to the principles already given (main clauses in Section 266, subordinate clauses in Section 272), it may be of use, for purposes of reference, to convert the examples of the eight normal types

given in Section 193. It will be seen that the distinction between some forms disappears:

	O. R.	*O. O.*
1. Present Particular.	*Si hoc dicit, errat.*	*Censeo, si hoc dicat, eum errare.*
		Censebam, si hoc diceret, eum errare.
2. Present General.	*Si hoc dicit, errat.*	(No difference from no. 1.)
	Si rosam vidit, putat ver incipere.	*Censeo, si rosam viderit, eum putare ver incipere.*
		Censebam, si rosam vidisset, eum putare ver incipere.
	Si quid dicas, creditur.	*Censeo, si quid dicas, credi.*
		Censebam, si quid diceres, credi.
3. Present Unreal.	*Si hoc diceret, erraret.*	*Censeo, si hoc diceret, eum erraturum fuisse.*[1]
		Censebam, si hoc diceret, eum erraturum fuisse.[1]
4. Past Particular.	*Si hoc dixit (dicebat), erravit (errabat).*	*Censeo, si hoc dixerit, eum erravisse.*
		Censebam, si id dixisset, eum erravisse.
5. Past General.	*Si hoc dicebat, errabat.*	*Censeo, si hoc dixerit, eum erravisse.*
		Censebam, si id dixisset, eum erravisse.
	Si peccaverat, poenas dabat.	*Censeo, si peccaverit, eum poenas dedisse.*
		Censebam, si peccavisset, eum poenas dedisse.
	Si quid dixisset, credebatur. (Silver Latin).	*Censeo, si quid dixisset, creditum esse.*
		Censebam, si quid dixisset, creditum esse.
6. Past Unreal.	*Si hoc dixisset, erravisset.*	*Censeo, si hoc dixisset, eum erraturum fuisse.*
		Censebam, si hoc dixisset, eum erraturum fuisse.
7. Future Ideal.	*Si hoc dicat, erret.*	*Censeo, si hoc dicat, eum erraturum esse.*
		Censebam, si hoc diceret, eum erraturum esse.

[1] See Section 282, Note 2.

	O. R.	*O. O.*
8. Future Logical.	*Si hoc dicet, errabit.*	(No difference from no. 7.)
	Si hoc fecerit (fut. pf.), *poenas dabit.*	*Censeo, si hoc fecerit* (pf. subj.), *eum poenas daturum.* *Censebam, si hoc fecisset, eum poenas daturum.*

281. In translating English 'unreal' conditions into Latin, difficulty arises when the main verb is passive, since there is no passive equivalent of the periphrastic infinitive in *-urum fuisse*. Latin authors themselves were at liberty to express the idea actively, or, when they required a verb which had no future participle in use, they were apt to fall back on the modal use of *possum* (cf. Section 200). The cumbersome periphrasis *futurum fuisse ut* . . . is usually given as the passive equivalent of *-urum fuisse*, but in fact only two examples of this have been noted: Caes. *B. C.* 3, 101, 3 *nisi nuntii de Caesaris victoria essent adlati, existimabant plerique futurum fuisse uti* (*oppidum*) *amitteretur.* 'Had not news of Caesar's victory been brought, the majority were of opinion that the town would have been lost.' Also Cic. *T. D.* 3, 69.

282. *Notes:*

(1) The distinction between the Present Particular and the Present General disappears, except when the generalizing *si*-clause had the perfect indicative. The difference between the Past Particular and the Past General disappears altogether.

(2) The imperfect subjunctive in the apodosis, whether it refers to the present or to the past, is represented in *O. O.* by *-urum fuisse.* Only the context can determine whether it is a Present or a Past Unreal that is being represented. Present: Cic. *N. D.* 1, 78 *quid censes? si ratio esset in beluis, non suo quasque generi plurimum tributuras fuisse?* 'What is your opinion? Is it not that, if reason existed in beasts, they would severally pay the highest tribute to their own species?' (*O. R. si ratio esset . . ., non . . . tribuerent?*). Livy 38, 47, 13 *stipendium scitote pependisse socios vestros Gallis, et nunc fuisse pensuros, si a me foret cessatum.* 'Know that your allies used to pay tribute to the Gauls, and would be paying it now, had my efforts been slackened.' (*O. R. . . . pendebant . . . et nunc penderent, si . . . foret cessatum.*) Past: Cic. *de Or.* 2, 230 *videmur quieturi fuisse, nisi essemus lacessiti.* 'It seems likely that we should have kept quiet, had we not been provoked.' (*O. R. quievissemus, nisi essemus lacessiti.*) Livy 3, 50, 7 *nec superstitem filiae futurum fuisse, nisi spem ulciscendae mortis eius habuisset.* 'Nor would he have survived his daughter, if he had not had hope of avenging her death.' (*O. R. nec superstes fuissem, nisi . . . habuissem.*)

As it is logically impossible for *-urum esse* to represent any idea which has not reference to the future (i.e. which is not still capable of fulfilment at the time of speaking), it is clear that the following passage ought to be emended: Caes. *B. G.* 5, 29 *Titurius clamitabat . . . Caesarem arbitrari profectum in Italiam; neque aliter Carnutes interficiendi Tasgeti consilium fuisse capturos, neque Eburones, si ille adesset, tanta contemptione nostri ad castra venturos esse. non hostem auctorem sed rem spectare. . . .* 'Titurius kept crying out that he thought Caesar had set out for Italy; not otherwise would the Carnutes have planned to kill Tasgetius, nor would the Eburones, if he were at hand, be approaching the camp with such contempt for us. He looked not to the enemy's advice, but to the facts . . .' Here it is clear that the *O. R.* must have been: *neque Eburones, si Caesar adesset . . . ad castra venirent* (or *venissent*). This cannot be represented by *venturos esse*, and it has been proposed to read . . . *venturos* (sc. *fuisse*, understood from above). *sese non hostem* . . . etc. The transposition of letters from *sese* to *esse* is a common type of palaeographical error.

(3) There is no means of distinguishing between the more vivid logical future conditional clause (with the indicative) and the Future Ideal (with the present subjunctive): Caes. *B. G.* 1, 44, 11 *nisi decedat, sese illum pro hoste habiturum. quodsi eum interfecerit, multis sese . . . gratum esse facturum.* 'If he did not withdraw, he would treat him as an enemy; and if he killed him, he would do what would be pleasing to many.' (*O. R. nisi decedes, te pro hoste habebo. quodsi te interfecero, multis gratum faciam.*) Cic. *Fin.* 3, 1 *voluptatem, si ipsa pro se loquatur, concessuram arbitror dignitati.* 'I think that Pleasure, if she were to speak for herself, would give way to Worth.' (*O. R. voluptas, si ipsa pro se loquatur, concedat dignitati.*) *Ibid.* 1, 39 *hoc ne statuam quidem dicturam pater aiebat, si loqui posset.* 'My father used to say that not even a statue would say this, if it could speak.' (*O. R. hoc ne statua quidem dicat, si loqui possit.*)

283. Circumstances under which the indicative may be used in the apodosis of an 'unreal' condition have been explained in Section 200. To these may be added the idiom *melius, longum, etc, erat* (*fuit*), 'It *would have been* better, tedious, etc.' These indicatives will naturally not require the periphrastic future-in-the past infinitive in *O. O.*: Cic. *Off.* 1, 4 *Platonem existimo, si genus forense dicendi tractare voluisset, gravissime et copiosissime potuisse dicere.* 'I think that Plato, had he wanted to practise forensic oratory, could have spoken with great weight and eloquence.' (*O. R. si voluisset, . . . potuit dicere.*) Livy 27, 20, 6 (*constabat*) *etiam si senatus Carthaginiensium non censuisset, eundum tamen Hasdrubali fuisse in Italiam.* 'It was agreed that, even if the Carthaginian senate had not proposed it, Hasdrubal would have had to go to Italy.' (*O. R. . . . eundum fuit.*) Tac. *Agr.* 4 *memoria teneo solitum ipsum narrare se prima in iuventa studium philosophiae acrius hausisse, ni prudentia matris coercuisset.* 'I remember that he himself used to relate that in his early youth he would have pursued the study of philosophy too eagerly, had not his mother's good sense restrained him.'

(*O. R. acrius hauriebam, ni . . . coercuisset*). Caes. *B. G.* 1, 14, 2 *Caesar respondit si (populus Romanus) alicuius iniuriae sibi conscius fuisset, non fuisse difficile cavere . . .* 'Caesar replied that if the Roman people had been conscious of having done any wrong, it would not have been difficult to take precautions . . .' (*O. R. si conscius fuisset, non fuit difficile. . . .*)

284. Repraesentatio

Both Cicero and the historians were in the habit of adding liveliness and variety of style to a narrative by assuming at will the point of view of the characters about whom they were writing. Thus, main verbs are often in the Historic Present, as if the writer were present on the spot and watching things happen. If the main verb in the Historic Present is a verb of speaking, or its equivalent, with subordinate clauses in the reported speech, strict grammar would require that this fiction should be kept up by using primary tenses of the subjunctive in the subordinate verbs. In fact, all authors pleased themselves, and used historic tenses or not, as it suited them: Caes. *B. G.* 1, 3, 4 *persuadet Castico ut regnum in civitate sua occuparet.* Cf. *ibid.* 1, 9, 4 *a Sequanis impetrat ut per fines suos Helvetios ire patiantur.* The great advantage of this trick of style is that, by changing the point of view in the same sentence, or in the course of the same report, greater emphasis can be laid on some points than on others, for the primary tenses are necessarily more vivid. Consequently we find that this device, known as *Repraesentatio*, is freely employed, even when the governing verb is not in the Historic Present: Livy 28, 32, 3 ff. *Scipio . . . nequaquam eodem animo se ire professus est ad vindicandum id scelus, quo civilem errorem nuper sanaverit . . . In exercitu suo se, praeterquam quod omnes cives aut socios Latinique nominis videat, etiam eo moveri quod nemo fere sit miles qui non aut a patruo suo Cn. Scipione, qui primus Romani nominis in eam provinciam venerit, aut a patre consule, aut a se sit ex Italia advectus.* – and so on, throughout the whole report of Scipio's speech. The tenses are those that were used by Scipio himself, and help to make the reader feel that he is present in the audience. For the shifting of the point of view in one and the same sentence, cf. Sall. *Cat.* 34 *ad haec Q. Marcius: Si quid ab senatu petere vellent, ab armis discedant.* This change of sequence is common both in Cicero and in the historians, and it is often difficult to see any reason for it other than desire for variety.

285. *Virtual* Oratio Obliqua

As has already been explained in Section 240, with examples under 242 (*b*), the subjunctive of *oratio obliqua* may be used in a subordinate clause, even when the main statement does not contain a verb of saying, thinking, or perceiving. This partial obliquity (virtual *oratio obliqua*) is probably commonest in the types of causal clause dealt with in the above sections, and in relative clauses, but is by no means confined to such. Indeed, all *final* clauses come under this heading, since they contain represented thought or intention.

A good example of this use of the subjunctive in a relative clause is Cic. *Att.* 2, 1, 12 *Paetus omnes libros quos frater suus reliquisset mihi donavit.* 'Paetus presented me with all the books which (he said) his brother had left.' By the use of the subjunctive *reliquisset* and the indirect reflexive *suus*, instead of *reliquerat* and *eius*, Cicero attributes this designation of the books to Paetus, and not to himself. The nuance can be rendered audibly in English by a parenthesis such as (*as he said*), (*as was thought*), etc., or visibly in writing by the insertion of inverted commas.

It is necessary to be aware of this idiom in order to avoid misinterpretation of many examples of the imperfect and pluperfect subjunctive, especially in conditional clauses, which might otherwise be mistaken for present or past 'unreals'. E.g. Caes. *B. C.* 3, 44, 1 *neque (Pompeius) munitiones Caesaris prohibere poterat, nisi proelio decertare vellet.* This does not mean 'Pompey could not have prevented Caesar's fortifications, *had he not been willing* to fight a battle', for he did not fight a battle at this time or prevent the circumvallation, and the sentence goes on . . . *quod eo tempore statuerat non esse faciendum.* The imperfect subjunctive *vellet* is due to virtual *O. O.*, representing Pompey's thought: *munitiones prohibere non possum, nisi . . . volo.* The sense therefore is: 'Nor could Pompey prevent Caesar's fortifications, *unless he were willing* to fight a battle.' For other examples cf. Sall. *Jug.* 25, 7 *timebat iram senatus, ni paruisset legatis.* 'He feared the anger of the senate, if he did not obey the envoys.' (Representing Jugurtha's thought: *Senatus irascetur, ni paruero.*) Livy 9, 29, 4 *nec . . . de inferendo bello agitat, quieturus haud dubie, nisi ultro arma Etrusci inferrent.* 'But he did not consider making war, intending doubtless to remain inactive, unless the Etruscans took the offensive.' (Representing the dictator's thought: *quiescam, nisi . . . inferent.*)

286. *The Retention of the Indicative in subordinate Clauses in* O. O.

The use of the subjunctive as a sign of indirectness, to represent the indicative of the *O. R.*, was a secondary development which was not yet so strictly observed in early Latin as it came to be in classical Latin. Nor was the rule so strictly observed in colloquial Latin, or in post-classical writers. In Plautus and Terence there are many examples of the indicative, where one would have expected the subjunctive, and both are found in different clauses in the same sentence: Plaut. *Bacch.* 735 *Chrysalus mihi usque quaque loquitur, nec recte, pater, quia tibi aurum reddidi, et quia non te fraudaverim.* 'Chrysalus keeps talking away at me everywhere, and talking harshly, father, because I restored the gold to you, and because I did not defraud you.' Here both *reddidi* and *fraudaverim* give Chrysalus' grounds for scolding, whereas in classical Latin *reddidi* would represent the speaker's views.

In Caesar and Cicero an indicative clause in the course of an indirect report is usually an explanatory parenthesis of the writer's own: Caes. *B. G.* 3, 2, 1 *per exploratores certior factus est ex ea parte vici quam Gallis concesserat omnes noctu discessisse, montesque qui impenderent a maxima multitudine teneri.* 'He was informed by scouts that from the part of the village which he had given up to the Gauls everyone had departed during the night, and that the mountains which overhung it were held by a great multitude.' From the use of the moods in this sentence it would appear that the clause describing the mountains formed part of the report, while that describing the part of the village did not.

287. The indicative is sometimes retained in a subordinate clause in *O. O.*, when it expresses an objective fact or a general truth, or when it is merely a circumlocution for something which might have been expressed by a single noun: Cic. *Fin.* 4, 61 *admirati sumus quid esset cur nobis Stoicos anteferres, qui de rebus bonis et malis sentirent ea quae ab hoc Polemone Zeno cognoverat.* 'We wondered why it was that you preferred the Stoics to us, when their views about good and evil were those which Zeno had taken over from Polemo.' *Id. Cat.* 3, 21 *quis potest esse tam mente captus qui neget haec omnia quae videmus deorum immortalium potestate administrari?* 'Who can be so mentally blind as to deny that all this visible world is governed by the power of the immortal gods?' (Here *haec omnia quae videmus* is a mere periphrasis for 'the visible world'.) *Id. Arch.* 20 *Marius eximie L. Plotium dilexit, cuius ingenio putabat ea quae gesserat posse celebrari.* 'Marius was exceedingly fond of L. Plotius, by whose genius he thought that his exploits might be celebrated.' (Here *ea quae gesserat* is a periphrasis for *res gestas suas.*)

288. It is noteworthy that the retention of the indicative is commoner after a primary than after a historic governing verb. The following passage is therefore typical: Cic. *de Div.* 2, 19 *si negas esse fortunam et omnia quae fiunt quaeque futura sunt ex omni aeternitate definita dicis esse fataliter, muta definitionem divinationis . . . quamquam dicebas omnia quae fierent futurave essent fato contineri.* 'If you deny the existence of chance, and say that all that comes to pass and will come to pass is determined by destiny from all eternity, then change your definition of divination. . . . Although you said that all that came to pass or would come to pass was fixed by destiny.' It would seem that, when the governing verb was in a past tense, the narrator felt it more difficult to express the thought of the subordinate clause from his own point of view.

It is not without significance that in a number of examples in which the indicative is retained even after a past tense, the more regular subjunctive would have caused real ambiguity. E.g., in the last example in Section 287, *ea quae gessisset* might have represented *ea quae gessero* rather than *ea quae gessi.* Cf. Caes. *B. G.* 1, 40, 5 *factum (esse) eius hostis periculum patrum nostrorum memoria, cum, Cimbris et Teutonis a C. Mario pulsis, non minorem laudem exercitus quam ipse imperator meritus videbatur*. 'Experience of that enemy had been gained within the memory of our fathers, at the time when, in the defeat of the Cimbri and Teutons by C. Marius, the army seemed to have earned no less credit than the general himself.' Here the date-giving *cum* with the indicative is important, for the context would allow *cum videretur* or *visus esset* to bear a concessive sense. Cf. also Cic. *Verr.* 4, 138 *petebatur . . . viderem.*

Finally, it is sometimes asserted that the future and future perfect indicative, after a primary governing verb, resist the change to the subjunctive more frequently than other tenses. However, in the passages usually cited, the subordinate clause is not necessarily oblique: Cic. *Off.* 3, 121 *tibi persuade te mihi multo fore cariorem, si talibus praeceptis laetabere.* 'Be assured that you will be much dearer to me, if you take pleasure in such precepts.' (But this means no more than: *certe carior eris, si . . . laetabere.*) *Id. de Sen.* 79 *nolite arbitrari me, cum a vobis discessero, nullum fore.* 'Do not think that, when I have departed from you, I shall be non-existent.' (= *haudquaquam nullus ero, cum . . . discessero.*)

289. *Relative Clauses in the Accusative and Infinitive in* O. O.

The use of the accusative and infinitive of *O. O.* in a relative clause which is not really dependent has been referred to in Section 230, Note. This usually occurs when the relative word is merely serving as a connection between two independent sentences (i.e. when *qui* = *et is*, *nam is*, *is igitur*, etc., or when *ubi* = *et ibi*, when *quare* = *et ea re*, etc.), but it can also occur in relative clauses of the parenthetic type, and, indeed, whenever a clause which is formally subordinate contains a statement which can be treated as independent: Caes. *B. G.* 1, 31, 7 *Aeduos . . . omnem equitatum amisisse: quibus proeliis fractos . . . coactos esse Sequanis obsides dare.* 'The Aedui had lost all their cavalry, and, broken by these battles, had been compelled to give hostages to the Sequani.' (Here *quibus proeliis* = *et iis proeliis.*) Livy 22, 53, 4 *nuntiat P. Furius Philus . . . nobiles iuvenes quosdam, quorum principem M. Caecilium Metellum* (sc. *esse*), *mare ac naves spectare.* 'P. Furius Philus reported that certain noble youths, whose leader was M. Caecilius Metellus, were thinking of taking to the sea and ships.'

The accusative and infinitive is also occasionally found after *ut* (or *quemadmodum*) in the combination *ut . . . ita* (*sic*), and also after *cum*, in the combination *cum . . . tum*, when the sense is 'not only . . . but also', so that the conjunctions are co-ordinating rather than subordinating: Cic. *Cl.* 138 *ex quo intellegi potuit . . . ut mare ventorum vi agitari, sic populum Romanum seditiosorum vocibus concitari.* 'From which it could be seen that, just as the sea is agitated by the violence of the winds, so the Roman people is roused by the utterances of seditious men.' (Or 'not only can the sea be roused . . . but also the Roman people . . .'.) *Id. Fin.* 4, 62 . . . *eisdem de rebus hos cum acutius disseruisse, tum sensisse gravius et fortius.* '(You had perceived that) the latter had not only argued in a more penetrating manner about the same matters, but had held more serious and stronger views.'

No hard and fast rule can be laid down about this use of the accusative and infinitive. An author may choose to regard the thought of the subordinate clause as an integral part of a larger period, in which case he will use the formally correct subjunctive, even where we should expect the accusative and infinitive: Caes. *B. G.* 2, 31, 4 *sibi omnes fere finitimos esse inimicos; a quibus se defendere, traditis armis, non possent.* 'Almost all their neighbours were their enemies; and they could not defend themselves against them, if they handed over their arms.'

Select Bibliography

BASSOLS DE CLIMENT, M., *Syntaxis latina*. 2 vols. Madrid, 1956.

BENNETT, C. E., *Syntax of Early Latin*. 2 vols. Boston, 1910.

BLASE, H., *Tempora und Modi* (in Landgraf's Hist. Gram. der lat. Sprache), 1903.

BLATT, F., *Précis de syntaxe latine*. (Collection 'Les Langues du Monde'), 1952.

COUSIN, J., *Bibliographie de la langue latine*, 1880–1948. Paris, 1951.

DELBRÜCK, B., *Vergleichende Syntax der Indogermanischen Sprachen*. 3 vols. Strassburg, 1893–1900.

DRAEGER, A., *Historische Syntax der lateinischen Sprache*. 2 vols. 1878–1881.

DRAEGER, A., *Syntax und Stil des Tacitus*. Leipzig, 1888.

ERNOUT, A., et THOMAS, F., *Syntaxe latine*. Paris, 1951.

GILDERSLEEVE, B. L., and LODGE, G., *Latin Grammar*. Macmillan, 1925.

GIUFFRIDA, G., *Principi di sintassi latina. Concetto e funzione del modo*. Turin, 1938.

HALE, W. G., *The Cum-constructions: their history and functions*. (Cornell Studies in Classical Philology, No. 1, 1887.)

HANDFORD, S. A., *The Latin Subjunctive*. Methuen, 1947.

HULLIHEN, W., *Antequam and Priusquam, with special reference to the historical development of their subjunctive usage*. Baltimore, 1903.

JURET, A. C., *Système de la syntaxe latine*. 2nd ed., 1933.

KREBS, J. P., *Antibarbarus der lateinischen Sprache*. Basel, 1886.

KROLL, W., *Die wissenschaftliche Syntax im lateinischen Unterricht*. Berlin, 1925.

KÜHNER, R., *Ausführliche Grammatik der lateinischen Sprache*. Rev. by Stegmann, R. 2 vols. Hannover, 1912.

LEBRETON, J., *Étude sur la langue et la grammaire de Cicéron*. Paris, 1901.

LEUMANN, M., und HOFMANN, J. B., *Lateinische Grammatik, Laut- und Formenlehre, Syntax und Stilistik*. (5th ed. of Stolz-Schmalz, in Müller's Handbuch), 1928.

LINDSAY, W. M., *Syntax of Plautus* (St. Andrews Univ. Publications), 1907.

LÖFSTEDT, E., *Syntactica*. Part I, 2nd ed., 1942; Part II, 1933.

LÖFSTEDT, E., *Vermischte Studien zur lateinischen Sprachkunde und Syntax*. Lund, 1936.

MAROUZEAU, J., *Traité de stylistique appliquée au Latin*. 2nd ed., Paris, 1948.

MEILLET, A., et VENDRYES, J., *Traité de grammaire comparée des langues classiques*. 2nd ed. Paris, 1948.

MÜLLER, C. F. W., *Syntax des Nominativs und Akkusativs*. (Suppl. to Landgraf's Hist. Gram.) Leipzig, 1908.

NÄGELSBACH, K. F. VON, *Lateinische Stilistik*. 9th ed. by I. Müller, 1905.

PALMER, L. R., *The Latin Language*. Faber and Faber, 1954.

RIEMANN, O., *Études sur la langue et la grammaire de Tite Live*. Paris, 1884.

RIEMANN, O., *Syntaxe latine*. 7th ed. rev. by A. Ernout, 1932.

ROBY, H. J., *A Grammar of the Latin Language from Plautus to Suetonius*. Part II, Syntax. 1892.

STOKOE, H. R., *The Understanding of Syntax*. Heinemann, 1937.

THOMAS, F., *Recherches sur le subjonctif latin, histoire et valeur des formes*. Paris, 1938.

VANDVIK, E., *Genetivus und Ablativus Qualitatis*. Oslo, 1942.

Index of Subject-matter

The numbers refer to the Sections

Latin Index

(*The numbers refer to the Sections*)

Index of Examples

(The figures in brackets refer to the Sections)